WHAT'S LAW GOT TO DO WITH IT?

Law, Politics, and the Media

Series Editor Keith J. Bybee

WHAT'S LAW GOT TO DO WITH IT?

*What Judges Do, Why They Do It,
and What's at Stake*

Edited by Charles Gardner Geyh

STANFORD LAW AND POLITICS
An Imprint of Stanford University Press
Stanford, California

Stanford University Press
Stanford, California

©2011 by the Board of Trustees of the Leland Stanford Junior University.
All rights reserved.

Printed in the United States of America on acid-free, archival-quality paper

Library of Congress Cataloging-in-Publication Data
What's law got to do with it? : what judges do, why they do it, and what's at stake /
Edited by Charles Gardner Geyh.
   pages cm.
Includes bibliographical references and index.
ISBN 978-0-8047-7532-8 (cloth : alk. paper) —
ISBN 978-0-8047-7533-5 (pbk. : alk. paper) —
1. Judicial process—United States. 2. Judges—United States. 3. Law—Political
aspects—United States. I. Geyh, Charles Gardner, editor of compilation
KF8775.A75W48 2011
347.73′14—dc22   2011008075

Typeset at Stanford University Press in 10/14 Minion

To Steve and Victoria

Nearly thirty years wasn't nearly enough

Contents

Figures and Tables

Figures

Tables

Acknowledgments

The project culminating in the publication of this volume began with a conference hosted at the Indiana University Maurer School of Law in March 2009. I would like to thank the Joyce Foundation for a generous grant that made the conference possible. Thanks likewise to Steve Burbank and Barry Friedman for their assistance in identifying authors and helping me to structure the conference. My dean and friend, Lauren Robel, lent significant institutional and personal support to the conference, for which I am deeply appreciative. And Archana Sridar, the law school's assistant dean for research, was instrumental to the success of the conference from start to finish. I'd also like to thank a great group of conference moderators: Bill Henderson, Jody Madeira, James Sample, and Jeff Yost. Finally, I want to thank the authors who presented papers at the conference and who, apart from being among the best scholars in the business, were a pleasure to work with: Larry Baum, Eileen Braman, Steve Burbank, Keith Bybee, Frank Cross, Barry Friedman, Mike Gerhardt, Jim Gibson, Melinda Gann Hall, Stefanie Lindquist, Andrew Martin, Mitch Pickerill, Dave Pozen, Ted Ruger, and Jeff Segal.

For their help with the introduction and in the editorial process, I'd like to thank my research assistants: Evelyn Gentry, Mark Plantan, Carrie Pytynia, and Andy Williams. Thanks likewise to Phillip Olsen, for exceptional research assistance during the summer prior to the conference. Finally, I'd like to express my appreciation to Rita Eads, as always, for her administrative assistance, to say nothing of her patience.

WHAT'S LAW GOT TO DO WITH IT?

Introduction

So What Does Law Have to Do with It?

Charles Gardner Geyh

D URING THE RENAISSANCE, the ermine became a symbol of purity that English royalty and later English judges adopted by adorning their robes with ermine fur. American judges forwent the fur but retained the symbol, for reasons that were nicely articulated by the Tennessee Supreme Court, writing in 1872:

> The idea that the judicial office is supposed to be invested with ermine, though fabulous and mythical, is yet most eloquent in significance. We are told that the little creature is so acutely sensitive as to its own cleanliness that it becomes paralyzed and powerless at the slightest touch of defilement upon its snow-white fur. A like sensibility should belong to him who comes to exercise the august functions of a judge .... But when once this great office becomes corrupted, when its judgment comes to reflect the passions or interests of the magistrate rather than the mandates of the law, the courts have ceased to be the conservators of the commonweal and the law itself is debauched into a prostrate and nerveless mockery. (Harrison v. Wisdom, 54 Tenn. [7 Heisk.] 99 [1872]).

In short, the ermine embodies the norm of impartial justice and the premise that judges are to bracket out extraneous influences on their decision-making and base their decisions upon applicable facts and law. If the story began and ended there, the answer to the question posed by the title of this volume, "What's law got to do with it?" would have to be: "Everything."

In the aftermath of the legal realism movement, a cadre of political scientists, inspired by principles of behavioral psychology, developed what they

1

dubbed the "attitudinal model" of judicial decision-making. Proponents pitted their attitudinal model against what they characterized as the "legal model," in studies of voting behavior on the Supreme Court (Segal and Spaeth 1993). They found that while judges say that they are following the law, in reality, their decisions are influenced more by their attitudes or ideological predilections. From this perspective, the myth of the ermine is just that, and despite its celebrated purity, the ermine is ultimately just another weasel. If so, what law has to do with it is essentially nothing.

For many years, the legal profession raised its ermines while the political science community nurtured its weasels, with only passing recognition that each was thinking of the same animal in fundamentally different ways. On those infrequent occasions in which one group acknowledged the other, it was typically in derisive or dismissive terms, for the limited purpose of observing that the other had misclassified its mammal in ways too obvious to take seriously. To the extent that there was a debate over the influences on judicial decision-making, it was a dichotomous one: judges were ermines, or they were weasels.

With the diversification of the menagerie in the 1990s, however, the ermine-weasel debate would take a turn for the complicated. Some political scientists challenged the premise of the attitudinal model that judges simply voted their policy preferences; rather, they posited, judges want to see their preferences implemented. For that to happen, the acquiescence, if not the support of other institutional actors—such as Congress or the president—can be essential. Judges therefore think strategically, the theory went, and adjust their decision-making to mollify or circumvent those who could thwart implementation of the judges' long-term policy objectives (Epstein and Knight 1998). Proponents of this "strategic choice" model thus postulate that judges are neither high-minded ermines nor weasels driven to satiate their ideological appetites, but clever, foxlike creatures, whose impulse to act upon their attitudes is tempered by savvy for the politically possible.

Still another cohort of political scientists, influenced by the thinking of social psychology, has questioned the premise underlying attitudinal and strategic choice models, that judges are driven by a single-minded desire to implement their vision of good public policy. Rather, they have argued, judges are social animals who desire respect and acceptance within their various communities to no less an extent than anyone else (Baum 2007). Thus, the argument goes, judicial decision-making is affected by the audiences that judges seek to impress, convince, or placate. The relevant audiences can be varied, and may include fellow judges, the bar, the media, the electorate, and others. Insofar as judges are an eager-to-please lot fixated upon ingratiating themselves to their audiences, the judicial mind-set would seem to be more closely akin to a puppy-dog than an ermine, fox, or weasel.

Then there are the economists. While economic analysis begot rational choice theories of legislative decision-making, which in turn spawned the strategic choice model discussed above, the relationship between strategic choice and traditional economic analysis of law is attenuated. The economic model rejects the suggestion that judicial decision-making can be explained by a desire to make good policy or make others happy. Rather, it presupposes a self-interested judge, who seeks to maximize the same things that all self-interested souls seek to maximize: income, power, prestige, leisure, and so on (Posner 1993). Fixed salaries and ethics rules constrain the influence of income on judicial decision-making, but judges may still structure their decision-making to maximize other interests, such as their prospects for appointment to higher judicial office (and the added power and prestige it entails) (Morriss, Heise, and Sisk 2005). In contrast to the ermine, weasel, fox, or puppy, the economic model's judge—who is driven by self-interested desires, is indifferent to the approbation of others, and has goals no loftier than indulging her own creature comforts—seems decidedly feline in orientation.

If analyzed superficially, this proliferation of models would simply seem to have enlarged the "either-or" debate over influences on judicial decision-making from two animals to five or six.[1] A closer look, however, reveals a gradual and perhaps fundamental shift in the way serious scholars think about judges and judicial decision-making. At the turn of the new millennium, political scientists and law professors began unprecedented collaborations on a range of empirical research projects. The net effect has been for each to take the others' work much more seriously than in the past, and to acknowledge with increasing frequency that the influences on judicial decision-making are complex and multivariate. As a consequence, few well-informed scholars would still argue that judges are exclusively foxes, or ermines, or weasels, or puppies, or cats; rather, there is an emerging consensus that judges are, well, foxermeaseluppycats.

For decades, law professors and political scientists were unwittingly engaged in a three blind men and the elephant remake, in which they, oblivious to each other, classified the same animal in different ways, with exclusive reference to the part they were holding. To complete the metaphor, the latest round of interdisciplinary research has been eye-opening. One objective of this volume is to chronicle the recently emerging, if limited, common-sense consensus among law professors, political scientists, and judges that the influences on judicial decision-making are varied, and that law has neither everything nor nothing to do with how judges decide cases—rather, it has *something* to do with it.

To herald this as a moment of interdisciplinary consensus is both notable and overstated. It is notable, in that it marks a turning point in the study of courts: we have, in effect, begun to carve a Rosetta stone enabling the two disciplines with the most to say about what judges do, to communicate in a language that each understands. So equipped, it is possible for the first time to appreciate the extent to which law professors, political scientists, and judges share the common view that law and politics each play a role in the decisions judges make.

Characterizing this as a "consensus" overstates the accord and conceals the profound disagreements that remain. Most, if not all, may agree that law has something to do with what judges do, but is that "something" meaningful enough to matter? The legal establishment has long thought so. It conceptualizes judges as significantly different from public officials in the so-called political branches of government, by virtue of the judge's duty to bracket out extraneous influences and apply the law. Judges have thus been afforded a measure of independence from external controls denied other public officials that affects how judges are selected, regulated, and removed. For judges and many law professors, then, judicial independence facilitates rather than denigrates the rule of law—but that assumes the primacy of law in relation to other influences on judicial decision-making. If "law" is toward the bottom of the list, as many political scientists maintain, judicial independence liberates judges to implement their other priorities, by acting on their ideological preferences; indulging in strategic gamesmanship; pandering to their favored audiences; or satiating their self-interest. From this perspective, judicial independence undermines, rather than facilitates, the rule of law.

In short, the discovery of the foxermeaseluppycat is no small matter, but it is a polymorphous creature that defies classification. Scholars acknowledge its existence and yet disagree as to what it looks like and whether it is better caged or allowed to roam free. The chapters of this volume chronicle both the struggle toward interdisciplinary consensus on what judges do, and the profound disagreements that remain.

In his stage-setting essay in Chapter 1, Professor Jeffrey Segal outlines the three dominant models of judicial decision-making—legal, attitudinal, and strategic choice—and highlights ongoing debates over their relative merits. This approach should be familiar to political scientists who study the courts, for it describes the field in terms of the differences separating the various schools of thought as they have emerged over the past generation.

Succeeding chapters orient themselves differently, by de-emphasizing what separates competing approaches and focusing instead on ways to reconcile or bridge the law-politics divide, embedded in the legal, attitudinal, and strategic choice models. In Chapter 2, Professor Stephen Burbank introduces complications, further explored by others in this volume, that offer insights into the difficulty of isolating the impact of law on judging. He emphasizes that the relationship between law and politics is not monolithic, but context-dependant, and may vary from court to court, issue to issue, and even case to case. He further argues that the relationship between law and politics is not dichotomous, because the law is necessarily written in terms sufficiently broad to accommodate discretion and consequently ideological (and other) influences. Here, Professor Segal takes issue, because in his view, defining law so flexibly enables it to explain everything, and so nothing—in other words, it is stated in terms so broad that its impact cannot meaningfully be verified or falsified. Burbank rejoins that while so capacious an understanding of law may complicate, if not undermine, the task of creating falsifiable hypotheses to test the respective influences of law and politics on judicial decision-making, he is unfazed, concluding, "I prefer the messiness of lived experience to the tidiness of unrealistically parsimonious models."

For Professor Lawrence Baum, on the other hand, a scholarly obsession with isolating the impact of law as distinct from politics is misdirected. In Chapter 3, Baum notes, consistent with the views of Cross and others, that law and policy are too intertwined to disentangle, and to that extent are less than a dichotomy. At the same time, more than just law and policy can hold sway with judges, whose decisions may also be influenced by the prospect of appointment to higher judicial office, the need for re-election, work-life balance, and the desire to preserve collegial relationships on a given court, among other considerations. To that extent, the universe of influences on judicial decision-making is much more than a dichotomy. Finally, Baum argues that when we do think about the law-policy dichotomy, we should concern ourselves more than most positive empirical scholars have with whether implementing ideological preferences is a judge's conscious motive, or is simply a subconscious effect of judicial decision-making, because the answer has significant normative implications.

In Chapter 4, Professor Frank Cross further explores the interplay between law and politics by characterizing the former as a subset of the latter. For him, pitting law against politics creates a false dichotomy. By its nature, law leaves room for judicial discretion and the discretion judges exercise is influenced by political ideology, among other factors. Law nonetheless operates as a constraint on judicial discretion, leaving judges to strike a pragmatic balance by making decisions they regard as sound.

If law is politics, however, is the task of isolating the relative influence of law on judicial decision-making hopeless? The legal academy's embrace of eclecticism and complexity in its study of judicial behavior, as evidenced in Professor Cross's chapter, is in tension with the impulse of positive scholars—such as Segal—toward simplicity and reducing the variable influences on judicial behavior to a minimum. As Theodore Ruger observed at a conference where the chapters in this volume were discussed, identifying a variable for "law" generous enough to satisfy legal scholars and yet parsimonious enough to meet the needs of positive empirical scholars, is "the elusive holy grail of interdisciplinary scholarship about judicial behavior."

Professors Eileen Braman and Mitchell Pickerill explore ways to get past these interdisciplinary impasses and reach greater accord on the complexity and nuance of judicial decision-making in Chapter 5. They explain the difficulty law professors and political scientists have had in understanding the relative influence of law on the decisions judges make in terms of "path dependency"—a term that they borrow from the work of scholars who have studied institutions (such as the courts), and turn on the scholars themselves. In effect, each discipline has its own path or way of thinking about the problems it studies, a path that structures its methods of analysis and constrains the extent to which those who walk the path are willing to deviate from it. They identify significant issues of "translation" involving the operationalization of concepts that can influence the perceived usefulness of research across disciplines, and recommend that political scientists and academic lawyers acquire a deeper appreciation for the ways in which scholars in other disciplines conceptualize concepts.

In Chapter 6, Professors Barry Friedman and Andrew Martin offer more specific guidance as to how the influence of law could be more productively studied. They suggest that for the most part the so-called legal model is not really a model at all. What political scientists have dubbed the legal model often is little more than a list of law-related factors that judges say matter to them when they make decisions. Without specifying under what circumstances or subject to what limitations those factors influence judicial decisions, such factors, by themselves, lack the explanatory or predictive qualities of a model. They note, however, that some limited efforts to model law show promise, and underscore the centrality of nuance to such undertakings. Thus, researchers looking to study the impact of law should think not only of the ways in which law constrains outcomes but also of the ways it channels judicial discretion; they should look beyond the U.S. Supreme Court and spend more time with the lower courts, where the regularity of law is more pervasive; they should look beyond constitutional law and pay greater attention to statutory and common law cases, where the pull of precedent is different and arguably greater; and they should look at more than votes to consider the impact of law on the opinions themselves.

In Chapter 7, Professor Stefanie Lindquist adds another influence on judicial decision-making to the mix: institutional structure. In a massive, groundbreaking study of state supreme courts, Lindquist has begun the process of documenting patterns and trends of decision-making across courts, to the end of exploring what influences the choices judges make. Some preliminary findings, reported here, show that courts are less likely to overturn their own precedent if their judges are appointed, rather than elected; if tenure on the court is longer, rather than shorter; and if the court is smaller rather than larger.

The first seven chapters show that the legal academy and the political science community have come a long way in a relatively short period of time. Gone is the period of isolation in which neither responded to the work of the other in a meaningful way. And going, if not gone, is each discipline's fixation on reducing its understanding of judicial decision-making to a single influence, which has given rise to otherworldly debates over whether judges follow the law or their policy preferences, as if the universe of influences on judicial decision-making is limited to those two choices, and as if those two choices were mutually exclusive. The new generation of interdisciplinary work is leaving dichotomous constructs behind in favor of a more nuanced and sophisticated understanding of what judges do. In short, what we see over the course of the first seven chapters is the gradual emergence of an interdisciplinary consensus acknowledging the convergence of multiple influences on judicial decision-making, including the legal, the political, and others.

This consensus, however, is a decidedly uneasy one, in part because of what it portends for the respective disciplines. Academic lawyers like Burbank and Cross (and neoinstitutional scholars like Baum) may be at peace with complexity and the possibility that the various influences on judicial decision-making cannot be completely reduced, isolated, or quantified, but positive political theorists like Segal find such conclusions unacceptable because they thwart the efforts of researchers to test the relative significance of law and other influences on judicial decision-making. Friedman and Martin, and Braman and Pickerill, in turn, seek ways to bridge the divide between the competing impulses to complicate and simplify, by exploring how empirical research can productively be pursued to the enlightenment of political scientists and law professors alike. And Lindquist's pioneering study of state courts opens the door to the next frontier of courts research, where the dialogue over what judges do and how to study it is sure to intensify.

Even if there is a rough consensus among most scholars that applicable law has something but not everything to do with judicial decision-making, there is no related consensus on where that takes us. For centuries, the legal establishment has defended an "independent judiciary" against proposals to impose greater political controls on judges and the decisions they make, on the grounds that such controls would interfere with the "rule of law," by intimidating judges into making choices that the majority (or whoever is positioned to control the courts) prefers rather than what the law requires. If, however, it is conceded that independent judges do more or less follow the rule of law, does that concession undermine the legal establishment's long-standing justification for judicial independence? The answer depends in part on how much law still has to do with it: if judicial independence comes at the cost of liberating judges to act upon extralegal influences, do those costs exceed the rule of law benefits judicial independence promotes? The answer may likewise depend in part on whether there are *other* justifications for judicial independence that warrant its preservation regardless of its mixed impact on the rule of law—such as the role judicial autonomy plays in promoting a due or fair process for litigants, or enabling sound, pragmatic decision-making.

The debate over whether judges should be appointed or elected is illustrative of how deeply divided the disputants remain despite progress toward consensus on an underlying question that fuels the debate—namely, what does law have to do with the decisions judges make? To the extent that independent judges follow the law, subjecting them to loss of tenure for decisions unpopular with an electorate unversed in what the law requires arguably replaces the rule of law with the rule of the mob, which augers in favor of selecting judges by appointment rather than election. On the other hand, to the extent that independent judges disregard the law and follow their ideological predilections, elections are a better way to promote accountability (and thereby promote institutional legitimacy) by ensuring that judicial preferences are more closely aligned with the preferences of the public judges serve.

Unsurprisingly, when it comes to judicial selection, the general agreement that judges are subject to an array of influences takes a back seat to disagreement over which influences predominate, with proponents of judicial elections typically highlighting the preeminence of ideology, and proponents of judicial appointment underscoring the primacy of law. At the nub of the judicial selection debate is a disagreement over whether judges are different from other public officials in ways that warrant a fundamentally different system of selection. Professor Matthew Streb's study in Chapter 8 reveals that when it comes to their election campaigns, legislators and judges (at the Supreme Court level, at least) are not that far apart. As he shows, these races have become comparably expensive, and comparably competitive. But such news will be greeted with alarm or huzzahs depending on what law has to do with the job judges perform—and whether one thinks that the kinds of legal decisions judges make are of a sort that the electorate should have an opportunity to influence directly.

In Chapter 9, Professor Melinda Gann Hall notes that the legal community generally regards contested judicial elections as ill suited to select capable, qualified judges, and as a threat to the independence of judges and the rule of law. She argues, with reference to empirical studies, that these concerns are grossly overblown. Rather, she posits that elections are democracy-enhancing, accountability-promoting, and foster rather than denigrate the rule of law by enabling the electorate to constrain judges from disregarding the law and implementing their personal ideological preferences.

David Pozen, on the other hand, is skeptical of such claims. In Chapter 10, he reasons that contested elections—by their nature—encourage judges to conform their interpretations of law to democratic preferences, and so become practitioners of "majoritarian judicial review." The dual effect of majoritarian judicial review, he argues, is to "usurp the achievements of previous generations by channeling interpretations toward contemporary understandings of the provisions they enacted," and to "usurp the achievements of future generations by foreclosing judicial innovations that might have helped generate, consolidate, and legitimize new understandings of the law." For Pozen, then, this "majoritarian circle" ultimately impoverishes rather than enhances democratic values.

The divide that separates Hall from Pozen is more than substantive—it is methodological as well. Pozen does not mount an empirical challenge to Hall's conclusions, but grounds his argument in political theory. For many within the legal academy, such an approach, which challenges the normative underpinnings of the argument Hall makes, is a familiar and compelling one. Many political scientists, however, may regard it as unhelpful insofar as it does not respond to the social science underlying Hall's claims.

How judges are to be selected and the extent to which they are independent from or accountable to the electorate, the political branches of government, or even themselves is ultimately determined not by academics but by the public and their elected representatives. If one accepts the premise that in a democratic republic, the legitimacy of government depends on the consent of the governed, then public perception matters. As Professor James Gibson explains in Chapter 11, that is particularly true of the judiciary:

> All political institutions need political capital in order to be effective, to get their decisions accepted by others, and be successfully implemented. Since courts are typically thought to be weak institutions—having neither the power of the "purse" (control of the treasury) nor the "sword" (control over agents of state coercion)—their political capital must be found in resources other than finances and force. For courts, their principal political capital is institutional legitimacy.

While the academic community may be close to an accord in its appreciation for the complex slurry of mixed motives underlying judicial decision-making, in the policy-making realm, the debate remains stubbornly binary. Court critics on the right have decried "activist judges" whom they accuse of disregarding the law and substituting their personal preferences, while court critics on the left bemoan "right-wing extremists" whose ideologically driven decisions are outside the political "mainstream." Meanwhile, the legal establishment has defended judges against attack from the left and right, arguing that independent judges are dedicated to upholding the law, and that efforts to intimidate judges and control their decision-making undermine judicial independence and the rule of law.

Despite the best efforts of court critics to undermine the public's faith in its judges, public confidence in courts remains considerably higher than for other political institutions. Gibson notes that ordinarily the legitimacy of political institutions is derived from electoral accountability, which may explain the public's continuing support for selecting judges in contested elections. In the case of unelected judiciaries, however, Gibson argues, legitimacy depends on the judges' perceived expertise and commitment to the rule of law. That may help to explain the legal establishment's long-standing mantra that judges are influenced by facts and law alone.

In Chapter 12, Professor Keith Bybee surveys a wealth of polling data that reveals that the public entertains conflicting views of judges both as impartial arbiters of law and as political actors influenced by their ideologies. In his Kentucky survey, Gibson makes a similar finding: while the vast majority of the public does want judges to follow the law, it also wants judges to protect the powerless against the powerful, and nearly half think that judges should be involved in politics because their role is to represent the political majority.

In sum, the public's view of what judges do (and should do) is eclectic and varied in ways not incompatible with the views expressed by many of the academicians writing in this volume. Court critics and defenders, in contrast, continue to make stark, dichotomous appeals to the public, to promote the image of judges as impartial guardians of the rule of law, or to erode public support for a judiciary they characterize as peopled with unprincipled, ideological zealots. To date, however, court critics have failed to gain traction, and, as Bybee notes, public confidence in an independent judiciary remains relatively stable and strong, despite widespread recognition that independent judges do more and less than simply follow the law.

The views of Indiana Supreme Court Justice Frank Sullivan, Indiana Court of Appeals Judge Nancy Vaidik, and U.S. District Judge Sarah Evans Barker, expressed in Chapter 13, simultaneously corroborate the emerging scholarly consensus that the influences on judicial decision-making are complex and multivariate, and underscore the distance that separates significant segments of political science from the legal establishment. Each judge underscores the centrality of law to the role they play and rejects the notion that attitude or ideology drives the decisions they make. Each, however, elucidates the complexities of their decision-making by describing the influences that affect their choices.

Justice Sullivan's answer to the question "What's law got to do with it?" is "Everything," but he nuances that conclusion with the observation that "politics and law are not mutually exclusive but rather inextricably bound," because "the very statutes and constitutional provisions that judges must interpret are products of politics and so cannot be interpreted without taking politics into account." Judge Vaidik sought to explain why scholars were so focused on extralegal explanations for judicial decision-making despite their relative insignificance in the minds of judges. She likened the "gap," where the law is unclear and appellate court judges exercise discretion subject to extralegal influences, to the gap between the teeth of David Letterman and Lauren Hutton: "It's a small gap, but it happens to be right in the middle of their face." As to how judges decide cases in that gap, Vaidik concluded that the answer is simply too complex to be captured by a unified model.

On this latter point Judge Barker concurred and elaborated. In addition to the "law," Barker pointed to the influences of her locale, the desire to avoid reversal, the dictates of the code of conduct, the need to manage her docket, a range of subconscious factors, and, most important, the facts of the case as relevant to her decision-making process. That leads her to conclude that empiricists must get "really close" to their judicial subjects if they hope to understand and explain the complexity of their decision-making.

To no small extent, this book illustrates how close and yet how far we are to a common understanding of what judges do and what to do about it. For example, Professor Gibson observes that law professors, political scientists, and judges may be "a lot closer than it appears":

> What judges do is to try to make fair decisions within the context of what's legally possible. . . . [We] probably believe that people differ in their perceptions of fairness, and [we] might even accept that those differences are ultimately tied to ideological views that individuals have—not that [ideology is] completely determinative, but, as I said, within the context of what's legally permitted.

On the other hand, Professor Gibson also observes of judges, law professors, and political scientists that "we have a fundamentally different view about what it is judges do." At bottom, Gibson, like many political scientists, is skeptical of arguments that independent judges are meaningfully constrained by law: "How can we even talk about rule of law, when we have 5–4 decisions?" he has asked, adding that when "there is no legally correct answer," how can the Court's decision "be anything but an ideological choice?" From his perspective, political scientists do not oppose the rule of law, but simply "don't believe it exists in the vast majority of cases that are decided at the appellate level."

In conclusion, scholars, judges, policy-makers, and the public have articulated complex and contradictory understandings of what law has to do with what judges do, whether it matters, and what—if anything—to do about it. This volume heralds the advent of an exciting new generation of interdisciplinary thinking about the decisions judges make. Gone are the eras of malign and benign interdisciplinary neglect, and fading fast are unproductive efforts to pit law against politics in a kind of death match for control of the judicial heart and mind, as if coexistence is not an option. As evidenced by the chapters that follow, in its place is a growing appreciation for the complexity of judicial decision-making, which offers a richer and more nuanced understanding of what judges do, but does so at the expense of complicating how we test and verify the intuitions that underlie such an understanding.

The implications of these developments for the participants in this ongoing discussion are provocative. To what extent is law reasonably characterized as a subset of politics? And to that extent, is it time for law professors to rethink legal education and what it means to teach law students to "think like lawyers" (and judges)? Should the legal establishment speak more candidly about the extralegal considerations that influence judicial decision-making—or is such a concession tantamount to admitting that the emperor has no clothes? Conversely, to what extent is politics reasonably characterized as a subset of law—in other words, to what extent can law be understood to subsume ideological, strategic, and other influences? Can political scientists abide this more capacious definition of law that animates the thinking of so many judges and lawyers? Can political scientists and academic lawyers take each other more seriously without ceding relevance to the other that each is loath to relinquish? Ultimately, and most important, what are the implications of these developments for the institutional legitimacy of the courts? The public may be at peace with courts that are subject to legal and extralegal influences, but what are the limits of its tolerance?

In short, the foxermeaseluppycat is a remarkable creature. The implications of its discovery are profound, and its proper care and feeding are critical to the operation of American government. It is hoped that the chapters that follow will benefit two distinct audiences: students and well-educated readers who seek an introduction to the latest learning on judicial politics and the rule of law; and scholars for whom this work presents the current state of the art in a rapidly moving field, and points the way for future research.

Notes

1. To the five models described above, one could add at least one more—the theory of "motivated reasoning." Cognitive psychologists theorize that judges' ideological predilections motivate them to interpret the law consistently with those predilections, which helps to explain why judges may honestly believe that they are simply following the law, even though their votes can often be correlated to their ideological preferences (Braman 2009; Simon 2004). I've omitted a discussion of cognitive psychology from the text, because it was not critical to the point I am making here, and—more important, perhaps—because I could not conjure an appropriate animal mascot.

References

Baum, Lawrence. 2006. *Judges and Their Audiences: A Perspective on Judicial Behavior.* Princeton: Princeton University Press.

Braman, Eileen. 2009. *Law, Politics, and Perception: How Policy Preferences Influence Legal Reasoning.* Charlottesville: University of Virginia Press.

Epstein, Lee, and Jack Knight. 1998. *The Choices Justices Make.* Washington, DC: CQ Press.

Morriss, Andrew, Michael Heise, and Gregory Sisk. 2005. "Signaling and Precedent in Federal District Court Opinions." *Supreme Court Economic Review* 13: 63.

Posner, Richard. 1993. "What Do Judges and Justices Maximize? (The Same Thing Everybody Else Does)." *Supreme Court Economic Review* 3: 1, 2.

Segal, Jeffery A., and Harold J. Spaeth. 1993. *The Supreme Court and the Attitudinal Model.* Cambridge: Cambridge University Press.

Simon, Dan. 2004. "A Third View of the Black Box: Cognitive Coherence in Legal Decision-Making." *University of Chicago Law Review* 71: 511, 542.

Harrison v. Wisdom, 54 Tenn. (7 Heisk.) 99 (1872).

I SETTING THE STAGE
The Debate over What Law Has
to Do with What Judges Do

1 What's Law Got to Do with It

Thoughts from "the Realm of Political Science"

Jeffrey A. Segal

CHIEF JUSTICE ROBERTS has declared himself to be a believer in precedent, a follower of the rule of law, an umpire calling balls and strikes:

> Somebody asked me, you know, "Are you going to be on the side of the little guy?" And you obviously want to give an immediate answer, but, as you reflect on it, if the Constitution says that the little guy should win, the little guy's going to win in court before me. But if the Constitution says that the big guy should win, well, then the big guy's going to win, because my obligation is to the Constitution. That's the oath." (Roberts 2005)

While this may have been mere show, it wasn't mere show just for the Judiciary Committee. In a recent speech at the University of Arizona's Rehnquist Center, Roberts declared that the shift to a Supreme Court filled exclusively with former appellate judges took constitutional law out of "the realm of political science" and onto "the more solid grounds of legal arguments. What are the texts of the statutes involved? What precedents control?"(Liptak 2009).

Let's leave aside for the moment the fact that Roberts's assertions are empirically false—justices who served on lower appellate courts are not more likely to abide by precedent, and are not less likely to vote ideologically than are judges without appellate court experience (Epstein et al. 2009). What is the realm of political science? A quick answer is that political science examinations of judicial decision-making have focused on four partially overlapping models of such behavior: the legal model, the historical institutional model, the attitudinal model, and the strategic model.

17

The Legal Model

The legal model in its various forms holds that judges are motivated to establish an accurate, clear, and consistent interpretation of the law (Baum 1997). They do so by applying the facts of the case to relevant statutory and constitutional text, the intent of those who established those texts, and the precedents established by previous courts interpreting those texts (Segal and Spaeth 2002). Within this general framework, three broad operationalizations of the legal model exist. The most extreme version of the legal model claims determinate answers to legal questions. While Frank Cross correctly claims that "most contemporary scholars no longer adhere to the strict determinate formalist model" (Cross 1997, 255), it is still possible to read that there are "internally correct answers to all legal questions" (Markovits 1998, 1), or that "any extreme thesis that the law is always or usually indeterminate is untenable" (Greenawalt 1992, 11). From the political science perspective, while the charge of "formalism" is readily hurled at those testing the legal model (for example, Gillman 2001), only one article of which I am aware tests a determinate model of judicial decision-making (Kort 1963).

More realistically, political scientists, borrowing conceptually from Dworkin (1978), have typically examined whether legal factors have a gravitational force on judicial decisions. Even within this framework, scholars differ on how strong the force of law is. Dworkin's notion of a strong gravitational force requires judges to find the correct answer to legal questions and disallows any "independent force" of a judge's convictions "just because they are his" (Dworkin 1978, 118).[1] Political scientists who have adopted a gravitational perspective on the influence of law nevertheless expect that policy preferences will play a substantial role in judicial decisions (Songer and Lindquist 1996; Spaeth and Segal 1999).

Beyond the gravitational models are postpositive legal models. According to Howard Gillman:

> In the version of the argument that might be called "post-positivist," legalists make claims, not about the predictable behavior of judges, but about their state of mind—whether they are basing their decisions on honest judgments about the meaning of law. What is post-positivist about this version is the assumption that a legal state of mind does not necessarily mean obedience to conspicuous rules; instead, it means a sense of obligation to make the best decision possible in light of one's general training and sense of professional obligation. On this view, decisions are considered legally motivated if they represent a judge's sin-

cere belief that their decision represents their best understanding of what the law requires. Burton [Steven J., Judging in Good Faith (Cambridge University Press, 1992), xi–xii, 44] has persuasively argued that this notion of "judging in good faith" is all we can expect of judges (Gillman 2001, 486).

Under the postpositivist approach, virtually any decision *can be* consistent with the legal model. And any decision *is* consistent with the model as long as the judge has sincerely convinced herself that the decision is legally appropriate. The most basic problem with this approach is clear: the model is not falsifiable in terms of which decisions judges actually make. By accepted standards of scientific research, the model cannot provide a valid explanation of what judges actually do (see, for example, the discussion in *Daubert v. Merrell Dow Pharmaceuticals, Inc.*, 1993, 593). The fact that law might be nuanced (Burbank, this volume) does not relieve its empirical supporters of the need to provide falsifiable tests of its influence.

It is difficult to know whether judges sincerely believe they are judging in good faith. The extensive psychological literature on motivated reasoning suggests that plausible arguments are all that are needed to create an overlap between prior views and a subjective belief in correct results (for example, Braman 2006; Baumeister and Newman 1994; Kunda 1990), thus suggesting that good faith will not be all that difficult to come by.

Modeling Law

Any hope of modeling law from a political science perspective is likely to require a gravitational approach. A deterministic account will almost certainly fail, particularly at the appellate level, as there is very little evidence that this is how judges rule. Alternatively, a postpositive account will never fail, as it offers no predictions about what a judge will do (Gillman 2001, 486). The gravitational approach, on the other hand, allows for comparative statics. It is also consistent with statistical models that allow for error terms, or unexplained variance.

To determine the impact of law is not much different than determining the impact of other social phenomena. Simply put, judges' decisions should change—not deterministically, but at the margins—as law changes, holding alternative phenomena constant. This is easiest to see in the case of vertical stare decisis. While the strategic implications of such models can be quite complex (Cameron, Segal, and Songer 2000), the essence of testing this requires little more than determining how lower court decisions change as higher court decisions change, after controlling for other relevant factors such as case characteristics and the preferences of lower court judges.

Text

When scholars make causal inferences that justices are influenced by text, too often they reach these conclusions from nothing more than the official writings of the justice in question (Karsten 1997; Kahn 1999). But as Harold Spaeth (1964) demonstrated decades ago, Frankfurter was able to convince scholars that he was a restraintist, despite ample evidence to the contrary, because he so often wrote about the need to defer in those cases in which he chose to do so. Similarly, the fact that Scalia readily claims to be constrained by text doesn't necessarily mean that he really is. Even Brennan, after all, was willing to make use of textual arguments in his opinions, at least when they helped him reach liberal results (Phelps and Gates 1991).

Sometimes, doctrinal-based scholarship makes a plausible case for reliance on text. This is especially true when the decisions appear to contradict the justice's broad policy values. It's impossible to imagine that anything other than a lack of any constitutional command could have led Black to vote to uphold Connecticut's silly birth control law. Similarly, Scalia's dedication to the confrontation clause (for example, *Maryland v. Craig*, 1990) lends an air of plausibility to his self-proclaimed originalism (Scalia 1997; for empirical support, see Barkow 2006).

How then can we systematically assess, through a priori measures and falsifiable tests, text as a potential explanation for the justices' behavior?[2] The fundamental problem in testing text—at least from a gravitational perspective—consists of validly measuring this factor. One possibility is to measure not law, but "the more solid ground of legal arguments" (Roberts 2009). This can be accomplished by examining the briefs filed by petitioners and respondents in cases heard before the Court. Under the adversary system of justice, one can rely on litigants to present the best possible set of arguments in their favor. If a plausible case can be made that a legal argument supports a party, that party will almost undoubtedly make that claim. While counsel will vary in quality and thus might miss some obvious claims, the principle that justices should not decide issues *sua sponte* largely limits the justices to those claims that are made by counsel. Thus, we can measure whether one or both parties make a text based claim, whether the other side disputes that claim, or whether the other side makes a counterclaim (Segal and Howard 2002).

These are certainly not ideal measures, but if Scalia is a textualist, he should be more willing to support a liberal litigant who makes an undisputed textual claim than a liberal litigant who makes a disputed textual claim, or, ceteris paribus, one who makes no textual claim at all.

Intent

Perhaps the biggest difference between political science and law school examinations of law involves the difference between the normative scholarship that largely drives law school scholarship—that is, writings that seek to answer what law should be—and the positive scholarship that typically drives political science scholarship—that is, writings that try to explain the influences on law (Friedman 2004). Thus, legal academics carefully examine many different flavors of framers' or legislative intent, finding profound normative differences between, say, semantic originalism and original intentions (Solum 2008). Positive political scientists have paid less attention to intent, in part because of paltry evidence that intent actually influences judicial decisions (Segal and Howard 2002), and in part because the concept of legislative or framers' intent does not make sense.

"Intent" is a concept that applies to individuals, not to groups. As Kenneth Shepsle (1992) appropriately noted, "Congress is a 'they,' not an 'it.'" Thus, legislative intent is an oxymoron (ibid., 244). The damage that the plural nature of legislatures causes to the concept of legislative intent is less severe if legislation is single-dimensional rather than multidimensional. With but a single dimension, it might be possible to argue that the intent of a law depends on the author of the legislation, committee reports on what the bill is intended to accomplish, the public positions of those who supported it, or as McNollGast have argued, on the pivotal legislators—the moderates who sit between the ardent proponents and ardent opponents—whose assent was necessary to secure passage of the law (McCubbins, Noll, and Weingast 1992).

This prescription falls apart when legislation is multidimensional. This can happen because an omnibus bill contains multiple issues or because preferences over a bill dealing with just one issue are not single peaked. Such multi-peaked preferences can occur over a single issue in a variety of circumstances: a legislator might prefer that we either expand a war or pull out rather than continue on a current course of stalemate; or, say, prefer that we allow either a wide variety of religious holidays or none rather than just those from mainstream religions.

Under these circumstances, group decisions, such as those made by leg-

TABLE 1.1

Hypothetical Choices of Three Groups
among Three Alternatives

	Legislator		
	1	2	3
First Choice	M	A	N
Second Choice	A	N	M
Third Choice	N	M	A

islatures, can cycle. Consider the preference ordering in Table 1.1. Legislator 1 prefers giving mainstream religious holidays off (M), followed by all religious holidays (A), followed by no religious holidays (N). In other words, Legislator 1's preference function is $_MP_AP_N$. Legislator 2 prefers to give all religious holidays off, followed by none, followed by mainstream: $_AP_NP_M$. Legislator 3's preference is to give no religious holidays, then mainstream, then all—that is, $_NP_MP_A$. With these alternatives, giving all holidays off defeats giving no holidays off, giving no holidays off defeats giving mainstream holidays off, but giving mainstream holidays off defeats giving all holidays off.

While we can make useful but disputable arguments as to legislative intent when preferences are transitive, to speak of legislative intent when preferences are not transitive is to speak of something that simply does not exist. Unfortunately for legislatures, and for judges who must interpret their actions, the likelihood of intransitive preferences increases monotonically as the number of voters and the number of alternatives increase (Jones et al. 1995). Moreover, as Nobel laureate Kenneth Arrow (1963) demonstrated, it is not possible to construct a voting system that avoids the possibility of cycling without diminishing individual freedom to order preferences; disrupting unanimous preferences; making preferences between alternatives dependent on the presence or absence of additional alternatives; or acquiescing to the dictatorial preferences of one over the many (see also Riker 1982, ch. 5; Easterbrook 1982).

Even without formal proof of this problem, group intent remains problematic. As Segal and Spaeth ask:

> After all, who were the Framers? All 55 of the delegates who showed up at one time or another in Philadelphia during the summer of 1787? Some came and went. Only 39 signed the final document. Some probably had not read it. Assuredly, they were not all of a single mind. Apart from the delegates who refused to

sign, should not the delegates to the various state conventions that were called to ratify the Constitution also be counted as Framers? (Segal and Spaeth 2002, 68–69)

Unfortunately, commentators too often exclude these persons from consideration.

The intent of framers of constitutional amendments also lacks clarity. For example, following the Civil War, Radical Republican Senator Charles Sumner (R-MA) insisted that "separate education deprived blacks of their Fourteenth Amendment rights" (Baer 1983, 96). Lyman Trumbull (R-IL), though, viewed equal protection as only covering the nineteenth century's restricted (by our standards) view of civil rights: "the right to go and come; the right to enforce contracts; the right to convey his property; the right to buy property—those general rights that belong to mankind everywhere" (ibid.). "So, two of the leading figures of the Thirty-ninth Congress fundamentally differed about what the Amendment they had enacted meant" (ibid., 97).

Apart from the contradictions found in the *Congressional Record*, its historic accuracy is dubious. Until 1978, members of Congress were free to add to, subtract from, edit, and insert remarks they never uttered on the floor of the House or the Senate, notwithstanding the requirement that the House and Senate records to be "substantially verbatim transcripts of floor debates and remarks" (McKinney 2008).

Whether it makes sense to talk of legislative intent or not, and whether it is normatively appropriate or not, intent does not appear to guide justices' decisions (Segal and Howard 2002). As Judge Richard Posner notes, the backward orientation of intent "enlarges a judge's legislative scope . . . by concealing that he is legislating" (Posner 2008, 103).

Precedent

Precedent may or may not be a stronger indicator of how judges decide cases than legislative intent, but at least it exists. Measuring precedent, though, is not a simple task. As noted above, one possibility for modeling text (and intent) is via legal arguments. This approach, though, probably would not work for precedent, for in nearly every case litigants will claim that precedent supports them, and that the other side's precedents do not.

An alternative approach to precedent begins by recognizing that in many cases Supreme Court decision-making would look exactly the same whether justices were influenced by precedent or not. Consider the Court's decision in

Roe v. Wade (1973). The majority found a constitutional right to abortion that could not be abridged without a compelling state interest. The dissenters found no such right. In subsequent cases, Justices Blackmun, Brennan, Marshall, and others continued to support abortion rights. While we could say that choices in these cases were based on the precedent set in *Roe*, it is just as reasonable to say that those justices would have supported abortion rights in subsequent cases even without the precedent in *Roe*. Thus, even in a system without a rule of precedent Justice Scalia would continue to support the death penalty, non-racial drawing of congressional districts, limited privacy rights, and so forth. When prior preferences and precedents are the same it is not meaningful to speak of decisions as being determined by precedent. For precedent to matter as an *influence* on decisions, it must achieve results that would not otherwise have obtained. As Judge Jerome Frank stated, "Stare decisis has no bite when it means merely that a court adheres to a precedent that it considers correct. It is significant only when a court feels constrained to stick to a former ruling although the court has come to regard it as unwise or unjust" (*Shaughnessy v. United States ex rel.* 1955, 719).

This suggests, correctly I think, that only judges who disagree with a prec-edent as an original matter can be *influenced* by it. This then poses the practical difficulty of knowing whether a judge disagrees with a precedent. By this crite-rion, judges who originally voted to establish a precedent can hardly be said to be influenced by it in subsequent cases, while educated guesses are all that can be made about the preferences of justices who join the Court following the es-tablishment of a precedent. But those who dissented from the established prec-edent might properly be considered potential candidates for being influenced by that precedent. Consistent with the gravitational approach, if the precedent established in the case influences them, that influence should be felt in some proportion of that case's progeny through the justices' votes and opinion writ-ing. Determining the influence of precedent requires examining the extent to which justices who disagree with a precedent move toward that position in some number of subsequent cases.

For instance, Justice Rehnquist dissented in the jury exclusion cases *Bat-son v. Kentucky* (1986) and *Edmonson v. Leesville Concrete Co.* (1991); he con-curred in *Georgia v. McCollum* (1992), providing a quintessential example of what it means to be constrained by precedent: "I was in dissent in *Edmonson v. Leesville Concrete Co.* and continue to believe that case to have been wrongly decided. But so long as it remains the law, I believe it controls the disposition of this case. . . . I therefore join the opinion of the Court" (p. 52). This operational definition of precedent—through the subsequent behavior of judges who originally dissented—is both reasonable and, unlike other definitions, falsifiable, and allows serious testing of perhaps the most crucial aspect of the legal model. Of course, nothing requires that a justice bend in any particular case, but the influence of precedent should be seen in some moderate percentage of cases.

Historic Institutionalism

Closely related to the legal model is historic institutionalism. This model grew from the "new institutionalism" propounded by March and Olsen (1984) and applied to law and courts by Rogers Smith (1988). In contrast to a then-dominant behavioralism, which viewed social behavior as largely distinct from the context in which it occurred, March and Olsen argued that institutions shape purposeful behavior. Though the new institutionalism was consistent with and was quickly adopted by rational choice scholars, it later splintered into a new subfield that became known as historic institutionalism (Smith 2008).

Historic institutionalism, in contrast to rational choice theory (discussed below), focuses on boundedly rational behavior, path dependence, and structural inequalities in power. It also rejects exogenous preferences, arguing instead that institutions played a role in constituting preferences (ibid., 47). "With respect to Supreme Court politics," the historic-institutionalist application to public law means "that the justices' behavior might be motivated not only by a calculation about prevailing opportunities and risks but also by a sense of duty or obligation about their responsibilities to the law and the Constitution, and by a commitment to act as judges rather than as legislators or executives" (Gillman and Clayton 1999)

Much research has followed from this application. Howard Gillman (1993), for example, argues that *Lochner*-era decisions do not represent conservative decisions by a conservative Court, but legal decisions by a Court "giving voice to the founders' conception of appropriate and inappropriate policymaking." Ronald Kahn argues that Supreme Court decision-making can best be understood as a *constitutive* process, by which "members of the Supreme Court believe that they are required to act in accordance with particular institutional and legal expectations and responsibilities" (Kahn 1999, 175). Thus, "[J]ustices must be principled in their decision-making process" (ibid., 176). At the core of a constitutive approach to Supreme Court decision-making are the following major premises: "First, the Court does not follow elections or politics, but views itself as autonomous from direct and indirect political pressure. Second, justices do not follow personal policy wants. Third, respect for precedent and principled decision-making are central to Supreme Court decision-making" (ibid., 177–78). This, of course, is not far from the traditional legal model.

The Attitudinal Model

In contrast to the legal model or historic institutionalism, many political scientists reject the notion that judges' legal decisions are directed toward legal accuracy. Rather, they believe that judges' legal decisions are often motivated by policy concerns. Two main branches of this position exist. First, the attitudinal model holds that judges' decisions directly correspond to their personal policy preferences. Second, the strategic model holds that judges are often constrained in their ability to reach such goals and thus must strategically defer to colleagues or external political actors.

Though the roots of the attitudinal model go back to C. Herman Pritchett (1948), if not the legal realists (Frank 1930; Llewellyn 1931), Glendon Schubert (1965) first provided a detailed attitudinal account of Supreme Court decision-making (see also Schubert 1974). Schubert assumed that case stimuli and the justices' values could be ideologically scaled. To illustrate: imagine a pair of affirmative action cases whose constitutionality the Court must determine. The first case involves a quota for admissions for minority applicants, the second simply involves minority preferences.

According to the attitudinal model, we can place these searches in ideological space. Since the program with quotas is more egalitarian than the program that simply provides preferences, the first program can be placed to the left of the second one. This is diagrammed in Figure 1.1, where A represents the first program and B the second. Presumably, any affirmative action program will locate on the line; depending on case characteristics the program will be to the left of A, between A and B (inclusive), or to the right of B. Schubert refers to the points on the line where the searches lie as j-points.

Next, we place the justices in ideological space. Consider three justices, 1, 2, and 3, who are, respectively, liberal, moderate, and conservative. They could easily be rank ordered on an ideological scale, with 1 on the left, 2 in the middle, and 3 on the right.

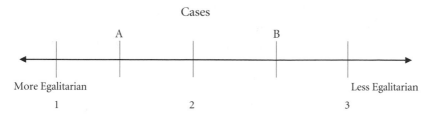

FIG. 1.1. The Attitudinal Model

With some additional information we might be able to go a bit further and say that Justice 1 is so liberal that he would uphold the quota-based affirmative action plan. Thus we could place Justice 1 to the left of Case A. Justice 2 might not be quite as liberal as Justice 1; she would not uphold the quota plan but would uphold the plan providing for racial preferences. Thus we could place Justice 2 to the right of Case A but to the left of Case B. Finally, Justice 3 might oppose all programs that take race into account. Thus we could place Justice 3 to the right of Case B. I place the justices in ideological space with the cases in Figure 1.1.

Schubert refers to the positions of the justices as their "ideal points" (i-points), though as we shall see the term is a misnomer. According to Schubert, a justice would vote to uphold all programs that are dominated by (that is, are to the right of) the justice's ideal point and would vote to strike all programs that dominate (that is, are to the left of) the justice's ideal point. If this is the situation the i-points represent not the ideal points of each justice, but the indifference point. Justice 1 upholds all searches to the right of her indifference point, rejects all searches to the left of her indifference point, and is indifferent whether searches at that point are upheld or overturned.

This model has several behavioral implications that can be tested, including the impact that case stimuli have on Court decisions (Segal 1984) and the influence that the justices' ideology has on their decisions. Consider the relationship in Figure 1.2. I place the justices' ideology, measured indirectly via a content analysis of newspaper editorial statements about each nominee from the time of his or her nomination by the president until the confirmation vote in the Senate, along the horizontal dimension. The vertical dimension presents the percentage of the time each justice cast a liberal vote in all of the cases between the 1953 and 2007 terms that are coded for ideological direction in Harold Spaeth's U.S. Supreme Court judicial database.

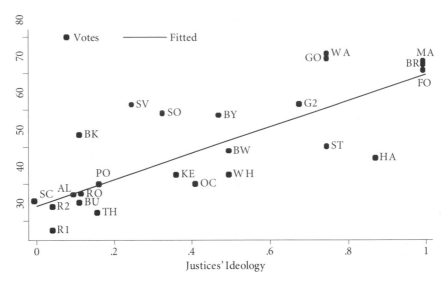

FIG. 1.2. Justices' Votes by Justices' Ideology (r = .79)

The diagonal line in Figure 1.2 represents the expected voting pattern given any justice's ideology. Justices above the line vote more liberally than expected; justices below the line vote more conservatively than expected. Overall, despite a couple of outliers, the justices vote pretty much as expected. The correlation coefficient, .79, demonstrates a tight fit between ideology and judicial behavior on the Supreme Court.

Schubert viewed the attitudinal model as a general model of political decision-making, without regard to organization or structure (Schubert 1965, 15–21). Institutions, though, matter, as lower court judges are not as free to engage in attitudinal behavior as Supreme Court justices are. Post-Schubert attitudinalists contend that the justices of the Supreme Court are able to decide cases based on their policy preferences because (1) they are a court of last resort and thus cannot be overruled by superior courts, (2) they have life tenure, (3) they lack ambition for higher office, and (4) docket control weeds out legally frivolous cases.

Judges below the Supreme Court cannot decide cases based on their personal policy preferences as they could readily be reversed by courts above them. An extensive literature demonstrates the influence of law and hierarchical authority on the decisions of lower court judges (See Songer 1990; Klein 2002; Baum 1978; Songer and Haire 1992; Songer, Segal, and Cameron 1994). When

U.S. Court of Appeals judge Samuel Alito voted to strike down New Jersey's partial birth abortion statute, he was undoubtedly expressing the Supreme Court's preference, not his own.

This is not to say that a lack of political finality necessarily characterizes all Supreme Court decisions. Congress can overturn judicial interpretations of statutory language and amendments can undo constitutional interpretation. Nevertheless, the fact that the president and the Senate choose the justices means that the justices' preferences will rarely be out of line with that of the dominant political coalition. And even if on some matters they are, the difficulty of overriding Supreme Court decisions, even statutory ones (see Henschen 1983), in a decentralized legislative environment means that the Court typically has little to fear from Congress.

Supreme Court justices also have little to fear from the public. Tenure concerns undoubtedly influence the decisions of state court judges (Hall 1987). Such judges react to factors such as public opinion, at least in highly salient areas (Kuklinski and Stanga 1979; Gibson 1980; Brace and Hall 1990). For example, judges sentence felons to longer prison terms as their reelections near (Huber and Gordon 2004). The evidence on life-tenured federal court judges, however, suggests little or no influence of public opinion.[3]

With regard to ambition, lower court judges may desire higher office and thus be influenced by significant political others. Lobbying for a Supreme Court seat from the lower courts, through speeches or through written opinions, is not uncommon. One interested in reaching the High Court could hardly vote his or her personal policy preferences on abortion during the Obama administration if those preferences were antichoice.

Finally, the Supreme Court controls its own docket. While this does not guarantee that the justices will vote their policy preferences, it is a requisite for their doing so. Many meritless cases undoubtedly exist that no self-respecting judge would decide solely on the basis of his or her policy preferences. If a citizen sought to have the AIG bailout declared unconstitutional, and if the Supreme Court had to decide the case, attitudinalists would not expect the votes in the case to depend on whether the justices favored the bailout. But because the Supreme Court does have control over its docket, the justices would refuse to decide such a meritless case. Those that the Court does decide tender plausible legal arguments on both sides.

The Strategic Model

The strategic model grows out of the fundamental belief in rational choice theory that human behavior is inherently interactive. Our best decisions in many instances depend on the decisions and actions taken by others. Of course, that is not always the case. In a perfectly competitive market, firms are price takers and they produce up to the point where marginal cost equals marginal revenue, regardless of what other firms do. In final-stage voting in an election with two candidates, a voter should choose the candidate she prefers most. In these and other situations where people face dominant strategies, their choice is the same no matter what others choose. In many situations, though—for example, imperfect competition, voting in primaries or three-candidate races, deciding cases that can be appealed to a higher court—the best choice depends on the actions and preferences of others. In those circumstances, humans must behave strategically, taking into account the reactions of relevant others in their environment. A justice writing an opinion for the Court must take into account the views of others in the majority decision coalition, or else she won't receive the votes needed to form a majority.

The strategic nature of choice is central to rational choice theory. William Riker provides a concise statement of the essence of the theory:

> Actors are able to order their alternative goals, values, tastes and strategies. This means that the relation of preference and indifference among the alternatives is transitive . . . . Actors choose from available alternatives so as to maximize their satisfaction (Riker 1990, 172).

Maximizing satisfaction requires rational foresight, the consideration of the consequences of one's decisions. This is strategic behavior.

As applied to the judiciary, the so-called separation of powers models examine the degree to which the courts should defer to legislative majorities in order to prevent overrides that result in policy worse than what the court might have achieved through sophisticated behavior. In the landmark work, Brian Marks carefully examined the placement of preferences in Congress that prevented *Grove City College v. Bell* (1984) from being overturned prior to 1986 (Marks 1988, 87–88). Consistent with the attitudinal model, Marks claimed that the justices simply voted their ideal points. Building on his work, subsequent neo-Marksist theorists argued that if the Court exercised rational foresight, it would not always choose its ideal point (see, for example, Ferejohn and Shipan 1990; Gely and Spiller 1990).

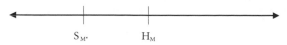

S_{M^*} H_M

FIG. 1.3. Simple pivotal model. Pivotal Politics model. H = House, S = Senate, $_M$ = Median. * = pivotal player. Model assumes that conservatives (on right) prefer legislation more than liberals (on left). * = pivotal player.

P H_{33^*} S_{33} S_{40} H_{50}

FIG. 1.4. Pivotal Politics model. P = President, H = House, S = Senate, Subscripts = percentile. * = pivotal player. Model assumes that conservatives (on right) prefer legislation more than liberals (on left).

To conceptualize the model, I use Krehbiel's (1998) notion of pivotal politics. Under Krehbiel's model, there are a variety of people who must support legislation for it to pass. In a single-chamber legislature with no agenda control, the pivotal person would be the median of the chamber (Black 1958). If there are two chambers and the legislation is preferred by those on the right as compared to those on the left, the pivotal player would be the leftmost of the two medians. If that player supported the legislation, so too would all of those to the median's right, as would the median of the other chamber and at least half the legislators in the other chamber. In Figure 1.3, that player would be the Senate median.

The possibility of a Senate filibuster complicates the game slightly. Now, instead of needing the support of the median or 50th percentile senator, the filibuster (under current rules for cloture) requires that legislation supported by conservatives receive the support of the 40th percentile senator (counting the most conservative member as the 99th percentile and the most liberal as the 1st percentile).

Presidential veto further complicates the game. Consider again override legislation favored by conservatives. The Court can withstand override if it has the support of

1. the House median, or
2. the Senate filibuster pivot, or
3. the president and either the 33rd percentile House member or the 33rd percentile Senate member.

Consider the preferences as laid out in Figure 1.4. The Court has made a liberal decision that conservatives would like to override. That override corresponds to a cutpoint, such that those to the right of the cutpoint prefer to override the Court while those to the left of the cutpoint would vote against the override legislation.

If the cutpoint is to the right of H_{50}, then no relevant players support override and the bill passes neither chamber. If the cutpoint is to the left of H_{50} but the right of S_{40}, the bill could pass both chambers but gets blocked by a filibuster in the Senate. If the cutpoint is between H_{33} and S_{33}, the bill passes both chambers and gets vetoed by the president. The veto is sustained by the House, as H_{33} does not support overriding the veto. Only if the cutpoint is at or below H_{33} does the Court get overturned. Thus, H_{33} is the pivotal player in this situation. Under the separation of powers model, if the Court is to the right of H_{33} its liberal decisions are safe from override. If the Court is to the left of H_{33}, it must place its decisions at (or just to the right of) H_{33} in order to avoid override.

These models can add gatekeepers to the model, such as majority party medians (Cox and McCubbins 2005; Cox and McCubbins 1993) or key committees (Shepsle and Weingast 1987).

What matters to the Marksist model is not who really controls the legislative process, but whom the Court believes controls the legislative process. As there is no apparent way of knowing this, many scholars have tried testing a set of plausible models hoping that the results are robust to legislative specification (Spiller and Gely 1992; Segal 1997; Bergara, Richman, and Spiller 2003; Segal, Westerland, and Lindquist 2011).

The Marksist model has been applied to both statutory and constitutional cases, but there are significant theoretical problems with each. In statutory cases, the Court is often faced with a binary choice: is pregnancy discrimination sex discrimination prohibited by the civil rights act? May the Food and Drug Administration regulate tobacco? To the extent that statutory cases are binary, the Court is never worse off from a policy perspective by choosing its ideal point. It is true that the Court's policy could be reversed, but unless there is a substantial cost to the Court from legislative override of statutory decisions—something that none of the proponents of the statutory model posit— the Court is never worse off than if it always chooses its ideal point.

The sliding standards of review in constitutional cases means that a Court that fails to compromise with Congress could end up with policies that are worse than it otherwise would have wanted. The problem here, is that Congress cannot legislatively override the Court's constitutional decisions.[4] Congress can restrict the institutional authority of the Court in a large number of ways (Rosenberg 1992; Segal, Westerland, and Lindquist 2011), but is unlikely to do so. This leads scholars such as Geyh (2006) to argue that the Court has a substantial degree of independence in such decisions. But that same lack of response by Congress leads rational choice scholars to exactly the opposite conclusion. As Rogers explains: "[We] do not observe justices being disciplined for their constitutional decisions because, as the SOP equivalent of nuclear war, the cost to them is so HIGH that they act strategically (to avoid) precisely that sort of devastating retaliation" (quoted in Segal and Westerland 2005). But certainly the Court can and does take positions at odds with those preferred by large majorities of senators and representatives, as its decisions of reapportionment (*Wesberry v. Sanders* 1964), flag burning (*United States v. Eichman* 1990), gun free school zones (*United States v. Lopez* 1995), and religious freedom restoration (*City of Boerne v. Flores* 1997) readily attest.

The separation-of-powers games vary the number of issue dimensions, the number of legislative chambers, the influence of committees, the existence of presidential veto, and so forth. But regardless of the specific assumptions made, these models assume that the Court will construe legislation as close to its ideal point as possible without getting overturned by Congress. The law that judges create is the result of this process.

Empirics

The legal approaches discussed above have led to some conditional positive findings of the impact of law in the judicial decision-making. At the Supreme Court, Spaeth and Segal (1999), for example, have found a small but discernable and systematic influence of stare decisis on the decisions of Supreme Court justices, while Segal and Howard (2002) have found a conditional impact of the plain meaning of text (but not intent) on the votes of conservative justices. So too, a large number of scholars have found evidence for the impact of doctrine or case stimuli on the justices' decisions (Bailey and Maltzman 2008; Richards and Kritzer 2002; Segal 1984).[5]

At the Court of Appeals we would expect to find greater influence of law, and by and large we do. Donald Songer and associates have clearly found an impact of Supreme Court preferences on Court of Appeal judges (Songer 1987; Songer, Segal, and Cameron 1994). In many cases the Courts of Appeals must issue rulings in the absence of guidance from the Supreme Court. Klein's (2002) examination of issues of first impression finds that Court of Appeals judges are motivated both by policy preferences and by a desire to make legally sound decisions. Cross (2007) finds a substantial role for doctrine in explaining Court of Appeals decisions. On the other hand, Hettinger, Lindquist, and Martinek (2006) claim that the impact of law on the courts of appeals is small and is generally overwhelmed by the impact of attitudinal or strategic factors.

At the state-court level, the presence of a state-level ERA does not have an overall influence on the likelihood of ruling in favor of litigants pressing sex-discrimination claims, though it does indirectly influence the probability that a court will use the strict-scrutiny standard (Baldez, Epstein, and Martin 2006). Moreover, there appears to be no impact of educational rights provisions in state constitutions on the decision of state supreme courts to strike down unequal funding provisions for public schools (Lundberg 2000). But constitutional rights to privacy do significantly increase the likelihood that state supreme courts will strike antiabortion statutes (Brace, Gann Hall, and Langer 1999).

Conclusion

You don't need to come from "the realm of political science" to reject the notion of judges as umpires. As Baum's chapter in this book notes, even umpires reject the Roberts notion of umpires. Judges, and particularly appellate judges, make both law and policy. The realm of political science has provided some clear examples of both. More interesting than the findings that separate law and policy is the work of Hansford and Spriggs (2006), who urge a convergence of the study of law and politics. Their systematic study of precedent on the Supreme Court finds that justices interpret precedent so as to move those precedents closer to their policy preferences. The justices, though, need to legitimate their decisions. Thus, law and politics are not separate; rather, the justices use law to make policy (ibid.).

Notes

1. This quotation concerns Dworkin's mythical judge Hercules, but Dworkin applies the technique to human judges as well (1978, 130). Dworkin's arguments are typically normative, but often have an empirical component to them as well. For example, "[J]udges are agreed that earlier decisions have gravitational force" (1978, 112), or "[J]udges characteristically feel an obligation to give what I call 'gravitational force' to past decisions" (Dworkin 1986, viii) are empirical statements, not normative ones.

2. Much of what follows here applies to intent as well, but intent has its own problems, as discussed below.

3. See, for example, Giles and Walker 1975 (finding no impact of public opinion on

district court decision-making); Kritzer 1979 (finding a spurious relationship between district court sentencing decisions and public opinion,); Mishler and Sheehan 1996 (suggesting that the relationship between judicial decisions and public opinion might be spurious); Stimson, MacKuen, and Erikson 1995 (finding a negligible relationship between Supreme Court decisions and public opinion); and Norpoth and Segal 1994 (finding a spurious relationship between public opinion and Supreme Court decisions).

4. This point is not without contention. Robert Dahl's (1957) famous article on judicial review notes Congress getting the final say on a variety of constitutional issues via ordinary legislation. Meernick and Ignagni (1997) credit Congress with the capability of overriding the Court's constitutional decisions via ordinary legislation. As Epstein and Knight (1998) note about the interbranch struggle over the Religious Freedom Restoration Act: "Shortly after the decision in *City of Boerne* was announced, Congress held hearings to discover how it might be circumvented. Therefore, the game over RFRA may not be over, with the possibility always existing that the Court will eventually buckle under." Of course, Congress and the states can override the Court via constitutional amendment, as they have done five times: the Eleventh Amendment (1798) overturned *Chisholm v. Georgia*, which had allowed individuals to sue states in federal courts; the Fourteenth Amendment (1868) overturned *Scott v. Sandford*, which had declared blacks ineligible for United States citizenship; the Sixteenth Amendment (1913) overturned *Pollock v. Farmer's Loan and Trust Company*, which had voided the federal income tax; the Nineteenth Amendment (1920) overruled *Minor v. Happersett*, which precluded the Fourteenth Amendment from guaranteeing women's suffrage; and the Twenty-sixth Amendment (1971) overturned *Oregon v. Mitchell*, which had struck a federal law permitting eighteen-year-olds to vote in state elections.

5. Richards and Kritzer claim that jurisprudential regimes guide Supreme Court decision-making, but they do not control for linear changes that are inconsistent with their approach that could have led to the same results. Lax and Rader (2010) find serious flaws with Richards and Kritzer's empirical findings.

References

Ariely, Dan. 2008. *Predictably Irrational: The Hidden Forces That Shape Our Decisions.* New York: HarperCollins.

Arrow, Kenneth. 1963. *Social Choice and Individual Values.* New Haven: Yale University Press.

Baer, Judith. 1983. *Equality under the Constitution.* Ithaca, NY: Cornell University Press.

Bailey, Michael, and Forest Maltzman. 2008. "Does Legal Doctrine Matter? Unpacking Law and Policy Preferences on the U.S. Supreme Court." *American Political Science Review* 102: 369–84.

Baldez, Lisa, Lee Epstein, and Andrew D. Martin. 2006. "Does the U.S. Constitution Need an ERA?" *Journal of Legal Studies* 35: 243–83.

Barkow, Rachel E. 2006. "Originalists, Politics, and Criminal Law on the Rehnquist Court." *George Washington Law Review* 74: 1043–77.

Batson v. Kentucky. 1986. 476 U.S. 79.

Baum, Lawrence. 1978. "Lower-Court Response to Supreme Court Decisions: Reconsidering a Negative Picture." *Justice System Journal* 3: 208–19.

———. 1997. *The Puzzle of Judicial Behavior.* Ann Arbor: University of Michigan Press.

Baumeister, Roy, and Leonard Newman. 1994. "Self-Regulation of Cognitive Inference and Decision Processes." *Personality and Social Psychology Bulletin* 20: 3–19.

Bazelon, Emily. 2006. "Invisible Men: Did Lindsey Graham and Jon Kyl Mislead the Supreme Court?" *Slate*, March 27. Available at http://www.slate.com/id/2138750/.

Bergara, Mario, Barak Richman, and Pablo T. Spiller. 2003. "Modeling Supreme Court Strategic Decision Making: The Congressional Constraint." *Legislative Studies Quarterly* 28: 247–80.

Black, Duncan. 1958. *The Theory of Committees and Elections.* Cambridge: Cambridge University Press.

Brace, Paul, and Melinda Gann Hall. 1990. "Neo-Institutionalism and Dissent in State Supreme Courts." *Journal of Politics* 52: 54–70.

Brace, Paul, Melinda Gann Hall, and Laura Langer. 1999. "Judicial Choice and the Politics of Abortion: Institutions, Context, and the Autonomy of Courts." *Albany Law Review* 62: 1265–1300.

Braman, Eileen. 2006. "Reasoning on the Threshold: Testing the Separability of Preferences in Legal Decision-Making." *Journal of Politics* 68 (May): 308–21.

Cameron, Charles, Jeffery Segal, and Donald Songer. 2000. "Strategic Auditing in a Political Hierarchy: An Informational Model of the Supreme Court's Certiorari Decisions." *American Political Science Review* 94: 101–15.

City of Boerne v. Flores. 1997. 521 U.S. 507.

Cox, Gary W., and Matthew D. McCubbins. 1993. *Legislative Leviathan: Party Government in the House.* Berkeley: University of California Press.

———. 2005. *Setting the Agenda: Responsible Party Government in the U.S. House of Representatives.* Cambridge: Cambridge University Press.

Cross, Frank B. 1997. "Political Science and the New Legal Realism: A Case of Unfortunate Interdisciplinary Ignorance." *Northwestern University Law Review* 92: 251–326.

———. 2007. *Decision Making in the U.S. Courts of Appeals.* Palo Alto: Stanford University Press.

Dahl, Robert. 1957. "Decision-Making in a Democracy: The Supreme Court as a National Policy-Maker." *Journal of Public Law* 6: 179-295.

Daubert v. Merrell Dow. 1993. 509 U.S. 579.

Dworkin, Ronald. 1978. *Taking Rights Seriously.* Boston: Harvard University Press.

———. 1986. *Law's Empire.* Boston: Harvard University Press.

Easterbrook, Frank H. 1982. "Ways of Criticizing the Court." *Harvard Law Review* 95: 802–32.

Edmonson v. Leesville Concrete Co. 1991. 500 U.S. 614.

Eisenstadt v. Baird. 1972. 405 U.S. 438.

Epstein, Lee, and Jack Knight. 1998. *Choices Justices Make.* Washington, DC: Congressional Quarterly Press.

Epstein, Lee, Andrew D. Martin, Kevin M. Quinn, and Jeffrey A. Segal. 2009. "Circuit Effects: How the Norm of Federal Judicial Experience Biases the Supreme Court." *University of Pennsylvania Law Review* 157.

Ferejohn, John, and Charles Shipan. 1990. "Congressional Influence on Bureaucracy." *Journal of Law, Economics and Organization* 6: 1–20.

Frank, Jerome. 1930. *Law and the Modern Mind*. New York: Brentano's.

Friedman, Barry. 2004. "The Importance of Being Positive: The Nature and Function of Judicial Review." *University of Cincinnati Law Review* 72: 1257–1303.

Gely, Rafael, and Pablo T. Spiller. 1990. "A Rational Choice Theory of Supreme Court Decision Making with Applications to the *State Farm* and *Grove City* Cases." *Journal of Law, Economics, and Organizations* 6: 263–300.

Georgia v. McCollum. 1992. 505 U.S. 42.

Geyh, Charles Gardner. 2006. *When Courts and Congress Collide: The Struggle for Control of America's Judicial System*. Ann Arbor: University of Michigan Press.

Gibson, James. 1980. "Environmental Constraints on the Behavior of Judges." *Law and Society Review* 14: 343–70.

Giles, Michael, and Thomas G. Walker. 1975. "Judicial Policy-Making and Southern School Segregation." *Journal of Politics* 37: 917–36.

Gillman, Howard. 1993. *The Constitution Besieged: The Rise and Demise of Lochner Era Police Power Jurisprudence*. Durham, NC: Duke University Press.

———. 2001. "What's Law Got to Do with It? Judicial Behavioralists Test the "Legal Model" of Judicial Decision Making." *Law and Social Inquiry* 26: 465–504.

Gillman, Howard, and Cornell W. Clayton. 1999. "Beyond Judicial Attitudes." In Cornell W. Clayton and Howard Gillman, eds., *Supreme Court Decision Making: New Institutionalist Approaches*. Chicago: University of Chicago Press.

Greenawalt, Kent. 1992. *Law and Objectivity*. New York: Oxford University Press.

Griswold v. Connecticut. 1965. 381 U.S. 479.

Grove City College v. Bell. 1984. 465 U.S. 555.

Hall, Melinda Gann. 1987. "Constituent Influence in State Supreme Courts: Conceptual Notes and a Case Study." *Journal of Politics* 49: 1117–24.

Hamdan v. Rumsfeld. 2006. 548 U.S. 557.

Hamdan Reply Brief. 2006. Available at http://www.hamdanvrumsfeld.com/HAMDAN-FINAL.march15.reply.pdf.

Hansford, Thomas G., and James F. Spriggs II. 2006. *The Politics of Precedent on the U.S. Supreme Court*. Princeton: Princeton University Press.

Henschen, Beth. 1983. "Statutory Interpretations of the Supreme Court." *American Politics Quarterly* 11: 441–58.

Hettinger, Virginia A., Stefanie A. Lindquist, and Wendy L. Martinek. 2006. *Judging on a Collegial Court: Influences on Federal Appellate Decision Making*. Charlottesville: University of Virginia Press.

Huber, Gregory A., and Sanford C. Gordon. 2004. "Accountability and Coercion: Is Justice Blind when It Runs for Office?" *American Journal of Political Science* 48: 247–63.

Jones, Bradford, Benjamin Radcliff, Charles Taber, and Richard Timpone. 1995. "Condorcet Winners and the Paradox of Voting: Probability Calculations for Weak Preference Orders." *American Political Science Review* 89: 137–44.

Kahn, Ronald. 1999. "Interpretive Norms and Supreme Court Decision Making: The Rehnquist Court on Privacy and Religion." In Cornell W. Clayton and Howard Gillman, eds., *Supreme Court Decision Making: New Institutionalist Approaches.* Chicago: University of Chicago Press.

Karsten, Peter. 1997. *Heart vs. Head: Judge-Made Law in Nineteenth Century America.* Chapel Hill: University of North Carolina Press.

Klein, David E. 2002. *Making Law in the United States Courts of Appeals.* New York: Cambridge University Press.

Kort, Fred. 1963. "Simultaneous Equations and Boolean Algebra in the Analysis of Judicial Decisions." *Law and Contemporary Problems* 28: 143–63.

Krehbiel, Keith. 1998. *Pivotal Politics: A Theory of U.S. Lawmaking.* Chicago: University of Chicago Press.

Kritzer, Herbert M. 1979. "Federal Judges and Their Political Environment: The Influence of Public Opinion." *American Journal of Political Science* 23: 194–207.

Kuklinski, James, and John Stanga. 1979. "Political Participation and Governmental Responsiveness." *American Political Science Review* 73: 1090–99.

Kunda, Ziva. 1990. "The Case for Motivated Reasoning." *Psychological Bulletin* 108: 480–98.

Lax, Jeffrey R. and Kelly T. Rader. "Legal Constraints on Supreme Court Decision Making: Do Jurisprudential Regimes Exist?" *Journal of Politics* 72: 273–84.

Liptak, Adam. 2009. "Roberts Sets Off Debate on Judicial Experience." *New York Times,* February 17, A14.

Llewellyn, Karl N. 1931. "Some Realism about Realism—Responding to Dean Pound." *Harvard Law Review* 44: 1222–64.

Lundberg, Paula J. 2000. "State Courts and School Funding: A Fifty-State Analysis." *Albany Law Review* 63: 1101–46.

March, James, and Johan P. Olsen. 1984. "The New Institutionalism: Organizational Factors in Political Life." *American Political Science Review* 78: 734–49.

Markovits, Richard S. 1998. *Matters of Principle: Legitimate Legal Argument and Constitutional Interpretation.* New York: New York University Press.

Marks, Brian. 1988. "A Model of Judicial Influence on Congressional Policymaking: *Grove City College v. Bell.*" Working Papers in Political Science, P-88–7, Hoover Institution, Stanford University.

Maryland v. Craig. 1990. 497 U.S. 836.

McCubbins, Matthew, Roger G. Noll, and Barry R. Weingast. 1992. "Positive Canons: The Role of Legislative Bargains in Statutory Interpretation." *Georgetown Law Journal* 80: 705–42.

McKinney, Richard. 2008. "An Overview of the Congressional Record and Its Predecessor Publications." Washington, DC: Law Librarian's Society. Available at http://www.llsdc.org/cong-record/.

Meernik, James, and Joseph Ignagni. 1997. "Judicial Review and Coordinate Construction of the Constitution." *American Journal of Political Science* 41: 447–67.

Mishler, William, and Reginald S. Sheehan. 1996. "Public Opinion, the Attitudinal Model, and Supreme Court Decision Making: A Micro-Analytic Perspective." *Journal of Politics* 58: 169–200.

Norpoth, Helmut, and Jeffrey A. Segal. 1994. "Popular Influence on Supreme Court Decisions." *American Political Science Review* 88: 711–24.

Phelps, Glenn A., and John B. Gates. 1991. "The Myth of Jurisprudence: Interpretive Theory in the Constitutional Opinions of Justices Rehnquist and Brennan." *Santa Clara Law Review* 31: 567–96.

Posner, Richard A. 2008. *How Judges Think.* Cambridge: Harvard University Press.

Pritchett, C. Herman. 1948. *The Roosevelt Court.* New York: Macmillan.

Richards, Mark J., and Herbert M. Kritzer. 2002. "Jurisprudential Regimes in Supreme Court Decision Making." *American Political Science Review* 96: 305–20.

Riker, William H. 1982. *Liberalism against Populism.* San Francisco: W. H. Freeman.

———. 1990. "Political Science and Rational Choice." In James E. Alt and Kenneth A. Shepsle, eds., *Perspectives on Positive Political Economy.* New York: Cambridge University Press.

Roberts, Chief Justice John G. 2005. Quoted in Liptak, Adam. 2005. "Court in Transition: The Context; Speaking Volumes." *New York Times,* September 16, A23.

———. 2009. Quoted in Liptak, Adam. 2009. "Roberts Sets off Debate on Judicial Experience." *New York Times,* February 17, A14.

Roe v. Wade. 1973. 410 U.S. 113.

Rosenberg, Gerald N. 1992. "Judicial Independence and the Reality of Judicial Power." *Review of Politics.* 54: 369–98.

Scalia, Antonin. 1997. *A Matter of Interpretation.* Princeton: Princeton University Press.

Schubert, Glendon. 1965. *The Judicial Mind.* Evanston, IL: Northwestern University Press.

———. 1974. *The Judicial Mind Revisited.* New York: Oxford.

Segal, Jeffrey A. 1984. "Predicting Supreme Court Decisions Probabilistically: The Search and Seizure Cases 1962–1981." *American Political Science Review* 78: 891–900.

———. 1997. "Separation of Power Games in the Positive Theory of Congress and Courts." *American Political Science Review* 91: 28–44.

Segal, Jeffery A., and Robert M. Howard. 2002. "An Original Look at Originalism." *Law and Society Review* 36: 113–38.

Segal, Jeffrey A., and Harold J. Spaeth. 2002. *The Supreme Court and the Attitudinal Model Revisited.* New York: Cambridge University Press.

Segal, Jeffrey A., and Chad Westerland. 2005. "The Supreme Court, Congress, and Judicial Review." *North Carolina Law Review* 83: 1323–52.

Segal, Jeffery A., Chad Westerland, and Stefanie Lindquist. 2011. "Congress, the Supreme Court, and Judicial Review: Testing a Constitutional Separation of Powers Model." *American Journal of Political Science:* 55: 89–104.

Shaughnessy v. United States ex rel. 1955. 349. U.S. 280.

Shepsle, Kenneth A. 1992. "Congress Is a "They," Not an "It": Legislative Intent as Oxymoron." *International Review of Law and Economy* 12: 239–56.

Shepsle, Kenneth A., and Barry R. Weingast. 1987. "The Institutional Foundations of Committee Power." *American Political Science Review* 81: 85–104.

Smith, Rogers. 1988. "Political Jurisprudence, the 'New Institutionalism,' and the Future of Public Law." *American Political Science Review* 82: 89–108.

———. 2008. "Historical Institutionalism and the Study of Public Law." In Keith E. Whittington, R. Daniel Kelemen, and Gregory A. Caldeira, *The Oxford Handbook of Law and Politics.* New York: Oxford University Press.

Solum, Lawrence B. 2008. "Semantic Originalism." Illinois Public Law Research Paper no. 07–24. Available at SSRN: http://ssrn.com/abstract=1120244.

Songer, Donald R. 1987. "The Impact of the Supreme Court on Trends in Economic Policy Making in the United States Courts of Appeals." *Journal of Politics* 49: 830–44.

———. 1990. "An Overview of Judicial Policymaking in the United States Courts of Appeals." In John B. Gates and Charles A. Johnson, eds., *The American Courts: A Critical Assessment.* Washington, DC: Congressional Quarterly.

Songer, Donald R., and Susan Haire. 1992. "Integrating Alternative Approaches to the Study of Judicial Voting: Obscenity Cases in the U.S. Court of Appeals." *American Journal of Political Science* 36: 963–82.

Songer, Donald R., and Stefanie A. Lindquist. 1996. "Not the Whole Story: The Impact of Justices' Values on Supreme Court Decision Making." *American Journal of Political Science* 40: 1049–63.

Songer, Donald R., Jeffrey A. Segal, and Charles M. Cameron. 1994. "The Hierarchy of Justice: Testing a Principal-Agent Model of Supreme Court–Circuit Court Interactions." *American Journal of Political Science* 38: 673–96.

Spaeth, Harold J. 1964. "The Judicial Restraint of Mr. Justice Frankfurter—Myth or Reality." *Midwest Journal of Political Science* 8: 22–38.

Spaeth, Harold J., and Jeffrey A. Segal. 1999. *Majority Rule vs. Minority Will: Adherence to Precedent on the U.S. Supreme Court.* New York: Cambridge University Press.

Spiller, Pablo T., and Rafael Gely. 1992. "Congressional Control or Judicial Independence: The Determinants of U.S. Supreme Court Labor-Relations Decisions, 1949–1988." *RAND Journal of Economics* 23: 463–92.

Stimson, James A., Michael B. MacKuen, and Robert S. Erikson. 1995. "Dynamic Representation." *American Political Science Review* 89: 54.

United States v. Eichman. 1990. 496 U.S. 765.

United States v. Lopez. 1995. 514 U.S. 549.

Wesberry v. Sanders. 1964. 376 U.S. 1.

2 On the Study of Judicial Behaviors

Of Law, Politics, Science, and Humility

Stephen B. Burbank

I T IS FITTING that I have been asked to help set the stage for this
volume by comparing legal and political science models of judicial
behavior and the light they shed on what judges do. I am not only a law professor; I am an old law professor. Moreover, a legal scholar commenting on an
article that I published in 1997 called it the work of a "committed formalist,"
which was not intended as a compliment (Neuborne 1997, 2094). Who better to
channel William Blackstone than an aged "committed formalist?"

In seeking to help set the stage for this volume, I first briefly review what
I take to be the key events and developments in the history of the study of
judicial behavior in legal scholarship, with attention to corresponding developments in political science. I identify obstacles to cooperation in the past—such
as indifference, professional self-interest, and methodological imperialism—as
well as precedents for cross-fertilization in the future.

Second, drawing on extensive reading in the political science and legal literatures concerning judicial behavior, I seek to identify the most important lessons that we have learned, or should have learned, to date, as the springboard
for progress in the future. The first lesson is that the relationship between law
and judicial politics (as I define them) is not monolithic; it varies among courts
and, even on the same court, among cases. As a result, we should speak of "judicial behaviors" rather than "judicial behavior." The second lesson is that there
is no dichotomy between law and judicial politics; they are complements, each
needing (or relying on) the other. The third lesson is that the mix of law and

judicial politics on any given court does or should result from institutional design decisions that reflect what the polity wants from that court.

Finally, I argue that, because the relevance of the enterprise in which we are engaged and its stakes transcend the world of scholarship, scholars who work in this area bear a special burden of responsibility.

A Troubled History

When I was a student at the Harvard Law School in the late 1960s and early 1970s, one might not have known that political scientists at the university studied courts (or more precisely the Supreme Court). I knew it, because as a Harvard undergraduate I had been privileged to take Government 154 from Robert McCloskey. Someone, perhaps Paul Freund, told me that McCloskey was the exception to the rule that Harvard Law School did not welcome political scientists. Whether or not that was true, precious few of McCloskey's insights, or those of other political scientists, made it into the courses I took or the course materials I studied.

My courses with Paul Freund *did* benefit from the influence that Thomas Reed Powell, his teacher and later colleague, had on that great constitutional scholar. But Powell was both a lawyer and a political scientist. His influence on Freund was that of a legal realist with acute analytical skills who paid close attention to judicial decisions, believed that ideas matter, and was on record that "[t]hose who see law as judicial whim or fiat are partly right, but only partly. Those who see law as *only* this or *only* that see but narrowly" (Freund 1956, 800).

In retrospect, the indifference to political science in that era is not a surprise, because Harvard Law School was still in the grip of the legal process approach (Kalman 1986). This was an effort to navigate between two strands of legal realism: its de(con)structive project of exposing the indeterminacy of law that (as some legal realists would have it) permits judges to pursue their own values while hiding behind the myth that the law made them do it, and its constructive project of seeking to develop policy through a value-neutral assembly and analysis of empirical data (facts). The latter (constructive) strand fell out of favor quickly, as law professors became discouraged by the time and money required to gather data, and by the seemingly slight payoffs, and with the effects of the Depression on funding (ibid.). The former (de[con]structive) strand, always living uneasily in Langdell Hall,[1] came increasingly under pressure with attacks on the Warren Court in the 1950s and the quest for neutral principles such attacks elicited (Wechsler 1959).[2] Long before that, however, both strands of legal realism had been caught up in controversy about scientific natural-ism during what Edward Purcell (1973) describes as "the crisis of democratic theory" that was caused by the rise of totalitarian governments on the left and the right in the 1920s and 1930s.

I have taught at law schools in one capacity or another since 1976. For many years thereafter, the study of judicial behavior in legal scholarship essentially did not exist. Even after technology facilitated, and funds became available for, empirical research, reducing obstacles that had discouraged legal realists in the 1930s, such research was not valued at most elite law schools.[3] Rather, law pro-fessors advanced *conceptions of judicial behavior*, and for a decade or more the most prominent such conceptions were advanced by scholars of polar opposite policy preferences and, usually, political persuasions.

On one side there were the adherents of Critical Legal Studies, latter-day realists with an attitude, if not a social agenda, who tended to confuse the ques-tion of what judges *can do* with the question of what they *ought to do* and who, in any event, did not systematically explore what judges *in fact do*. On the other side there were the adherents of Law and Economics, whose agenda was to explain law through microeconomic theory and, to the extent they were concerned about judicial behavior, to explain it through an economic theory of human behavior (Posner 1995). Richer than the conception of judicial behavior held by most adherents of Critical Legal Studies, for many years this too was, nevertheless, a theory undisciplined by facts.

Finally, in that area of legal scholarship most likely to overlap with, and be informed by, political science—constitutional law—judges "behaved" either in a world of doctrine or in a world of theory. In neither sphere, with few excep-tions, was the scholarship of law professors informed by quantitative analy-sis or by the insights of traditional political science, perhaps because the legal scholars in question "were more interested in shaping the law than explaining it" (Keck 2007, 511; see also Friedman 2006, 263).

Until quite recently political scientists had good reason for the complaint that law professors ignored their work. To their great credit, the same was not true in the other direction. Legal realism is acknowledged as one of the intellec-tual inspirations of the attitudinal model of judicial behavior (Segal and Spaeth 2002). In addition, although rational choice (strategic) theory was evident in the law and courts subfield as early as the 1950s, political scientists have generously credited law professors, economists, and business school professors with reviving it by demonstrating its potential (Epstein and Knight 2003; Brenner 2003).

Admirable as the willingness of political scientists to follow a scholarly Golden Rule has been, it renders more puzzling the certitude that some of them have occasionally displayed in their dismissive treatment of the notion that law may play a role in the behavior of the justices of the U.S. Supreme Court (Segal and Spaeth 2002; see Keck 2008). For one who is conversant with the intellectual (and moral) dilemmas that scientific naturalism was thought to pose in the 1930s, Thomas Reed Powell's observation about those who "see but narrowly" is wise counsel in favor of humility. One would have thought the same of the cautions expressed by C. Herman Pritchett, "the first pioneer in what became the leading body of research on judicial behavior" (Baum 2003, 71). Pritchett observed that "political scientists, who have done so much to put the 'political' in 'political jurisprudence' need to emphasize that it is still 'jurisprudence.' It is judging in a political context, but it is still judging; and judging is still different from legislating or administering"(1969, 42).[4]

Law professors have not been the only, and probably not the primary, targets of criticism by those who deny the influence of law. After all, Pritchett's caution was a response to what Lawrence Baum has termed "a degree of intolerance across methodological divides [within political science], especially directed by quantitative scholars toward those who do qualitative research" (2003, 69).[5]

Indeed, perhaps the real intended audience for criticisms of "outdated immersion in legal rules and legal doctrine" were "mainstream" political scientists, since, "[by] demonstrating that the study of judicial behavior was amenable to statistical analyses, [quantitative law and courts scholars] could thereby prove [their] bona fides as card-carrying social *scientists*" (Scheingold 2008, 748).

The Present Situation

Even if still viewed with suspicion at some law schools—and hence, a risky scholarly path for the untenured—empirical research on legal institutions, including courts,[6] seems poised to fulfill the promise that eluded the legal realists, albeit without the pretense of value-agnostic pragmatism.[7] More to the point of this volume, for close to two decades scholars teaching at law (and business) schools have been making important contributions to the literature on judicial behavior, particularly (as discussed above) by developing and testing rational choice models of judicial behavior (Eskridge 1991; Revesz 1997; Cross and Tiller 1998; Harvey and Friedman 2006; Cross 2007; Posner 2008; Landes and Posner 2008; Kim 2009). Others, whether or not themselves conducting original empirical research, have begun regularly to consult the political science literature on courts and judicial behavior, and, unencumbered by turf wars, to find nourishment "across methodological divides" (Friedman 2006).

An overwhelming majority of judges are probably ignorant of the political science literature on judicial behavior. Some judges read law reviews, however, and because those teaching in law schools tend to publish in law reviews, some of their articles on judicial behavior came to the attention of judges and elicited responses (Edwards 1998; Wald 1999). Although at times reminiscent of methodological intolerance in political science, more recently these interventions have suggested a dialogue holding the potential for all participants to learn (Edwards 2003; Edwards and Livermore 2009).

The same, I hope and would like to believe, is true of the relationship between law professors and quantitatively oriented political scientists.[8] Apart from the conference that led to this volume, there are many reasons for optimism. I will suggest three.

First, it cannot hurt that, after decades of neglect which, after a while, must have seemed malignant rather than benign, law professors and law schools are paying attention to the work of judicial behavior scholars in political science. The attention paid comes in many forms: citations in the legal literature, invitations to present work in seminars for law school faculty and/or students, invitations to coauthor with law faculty, increasing opportunities to publish in law reviews,[9] and, perhaps most important for the interdisciplinary enterprise, appointments to law school faculties.

Second, it is hard to ignore the energy, creativity, and research results of those scholars, including law professors, who have taken up the challenge by quantitative political scientists to demonstrate by acceptable (that is, of course, quantitative) methods that law matters, including on the Supreme Court, and how it matters (Richards and Kritzer 2002; Kritzer and Richards 2003, 2005; Kastellec and Lax 2008; Cross 2007; Johnson, Spriggs, and Wahlbeck 2007; Bailey and Maltzman 2008). To the extent that such efforts are deemed successful, the narrowly instrumental theory that the justices (or judges more generally) are autonomous, unifocal, and unidimensional personal-policy-preference machines (Benesh 2003) that underlies the attitudinal model and, without the assumption of complete autonomy, the work of some rational choice scholars (Bloom 2001), has lost any claim to monopoly power. "Justices are not simply life-tenured policy maximizers" (Bailey and Maltzman 2008, 282).

Third, at the same time that some scholars have sought to meet the challenge to model law, other scholars have begun to take a close look at the "science" undergirding the work of those issuing the challenge. The number and variety of fundamental assumptions, operating principles, and concrete choices that have been questioned, particularly within the last few years, are impressive (Kritzer 1996; Gillman 2001; Friedman 2006; Shapiro 2009; Fischman and Law 2008; Landes and Posner 2008; Kim 2009; Kastellec and Lax 2008; Braman 2008; Edwards and Livermore 2009). Many of the demonstrated problems can be fixed. Yet, now that there is good reason, on their own terms, to question quantitative political scientists' monopoly of knowledge about the wellsprings of judicial behavior, other problems in the specification and testing of their models and with their data—such as behavioral or observational equivalence (or collinear variables) (Segal 1984; Friedman 2006; Stras 2006; Bailey and Maltzman 2008; Fischman and Law 2008),[10] inability to accommodate cases presenting multiple issues (Young 2002; Braman 2008; Shapiro 2009), selection bias (Kastellec and Lax 2008), coding bias (Harvey and Woodruff 2009; Harvey 2008; Fischman and Law 2008), and systematic coding errors (Stras 2006; Landes and Posner 2008, Shapiro 2009)[11]—may prompt greater humility, perhaps helping to bridge the methodological divide.[12]

What, then, do I see as the state of current knowledge about judicial behavior? The framework I have chosen to describe it is drawn from work on judicial independence and accountability, particularly interdisciplinary work with Barry Friedman (1999; Burbank and Friedman 2002a; Burbank and Friedman 2002b). Accountability to law is an important source of constraint (or selfrestraint; Kramer and Ferejohn 2002) posited by those who resist claims that judges are completely independent to decide as they wish. A putative dichotomy between independence and accountability thus maps well on to a putative dichotomy between "judicial politics," *defined for this purpose as the pursuit of a judge's preferences on matters of policy relevant in litigation*, and "law," *defined for this purpose as known and established (but not necessarily determinate) law*. This way of framing the inquiry recalls the turf war in the law and courts subfield of political science. Imagine my surprise when, having learned from one group of political scientists that Supreme Court justices are accountable to elected politicians (Dahl 1957; McCloskey 2005) and thus that judicial independence is a myth (Rosenberg 1991; Jacob 1962), I learned from another group of political scientists that Supreme Court justices are wholly independent, and thus that judicial accountability is a myth (Segal and Spaeth 2002).

For Contextualism
The first lesson that I take from a review of the judicial behavior literatures is that, just as it is an error to treat judicial independence (and accountability) as a monolith (Burbank and Friedman 2002b), so, in describing judicial behavior, *it is an error to assert or assume that the relationship between "judicial politics" and "law" is or should be the same with respect to every judge in a particular judicial system, or indeed that it is or should be the same even for judges on the same court in every type of case.*[13] In sum, we should speak not of "judicial behavior" but of "judicial behaviors" (Friedman, 2006).

For many years these points were obscured as a result of the long virtual monopoly that studies of the U.S. Supreme Court held in the public law subfield of political science (M. Shapiro 2008, 769). Even today the variousness of the relationship between "law" and "judicial politics" may be obscured by the occasional failure of scholars to confine descriptions of their results, and their claims, to the judges, courts, and cases in fact studied and/or their apparent reluctance to acknowledge that judges on different courts are influenced in different ways and to different degrees, including by "law," even after that should have been clear (Segal and Spaeth 2002, 10, 92–93, 235; Spaeth 2008, 753; compare Segal, this volume, 24, with ibid., 28).

Those promoting the attitudinal model have never satisfactorily explained unanimous decisions of the Supreme Court, which in recent years have accounted for 30 to 40 percent of the Court's output. And these percentages are "misleading" because they "ignore the petitions for certiorari that the Justices turn down because they are not minded to disturb a precedent for which they would not have voted in the first place, and the petitions that are never filed because the Court would be sure to deny them on the basis of established precedent or clear constitutional or statutory language" (Posner 2008, 50; see also Gerhardt 2008).[14] Even if an explanation for unanimous decisions other than a shared view of what fidelity to law requires were plausible, such an explanation presumably would contemplate behavior different from that evinced in 5–4 decisions. Moreover, even if one were willing to accept the test of adherence to precedent used by Segal and Spaeth in their attempt quantitatively to falsify the operation of the legal model on the Supreme Court (2002; see also Segal, this volume, 23–25), that would tell us nothing about the role of precedent on the lower federal (or state) courts. In fact, as many scholars have pointed out, their test confuses judicial roles, neglecting the fact that the legal norms concerning precedent that govern Supreme Court justices are different from those that govern the judges of other courts (Gillman 2001; Gerhardt 2003; Friedman 2006).[15] Moreover, recently other scholars have provided "evidence that non-policy factors [including precedent] influence Supreme Court justices and that the extent of such influence varies across individual justices in interesting ways" (Bailey and Maltzman 2008, 369).

The attitudinal model requires that the justices not be constrained by Congress (or by the Executive Branch), which is the most obvious reason why its proponents have resisted contrary findings by those testing rational choice models designed to determine whether the justices act strategically in anticipation of responses by Congress (Segal and Spaeth 2002, 106–9, 346). In unpublished work perhaps stimulated by Harvey and Friedman's study that yielded "fairly robust support, across different models of the legislative process, for the hypothesis of a constitutionally constrained Court" (2006, 553), Professor Segal proves (again) that his commitment to scholarship is stronger than his commitment to the attitudinal model (Segal, Westerland, and Lindquist 2009). In a paper describing a study of the Court's decisions in cases challenging the constitutionality of federal statutes, he reports statistical results that lead him to conclude that there may be an "institutional maintenance effect"—justices moderating their use of the power of judicial review out of concern, not about the fate of a particular decision, but about the Court's ongoing ability to function independently.

There is something deeply unsettling about an account of judicial behavior, even if confined to the justices of the Supreme Court, that consigns, if not all of the effort of the lawyers briefing and arguing cases before them, then the opinions that fill the U.S. Reports, to the category of window-dressing. The attitudinalists' response to criticisms reflecting that discomfort has been the assurance that they are not claiming conscious dissembling, coupled with invocation of the phenomenon of motivated reasoning, about which, however, they profess agnosticism (Segal and Spaeth 2002, 433). If, however, the justices are acting strategically, modifying their behavior in anticipation of, or response to, other actors, it is not clear that there is any room for motivated reasoning. That helps to explain why some strategic accounts, as for instance of stare decisis on the Supreme Court, are so controversial in certain quarters (Bloom 2001; Edwards 2003).

Increasingly over the past thirty years, political scientists and law professors have studied judicial behavior on courts other than the U.S. Supreme Court. By exposing the influence of precedent and of law more generally on lower court judges, scholars have confirmed that judicial behavior is not monolithic (Cross 2007; Sisk and Heise 2005). It has not been clear, however, whether findings of widespread obedience to Supreme Court precedent on the courts of appeals—findings acknowledged by Segal and Spaeth (2002, 96)[16]—reflect the influence of law or simply strategic behavior to avoid reversal. The latter explanation became increasingly implausible as the Supreme Court's appetite for work became more anorexic. Moreover, as noted by Professor Cross, "[T]he studies to date have shown only very limited evidence of hierarchical strategic decision making by circuit courts" (2007, 103). Cross's own results suggest that "circuit court judges do not anticipatorily repudiate old precedents but instead aggressively follow old precedents that are presumptively unattractive to the current Supreme Court" (ibid., 104–5).

Recent work by Professor Kim confirms the existence of panel effects—different voting behavior by court of appeals judges on ideologically heterogeneous than on ideologically homogeneous panels—in sex discrimination cases (2009). She too finds no support for the view that such behavior (on the part of those in the ideological majority) reflects a strategic response to possible reversal by the Supreme Court, and for that and other reasons she rejects the "whistleblowing" hypothesis posited by Cross and Tiller (1998). She does find, however, that such behavior is correlated with the proximity of the minority panel member's preferences to those of the circuit median judge, which is consistent with strategic behavior to avoid reversal by the en banc court of appeals.

To her credit, Professor Kim discusses possible alternative explanations for her findings, in particular deliberative accounts that focus on the internal dynamics of a panel. However, her distinction between "the dynamics internal to the judicial panel" and "interaction between the appellate judges on a panel and the other actors in the judicial system" (2009, 1333–34) is potentially misleading. Although courts of appeals accomplish (almost all of their) decisional work through panels of three judges, the court as a whole bears responsibility for the law of the circuit. That the judges take their responsibility very seriously is suggested by rules forbidding one panel from overruling the legal ruling of another and by intracourt opinion dissemination practices that permit all judges to see what their colleagues are doing (or proposing to do) without having to rely on disappointed litigants.[17] Perhaps we should not conceive of the deliberations or dialogue occurring when panel members have different views as restricted to the panel. Conversely, strategic behavior need not be confined to maximizing a judge's preferences as to policy. As often pointed out, rational choice models can accommodate a preference for law (Epstein and Knight 2003; Posner 2008).

Professor Kim's admirable acknowledgment of the problem of behavioral or observational equivalence causes her to be appropriately cautious in reporting her findings and in making claims. My point here is only that consideration of her posited deliberative/strategic dichotomy underscores the extent to which both the attitudinal model and rational choice models based solely on a preference for policy deny any consequential role on a plural court for dialogue about law (Edwards 2003; Edwards and Livermore 2009; Whittington 2000). Particularly if motivated reasoning is not an available refuge, but in any event, one can only wonder why judges, including the justices, spend so much time talking, and talking about, law, not just publicly (as at oral argument or in opinions), but to each other (Johnson, Spriggs, and Wahlbeck 2007).[18]

All of this suggests that just because parsimony is *useful* in modeling for purposes of statistical analysis does not mean that the results of those analyses are *sufficient* for thinking about human behavior, about law, or for that matter about politics.

Unlike the attitudinal model, a strategic model narrowly focused on pursuit of personal policy preferences at least acknowledges that judicial behavior is like the behavior of other government actors in at least one respect: it is shaped or constrained by institutional context.[19] Neither model, however, leaves room for other influences—such as, for instance, insecurity (Burbank 2007a)—that might complicate the judicial utility function with elements that do not lead invariably to pursuit of a judge's personal policy preferences. Yet, whatever the merits of the psychological theories that informed the attitudinal model of judicial behavior (Segal and Spaeth 2002), scholarship in the intervening decades has provided accounts of human behavior that, in their complexity, accord far better with the sense that most of us have about what motivates (or, more precisely, can motivate) human beings (Posner 2008).

In this light, it is not surprising to learn that, even on that most political of all American courts, the Supreme Court of the United States, the justices respond to a variety of audiences, with the result that their behavior cannot be explained in a single dimension (Baum 2006; see also Peretti and Rozzi,

2008), or that "observed changes in judges' voting positions on final votes result from factors other than changes in preferences and issue content" (Meinke and Scott 2007, 933). Other scholars, studying court of appeals chief judges, have found that "the judicial utility function includes non-policy as well as policy concerns" (George and Yoon 2008, 8). Finally, studies have indicated that, *on certain courts and in certain types of cases*, personal characteristics such as religion (Sisk, Heise, and Morriss 2004) and sex (Boyd, Epstein, and Martin 2007) may influence judicial behavior, and that judges are subject to unconscious bias (Rachlinski, Johnson, Wistrich, and Guthrie 2007). In sum, "Ringing changes on the 'political' might seem to exhaust the possible nonlegalist factors in adjudication. It does not begin to" (Posner 2008, 10).

We can all agree that "social scientists should develop realistic and generalizable explanations of social behavior" (Epstein and Knight 2003, 210). Science has told us where human beings come from (Shubin 2008). It has not yet been able to tell us very much about the human brain (Morse 2006, 2008).[20] Even when confined to the Supreme Court, the attitudinal model is implausible (*not* "realistic") as a self-sufficient theory of judicial behavior, not just because it strips judging of "law" and institutional context. Both it and narrowly instrumental strategic models are implausible because they strip judges of their humanity, reducing human behavior to the single-minded pursuit of a narrow set of goals. Recent studies contradict the narrow supposition of these models' proponents, suggesting that, to the contrary, it is not just "law" that must be considered in the mix with "judicial politics" and that, as with "law," whether and when other influences affect judicial behavior is context-dependent.

Against Dichotomies

The second lesson I take from a review of the judicial behavior literatures is that, just as it is an error to posit a dichotomy between judicial independence and judicial accountability (Burbank and Friedman 2002b), so, *in describing judicial behavior, it is an error to posit a dichotomy between "law" and "judicial politics." Instead, like judicial independence and accountability, "law" and "judicial politics" are different sides of the same coin. They are not opposites but rather complements.*

This proposition may be logically anterior to the first, and it is implicit in the way in which I framed some of that discussion, in particular by referring to "the relationship between 'judicial politics' ... and 'law,'" and the "mix of 'law' and 'judicial politics.'" I chose this order instead, because the evidence adduced above suggesting that "law" matters on all courts at least some of the time should make it clear that a "law"/"judicial politics" dichotomy is untenable with respect to those courts and may make it easier to rethink the relationship between them more generally. On the view I take here, the answer to the question at the center of this volume—What's law got to do with it?—depends in important measure on how one defines law.

Those who deny judicial independence have tended to think in absolute terms (that is, independence *or* accountability, not independence *and* accountability), to neglect the role that dialogic processes play in a system of separated but interdependent lawmakers, and to confuse influence with control (Burbank 1999). Those who deny that "law" matters (judicial accountability) have tended to model and code in absolute, unidimensional terms, to deny (because, for some, their theory demands it) the influence of dialogic processes, and to confuse the results of statistical tests confirming the influence of one variable in an impoverished model with proof of their prophecy.

My proposition, however, is not just that different models of judicial behavior should be regarded as complements because "each model accurately captures some of what every judge does some of the time, and . . . no single model is likely to describe any judge all of the time" (Robbennolt, MacCoun, and Darley 2008, 1–2). Judge Posner has warned that "one must be careful about dividing judicial decisions (or judges) into legalist and political, or, what is closely related, asserting a Manichean dualism between law and politics. The dualism only works when 'law' is equated to legalism, and that is too narrow" (2008, 8; see also 47; Edwards and Livermore 2009). Or again, "The middle ground is not the idea that adjudication is part 'law' and part 'ideology.' . . . Law is suffused with ideology" (Posner 2008, 43).

Other scholars have also observed that "law" and "judicial politics" "are not, in fact, mutually exclusive categories: the 'law' may explicitly give room for a judge's 'ideology' to operate" (Fischman and Law 2008, 6). In that regard, consideration of the many roles that, without apology or disguise, judicial discretion plays in "law" suggests that the territory where "judicial politics" are part of (cannot usefully be distinguished from) "law" is substantial (Gillman 2001). It also suggests that, like decisions about formalism (Schauer 1988), decisions about discretion (and hence about the proper role for "judicial politics" in "law") have to do with power, "because institutional values argue for allocating different types of power between different levels of the judiciary" (Kim 2007, 442).

This relationship between (not opposition of) "law" and "judicial politics" was at one time obscured by the claims of lawyers, scholars, and judges who were concerned to establish, preserve, or augment their professional power by minimizing judicial agency in (or, as opposed to) "law" (including even, or especially, the common law). More recently, it has been obscured by anachronistic insistence on such claims by political scientists who have been concerned to establish, preserve, or augment disciplinary power by maximizing judicial agency in (or as opposed to) "law." Critical to acceptance of this proposition by both groups is a willingness to renounce reductionist thinking (Clayton 2003, 308), even at the risk of losing professional power. Like a "[m]onolithic brain explanation of complex behavior," a monolithic social science explanation of judicial behavior is almost always "radically incomplete" (Morse 2006, 464).

Professor Kim's valuable discussion of judicial discretion has both positive and normative dimensions. Confident that she, Judge Posner (2008), Judge Edwards and Mr. Livermore (2009), and others in law and political science (for example, Gillman 2001) are correct as a descriptive matter when they insist on a more nuanced view of law that recognizes the "interpenetration of law and [judicial] politics" (Whittington 2000, 631), I will not pause long over the objection that such accounts are nonfalsifiable (Segal and Spaeth 2002, 48 n. 12, 433; Segal, this volume, 19).

One response to that objection is a reminder that a person whose only tool is a hammer is prone to see only nails. Another is to recall the reasons for humility, canvassed above, given how the science of modeling and statistics has fared even with models not at all nuanced in this respect. A more hopeful response is that the relevant science (which, after all, has come a long way since the realists' forays into the empirical world) may one day catch up to the complexity of the enterprise, and that in the meanwhile, as recent work suggests, some law can be modeled and its influence tested through statistical manipulation. For the rest, and given that the stakes are not limited to the world of scholarship, I prefer the messiness of lived experience to the tidiness of unrealistically parsimonious models.

Like those responsible for legal processes, legislative and judicial, scholars who study those processes and the human beings who make them work should seek enlightenment from science. At the end of the day, however, just as "it may be a mistake to let science furnish not only evidence with which we adjudicate controversies but the standards for deciding whether evidence can be considered" (Burbank 1996; see also Lempert 2009), so too may some judicial behavior elude the scientific techniques by which we seek to pin down phenomena in the natural world (Edwards 2003).

In thus rejecting the belief of some realists "that truth [is] wholly dependent on empirically established facts," I do not side with the rational absolutists' belief "that human reason [can] discover certain universal principles of justice by philosophical analysis of the nature of reality" (Purcell 1973, 176). I simply opt for an epistemology that seems appropriate in light of how little we know about the causal mechanisms of human behavior, mindful that "[it] defies the imagination that one new methodology or theoretical assumption is going to topple all previous efforts to understand the human condition" (Wolfe 2008, 55).

This is not the occasion to delve deeply into the normative dimensions of Professor Kim's account of judicial discretion. Yet, some consideration of those dimensions is appropriate, if only as a way to anticipate questions likely to be raised by the proposition that "law" and "judicial politics" are complements or different sides of the same coin. I have already indicated that complementarity means more than existing side by side. But if it is true that "law" is "suffused with" "judicial politics" (Posner 2008, 43), do we not confront again the dilemma that bedeviled the realists: "[H]ow could the idea of the subjectivity of judicial decision be squared with the doctrine that free men should be subject only to known and established law?" (Purcell, 1973, 94).

Professor Kim posits that judicial discretion exists in part because "social needs demand some measure of flexibility in the application of legal rules" (2007, 442). She thus helps us to understand that "judicial politics" are a complement to "law" not only as the necessary price, in a human construct, of filling interstices and resolving indeterminacies. "Judicial politics" are also a complement to "law," because "law" needs their mediating influence (Scheppele 2002). It is equally true, however, that for reasons that span the legal landscape—from the predictability and even-handedness that a well-functioning market economy requires, to the respect for other lawmaking institutions that constitutional democracy requires—"judicial politics" need the restraining influence of "law." *In other words, known and established (but not necessarily determinate) law and the pursuit of a judge's preferences on matters of policy relevant in litigation are complements in the sense that, like judicial independence and accountability, they need (or at least must rely on) each other.* To acknowledge that normative views about the proper balance between them as to any particular judge or court may differ (see the first proposition above) or that, even on the same normative view and as to the same judge or court, the proper balance may change over time, is not to deny that, on some courts and in some cases,

(1) "law" without "judicial politics" would be weak and feeble, or (2) "judicial politics" without "law" would be dangerous.[21] *Moreover, it is not to deny that the two in combination can constitute law as it is generally understood.*

Judge Posner argues that "the reasons for the legislative character of much American judging lie so deep in our political and legal systems and our culture that no feasible reforms could alter it" (2008, 15). One useful perspective on the historical influences to which he alludes is provided by the history of equity. That American lawyers, scholars, and judges in the nineteenth and early twentieth centuries could with straight faces have denied the role of judicial agency in (or as opposed to) law is, from a historical perspective, hardly surprising. Apart from the advantages of such a position as a means to establish, preserve, or augment professional power, the common law looked relatively determinate and quite free of "judicial politics" when compared with the system of equity with which it had long been in competition and remnants of which survived the Revolution, reshaped in its image. Following Maitland's insight that equity presupposed the existence of common law, Professor Subrin observed:

> In assessing the place of equity practice in the overall legal system, it is critical to realize the extent to which the common law system operated as a brake. One could not turn to equity if there was an adequate remedy at law. Equity grew interstitially, to fill in the gaps of substantive common law (such as the absence of law relating to trusts) and to provide a broader array of remedies—specific performance, injunctions, and accounting. Equity thus provided a "gloss" or "appendix" to the more structured common law. An expansive equity practice developed as a necessary companion to common law. (1987, 920)

This is one way, as a normative matter, to think about the relationship between "law" and "judicial politics." *Or at least it is once one recalls that equity was and is a species of law as it is generally understood.* Again, the balance between them will vary within a judicial system and across the litigation landscape, and it will vary over time.

It is often said that "we are all legal realists now" (Kalman 1986, 229). Certainly, very few if any lawyers believe today that a constitutional case can be decided in the mechanistic way that Justice Owen Roberts described.[22] Yet, it is probably true that the lawyers of every generation need to relearn the lessons of legal realism. One such lesson is that, even when a legal provision does not invite the infusion of judicial policy preferences, it may be sufficiently indeterminate that judges so inclined can deploy their power to try to implement their personal policy preferences. Another lesson is that undisciplined pursuit of judicial policy preferences is difficult to square with the assumptions of a system that aspires to democracy under law.

As this discussion suggests, however, the lessons of legal realism are misleading to the extent that they imply a dichotomy between "law" and "judicial politics." The critical concept is that of discipline, and it operates in both directions. In one direction, cynicism engendered by a monolithic (and dichotomous) conception of both law and politics makes it too easy to ignore the extent to which "law" must rely on "judicial politics" in order to avoid (1) crippling formalism (because the gaps and indeterminacies, planned and unplanned, that result from avoiding it will be filled by human beings who have policy preferences), and (2) socially destabilizing unfairness (because, as Hamilton observed, independent judges are needed to provide relief from, by mitigating the severity and confining the operation of, "unjust and partial laws") (Hamilton 1961; Burbank 1999). Judge Posner describes "the legislative character of much American judging" as "not such a terrible thing" (2008, 15).[23] Professor Ramseyer goes further. In his view, "That [judges] act politically in political cases simply reflects their essential independence. That politics matters should not embarrass. To the extent judicial independence is a good, it should engender pride" (2008, 3). If this does not assume a dual dichotomy, it invites attention to the constraining influence, promoting accountability, of "law."

In the other direction, I find persuasive Kritzer and Richards's argument that "the justices create jurisprudential regimes to provide guidance to other political actors [including other courts] and to themselves," and that "the goal here is consistency" (2005, 35). Moreover, a legal system disciplines "judicial politics" not only when it provides guidance through law that is determinate, but also by means of practices, norms, and customs that have accreted around the judicial office,[24] of which adherence to precedent is the most important. Such practices, norms, and customs can themselves be regarded as instantiations of a penchant for self-discipline (Kramer and Ferejohn 2002) that acknowledges the sources of, and constraints on, institutional power in a system of separate but interdependent lawmaking institutions (Cross 2007; McCloskey 2005). In this too, the relationship between "law" and "judicial politics" is akin to the relationship between judicial independence and judicial accountability (Geyh, 2006; Burbank and Friedman 2002b).

Institutional Design

The third lesson I take from a review of the judicial behavior literatures is that, as with judicial independence and judicial accountability, *the quantum and quality, or mix, of "law" and "judicial politics" depends, or should depend, on what a particular polity wants from its courts.*

This proposition can be viewed as a normative corollary to, or partial restatement of, the proposition that it is an error to think that the relationship between "judicial politics" and "law" is or should be the same with respect to every judge (court) in a particular judicial system, or that, even with respect to judges on the same court, it is or should be the same in every type of case. It echoes Professor Schauer's suggestion that formalism (or what Judge Posner calls "legalism") "ought to be seen as a tool to be used in some parts of the legal system and not in others" (1988, 547), as it does, conversely, Professor Kim's argument that judicial discretion exists in part "because institutional values argue for allocating different types of power between different levels of the judiciary" (2007, 442).

The fact that quantitative judicial behavior scholarship, standing alone, cannot answer questions of institutional design is, of course, no reproach. Properly conceived and properly implemented, such research could be of enormous benefit to those responsible for institutional design who are interested, or can be persuaded to take an interest, in knowing what judges in fact do and why they do it. In order to be "properly conceived" for these purposes, the research will have to reflect attention to Professor Friedman's concern that quantitative scholarship too often has lacked "normative bite" (2006, 262), a concern recently echoed in Professor Wolfe's observation that "[t]echnique comes first in the new [behavioral] economics, just as it did in the old, and conclusions follow" (2008, 53). It may also be true that, before research of this type and with this potential is undertaken, those capable of conducting it will have to broaden their (research) horizons to include questions of "[p]ower and authority" (Whittington 2000, 631) that they have hitherto neglected.

On the assumption that future quantitative research will be designed to address institutional questions of import, the failure or inability of some theories or models of judicial behavior to acknowledge or accommodate the documented phenomenon of preference change (or "drift") (Epstein, Martin, Quinn, and Segal 2007; Ruger 2005; Burbank 2007a) will limit their ability to inform wise public policy even if their other assumptions and methodologies are accepted. Of greater concern, the apparent reluctance of some quantitative scholars to embrace and move on from evidence that judicial behavior is not monolithic, even on the same court, and even if that court is the U.S. Supreme Court, is antithetical to the development of wise public policy.

There are many examples of reforms of the judiciary that have not turned out the way those responsible for them intended, or have turned out in ways they could never have imagined. Thus, although we may assume that Congress created the federal courts of appeals in 1891 in order to lessen the docket burden of the Supreme Court, it is not clear that the legislation would have passed but for the perception that district courts (judges) lacked adequate legal accountability (Geyh 2006). As a result of a number of other alterations in the relevant landscape, however, district courts have been re-empowered (Yeazell 1994).

The Congress that in 1925 acceded to the justices' request to make the Court's docket almost entirely discretionary surely did not imagine the effects of that legislation. As recounted by Professor Hartnett (2000), their putative surprise could be explained in part by the failure of subsequent courts to keep almost all of the promises that the justices made to Congress when seeking the legislation. More consequential by far, Hartnett suggests (following a number of political scientists [Provine 1980; Pacelle, 1991]), has been the doctrinal freedom that release from the obligation to police its consequences has afforded, coupled with the power that the Court seized by unilaterally "claim[ing] the authority to issue limited grants of certiorari, that is, to decide only a particular issue in a case, ignoring the other issues" (Hartnett 2000, 1705).

It is not clear which, if any, of the institutional design decisions that these examples reflect would have been changed if those making them had available relevant quantitative and qualitative political science research (of the sophistication and quality that can be expected today) and/or legal scholarship informed by the fruits of such research. One is not left entirely to speculation, however, about the possible impact of such scholarship on the assessment of current proposals affecting the institutional design of the judiciary. In order to reach an informed judgment about the claims made by those promoting a nonrenewable eighteen-year term for Supreme Court justices (Cramton and Carrington 2006), recourse to history and to both quantitative and qualitative research in political science is essential. The relevant research concerns not just the Court itself, but what the public knows about the Court and how (as bearing on legitimacy), and the behavior of interest groups (Burbank 2006).

Conclusion

We have made great progress in the study of judicial behaviors, and law professors interested in that subject owe a large debt to scholars in political science. Their work, quantitative and qualitative, has enriched our knowledge and provided us with new tools and perspectives. In devoting attention to the more extreme claims of some quantitative political scientists, I do not mean to diminish either their contributions to this body of knowledge or the potential that their work holds to enable additional advances. Just as it is a mistake to banish law and other influences from the behavioral landscape, even at the Supreme Court of the United States, so is it a mistake to neglect the numerous insights that the attitudinalists and other like-minded (as to judicial preferences) scholars have provided, and continue to provide, that shed light on an extraordinarily complex subject.

I have argued that the record to date counsels humility about our capacity definitively to pin down the causal mechanisms of judicial behaviors and that, for this and other reasons, it also counsels embrace of methodological pluralism. These are not, however, the only reasons for scholars to abandon their intra- and interdisciplinary turf wars, to resolve to help, and learn from, each other, and to pay close attention to the ways in which they present their findings and state their claims.

Four years ago, I described the state of interbranch relations affecting the judiciary, expressing concern that we might be moving toward a system in which "law itself would be seen as nothing more than ordinary politics, and it would become increasingly difficult to appoint (elect, or retain) people with the qualities necessary for judicial independence, because the actors involved would be preoccupied with a degraded notion of judicial accountability" (Burbank 2007b, 910, 916). It may be that these risks have diminished at the federal level with the loss of power of those primarily responsible for the strategies I identified and the attacks on courts that were designed to implement them. Even if so, however, recrudescence is possible, and, in any event, the federal courts are responsible for only a very small portion of the judicial business in this country. It thus remains important that scholars not contribute to the process of assimilating the law made by judges to ordinary politics unless they are confident, and have adequate reason to be confident, about their findings and the inferences they draw from them (Sisk and Heise 2005; Edwards and Livermore 2009).

Professor Gillman has cautioned judicial behavior scholars to consider "the potential real world consequences of this debate [between thinking of law as behavioral uniformity and thinking of it as good faith deliberation]" (2001, 497). Judge Posner has observed that the "attitudinalists' traditional preoccupation with politically charged cases decided by the Supreme Court creates an exaggerated impression of the permeation of American judging by politics" (2008, 27–28). He has also pointed out that the trend toward selecting "judges who will be politically dependable . . . is the triumph of the attitudinal school" (ibid., 169).

This is not a plea that "valid social research should not be undertaken in order to protect cherished myths" (Segal and Spaeth 2002, 429). There is a difference between the merit of a research topic and of a model used to explore it, as there is between the merit of a model and the methods by which, and the data with which, it is tested. In any event, one need not be a mythologist to believe that, the more obvious the real world implications of research, the more important it is that researchers attend carefully not just to their models, methodology, and data but also to their findings and the claims that those findings reasonably support. The ability of policy-makers who are so inclined *not* to "see but narrowly" (Freund, 1956, 802) when considering institutional design (and other) questions affecting the judiciary depends critically on the willingness and ability of scholars to abjure methodological imperialism and to recognize the value of pluralism in perspective as well as methodology.

Notes

1. "Introduced originally into American legal education in 1871 by Christopher C. Langdell, the dean of Harvard Law School, the case method rested on the assumption that a close study of past judicial decisions would reveal the basic principles and rules of the law that had led to the various decisions" (Purcell 1973, 75).

2. "But saluting these content-free, technocratic-seeming precepts is to adjudicating as spring training is to the baseball season. The precepts are warm-up measures. Closure requires agreement on substance. Without that, the choice of neutral principles is up in the air. No more than legal realism could legal process offer a substitute for legalism on the one hand and politics and emotion on the other" (Posner 2008, 236).

3. Whether one deems empirical work by scholars of law and society (Mather 2008) an exception to this proposition may depend on one's views about "elite law schools."

4. Professor Spaeth has recently reiterated his insistence that Pritchett's "assertion that judging is different from the free choice of congresspersons or administrators is simply false" (Spaeth 2008, 753).

5. Professor Spaeth's recent description of "a vehement antibehavioral onslaught" (2008, 757) is a useful reminder that the intolerance within political science has run in both directions. Gillman refers to a "symmetry of frustration" (2001, 484).

6. The empirical legal studies (ELS) movement is broader than portrayed by Keck, who described it "as the new law school equivalent of what political scientists usually call 'judicial behavior' research" (2007, 512). Moreover, the account in the text does not include either economists or psychologists who do empirical work and who have been hired by law schools in increasing numbers.

7. "Legal pragmatism is disciplined by a structure of norms and doctrine, commonly expressed in standards such as negligence, good faith, and freedom of speech, that tells judges what consequences they can consider and how (in what relation to each other, for example). Take away the framework and what judges do does not merit the word 'law'" (Posner 2008, 362).

8. Dialogue about judicial behavior among legal scholars and qualitative political scientists is well established (Keck 2007).

9. Those aware that law reviews are not peer reviewed may ask, "What is second prize?" As the earlier reference to the debate (and ultimately dialogue) between scholars teaching in law schools and judges suggests, the benefit is the greater opportunity that publication in law reviews affords actually to reach and affect those being studied (and others with whom judges interact).

10. Segal and Spaeth assert that "[w]hen prior preferences and precedents are the same, it is not meaningful to speak of decisions being determined by precedent" (2002, 290). The obverse is equally true. "In this formulation, what is important is not whether the justices are acting on the basis of law or politics; that question is likely to be difficult to answer other than by fiat—naming certain commitments 'legal' and other 'political'" (Keck 2007, 550). Compare Segal (1984) with Segal and Spaeth (2002).

11. "Variables may also not bear the meaning attributed to them because of coding conventions or coding errors. Readers of empirical work should always look behind the language in which results are presented for information about how a concept has been *operationalized*, which is to say instantiated in the data" (Lempert 2009, 244).

12. Methodological humility seems appropriate for the anterior reason that, once one recognizes that most judges, most of the time, seek to advance a variety of preferences, one confronts the fact that "it is difficult to test formal models when multiple goals are being pursued" (Brenner 2003, 280).

13. Compare Professor Kritzer's description of Martin Shapiro's anticipation of "what we today call the new institutionalism" (2003, 387):

> The thrust of Shapiro's analysis is that the Supreme Court's role in the policy process varies substantially from area to area. The variations depend on factors such as the need for technical expertise, the level of detail involved in the area, the constitutional or statutory nature of the issues, and the nature of the policy implementation process (ibid., 390).

For the view that "[e]mpirical and normative studies of circuit courts must take into account their unique historical, geographic and legal characteristics," see George and Yoon, 2008, 50.

14. "Focusing on non-unanimous cases or on controversial issue areas, as some of Spaeth's work does, misses these easy cases, thereby underestimating the strength of the legal model" (Benesh 2003, 124). Compare in that regard the explanation given for the view that the Court's control over its docket "is a requisite for" the justices voting their policy preferences: "Many meritless cases undoubtedly exist that no self-respecting judge would decide solely on the basis of his or her policy preferences" (Segal and Spaeth 2002, 93; Segal, this volume, 29). Professor Spaeth has recently sought to explain unanimous decisions as caused by "indifference." Thus, "At the Supreme Court level, decisions of limited applicability, such as those involving narrow tax questions, matters of arcane civil procedure, or the preemptive effect of federal legislation [*sic*], may also engender indifference" (2008, 762).

15. Professor David Shapiro has provided a good recent summary of the empirical literature on the role of precedent on the Supreme Court (2008, 938–40).

16. In his contribution to this volume, having acknowledged that "we . . . find greater influence of law" in the courts of appeals, Professor Segal uses as an example work by Donald Songer and others who "have clearly found an impact of Supreme Court preferences on Court of Appeals judges" (Segal, this volume, 33). Like the rest of the paragraph of which it is a part, this seems to me unnecessarily grudging concerning the influence of what we should all be willing to call law (however it started out).

17. Professor Kim does suggest that "[b]ecause of the routine, ongoing interactions among judges within a circuit, the views of their immediate colleagues will be far more salient for panel members when they deliberate than the preferences of the Supreme Court" (2009, 1369).

18. "Jack Knight and Lee Epstein note that stare decisis serves as an important norm constraining justices from being 'motivated by their own preferences' because, inter alia, attorneys rely primarily on precedents, the justices invoke them at conference and in their opinions, and cases overruled amount to only a minuscule percentage of those available for overruling. At the very least, then, precedent shapes strategic behavior by advocates and judges—even those who may put little stock in the doctrine. Presumably they do so not because they are all engaged in a collective effort of self-deception but because some significant percentage of those who decide do consider precedent an important factor in reaching a result" (D. Shapiro 2008, 939–40).

19. Strategic models typically neglect the fact that "law, like other institutions, is created by actors (justices) with political goals (attitudes) whose subsequent decisions are then in turn influenced but not determined by the institutional structure they have created" (Kritzer and Richards 2005, 35).

20. "Absent the ability to peer inside a judge's mind and observe a thing called 'ideology' at work, the only way to measure 'ideology' is to focus upon some observable trait or behavior that is correlated with, or indicative of, ideology" (Fischman and Law 2008, 8–9).

21. "An accountable judiciary without any independence is weak and feeble. An independent judiciary without any accountability is dangerous" (Burbank 2003, 325).

22. "When an act of Congress is appropriately challenged in the courts as not

conforming to the constitutional mandate the judicial branch of the Government has only one duty,—to lay the article of the Constitution which is invoked beside the statute which is challenged and to decide whether the latter squares with the former" (*United States v. Butler*, 62).

23. Compare the view of the legal realist Max Radin: "But in that great mass of transactions which will not fit readily or quickly into established types, or will fit into one just as easily as another, the judge ought to be a free agent. We need not fear arbitrariness. Our Cokes and Mansfields and Eldons derive their physical and spiritual nourishment from the same sources that we do. They will find good what we find good, if we will let them" (1993, 198).

24. "The 'constraining rules' operating on judicial actors may not be directly legible off the legal text. Indeed, there may be formal rules and informal norms internal and particular to judicial institutions that shape and constrain judicial conduct by providing, as historical institutionalists put it, 'the content of the identities, preferences, and interests that actors [can] embrace and express'" (Hilbink 2008, 1099–1100).

References

Bailey, Michael A., and Forrest Maltzman. 2008. "Does Legal Doctrine Matter? Unpacking Law and Policy Preferences on the U.S. Supreme Court." *American Political Science Review* 102: 369–84.

Baum, Lawrence. 2003. "C. Herman Pritchett: Innovator with an Ambiguous Legacy." In Nancy Maveety, ed., *The Pioneers of Judicial Behavior*. Ann Arbor: University of Michigan Press, 57–77.

———. 2006. *Justices and Their Audiences: A Perspective on Judicial Behavior*. Princeton: Princeton University Press.

Benesh, Sara C. 2003. "Harold J. Spaeth: The Supreme Court Computer." In Nancy Maveety, ed., *The Pioneers of Judicial Behavior*. Ann Arbor: University of Michigan Press, 116–47.

Bloom, Anne. 2001. "The 'Post-Attitudinal Moment': Judicial Policymaking through the Lens of New Institutionalism." *Law and Society Review* 35: 219–30.

Boyd, Christina L., Lee Epstein, and Andrew D. Martin. 2007. *Untangling the Causal Effects of Sex on Judging*. Available at http://ssrn.com/abstract=1001748.

Braman, Eileen. 2008. "A Motivated Reasoning Approach to the Commerce Clause Interpretation of the Rehnquist Court." Midwest Political Science Association.

Brenner, Saul. 2003. "David Rohde: Rational Choice Theories." In Nancy Maveety, ed., *The Pioneers of Judicial Behavior*. Ann Arbor: University of Michigan Press, 270–83.

Burbank, Stephen B. 1996. "The Good, the Bad and the Ugly." *Judicature* 79: 318–22.

———. 1999. "The Architecture of Judicial Independence." *Southern California Law Review* 72: 315–51.

———. 2003. "What Do We Mean by 'Judicial Independence'"? *Ohio State Law Journal* 64: 323–39.

———. 2006. "Alternative Career Resolution II: Changing the Tenure of Supreme Court Justices." *University of Pennsylvania Law Review* 154: 1511–50.

———. 2007a. "The Greening of Harry Blackmun." *Northwestern University Law Review Colloquy* 101: 137–42.

———. 2007b. "Judicial Independence, Judicial Accountability, and Interbranch Relations." *Georgetown Law Journal* 95: 909–27.

Burbank, Stephen B., and Barry Friedman, eds. 2002a. *Judicial Independence at the Crossroads: An Interdisciplinary Approach.* Thousand Oaks, CA: Sage Publications.

———. 2002b. "Reconsidering Judicial Independence." In *Judicial Independence at the Crossroads*, 9–42.

Clayton, Cornell W. 2003. "Edward S. Corwin as Public Scholar." In Nancy Maveety, ed., *The Pioneers of Judicial Behavior.* Ann Arbor: University of Michigan Press, 289–315.

Cramton, Roger D., and Paul C. Carrington, eds. 2006. *Reforming the Court.* Durham, NC: Carolina Academic Press.

Cross, Frank B. 2007. *Decision Making in the U.S. Courts of Appeals.* Stanford: Stanford University Press.

Cross, Frank B., and Emerson H. Tiller. 1998. "Judicial Partisanship and Obedience to Legal Doctrine: Whistleblowing on the Federal Courts of Appeals." *Yale Law Journal* 107: 2155–76.

Dahl, Robert. 1957. "Decision Making in a Democracy: The Supreme Court as a National Policy-Maker." *Journal of Public Law* 6: 279–95.

Edwards, Harry T. 1998. "Collegiality and Decision Making on the D.C. Circuit." *Virginia Law Review* 84: 1335–70.

———. 2003. "The Effects of Collegiality on Judicial Decision Making." *University of Pennsylvania Law Review* 151: 1639–90.

Edwards, Harry T., and Michael A. Livermore. 2009. "Pitfalls of Empirical Studies That Attempt to Understand the Factors Affecting Appellate Decisionmaking." *Duke Law Journal* 58: 1895–1989.

Epstein, Lee, and Jack Knight. 2003. "Walter F. Murphy: The Interactive Nature of Judicial Decision Making." In Nancy Maveety, ed., *The Pioneers of Judicial Behavior.* Ann Arbor: University of Michigan Press, 197–227.

Epstein, Lee, Andrew D. Martin, Kevin M. Quinn, and Jeffrey A. Segal. 2007. "Ideological Drift among Supreme Court Justices: Who, When, and How Important?" *Northwestern University Law Review* 101: 1483–1542.

Eskridge, William N., Jr. 1991. "Overriding Supreme Court Statutory Interpretation Decisions." *Yale Law Journal* 101: 331–417.

Fischman, Joshua B., and David S. Law. 2009. "What Is Judicial Ideology, and How Should We Measure It?" *Washington University Journal of Law and Policy* 29: 133–214.

Freund, Paul A. 1956. "Thomas Reed Powell." *Harvard Law Review* 69: 800–803.

Friedman, Barry. 2006. "Taking Law Seriously." *Perspectives on Politics* 4: 261–76.

George, Tracey E., and Albert H. Yoon. 2008. "Chief Judges: The Limits of Attitudinal Theory and Possible Paradox of Managerial Judging." *Vanderbilt Law Review* 61: 1–61.

Gerhardt, Michael J. 2003. "Attitudes about Attitudes." *Michigan Law Review* 101: 1733–63.

———. 2008. *The Power of Precedent*. Oxford: Oxford University Press.

Geyh, Charles Gardner. 2006. *When Courts and Congress Collide*. Ann Arbor: University of Michigan Press.

Gillman, Howard. 2001. "What's Law Got to Do with It? Judicial Behavioralists Test the 'Legal Model' of Judicial Decision Making." *Law and Social Inquiry* 26: 465–504.

Hamilton, Alexander. 1961. "The Federalist No. 78." In Clinton Rossiter, ed., *The Federalist Papers*. New York: New American Library, 464–72.

Hartnett, Edward A. 2000. "Questioning Certiorari: Some Reflections Seventy-Five Years after the Judges' Bill." *Columbia Law Review* 100: 1643–1738.

Harvey, Anna. 2008. *What Makes a Judgment "Liberal"? Coding Bias in the United States Supreme Court Judicial Database*. Available at http://ssrn.com/abstract=1120970.

Harvey, Anna, and Barry Friedman. 2006. "Pulling Punches: Congressional Constraints on the Supreme Court's Constitutional Rulings, 1987–2000." *Legislative Studies Quarterly* 31: 533–62.

Harvey, Anna, and Michael J. Woodruff. 2009. *Confirmation Bias in the United States Supreme Court Judicial Database*. Available at http://ssrn.com/abstract=1393613.

Hilbink, Lisa. 2008. "From Comparative Judicial Politics to Comparative Law and Politics." *Law and Politics Book Review* 18: 1098–1102.

Jacob, Herbert. 1962. "The Courts as Political Agencies: An Historical Analysis." In Kenneth N. Vines and Herbert Jacob, eds., *Tulane Studies in Political Science* 8: 9–50.

Johnson, Timothy R., James F. Spriggs II, and Paul J. Wahlbeck. 2007. "Oral Advocacy before the United States Supreme Court: Does It Affect the Justices' Decisions?" *Washington University Law Review* 85: 457–527.

Kalman, Laura. 1986. *Legal Realism at Yale: 1927–1960*. Chapel Hill: University of North Carolina Press.

Kastellec, Johnathan P., and Jeffrey R. Lax. 2008. "Case Selection and the Study of Judicial Politics." *Journal of Empirical Legal Studies* 5: 407–46.

Keck, Thomas M. 2007. "Party Politics or Judicial Independence? The Regime Politics Literature Hits the Law Schools." *Law and Social Inquiry* 32: 511–44.

———. 2008. "Law, Politics, and Political Science." *Law and Politics Book Review* 18: 1103–10.

Kim, Pauline T. 2007. "Lower Court Discretion." *New York University Law Review* 82: 383–442.

———. 2009. "Deliberation and Strategy on the United States Court of Appeals." *University of Pennsylvania Law Review* 157: 1319–81.

Kramer, Larry D., and John Ferejohn. 2002. "Independent Judges, Dependent Judiciary: Institutionalizing Judicial Restraint." *New York University Law Review* 77: 962–1039.

Kritzer, Herbert M. 1996. "The Data Puzzle: The Nature of Interpretation in Quantitative Research." *American Journal of Political Science* 40: 1–32.

———. 2003. "Martin Shapiro: Anticipating the New Institutionalism." In Nancy Maveety, ed., *The Pioneers of Judicial Behavior*. Ann Arbor: University of Michigan Press, 387–417.

Kritzer, Herbert M., and Mark J. Richards. 2003. "Jurisprudential Regimes and Supreme Court Decision Making: The Lemon Regime and Establishment Clause Cases." *Law and Society Review* 37: 827–40.

———. 2005. "The Influence of Law in the Supreme Court's Search-and-Seizure Jurisprudence." *American Politics Research* 33: 33–55.

Landes, William M., and Richard A. Posner. 2008. *Rational Judicial Behavior: A Statistical Study*. Available at http://ssrn.com/abstract=1126403.

Lempert, Richard. 2009. "The Significance of Statistical Significance: Two Authors Restate an Incontrovertible Caution. Why a Book?" *Law and Social Inquiry* 34: 225–49.

Mather, Lynn. 2008. "Law and Society." In Keith E. Whittington, R. Daniel Kelemen, and Gregory A. Caldeira, eds., *The Oxford Handbook of Law and Politics*. Oxford: Oxford University Press, 681–97.

Meinke, Scott R., and Kevin M. Scott. 2007. "Collegial Influence and Judicial Voting Change: The Effect of Membership Change on U.S. Supreme Court Justices." *Law and Society Review* 41: 909–38.

McCloskey, Robert G. 2005. *The American Supreme Court*. 4th ed. rev. Sanford Levinson. Chicago: University of Chicago Press.

Morse, Stephen J. 2006. "Brain Overclaim Syndrome and Criminal Responsibility: A Diagnostic Note." *Ohio State Journal of Criminal Law* 3: 397–412.

———. 2008. "Determinism and the Death of Folk Psychology: Two Challenges to Responsibility from Neuroscience." *Minnesota Journal of Law, Science and Technology* 9: 1–35.

Neuborne, Burt. 1997. "Innovation in the Interstices of the Final Judgment Rule: A Demurrer to Professor Burbank." *Columbia Law Review* 97: 2091–2101.

Pacelle, Jr., Richard L. 1991. *The Transformation of the Supreme Court's Agenda*. Boulder, CO: Westview.

Peretti, Terri, and Alan Rozzi. 2008. *Modern Departures from the U.S. Supreme Court: Party, Pensions, or Power?*. Available at http://ssrn.com/abstract=1307845.

Posner, Richard A. 1995. *Overcoming Law*. Cambridge: Harvard University Press.

———. 2008. *How Judges Think*. Cambridge: Harvard University Press.

Pritchett, C. Herman. 1969. "The Development of Judicial Research." In Joel B. Grossman and Joseph Tanenhaus, eds., *Frontiers of Judicial Research*. New York: Wiley, 27–42.

Provine, Doris M. 1980. *Case Selection in the United States Supreme Court*. Chicago: University of Chicago Press.

Purcell, Edward A., Jr. 1973. *The Crisis of Democratic Theory: Scientific Naturalism and the Problem of Value.* Lexington: University Press of Kentucky.

Rachlinski, Jeffrey J., Sheri Lynn Johnson, Andrew J. Wistrich, and Chris Guthrie. 2007. "Does Unconscious Racial Bias Affect Trial Judges?" *Notre Dame Law Review* 84: 1195–1246.

Radin, Max. 1993. "The Theory of Judicial Decision: Or How Judges Think." In William W. Fisher, Morton J. Horowitz, and Thomas A. Reed, eds., *American Legal Realism.* Oxford: Oxford University Press, 195–98.

Ramseyer, J. Mark. 2008. "Predicting Court Outcomes through Political Preferences: The Japanese Supreme Court and the Chaos of 1993." Available at http://ssrn.com/abstract=1326548.

Revesz, Richard L. 1997. "Environmental Regulation, Ideology, and the D.C. Circuit." *Virginia Law Review* 83: 1717–69.

Richards, Mark J., and Herbert M. Kritzer. 2002. "Jurisprudential Regimes in Supreme Court Decision Making." *American Political Science Review* 96: 305–20.

Robbennolt, Jennifer K., Robert J. MacCoun, and John M. Darley. 2010. "Multiple Constraint Satisfaction in Judging." In David Klein and Gregory Mitchell, eds., *The Psychology of Judicial Decision Making* 27–40.

Rosenberg, Gerald N. 1991. *The Hollow Hope: Can Courts Bring about Social Change?* Chicago: University of Chicago Press.

Ruger, Theodore W. 2005. "Justice Harry Blackmun and the Phenomenon of Judicial Preference Change." *Missouri Law Review* 70: 1209–31.

Schauer, Frederick. 1988. "Formalism." *Yale Law Journal* 97: 509–48.

Scheingold, Stuart A. 2008. "The Path of the Law in Political Science: De-centering Legality from Olden Times to the Day before Yesterday." In Keith E. Whittington, R. Daniel Kelemen, and Gregory A. Caldeira, eds., *The Oxford Handbook of Law and Politics.* Oxford: Oxford University Press, 737–51.

Scheppele, Kim Lane. 2002. "Declarations of Independence: Judicial Reactions to Political Pressure." In Stephen B. Burbank and Barry Friedman, eds., *Judicial Independence at the Crossroads: An Interdisciplinary Approach.* Thousand Oaks, CA: Sage Publications, 227–79.

Segal, Jeffrey A. 1984. "Predicting Supreme Court Cases Probabilistically: The Search and Seizure Cases, 1962–1981." *American Political Science Review* 78: 891–900.

Segal, Jeffrey A., and Harold J. Spaeth. 2002. *The Supreme Court and the Attitudinal Model Revisited.* New York: Cambridge University Press.

Segal, Jeffrey, Chad Westerland, and Stefanie A. Lindquist. 2011. "Congress, The Supreme Court and Judicial Review: Testing a Constitutional Separation of Powers Model." *American Journal of Political Science* 55: 89–104.

Shapiro, Carolyn. 2009. "Coding Complexity: Bringing Law to the Empirical Analysis of the Supreme Court." *Hastings Law Journal* 60: 477–537.

Shapiro, David L. 2008. "The Role of Precedent in Constitutional Adjudication: An Introspection." *Texas Law Review* 86: 929–57.

Shapiro, Martin. 2008. "Law and Politics: The Problem of Boundaries." In Keith

E. Whittington, R. Daniel Kelemen, and Gregory A. Caldeira, eds., *The Oxford Handbook of Law and Politics*. Oxford: Oxford University Press, 767–74.

Shubin, Neil. 2008. *Your Inner Fish: A Journey into the 3.5 Billion-Year History of the Human Body*. New York: Pantheon Books.

Sisk, Gregory C., and Michael Heise. 2005. "Judges and Ideology: Public and Academic Debates about Statistical Measures." *Northwestern University Law Review* 99: 743–803.

Sisk, Gregory C., Michael Heise, and Andrew P. Morriss. 2004. "Searching for the Soul of Judicial Decisionmaking: An Empirical Study of Religious Freedom Decisions." *Ohio State Law Journal* 65: 491–614.

Spaeth, Harold J. 2008. "Reflections about Judicial Politics." In Keith E. Whittington, R. Daniel Kelemen, and Gregory A. Caldeira, eds., *The Oxford Handbook of Law and Politics*. Oxford: Oxford University Press, 752–66.

Stras, David R. 2006. "The Incentives Approach to Judicial Retirement." *Minnesota Law Review* 90: 1417–46.

Subrin, Stephen N. 1987. "How Equity Conquered Common Law: The Federal Rules of Civil Procedure in Historical Perspective." *University of Pennsylvania Law Review* 135: 909–1002.

Wald, Patricia M. 1999. "Colloquy: A Response to Tiller and Cross." *Columbia Law Review* 99: 235–61.

Wechsler, Herbert. 1959. "Toward Neutral Principles of Constitutional Law." *Harvard Law Review* 73: 1–35.

Whittington, Keith E. 2000. "Once More Unto the Breach: Postbehavioralist Approaches to Judicial Politics." *Law and Social Inquiry* 25: 601–34.

Wolfe, Alan. 2008. "Hedonic Man." *New Republic*, July 9, 2008, 47–55.

Yeazell, Stephen C. 1994. "The Misunderstood Consequences of Modern Civil Process." *Wisconsin Law Review* 1994: 631–78.

Young, Ernest A. 2002. "Judicial Activism and Conservative Politics." *Colorado Law Review* 73: 1139–1216.

CASES CITED

United States v. Butler. 1936. 297 U.S. 1.

II DISTINGUISHING LAW
FROM OTHER INFLUENCES
ON JUDICIAL DECISION-MAKING

3   Law and Policy

More and Less than a Dichotomy

Lawrence Baum

WITHIN AND BEYOND THE ACADEMIC WORLD, the most frequent question about judicial behavior is the balance between law and policy.[1] To what extent do judges act to make good law, and to what extent do they act to make good public policy?

Some participants in the debate over this question depict judging as entirely law-oriented or entirely policy-oriented.[2] The all-legal position is expressed most often by judges themselves, as it was in Chief Justice John Roberts's analogy between judges and baseball umpires at his confirmation hearing (U.S. Senate 2005, 55). The all-policy position is expressed most often by political scientists whose models of decision-making exclude legal considerations (Segal and Spaeth 2002). In contrast, many people who address this issue argue that judges act on the basis of both legal and policy considerations (Gillman 2001b; Whittington 2000).

Regardless of their positions in this debate, however, scholars and others typically treat law and policy as separate and separable. Scholars also tend to treat legal and policy considerations as the only valid explanations of judicial decision-making; other motives that might affect judges' choices are left aside. Thus judging is analyzed as a dichotomy between law and policy, in which judges' choices can be understood in terms of the relative weights of those two considerations alone.

This perspective on judging has provided the basis for a great deal of fruitful research, but it oversimplifies the reality of judging. In this chapter I explore some of the complexities of the relationship between law and policy in judging. After addressing some important conceptual issues concerning law and policy, I turn to two theoretical complexities. The first concerns the difficulty of separating legal and policy considerations in judges' decision-making. The second concerns the role of considerations other than law and policy in decision-making. After working through these complexities, I consider their implications for our understanding of judging.

Two Conceptual Issues

The first conceptual issue to address is the meaning of "law" and "policy" as elements in decision-making. As frequently as these terms are used in discussions of judging, their meaning is often unclear. This is primarily because both categories have multiple facets.

In their chapter in this book, Barry Friedman and Andrew Martin appropriately emphasize the multiple meanings of law as an element in judicial decision-making. The most obvious type of law-oriented decision-making is one in which judges make choices on the basis of legal sources—the text of the laws to be interpreted, the intent of the writers of those laws, and applicable judicial precedents. In the political science scholarship on Supreme Court decision-making, the most attention is given to the justices' treatment of the Court's precedents (for example, Spaeth and Segal 1999). This focus reflects the visibility of decisions that abrogate precedents and the relative ease of analyzing the justices' responses to precedents.

But judges' opinions routinely, and appropriately, emphasize text and intent as sources of law. Actual reliance on those sources constitutes law-oriented behavior just as giving weight to precedent does (see Howard and Segal 2002). Justice Clarence Thomas argues in opinions that the Court should discard whole lines of precedent because the doctrines reflected in those precedents have departed from his reading of the original meaning of the text of the Constitution.[3] If his argument is an accurate description of the path he takes to decisions, his behavior is as law-oriented as that of a justice who consistently adheres to precedent.

Certain forms of judicial behavior are sometimes interpreted as law-oriented even though they do not relate directly to ways of reaching decisions. One example is working to achieve consistency in the law through such means as conforming a court's doctrinal positions to the positions of other, coordinate courts (such as other federal courts of appeals) on the same issue. A variant of this behavior for a court with discretionary jurisdiction is accepting cases in order to resolve lower-court disagreements about the meaning of the law (Perry 1991, ch. 9).

Like efforts to make good law, efforts to make good policy can take multiple forms. For one thing, judges might care primarily about outcomes for litigants or primarily about the legal doctrines that their court announces. In quantitative research, it is a nearly universal practice to code the policy content of court decisions in terms of outcomes rather than doctrine. That practice is mostly a matter of convenience, reflecting the difficulty of measuring the content of doctrine. However, it also reflects a legacy of legal realism, the belief that judges care more about who wins and loses than about the content of opinions. That belief is unrealistic for supreme courts that establish doctrinal rules for a whole court system. Members of those courts may care far less about who wins and loses a specific case than about doctrine that determines the broader policy implications of court decisions (see Wahlbeck 1997).

Another distinction has received growing attention in the past two decades. A policy-oriented judge might act "sincerely," simply taking the position that accords most closely with the judge's policy preferences. This conception is reflected in the pure version of the attitudinal model of Supreme Court decision-making that long dominated political science scholarship (Schubert 1965; Segal and Spaeth 2002).

Alternatively, a judge who seeks to make good policy might act strategically, taking into account the prospective behavior of other judges on an appellate court and of individuals and institutions outside the judge's court.[4] These strategic considerations could lead judges to depart from their preferred positions in the interest of achieving the most desirable court decision (Maltzman, Spriggs, and Wahlbeck 2000) or the most desirable result after other courts, other branches of government, and the public have responded to a decision (Langer 2003; McGuire and Stimson 2004). Strategic behavior is more likely to thrive if judges focus on doctrine rather than outcomes for the litigants, because there are usually more alternative formulations of doctrine than alternative outcomes.

In practice, sincere and strategic judges might not behave very differently across the set of cases they decide. Strategic considerations may require only occasional and limited departures from judges' most preferred positions. But in motivational terms, sincere and strategic judges are fundamentally different.

Indeed, the two models of policy-oriented judging have roots in disciplines with quite different assumptions about human behavior, psychology (for sincere judges) and economics (for strategic judges).

Strategic models have achieved a degree of dominance in the study of judicial behavior, especially in political science (Epstein and Knight 2000). But the extent to which judges behave strategically, the forms of their strategy, and the degree to which strategic considerations move judges away from their preferred positions remain open questions. Because of this uncertainty, it is necessary to take into account both sincere and strategic conceptions of judicial action in assessing the roles of legal and policy considerations in decision-making.

Thus law and policy as elements in judicial decision-making each have multiple meanings in several respects. The complexity of these concepts makes it more difficult to speak in a meaningful way about legal and policy considerations in judges' choices. The absolute and relative importance of those considerations may vary considerably depending on how we define law and policy.

A second conceptual issue is the distinction between motivation and effects. Inquiries into the roles of legal and policy considerations in judicial decisions might be directed at either of two questions. The first concerns judges' motivations: are they trying to make good law, good policy, or some combination of the two? The second concerns the effects of different considerations: to what extent are judges' choices a product of the law and of judges' policy preferences? These two questions are frequently conflated in discussions of judging and research on judicial behavior, but they should be kept distinct.

The differences between motivation and effects can be illustrated with two influential theories of judicial behavior. The first is the version of the attitudinal theory of Supreme Court decision-making that Jeffrey Segal and Harold Spaeth (2002, 93–96) have presented, one in which institutional attributes of the Supreme Court make policy dominant over law. The most important attribute is the Court's control over its agenda. The justices generally choose cases in which the application of the law is ambiguous, and in those cases they could easily offer legal justifications for decisions favoring either side.[5] As a result, the law falls out, and decisions are based instead on the justices' conceptions of good policy. A key implication of Segal and Spaeth's argument is that even a justice who seeks only to follow the law would still make decisions on the basis of policy preferences, because the ambiguity of the law allows those preferences to color the justices' reading of the law.

Segal and Spaeth (ibid., 433 n. 10) allude to this implication when they cite the theory of motivated reasoning in social psychology. In that theory (Kunda 1990), people's efforts to achieve the "accuracy" goal of getting to the most justifiable decision can conflict with their "directional" goal of reaching a decision they prefer, a goal that shapes their judgment at a conscious or unconscious level. The impact of directional goals increases with the degree of ambiguity about what is the most justifiable decision. This theory has a direct application to judicial decision-making, if good law is treated as the accuracy goal and good policy as the directional goal (Braman and Nelson 2007; Braman 2009, ch. 1). As the theory suggests, a Supreme Court justice might want to follow the law but actually reach decisions that are based on only the justice's conceptions of good policy.

In sharp contrast is the strategic theory of decision-making that Lee Epstein and Jack Knight have presented. In that theory, Supreme Court justices care only about making good policy. But because justices are strategic, they think about how other people will respond to choices they might make. One result, as Epstein and Knight (1998, 163–77) see it, is that justices give considerable weight to precedent because they want to maintain the legitimacy of the Court and its decisions. The public expects the justices to follow precedent, so they do so. Thus we have a situation directly opposite from one of the possibilities that Segal and Spaeth suggest. Here, justices intend only to make good policy, but in fact one legal consideration exerts considerable impact on their choices.

These formulations underline the potential for divergence between judges' intentions and the determinants of their choices. Most empirical scholarship, especially quantitative work, analyzes the determinants of judicial choice. The findings of those studies provide a basis for cautious inferences about judges' motivations, but they usually tell us nothing directly about motivation.

The Intertwining of Legal and Policy Considerations

I turn now to the theoretical complexities that are the central concerns of this chapter. The first relates to both judges' motivations and the effects of various considerations on their choices. As noted earlier, empirical analyses of the roles of legal considerations and policy preferences in judicial decision-making tend to treat the two as separate contributors to judicial choice. My argument, in contrast, is that those roles cannot be fully separated from each other. It is not simply that both legal and policy considerations affect decisions. Rather, the determinants of decisions and the motivations on which judges act are impossible to apportion between law and policy. In statistical terms, any effort to ascertain the proportion of the variance in judicial behavior that can be ascribed to the law and the proportion that can be ascribed to judges' policy preferences inevitably will fail. The fundamental reason is that legal and policy considerations are intertwined in the processes through which judges make their choices.[6]

One way in which the two types of considerations are intertwined is straightforward: there are some situations in which legal and policy considerations would lead to the same judicial choices. Scholars usually think of these situations in terms of a methodological concept, behavioral equivalence, which means that we cannot distinguish between two possible causes of a pattern of behavior when the effects of the two causes would be the same. In this situation, it is often assumed that one or the other of the possible causes is actually dominant, even though that dominance cannot be ascertained. But in the case of law and policy, it is likely that both sources of behavior operate and combine in their effects.

An example is adherence by Supreme Court justices to the Court's own precedents. As Epstein and Knight argue, justices might give weight to the Court's precedents because they seek to maintain the Court's legitimacy with the public and thus advance their policy goals.[7] Their formulation could be modified to encompass elite groups that have particular impact on the Court's efficacy as a policy-maker, such as officials in the other branches of government.

Perhaps the justices take the Court's precedents into account only because they care about external audiences that can affect the achievement of justices' policy goals. It might instead be that justices take precedent into account only because of their own belief that adherence to precedent is desirable in itself, a legal consideration. But almost surely, both motives operate. Careful analysis of the conditions under which justices adhere to precedent or depart from it may provide some sense of their relative importance.

Another example also involves precedent, but here the issue is adherence by judges to the precedents of courts that stand above them in a court hierarchy. The traditional interpretation of this adherence is legal: judges adopt the doctrines of higher courts because they believe that is their duty under the law. Scholars who work from strategic models posit instead that judges follow the lead of higher courts as a means to advance their policy goals. If a court of appeals panel adopts its members' most preferred position but suffers a Supreme

Court reversal as a result, the impact will be to move judicial policy further from that preferred position. Thus policy-minded judges have an incentive to adhere to the Court's precedents (Songer, Segal, and Cameron 1994).

It may be possible to differentiate between alternative motivations in their impact on lower courts' responses to courts above them, because legal and policy considerations sometimes lead in different directions for lower court judges. In particular, the policy-minded judge would tend to depart from a Supreme Court precedent when there was reason to think that the Court's policy position had changed since the precedent was issued, while a law-minded judge would tend to follow the precedent in that situation (see Caminker 1994). But most of the time, legal and policy considerations each induce judges to follow the precedents of a higher court, and under that condition the two reinforce each other.

In a second kind of intertwining, legal and policy considerations do not lead to exactly the same behavior, but their effects are closely linked. One important example is the concept of jurisprudential regimes, developed by Mark Richards and Herbert Kritzer. As Richards and Kritzer (2002, 308) describe the concept, a jurisprudential regime is "a key precedent, or a set of related precedents, that structures the way in which the Supreme Court justices evaluate key elements of cases in arriving at decisions in a particular legal area."

As Richards and Kritzer see it, once the Court creates an analytic framework for a particular type of case, the existence of that framework structures the justices' thinking and thus affects the positions they take. The key manifestation of jurisprudential regimes is increases in the weight that the justices give to factors that are emphasized by the new legal rules. Thus, after the Court established its three-level framework for freedom of expression cases in two 1972 decisions, this new jurisprudential regime might cause justices to favor free speech claims more frequently when the framework called for strict scrutiny of regulations and less frequently when the framework called for lenient scrutiny (ibid.).

Richards and Kritzer tested their argument empirically in four policy areas (ibid.; Kritzer and Richards 2003, 2005; Richards, Kritzer, and Smith 2006). In each area they found that jurisprudential frameworks did change the impact of relevant case attributes on the Court's collective decisions and on the positions of justices who served both before and after the creation of a regime. Although their evidence is subject to multiple interpretations, it provides substantial support for the argument that legal frameworks influence the justices' choices.

One possible objection to Richards and Kritzer's line of analysis is that jurisprudential regimes are not imposed on the justices by an external source; rather, the justices create those regimes themselves. Richards and Kritzer (2002, 306) readily accept the proposition that jurisprudential regimes reflect the justices' policy preferences. However, their evidence seems to demonstrate that even the justices who created a regime shift in their decisional tendencies in ways that we would expect from the content of a regime.

This evidence underlines the intertwining of legal and policy considerations. The justices create legal frameworks that they find compatible with their policy preferences. Having done so, they allow the frameworks to move them in directions that they found attractive when they settled on those frameworks. As a result, a framework sometimes leads them to results in particular cases that they would not have reached in its absence.

Another example of this second kind of intertwining concerns judges' personal philosophies of legal interpretation. Some judges, especially Supreme Court justices, proclaim their adherence to particular approaches to legal interpretation. On the current Court, the most prominent example is Justice Scalia's emphasis on the text of legal provisions as opposed to the intent of those who wrote these provisions (see Scalia 1997). The limited weight that Justice Thomas gives to precedent, including long-standing doctrines for interpreting the Constitution, is another example. And Justice Breyer (2008) has articulated his own approach to interpretation of the Constitution.

These philosophies are largely reflections of the justices' policy preferences. When justices choose ways of interpreting the law, they understand the kinds of policies that those ways will favor and disfavor. Moreover, the influence of these philosophies on judges' positions in cases should not be exaggerated: any legal philosophy provides considerable leeway in deciding specific cases.

Yet the adoption of a legal philosophy creates mechanisms by which that philosophy can affect judges' positions. One mechanism is like the effect that Richards and Kritzer ascribe to jurisprudential regimes: a personal philosophy of legal interpretation structures the way that a judge thinks about cases. Another mechanism concerns judges' self-image and the image they want to project to other people. By and large, judges want to see themselves, and to have their audiences see them, as acting on a legal basis. Allowing themselves to be diverted from their most preferred policy positions by a legal philosophy they have proclaimed fosters that image.

Justice Scalia provides an especially clear example of this mechanism. At his public appearances he frequently emphasizes his adherence to a conception of the law that requires him to cast votes he does not like. In this context he regularly cites his vote to strike down the state law against flag burning in *Texas v. Johnson* (1989) (for example, Talbot 2005, 43).

It is an open question how much judges' legal philosophies actually affect their choices in cases. Moreover, this is a difficult question to analyze empirically. The important point for this discussion is that any impact of these philosophies represents an intertwining of legal and policy considerations.

A final and somewhat different kind of intertwining involves the formation of judges' policy preferences. Students of judicial behavior give limited attention to preference formation, except for analyses of the relationship between judges' personal attributes and the ideological or issue-specific positions they take in decisions (for example, Tate 1981; Brudney, Schiavoni, and Merritt 1999).[8] Thus, a discussion of the sources of judges' policy preferences must be largely speculative.

Undoubtedly, the people who become judges, like other politically aware people, gain their policy preferences from an array of sources. For judges, one source is education and experience in the law. Because prospective and practicing lawyers often encounter policy issues within the framework of existing legal rules, that framework potentially shapes lawyers' conceptions of good policy (Stier and Brenner 2008, 5).[9] If jurisprudential regimes can influence the ways that judges analyze cases, the same regimes can influence the ways that law students think about policy issues.

There may be a second and more powerful way in which legal rules affect the policy preferences of present and future judges. Law students, lawyers, and judges make arguments in terms of the law. Psychologists have demonstrated that behavior can have considerable impact on attitudes, and one example is the effect of advocacy on advocates' support for the positions they have voiced (Eagly and Chaiken 1993, ch. 11). The act of making legal arguments could be expected to have that kind of effect (see Braman 2009, 23–25). Thus, working in the law can produce a closer alignment between the state of the law and a lawyer's policy preferences.[10]

The strength of this mechanism should not be exaggerated. For one thing, legal doctrines on most issues are contested, so that law students and practicing lawyers see more than one point of view. For another, both groups are accustomed to assessing the state of the law critically. And most people who become lawyers have ideological positions through which they filter what they learn about legal doctrine.

Nonetheless, the legal rules that future judges encounter and that they employ to make their arguments are likely to shape their conceptions of desirable policy. And if this is true, then the impact of those preferences is partly the impact of the law. For this reason, statistical relationships between measures of policy preferences and measures of judicial behavior may say something about the impact of the law as well as the impact of policy considerations.

Law, Policy, and Judicial Motivations

Scholarship on human behavior in psychology emphasizes issues of both motivation and cognition. In contrast, students of judicial behavior give quite limited attention to cognition. Instead, their focus is on the goals that judges seek to advance through their choices as decision-makers.[11]

The conception that the only goals relevant to judicial decision-making are legal and policy considerations is narrow, in that it excludes a wide array of human motivations that might affect judges' choices. That conception is also shallow: it sets aside inquiry into what judges gain from their efforts to make good law or good policy—that is, the basic motivations that underlie those goals.

The narrowness of this conception is self-evident. Even taken together, good law and good policy represent a small slice of the goals that we could expect judges as people to hold. The question is whether the situations in which judges make their choices on the bench render goals other than law and policy irrelevant to those choices. The standard view of the Supreme Court is that its institutional attributes have that effect. To a lesser extent, scholars hold the same view of judges on other courts.

Certainly, attributes of the situations in which judges make decisions do limit the range of goals on which they act. The most obvious example is the life terms of Article III federal judges, which essentially rule out any concerns about maintaining their positions. Yet scholars have gone too far, dismissing or ignoring goals that might well affect judges' choices.[12]

Career considerations are a good starting place. Although Article III federal judges enjoy nearly complete job security, lower-court judges are not guaranteed promotions. It is a reasonable assumption that most judges would prefer to be promoted. As one court of appeals judge put it, "Every magistrate judge is a district judge in waiting; every district judge is a circuit judge in waiting; every circuit judge is an associate justice in waiting . . . ." (Kozinski 2004, 1104).

Perhaps ambition has little impact on judges' decisions, for any of several reasons: they perceive that their decisions do not affect their prospects for promotion, this effect is difficult to predict, or (for court of appeals judges) promotions are infrequent. We have only limited evidence on how, and how much, an interest in promotion plays into the choices of federal judges. Still, the evidence we do have suggests that the potential for promotion affects those choices (Cohen 1991, 1992; Sisk, Heise, and Morriss 1998; Taha 2004; Morriss, Heise, and Sisk 2005). And within the federal court system, magistrate judges, bankruptcy judges, and judges on Article I courts do not enjoy life tenure. For those judges, maintaining their positions may be an important concern.

Job security is even more salient for the great majority of state judges, judges who also lack life tenure. Scholars have recognized the potential effect of insecure tenure on state judges, and they have found evidence that the actual effect is substantial in some situations (Hall 1987, 1992; Huber and Gordon 2004; Gordon and Huber 2007; Shepherd 2009). Other career considerations may also be important. These considerations include favorable assignments within a judge's existing court, promotion to a higher court or to the position of chief judge, and securing remunerative or prestigious positions outside the judiciary.

Even at the state level, scholars tend to treat career considerations as a constraint on judges who care primarily about the content of the decisions they make rather than as goals in themselves. This is not necessarily the case. Rather, some judges may be most interested in career advancement, so that the legal and policy content of their decisions is a means to that end, rather than the other way around.

A cluster of goals that receives little attention concerns the quality of a judge's work life. In the standard models of judicial behavior, these goals are present only on the fringes if at all. Unlike most other human beings, judges are assumed to have little interest in their workloads. Nor do they care about good relations with their fellow workers except as a means to advance their policy agendas.

We know that the reality is different. Especially in urban trial courts, some judges find themselves overwhelmed with their caseloads, and simply disposing of cases often becomes their dominant concern. Even when judges are not overwhelmed, some of them demonstrate an interest in working less rather than more. The local trial judge who effectively works part-time is a staple of newspaper investigations of the courts (for example, Farrell 1990).

At the other end of the judicial hierarchy, even some Supreme Court justices are reputed to give less than full time to their work (for example, Woodward and Armstrong 1979, 270). The sharp decline since the 1980s in the number of cases that the Court accepts for full decisions might be explained in several ways (Hellman 1996; O'Brien 1997; Greenhouse 2006). But whatever set of factors explains this decline, the fact remains that it would not have occurred if the justices wanted only to maximize their impact on federal law or public policy. Whether consciously or not, the justices have effectively traded influence for a more leisurely work life.

Relationships among judges on an appellate court are an interesting matter. Long ago, political scientist Walter Murphy (1964, ch. 3) explored the ways that strategically inclined Supreme Court justices might advance their policy goals through their relations with colleagues. Current scholarship analyzes interactions among judges simply as a means to an end (for example, Maltzman, Spriggs, and Wahlbeck 2000).

Yet it would be surprising if judges cared about relationships with their colleagues only as a means to advance their policy goals. Judges on some courts have frequent face-to-face interactions with each other; others do not. But in either instance, judges' job satisfaction is affected by how they get along with other judges, and surely most judges care about what their colleagues think of them (see Cooper 1995). These goals can affect the level of consensus on a court, to take the most obvious example.

Thus judges have and act on goals that go beyond making good law and good policy. In that sense, the standard conception of judging is unduly narrow. It might be that these other goals are generally peripheral, greatly outweighed by legal and policy considerations. But this is not self-evident, even though it frequently is treated as such.

This discussion raises the question of how it is that judges could be strongly devoted to good law and good policy in their decision-making. Why would those goals outweigh such basic interests as career advancement and the respect of professional peers? Students of judicial behavior have barely touched that question, and that is the sense in which the standard conception of judging is shallow.

This question of motivation gains force from the fact that judges' efforts to make what they see as good law and good policy have little to do with their self-interest. The basic irrelevance of self-interest is especially striking for strategic models of judging, models in which judges expend considerable effort to identify the best means to advance their visions of good policy. What is the basis for that effort?

If we step back a bit, it is not difficult to identify reasons why judges might act on legal or policy goals. Psychologist David Winter (2002, 2003) has described three basic needs on which political leaders act: achievement, power (which includes prestige), and affiliation. Efforts to advance good law or good policy can be motivated by these needs: the satisfaction of furthering the public good as the judge sees it, the somewhat different satisfaction gained from exercising influence within a court, winning the regard of fellow lawyers and judges, or strengthening ties with people who are close to a judge by supporting values that the judge shares with them.

Depending on the relative importance of these needs to judges and the ways they seek to meet those needs, judges might be inclined to emphasize either legal or policy considerations in their decisions. Similarly, they might be inclined to act sincerely or strategically. A judge who cares most about prestige among legal professionals, for instance, could be expected to act in ways that establish a reputation for devotion to the law. An appellate judge who is interested in power in a narrow sense would devote greater efforts to shaping collective decisions than a judge for whom power was of little interest.

Of course, the same needs might lead judges to deemphasize legal and policy considerations in favor of quite different considerations. For instance, a judge for whom achievement is important might seek to advance to the highest position possible. Such a judge could focus on developing a judicial record that would maximize the chances of promotion.

Thus the law-policy dichotomy should be put in a broader and deeper context. We can think of efforts to make good law or good policy as proximate goals that stand alongside other goals such as career advancement and a satisfying work life. In turn, those proximate goals can be understood as manifestations of deeper needs that judges seek to fulfill consciously or unconsciously. This perspective facilitates a full inquiry into the motivational process that shapes judges' choices.

Implications

Scholars have amply demonstrated the benefits of thinking about judicial behavior in terms of a dichotomy between legal and policy considerations. But this conception also has clear limitations.

The most fundamental limitation to the law-policy dichotomy is that it does not fully capture either the realities of judging or the issues that are relevant to an understanding of judicial decision-making. The intertwining of legal and policy considerations and the breadth and complexity of judicial motivations limit the value of the standard dichotomous framework for explanation.

Some of these themes can be illustrated by returning to the example of Justice Antonin Scalia (see Zlotnick 1999). Justice Scalia attracts admirers who see him as someone who interprets the law properly and who avoids the sin of deciding cases on the basis of his policy preferences (for example, Ring 2004, 1–21; Weizer 2004, 5–21). Scalia's own opinions and public statements make it clear that he is among the admirers. Meanwhile, his detractors view him as someone who espouses a legal philosophy that provides a convenient cover for votes and opinions that accord with his conception of good policy (for example, Chemerinsky 2000).

The distinction between motive and effect helps to bridge the gap between admirers and detractors. To the extent that the effects of legal and policy considerations actually can be separated, it is a reasonable judgment that Scalia's votes and opinions reflect his policy preferences considerably more than he claims. But this does not mean that he does not believe those claims himself. Indeed, like Felix Frankfurter on an earlier Court (Hirsch 1981, 148, 167, 170, 173, 190), Scalia seems to believe that he differs from most of his colleagues by adhering to a philosophy of legal interpretation that prevents his views about policy from coming into play in his decisions.[13] And like other people in a similar situation, he can maintain that belief despite evidence that some observers find compelling. After all, he too can point to evidence—his votes and opinions that take liberal positions.

If this interpretation of Scalia's behavior as a justice is reasonable, it points to the value of digging more deeply into motivations than the dichotomy between law and policy does. It is important to everyone how they think of themselves and how they perceive that others think of them. Scalia has adopted a self-image that he finds pleasing, and his frequent descriptions of his behavior in terms consistent with that self-image indicate how much he wants other people to adopt the same image of him. In turn, the success he has achieved in that effort and the regard in which he is held by audiences that are important to him reinforce his self-image.[14] And what is true of Justice Scalia is true of other judges as well, even those whose presentations of themselves are far less prominent.

Moving beyond the law-policy dichotomy has normative implications. One implication follows from the distinction between intent and effects. Criticisms of judges on the ground that they let extralegal considerations affect their judgments may be largely misdirected. Many and perhaps most judges exert considerable effort to base their choices on legal considerations. If we believe that this is the most (or only) appropriate behavior for judges, the judges who make more of an effort to follow the law merit praise, and we might want to implore less law-oriented colleagues to change their ways.

At the same time, however, we need to keep in mind that judges cannot banish extralegal considerations from their choices. Faced with cases in which the application of the law is ambiguous, judges inevitably perceive the contending arguments through a filter created by their own conceptions of good policy. This is especially true on the Supreme Court, where cases typically have strong legal arguments on both sides. Criticism of judges for this inevitable behavior seems unjustified.

In this context, it is useful to return to Chief Justice Roberts's analogy between judges and umpires. Two major league umpires have made the same analogy, focusing on their calling of balls and strikes, but they make a quite different point from the one Roberts made (Weber 2009, 172). One umpire said that "it's like the Constitution. The strike zone is a living, breathing document." The other asked, "Have you ever read *Roe v. Wade*? It's very clear. What it says is *very* clear. And we've still been fighting for twenty-five or thirty years over what it means." As the two umpires saw it, in the words of the writer who talked with them, "calling balls and strikes" is "a kind of political enterprise, an activity requiring will and conscience and a point of view." And they captured the reality that judging is at least partly the same kind of enterprise.

When Supreme Court nominees assure the Senate Judiciary Committee that their policy preferences will have little effect on their behavior,[15] they are denying this reality. It is impossible to know whether these nominees actually believe what they are saying. It may be better if they do not believe it, because only those people who realize that they engage in motivated reasoning can work to reduce its effects.

The susceptibility of judges to motivated reasoning is one example of the larger reality that judges are human, acting on motivations that have more similarities to, than differences from, those of other people.[16] It may be pointless to ask that judges behave in a way that does not reflect those motivations. We might prefer that judges not act to improve their career prospects, to reduce their workloads, or to win the admiration of people whose opinions they care about. But undoubtedly many judges act on each of those goals, either consciously or unconsciously. It is easy to understand why state judges might issue heavier sentences as the next election nears (Huber and Gordon 2004), whether or not those judges are aware of that pattern in their sentences.

One central lesson of psychological research is that human behavior is less a product of people's inherent traits and more a product of the situations in which they act than we generally realize (Ross and Nisbett 1991). Efforts to improve the quality of judging, no matter how quality is defined, are more likely to succeed when they focus on the conditions under which judges act rather than on imploring judges to behave differently. The life tenure of federal judges does not eliminate policy-oriented judging, but it does reduce the effects of one kind of self-interest. People who seek to improve the quality of state courts by changing formal selection rules may pin too much hope on those rules, but their emphasis on situations rather than people is sound.

For scholars whose interest is in issues of explanation, my argument is that the conception of law and policy as a dichotomy has limitations as a framework for analysis of judicial behavior. By recognizing both the complexities of legal and policy considerations as elements in judges' choices and the elements of judging that a focus on law and policy omits, we can gain a broader and deeper sense of how judges make their decisions.

Notes

This chapter has been strengthened by valuable suggestions from Eileen Braman and Daniel Lempert.

1. The themes of this book distinguish not between law and policy but between law and politics. Policy-oriented judging can be understood as a subset of political judging, what Sanford Levinson (2001) and Howard Gillman (2001a, 7) called "high" politics as distinguished from the "low" politics of political considerations in the colloquial sense of the term—considerations such as partisan interests.

2. Jeffrey Segal's chapter in this book provides an excellent overview and analysis of positions in this debate.

3. Over eight days in June 2005, for instance, Thomas articulated his opposition to major constitutional doctrines involving the commerce clause (*American Trucking Associations v. Michigan Public Service Commission*), the takings clause (*Kelo v. City of New London*), and the due process clause of the Fourteenth Amendment (*Van Orden v. Perry*).

4. Strategic behavior is generally conceived of as a means to advance policy goals, but judges might also act strategically in behalf of legal goals.

5. As Frank Cross points out in his chapter in this book, the Supreme Court stands out in that the average degree of legal ambiguity in the cases it hears is considerably higher than in courts that do not have nearly complete discretion to accept or reject cases; the Court hears almost nothing but "hard" cases.

6. Even if the effects of legal and policy considerations were not intertwined, other measurement problems would make the task of ascertaining the impact of those considerations quite difficult.

7. For another formulation in which justices use precedent to advance their policy goals, see Hansford and Spriggs (2006).

8. There is a vast body of research on preference formation in psychological research on attitudes (Eagly and Chaiken 1993, chs. 5–13), and political scientists have given attention to this issue (Druckman and Lupia 2000). This work focuses on the mass public, and limited attention has been given to preference formation in political elites.

9. This discussion builds on the point made by Stier and Brenner.

10. This process might help to account for the finding by McClosky and Brill (1983, 247) that "elite" lawyers were especially favorable to the civil liberties that have legal protection.

11. In this section I refer to goals, motivations, and needs. In general, I use the term "goals" to refer to specific things that judges want to accomplish, such as achieving good policy or keeping a judgeship. I treat motivations and needs as more fundamental, providing bases for judges' goals.

On applications of psychological research on motivation and cognition to judicial decision-making, see Klein and Mitchell (2010).

12. This discussion draws from Baum (2006, 11–14). On multiple goals in judicial decision-making, see Robbennolt, MacCoun, and Darley (2010).

13. An especially clear expression of Scalia's view of himself and other justices is his 2005 speech at the Woodrow Wilson International Center for Scholars. A transcript is posted at http://www.cfif.org/htdocs/freedomline/current/guest_commentary/scalia-constitutional-speech.htm.

14. This perspective underlines the importance of Scalia's departures from standard conservative positions on some issues. Those departures help both his audiences and himself to interpret his behavior in the way he wishes, and it is not surprising that he calls attention to those departures. Consciously or unconsciously, his incentive to make such departures may well affect some of his votes and opinions.

15. Along with the example of John Roberts that was cited earlier (U.S. Senate 2005, 55), see U.S. Senate (1971, 19, 77–78) (William Rehnquist) and U.S. Senate (1991, 110, 126) (Clarence Thomas).

16. The extent of any differences in motivation is an open question. Thomas Jefferson, no friend of the judiciary, saw no differences. "Our judges are as honest as other men, and not more so. They have, with others, the same passions for party, for power, and the privilege of their corps" (Ford 1899, 160). Because judges are not a random sample of the general population, however, it is almost certain that their motiva-

tions differ systematically from those of the average person in some respects. For one thing, judgeships are more likely to appeal to people with certain sets of motivations. But it is doubtful that these differences are overwhelming.

On similarities and differences between judges and other people in reasoning processes, see Alexander and Sherwin (2008) and Schauer (2010).

References

Alexander, Larry, and Emily Sherwin. 2008. *Judicial Reasoning Demystified*. New York: Cambridge University Press.

Baum, Lawrence. 2006. *Judges and Their Audiences: A Perspective on Judicial Behavior*. Princeton.: Princeton University Press.

Braman, Eileen. 2009. *Law, Politics, and Perception: How Policy Preferences Influence Legal Reasoning*. Charlottesville: University of Virginia Press.

Braman, Eileen, and Thomas E. Nelson. 2007. "Mechanism of Motivated Reasoning?" *American Journal of Political Science* 51: 940–56.

Breyer, Stephen. 2008. *Active Liberty: Interpreting a Democratic Constitution*. New York: Oxford University Press.

Brudney, James J., Sara Schiavoni, and Deborah J. Merritt. 1999. "Judicial Hostility toward Labor Unions? Applying the Social Background Model to a Celebrated Concern." *Ohio State Law Journal* 60: 1675–1771.

Caminker, Evan H. 1994. "Precedent and Prediction: The Forward-Looking Aspects of Inferior Court Decisionmaking." *Texas Law Review* 73: 1–82.

Chemerinsky, Erwin. 2000. "The Jurisprudence of Justice Scalia: A Critical Appraisal." *University of Hawaii Law Review* 22: 385–401.

Cohen, Mark A. 1991. "Explaining Judicial Behavior or What's 'Unconstitutional' about the Sentencing Commission?" *Journal of Law, Economics, and Organization* 7: 183–99.

———. 1992. "The Motives of Judges: Empirical Evidence from Antitrust Sentencing." *International Review of Law and Economics* 12: 13–30.

Cooper, Phillip J. 1995. *Battles on the Bench: Conflict inside the Supreme Court*. Lawrence: University Press of Kansas.

Druckman, James N., and Arthur Lupia. 2000. "Preference Formation," *Annual Review of Political Science* 3: 1–24.

Eagly, Alice H., and Shelly Chaiken. 1993. *The Psychology of Attitudes*. Fort Worth: Harcourt Brace Jovanovich.

Epstein, Lee, and Jack Knight. 1998. *The Choices Justices Make*. Washington, DC: CQ Press.

———. 2000. "Toward a Strategic Revolution in Judicial Politics: A Look Back, a Look Ahead." *Political Research Quarterly* 53: 625–61.

Farrell, John Aloysius. 1990. "Half-Day Justice." *Boston Globe*, September 23, 1, 34.

Feldman, Stephen M. 2005. "The Rule of Law or the Rule of Politics? Harmonizing the Internal and External Views of Supreme Court Decision Making." *Law and Social Inquiry* 30: 89–135.

Ford, Paul Leicester, ed. 1899. *The Writings of Thomas Jefferson*, vol. X. New York: G. P. Putnam's Sons.

Gillman, Howard. 2001a. *The Votes That Counted: How the Court Decided the 2000 Presidential Election*. Chicago: University of Chicago Press.

———. 2001b. "What's Law Got to Do with It? Judicial Behavioralists Test the 'Legal Model' of Judicial Decision Making." *Law and Social Inquiry* 26: 465–504.

Gordon, Sanford C., and Gregory A. Huber. 2007. "The Effect of Electoral Competitiveness on Incumbent Behavior." *Quarterly Journal of Political Science* 2: 107–38.

Greenhouse, Linda. 2006. "Case of the Dwindling Docket Mystifies the Supreme Court." *New York Times*, December 7, A1, A30.

Hall, Melinda Gann. 1987. "Constituent Influence in State Supreme Courts: Conceptual Notes and a Case Study." *Journal of Politics* 49: 1117–24.

———. 1992. "Electoral Politics and Strategic Voting in State Supreme Courts." *Journal of Politics* 54: 427–46.

Hansford, Thomas G., and James F. Spriggs II. 2006. *The Politics of Precedent on the U.S. Supreme Court*. Princeton: Princeton University Press.

Hellman, Arthur D. 1996. "The Shrunken Docket of the Rehnquist Court." *Supreme Court Review* 1996: 403–38.

Hirsch, H. N. 1981. *The Enigma of Felix Frankfurter*. New York: Basic Books.

Howard, Robert M., and Jeffrey A. Segal. 2002. "An Original Lack at Originalism." *Law and Society Review* 36: 113–37.

Huber, Gregory A., and Sanford C. Gordon. 2004. "Accountability and Coercion: Is Justice Blind When It Runs for Office?" *American Journal of Political Science* 48: 247–63.

Klein, David, and Gregory Mitchell, eds. 2010. *The Psychology of Judicial Decision Making*. New York: Oxford University Press.

Kozinski, Alex. 2004. "The *Real* Issues of Judicial Ethics." *Hofstra Law Review* 32: 1095–1106.

Kritzer, Herbert M., and Mark J. Richards. 2003. "Jurisprudential Regimes and Supreme Court Decisionmaking: The *Lemon* Regime and Establishment Clause Cases." *Law and Society Review* 37: 827–40.

———. 2005. "The Role of Law in the Supreme Court's Search and Seizure Jurisprudence." *American Politics Research* 33: 33–55.

Kunda, Ziva. 1990. "The Case for Motivated Reasoning." *Psychological Bulletin* 108: 480–98.

Langer, Laura. 2003. "Strategic Considerations and Judicial Review: The Case of Workers' Compensation Laws in the American States." *Public Choice* 116: 55–78.

Levinson, Sanford. 2001. "Return of Legal Realism." *Nation*, January 8, 8.

Maltzman, Forrest, James F. Spriggs II, and Paul J. Wahlbeck. 2000. *Crafting Law on the Supreme Court: The Collegial Game*. New York: Cambridge University Press.

McClosky, Herbert, and Alida Brill. 1983. *Dimensions of Tolerance: What Americans Believe about Civil Liberties*. New York: Russell Sage Foundation.

McGuire, Kevin T., and James A. Stimson. 2004. "The Least Dangerous Branch Revisited: New Evidence on Supreme Court Responsiveness to Public Preferences." *Journal of Politics* 66: 1018–35.

Morriss, Andrew P., Michael Heise, and Gregory C. Sisk. 2005. "Signaling and Precedent in Federal District Court Opinions." *Supreme Court Economic Review* 13: 63–97.

Murphy, Walter F. 1964. *Elements of Judicial Strategy*. Chicago: University of Chicago Press.

O'Brien, David M. 1997. "Join-3 Votes, The Rule of Four, the *Cert.* Pool, and the Supreme Court's Shrinking Plenary Docket." *Journal of Law and Politics* 13: 779–808.

Perry, H. W., Jr. 1991. *Deciding to Decide: Agenda Setting in the United States Supreme Court*. Cambridge: Harvard University Press.

Richards, Mark J., and Herbert M. Kritzer. 2002. "Jurisprudential Regimes in Supreme Court Decision Making." *American Political Science Review* 96: 305–20.

Richards, Mark J., Herbert M. Kritzer, and Joseph L. Smith. 2006. "Does *Chevron* Matter?" *Law and Policy* 28: 444–69.

Ring, Kevin A., ed. 2004. *Scalia Dissents: Writings of the Supreme Court's Wittiest, Most Outspoken Justice*. Washington, DC: Regnery.

Robbennolt, Jennifer K., Robert J. MacCoun, and John M. Darley. 2010. "Multiple Constraint Satisfaction in Judging." In David Klein and Gregory Mitchell, eds., *The Psychology of Judicial Decision Making*. New York: Oxford University Press, 27–39.

Ross, Lee, and Richard A. Nisbett. 1991. *The Person and the Situation: Perspectives of Social Psychology*. New York: McGraw-Hill.

Scalia, Antonin. 1997. *A Matter of Interpretation*. Princeton: Princeton University Press.

Schauer, Frederick. 2010. "Is There a Psychology of Judging?" In David Klein and Gregory Mitchell, eds., *The Psychology of Judicial Decision Making*. New York: Oxford University Press, 103–20.

Schubert, Glendon. 1965. *The Judicial Mind: Attitudes and Ideologies of Supreme Court Justices 1946–1963*. Evanston, IL: Northwestern University Press.

Segal, Jeffrey A., and Harold J. Spaeth. 2002. *The Supreme Court and the Attitudinal Model Revisited*. New York: Cambridge University Press.

Shepherd, Joanna M. 2009. "Are Appointed Judges Strategic Too?" *Duke Law Journal* 58: 1589–1626.

Sisk, Gregory C., Michael Heise, and Andrew P. Morriss. 1998. "Charting the Influences on the Judicial Mind: An Empirical Study of Judicial Reasoning." *New York University Law Review* 73: 1377–1500.

Songer, Donald R., Jeffrey A. Segal, and Charles M. Cameron. 1994. "The Hierarchy of Justice: Testing a Principal-Agent Model of Supreme Court-Circuit Court Interactions." *American Journal of Political Science* 38: 673–96.

Spaeth, Harold J., and Jeffrey A. Segal. 1999. *Majority Rule or Minority Will: Adherence to Precedent on the U.S. Supreme Court*. New York: Cambridge University Press.

Stier, Marc, and Saul Brenner. 2008. "Does Precedent Influence the Justices' Voting on the U.S. Supreme Court? A Theoretical Argument." *Law and Courts* 18 (1): 4–10.

Taha, Ahmed E. 2004. "Publish or Paris? Evidence of How Judges Allocate Their Time." *American Law and Economics Review* 6: 1–27.

Talbot, Margaret. 2005. "Supreme Confidence: The Jurisprudence of Justice Antonin Scalia." *New Yorker*, March 28, 40–55.

Tate, C. Neal. 1981. "Personal Attribute Models of the Voting Behavior of U.S. Supreme Court Justices: Liberalism in Civil Liberties and Economic Decisions, 1946–1978." *American Political Science Review* 75: 355–367.

U.S. Senate. 1971. *Nominations of William H. Rehnquist and Lewis F. Powell, Jr.* Hearings before the Committee on the Judiciary, 92nd Congress, 1st Session.

———. 1991. *Nomination of Judge Clarence Thomas to Be Associate Justice of the Supreme Court of the United States.* Hearings before the Committee on the Judiciary, 102nd Congress, 1st Session.

———. 2005. *Confirmation Hearing on the Nomination of John G. Roberts, Jr. to Be Chief Justice of the United States.* Hearings before the Committee on the Judiciary, 109th Congress, 1st Session.

Wahlbeck, Paul J. 1997. "The Life of the Law: Judicial Politics and Legal Change." *Journal of Politics* 59: 778–802.

Weber, Bruce. 2009. *As They See 'Em: A Fan's Travels in the Land of Umpires.* New York: Scribner.

Weizer, Paul I. 2004. *The Opinions of Justice Antonin Scalia: The Caustic Conservative.* New York: Peter Lang.

Whittington, Keith E. 2000. "Once More Unto the Breach: PostBehavioralist Approaches to Judicial Politics." *Law and Social Inquiry* 25: 601–34.

Winter, David G. 2002. "Motivation and Political Leadership." In Linda O. Valenty and Ofer Feldman, eds., *Political Leadership for the New Century: Personality and Behavior among American Leaders.* Westport, CT: Praeger, 25–47.

———. 2003. "Measuring the Motives of Political Actors at a Distance." In Jerrold M. Post, ed., *The Psychological Assessment of Political Leaders.* Ann Arbor: University of Michigan Press, 153–77.

Woodward, Bob, and Scott Armstrong. 1979. *The Brethren: Inside the Supreme Court.* New York: Simon and Schuster.

Zlotnick, David M. 1999. "Justice Scalia and His Critics: An Exploration of Scalia's Fidelity to His Constitutional Methodology." *Emory Law Journal* 48: 1377–1429.

Court Decisions

American Trucking Associations v. Michigan Public Service Commission. 2005. 545 U.S. 429.

Brown v. Board of Education. 1954. 347 U.S. 483.

Chevron U.S.A. v. Natural Resources Defense Council. 1984. 467 U.S. 837.

Kelo v. City of New London. 2005. 545 U.S. 469.

Lemon v. Kurtzman. 1971. 403 U.S. 602.

Texas v. Johnson. 1989. 491 U.S. 397.

Van Orden v. Perry. 2005. 545 U.S. 677.

4   Law *Is* Politics

Frank B. Cross

JUDICIAL DECISION-MAKING is commonly analyzed by contrasting the legal model with the attitudinal model (Segal and Spaeth 2002). This formulation can be misleading. The law, including that used by judicial decisions, is a subset of politics. The fundamental definition of politics is something like "the art and science of government." Because the judicial system is a central part of our government, it is a central part of our politics. Just as statutes are a product of our political system, so are judicial decisions. As Judge Posner puts it, "[L]aw is shot through with politics" (Posner 2008, 9).

The research on the determinants of judicial decision-making remains important, but not for the simplistic reasons commonly expressed. Empirical research has clearly demonstrated that judicial ideology is a statistically significant determinant of judicial outcomes. This is sometimes portrayed as a disproof of the legal model and evidence that judges are violating their authority and not making decisions according to law. In fact, such ideological decision-making may well be decision-making according to law, as it is a subset of politics. Theoretically, a judiciary might be instructed by a legislature, or the constitution, to make ideological decisions, in which case the courts would be carrying out the law with such ideology. While such an express extreme delegation is far from the rule in the United States, the delegation of some ideological decision-making is not.

The judiciary makes political decisions, either because that is the intent of the elected branches or because it is inevitable. Such decisions are not purely political, because the judiciary is considerably constrained by the content of the law and other practical political considerations, such as the attitudes of the elected branches. I contend that the federal judiciary is pursuing this model effectively. Judges don't always get it right, but the political system constrains substantial errors. The relevant question is how the system may be tweaked, not to eliminate judicial politics but to restrain errors insofar as possible.

The Inevitable Presence of Judicial Politics

The hypothesized legal model suggests that judges should decide solely according to accepted legal materials, sometimes referred to as formalism. Yet this hypothesized ideal is unrealizable because of the indeterminacy of language. While some may have exaggerated this indeterminacy, some indeterminacy is inevitable. "Statutes and constitutions are riddled with ambiguous language" (Lindquist and Klein 2006, 137). When formalistic law underdetermines a judicial decision, judges must use extralegal factors. When doing so, the ideal judge reaches the "best" political decision, with "political" simply meaning governance. In deciding what is "best," judges are inevitably influenced by their personal characteristics, which incorporate their ideology.

Direct Legislative Delegation to the Judiciary

In theory, judges simply apply the law given to them by the legislature (save for their common law authority). Judges are viewed as agents who are to do the bidding of their congressional principal. In practice, however, judges exercise considerable discretion on the meaning of that law, not because they exceed the bounds of their judicial authority but because the legislature delegates judges that discretionary authority. This is most obviously true when Congress passes a statute with language so vague that it compels judicial gap-filling in applications to individual cases.

The classic example of this delegation can be found in the nation's initial antitrust statute, the Sherman Act. The statutory language of Section 1 was a vague and general proscription of combinations in restraint of trade. In the ensuing century, courts fleshed this language out with detailed rules for different types of business policies. Judicial interpretations have evolved over time, with some prior doctrines overturned. All this gloss was simply added to a statute, and Congress has seldom intervened in the judicial product. The legislature appears happy to delegate details of antitrust law and reasonably satisfied with the outcome of that delegation.

The notion of delegation of policy-making authority to the judiciary is not limited to older historical context. The 1980 passage of the Comprehensive Environmental Response Compensation and Liability Act also witnessed clear cases where Congress delegated significant liability issues to resolution by the courts, rather than adopting statutory standards. Similarly, in the Private Securities Litigation Reform Act, which set standards for private rights of action under federal securities laws, the legislature ducked important issues, "leaving it to the courts to flesh out the [ambiguous] statutory standard with meaning" (Cross 2008a, 8).

The classic exposition of delegation of policy-making authority to the judiciary was written by Mark Graber, who takes the theory beyond statutory interpretation to constitutional rulings, which are generally considered the apogee of discretionary judicial authority. He suggests that the judiciary engages in aggressive policy-making "only when the dominant national coalition is unable or unwilling to settle some dispute" (Graber 1993, 36).

Graber's vision of delegation to the judiciary is a relatively cynical one, in which the elected branches of government use delegation to dodge responsibility for resolving an important policy question. He suggests that elected officials "encourage or tacitly support judicial policymaking both as a means of avoiding responsibility for making tough decisions and as a means of pursuing controversial policy goals that they cannot publicly advance through open legislative and electoral politics" (ibid., 37). The approach allegedly serves the political status quo. In such cases, politicians "try to straddle [the subject] . . . and to nominate candidates who are uncommitted and able to make gestures in both directions, all the while hoping that the issue will somehow solve itself or disappear" (Sundquist 1983, 307). Such action has a whiff of illegitimacy, though it shifts the illegitimacy from the judicial branch to the elected branches.

In fact, there is a much better and wholly legitimate reason for this delegation—the judiciary will offer better governance for the particularized questions than will the elected branches. An efficient government organization would empower the branch best suited for resolving these questions, and that branch may sometimes be the judiciary. It may be that some issue requires government supervision, yet the legislature lacks the knowledge to set clear requirements for all the future cases that may arise. It may be that "the best way to resolve certain intractable policy questions is to give judges the discretion to apply flexible principles as they design outcomes that meet the unique circumstances of individual cases" (Lovell 2003, 8). Judicial decisions have the ability to be "sensitive to unintended or harmful policy consequences in individual cases"

(Peretti 1999, 243). This reflects a wise, pragmatic approach to policy-making that "leaves the task of fine-tuning statutes to judges" (Posner 2008, 215).

It is impossible to universally discern the motivations for delegation to the judiciary. Some cases may be political, others pragmatic. Because there are hundreds of legislators voting on statutes, it may be that both factors are operating in any single case. Identifying the rationale for delegation is not critical, though, for a finding that delegation is present. Moreover, even if the motivating rationale were purely political, the result may be a promising pragmatic one.

Background Delegation to the Judiciary

In addition to intentional delegation of political decision-making authority to courts, some such authorization is inevitable. Courts must apply legal authority to the divergent facts of a myriad of cases that arise under prevailing legal authority. In *The Federalist*, James Madison wrote that all new laws, "though penned with the greatest technical skill and passed on the fullest and most mature deliberation," are nonetheless to some degree "obscure and equivocal." With technological and other changes in society, statutes "will constantly be applied to new circumstances which may not even have existed at the time of their passage," but courts nevertheless must "somehow interpret the language to rule on the case" (Cross 2008a, 6).

When Congress passes a statute, it may *try* to fill every gap, giving directions for all circumstances, but the legislature cannot foresee all circumstances. When Congress passed the Clean Air Act, it contemplated conventional air pollutants, such as particulates, but did not foresee the climate change issue. Moreover, words are inescapably ambiguous. While they may have a core meaning that is clear in many cases, there are always cases on the margin that may or may not fall within the statutory requirements. The need for compromises among legislators also makes it more difficult to spell out clear answers to all interpretive questions. This fact is even more true of constitutions, which are necessarily less detailed, given the relative difficulties of amendment.

Even in the case of background delegation, there is some conscious delegation to discretionary judicial decision-making. The legislature delegates interpretive authority to agencies, in rule-making or adjudication, as well as to courts. Matthew Stephenson (2008) has recently modeled this choice. He suggests that this choice is based on politics, but also on institutional characteristics. Stephenson hypothesizes that the judiciary will be more consistent over time in its interpretation of a statute.

While legislatures plainly delegate considerable authority to administrative agencies, they clearly empower courts and apparently prefer them to agencies. The Administrate Procedure Act gives courts the authority to review agency decisions and even delegates to courts the power to decide matters of law, such as statutory interpretation. In *Chevron*, the Supreme Court delegated back some legal interpretive authority to agencies, but it still retained the last word and ability to determine those issues.

Statutes unavoidably delegate discretionary authority to the courts, and this delegation is even more profound on constitutional issues. The courts are therefore a central part of our political governance system. Because questions are underdetermined by law, judges must use extralegal bases for their resolution, inevitably involving ideologically informed judgments.

The Inevitable Limitations of Judicial Politics

While judiciaries make political decisions, they are not utterly political, and their politics operate in a different fashion than that of legislatures (Burbank, this volume). This is true for institutional reasons alone. The position of the judiciary is not such a strong one that it can impose its will, without regard to the political views of other governmental branches. Moreover, there is ample reason to believe that the judiciary has sincere commitment to the law, independent of its political motivations. Consequently, there is reason to believe that judicial politics is bounded.

The Judiciary's Role in Government

Although the judiciary is inevitably a part of politics, it plays a different role from that of the legislature. Congress sets its own agenda, constrained only by the broad limits of the Constitution. Congress typically tackles the issues of most concern to the public. Congress also may appropriate more or less money to advance different ends. The courts, by contrast, may hear only cases or controversies brought to them by third parties and may rule only on the facts of those cases. Some issues are simply not on the judicial agenda, and these include some of the most important governance questions. The Court has little input into foreign policy. Macroeconomic policy is outside the purview of the justices.

In addition to addressing different issues, the courts use different procedures. Although judges are part of politics, they use legal model methods, and "there are cases in which justices vote for results that they would not support were they legislators whose constituents permitted them a free choice" (Posner 2008, 281). While the nature of such a ruling may have an effect well beyond the case facts, the judiciary lacks the power of the "purse or sword" to implement its rulings and hence remains highly dependent on the elected branches to effect its holdings (Friedman 2005).

Numerous institutional features of the American system limit the political authority of the judiciary. The elected branches have retained authority to check its exercise of discretion (Cross and Nelson 2001). The impeachment authority is potentially available, and legislative criticisms and threats may concern judges. Congress controls the resources available to courts and determines whether judicial pay is increased or left constant. The courts are wholly reliant on the other branches to implement their decisions. There are numerous tools by which the other branches of government can restrain the influence of courts, and justices respond to these tools (ibid.). Courts need political capital to have power and must husband it (Gibson, this volume).

There is also evidence that the courts are responsive to public opinion, though their independence was meant to insulate them from such influence. A study of opinions issued in the Warren and Burger courts found that the Court appeared to be "highly responsive to majority opinion" (Mishler and Sheehan 1993). Other research (Marshall 1989) demonstrates that unpopular decisions are more likely to be reversed. Judges may be concerned for public backlash, or they may simply be influenced by the same societal circumstances driving public opinion. In either case, the courts are not operating in an arbitrary, ideological, and countermajoritarian fashion.

The standard vision of judicial power is that the Court cannot long block the desires of a "dominant political coalition" (Funston 1975). This approach acknowledges that the Court can block the prevailing coalition for some period of time. Justices have sometimes "engaged in classic countermajoritarian behavior . . . in those relatively brief periods when members of a newly formed dominant national coalition have not yet had the time necessary to install their adherents on the bench" (Graber 1993, 38). Thus, the Court for a time frustrated aspects of Roosevelt's New Deal reform efforts, though new appointments switched the court.

Political Constitution of the Judiciary

A key element of the political nature of the judiciary can be found in the selection of judges. While some nations have neutral meritocratic selection methods, that is not true of the United States. Federal judges are chosen by politicians.

Aware of the inevitable influence of judicial ideology on judicial decisions, these selecting politicians make that a key component of their selection.

When appointing justices, "[p]residents are almost always motivated by the potential nominee's political philosophy" (Hulbary and Walker 1980, 189). An extensive historical review of Supreme Court appointments found that "political and ideological compatibility . . . has arguably been *the* controlling factor" in presidential nominations (Abraham 1992, 6). Presidents do not disregard other factors, such as qualifications, but ideological compatibility is nearly essential, and recent years have seen the ideological influence migrate to circuit court appointments as well as those of the Supreme Court.

Presidential appointments are checked by the need for Senate confirmation, especially when the Senate is controlled by a different party. While most nominees are confirmed, this may simply be due to the president's anticipation of potential resistance and choice of a nominee likely to be acceptable to the Senate (Peretti 1999). The selection of a Supreme Court justice will depend on the political alignment of both the president and Congress.

Judicial appointments "will thus over time spell the direction of constitutional law" (Friedman 2005, 279). The Court therefore responds somewhat more slowly than do the elected branches, a tendency that enhances stability of the political system and checks the impulses of immediate majorities. Efforts to expedite this process, such as Roosevelt's court-packing plan, have failed. But the infamous "switch in time" that produced affirmance of New Deal actions demonstrates that the Court can be more responsive to strong pressures of politics and public opinion.

Even absent political appointment influence and court-packing, the expressly political branches have the ability to influence judicial output, when the ideological inclinations of the Court diverge from those of Congress and the president. The most obvious ability, in a statutory context, lies in the legislature's ability to pass a new law that overrides judicial interpretations of existing authority. This practice has been extensively explained and studied by William Eskridge (1993). This occurred in the labor law context, where Congress modified the law in a more prolabor direction, after courts had been unduly promanagement, though even this statute "empowered judges" to make decisions in areas of the law (Lovell 2003, 225).

The elected branches may influence the Court even in its constitutional decisions. The other branches have numerous tools by which to channel the Court, and the public opinion that influences Congress and the president likewise appears to affect judicial rulings. When the Warren Court ruled for the rights of communists in domestic security cases in the late 1950s, congressional backlash "convinced Frankfurter that the Court could not sustain itself against such intense opposition and led him to join the more conservative justices to create an impregnable five-vote bloc" that retreated from the earlier decisions (Powe 2000, 179).

Although restraints on the Court are not commonly deployed, the threat of their use keeps the Court in check (Friedman 2005). Evidence of judicial restraint can be found in the Court's common deference to the position of the executive branch's solicitor general, even when that officer takes positions that appear ideologically contrary to that of the Court (Segal 1988). Case studies have demonstrated this effect as well; when pursuing a desegregation agenda the Court moderated its outcomes "to insure policy success" in the face of perceived public resistance (Peretti 1999). On other occasions, though, the public embraced a Court opinion, and its implementation proceeded expeditiously (Powe 2000, 203).

Limitations of the Research on Judicial Politics

The considerable empirical research on judicial decision-making shows a plain and consistent effect of judicial ideology on court outcomes. In fact, the empirical evidence is not so strong in its implications. The research reveals some ideological effect, but a much weaker one than commonly claimed. Judicial ideological decision-making is moderated by other institutions and preferences of judges themselves. This section reviews the limits of the research and how the attitudinal model effects have been sometimes exaggerated.

The U.S. Supreme Court database, the most common source for such research, has been criticized for ignoring legal factors and unreliably reporting the legal provisions at issue. Subjectivity and the coders' knowledge of how justices voted may have biased their coding, and various other coding questions have been identified (Burbank, this volume). Landes and Posner have similarly challenged the accuracy of coding outcomes in the most commonly used database for study of circuit court opinions (Landes and Posner 2008).

The coding questions cannot disqualify the findings of the empirical research on ideological judicial decision-making. Studies have produced similar attitudinal findings, without use of the prevailing databases and their associated coding questions (Cross 2008a, 188). A casual scan of Supreme Court voting patterns makes clear that conservative justices commonly reach outcomes that are generally considered conservative, while more liberal justices reach opposite outcomes. Nevertheless, the legitimate questions about case coding in the existing databases, especially the widely used U.S. Supreme Court Database, should give pause about relying too strongly on findings that they yield.

The claims of ideological judicial decision-making also falter on the frequency of unanimous opinions of the Supreme Court. It is in the unanimous cases that outcomes can be "explained by the presence of a very clear precedent" (Klein 1984, 112). Thus, when the law is truly determinate, it in fact directs the outcomes at the Supreme Court. Some suggest that this is not the case and that unanimous decisions occur only in the presence of an unusually ideologically extreme lower court decision, beyond the ideological positions of even the most extreme justices of the Supreme Court. This theory cannot explain the occurrences of unanimous affirmances. In addition, a study of unanimous reversals and the decisions below found that the cases being reviewed by the Court found that they were not rendered by "rogue ideologues" on the circuit courts but instead by judges with ideologies paralleling that of the Supreme Court (Songer 2005). Nor was there a profound difference between the lower court ideologies in cases that saw unanimous liberal and unanimous conservative reversals. Unanimous decisions may tend to occur in cases with a lesser ideological charge, but they demonstrate that justices care about more than mere ideology.

Unanimous decisions demonstrate that the justices are not pure ideological politicians. The frequency of nonunanimous decisions and the systematic ideological variances in the justice-votes, though, demonstrates that justices sometimes produce decisions driven by their political preferences. The most plausible explanation for these results is that justices adhere to the law when clearly determinate, even though contrary to their political preferences, but allow their ideologies influence when the law itself underdetermines the outcome.

The research on judicial ideological decision-making also confronts selection effects that may produce misleading conclusions. This is especially profound at the Supreme Court level, where the decision to accept a case for decision is highly discretionary. The Court chooses to review only a small fraction of the cases appealed. It could be that the Court simply declines to review those decisions in which the law is clear, and, "if so, [this genuine legal] constraint never would show up in studies that look only to granted cases" (Friedman 2006, 271). This thesis is evidenced by the Court's tendency to take cases on which the circuit courts have split on the legal questions. The presence of such a circuit split is evidence that the law is not dispositive, leaving extralegal factors as critical to resolution of the outcome. This prospect is confirmed by empirical evidence demonstrating that decisions on certiorari are not ideologically driven but instead reflect legal evaluations. A recent study suggests that the Court's certiorari decisions are influenced by the ideological composition of Congress, with the Court avoiding cases that could greatly displease contemporaneous legislators (Harvey and Friedman 2008).

A similar, though lesser, selection effect occurs at lower court levels, in which judges have less discretion in choosing cases to accept. Pursuing a case is costly for litigating parties. Plaintiffs are unlikely to bring a case that is a sure loser; if the law is an important factor in decision-making, the cases that plaintiffs will lose on the law will never appear in court. Moreover, defendants may settle a case in which their side is a clear loser on the law, so those cases will also be absent from the corpus of decisions to be analyzed empirically.

This consequence is set out in seminal research by George Priest and Benjamin Klein (1984). They modeled parties' decisions to pursue cases to final court outcomes. Their hypothesis was that clear cases would be settled and never produce a trial. It is the close cases on the law that produce judicial decisions, and those cases, where the law is less determinate, are the ones where extralegal factors such as ideology are most likely to appear. Hence, even if the law dictated most potential judicial outcomes when it was clear, decisions could nonetheless appear ideological.

The potentially distorting features of selection effects find some support in the empirical research on ideological judicial decision-making. The selection effects would predict the most ideological decision-making at the Supreme Court level where the selection effects are most profound. They would also predict somewhat more ideological decision-making in circuit courts, as opposed to district courts, because the additional costs of appeal would screen out more relatively clear cases. A meta-analysis of research on different levels of the federal judiciary found some evidence of attitudinal decision-making throughout, but its extent declined from the Supreme Court, to the circuit courts, to the district courts (Pinello 1999).

The data on selection effects are again consistent with my hypothesis about the political role of the Court. Justices screen out many of the relatively clear legal outcomes (though not all, as evidenced by unanimous opinions), so that the cases they decide are those in which the law is somewhat indeterminate, either due to conscious delegation to the Court or inevitable linguistic imprecision and background delegation. This is the proper political role for the judiciary in my model.

Another crucial limitation on the attitudinalist research, especially at the Supreme Court level, is the focus on outcomes rather than opinions. Most of the research simply examines whether the result in the case favored the party taking the conservative position or the liberal position, using traditional and accepted criteria for ideological direction. It is much easier to code the direction of the outcome than the content of the opinion, but such coding ignores the key element of the decision and consequently can produce misleading results.

Even Segal and Spaeth have observed that it is the "opinion of the Court" that constitutes the core of the Court's policy-making process (Segal and Spaeth 2002). The significance of opinion content is evident from the number of concurrences found at the Supreme Court level. If the Court's product was simply that of the outcome, justices would simply join the majority opinion or dissent, there would be no reason to issue a concurrence. The language of the opinion matters.

Consider the opinion in *Planned Parenthood of Southeastern Pennsylvania v. Casey*. This was chosen as a vehicle for overturning reproductive rights. The majority of the Court rejected this effort and reaffirmed *Roe*. However, the majority opinion altered the existing framework, shifting from the trimester standard to an "undue burden" standard and upheld state requirements for informed consent, a waiting period, parental consent, and other abortion rights restrictions of state law. The *Casey* decision was clearly one that shifted the law in a conservative direction, but it was *much* less conservative than it might have been.

The key question about Supreme Court rulings is not their outcome but their opinion's content. Most studies do not capture this essential element. The key votes in *Casey* emphasized the importance of stare decisis as a basis for the reluctance to overturn *Roe*. The law apparently mattered to the crucial issue in the case. Thus, the content of opinions, the key product of courts, can be driven in part by ideological concerns but also by the preexisting law, the political environment, and other factors.

Barry Friedman examined recent decisions on affirmative action and found that "looking to outcomes rather than opinions leads to the wrong conclusion of what the court 'did'" (Friedman 2006, 266). The same justices reached different outcomes but employed the same criteria for evaluating affirmative action programs. Had only one of these cases come before the Court, empirical re-searchers might have concluded that it demonstrated a conservative (or liberal) paradigm, but that would have been but an artifact of the particular case facts decided. Professor Friedman goes on to observe that a simple comparison of the voting records of Justices Rehnquist and Thomas makes them appear quite similar, but "if one reads the decisions authored by these justices, it is apparent that the two are quite different in ways that have great significance for the law" (ibid., 267).

The opinions of the Supreme Court create the standard by which lower courts render future decisions and influence the actions of private parties and the judicial challenges that they subsequently bring. Any study of the true na-ture of judicial decision-making must consider the content of opinions, yet this has seen little empirical research. To understand the effect of the law, one must study the law, not simply case outcomes.

Although the law is notoriously difficult to study in an empirical fashion, some findings are suggestive of its influence on judicial decisions. A study of Supreme Court decisions in cases with circuit conflicts found that the Court was more likely to adopt the policy adopted by most circuits, with less dis-sent, and that adopted by more expert circuit court judges, even controlling for ideological influences (Lindquist and Klein 2006). At the circuit court level, the study of the power of procedural legal commands is more readily available. For example, such courts are legally commanded to give deference to aspects of the decisions they review. They are to defer to factual findings of lower courts and, in varying degrees, to administrative agencies. If judges were so deferential, one would expect a relatively high affirmance rate, regardless of their ideological preferences. This is true to a degree that dwarfs their ideological preferences (Cross 2007).

Notwithstanding these limitations, the empirical research on attitudinalism contains revealing findings. They produce consistent, statistically significant findings of ideological influence, even with different sources of data. Former judge Wald, who has criticized quantitative research on judicial ideology, has herself conceded that the "judge's political orientation *will* affect decisionmak-ing" (Wald 1985, 895). The above challenges to attitudinalism are limitations on the theory, not complete rejections of its findings. I next consider the rationale or process by which judges, especially Supreme Court justices, render ideologi-cal decisions.

Even when judges produce apparently ideological decision-making, they may well be "engag[ing] in good-faith efforts to find the most persuasive solutions to complex legal puzzles" (Lindquist and Klein 2006, 136). The evidence of ideological decision-making patterns does not refute this hypothesis. Because of the factors above, including selection effects and opinion content, the law may have a profound effect on decisions even in cases where outcomes appear ideological. Those opinions may not even involve *any* conscious ideological choice of the sort associated with legislative decisions.

The theory of motivated reasoning suggests that different judges will assess the same information differently, depending on their backgrounds and fundamental values (Braman and Nelson 2007). Attitudinalists have concurred that their findings on ideological decision-making could be explained by the "human reflex" to "convince oneself of the propriety of what one prefers to believe—motivated reasoning" (Howard and Segal 2002).

Motivated reasoning, however, is subject to "reasonableness constraints" (Boiney et al. 1997). For example, the accuracy of decision-making is enhanced when the stakes for the decision are higher, when the decision must be justified, and when decision will be made public. Such circumstances often apply to judicial decisions. The presence of stronger arguments contrary to preferences reduces the influence of motivations (Jain and Maheswaran 2000; Kunda 1990). The limitations of the power of motivated reasoning are apparent from the numerous unanimous opinions of the Supreme Court and other cases in which justices appear to vote contrary to their ideological preferences. One would anticipate that the influence of such motivated reasoning is at its apex when the law is relatively less determinate, which is consistent with the findings of empirical research.

Judge Posner largely ascribes the results of the empirical findings through this subconscious effect, noting that people can see the "same thing" but interpret it in "opposite ways" (Posner 2008, 97). Yet he also notes that judges sometimes engage in more traditional political, or "legislative," decision-making. The following section describes this process and why it is a beneficial aspect of our political system.

Pragmatism and Appropriate Judicial Politics

Judicial decision-making, including its exercise of political discretion, may be viewed as a form of pragmatism, simply seeking the optimal policy for our government. If so, one might find patterns of ideological decision-making even though judges are not consciously considering ideology when making decisions. This section begins by describing the practical nature of judicial pragmatism, which may explain the empirical findings. Then I set forth the affirmative case for such pragmatism as sound political governance.

The Nature of Pragmatic Judicial Decision-making

Judge Posner contends that the "word that best describes the average American judge at all levels of our judicial hierarchies . . . is 'pragmatist'" (ibid., 230). The pragmatic judge balances his or her political discretion with the pursuit of traditional legal model standards. Some commitment to traditional legal decision-making is surely essential to judicial legitimacy, and it also is pragmatic, insofar as it produces more predictability.

Rigid adherence to formal legalism does not, and should not, describe our judicial practice. Brian Tamanaha suggests that "a greater proportion of contemporary judges are judicial pragmatists" (Tamanaha 2007, 490). In statutory interpretation cases, Thomas Merrill contends that American judges "have been pragmatists" for "most of our history" (Merrill 1994, 351). A survey of circuit court judges reported that "common sense," in addition to the law, was a "very important" determinant of their decisions (Howard 1981, 164). While judges may have always used pragmatism, its use appears to be increasing over the past decade (Cross 2008b).

The Posnerian pragmatist seeks the best result for a given case. "Best," in this context, does not necessarily mean the fairest outcome for the parties or even the optimal legal policy for the nation as a whole. Judges realize the value of the traditional legal model; indeed, their training inculcates them in its importance (Cross and Nelson 2001, 1479–81). Judges have strong incentives to adhere to traditional legal methodologies for decisions. Even if judges had no training or taste for legal decision-making, a pragmatist would adhere to its method, because it contributes to pragmatic results (Posner 2008). Consequently, they will adhere to clear legislative direction, or precedent, unless it produces absurd results. Empirical research demonstrates that the content of opinions shapes the content and result of future opinions (Richards and Kritzer 2002). This pragmatism involves "common sense, respect for precedent, and an appreciation of society's needs" (Farber 1992, 536).

The pragmatic judge considers the systemic effects of his or her ruling, including the value of stare decisis. Goodness may depend substantially on the materials of the law, insofar as they are applicable. David Klein notes that "judges find the search for good answers to legal questions intrinsically rewarding" (Klein 2002, 11–12). Where the law is indeterminate, goodness is not purely legal, though, but influenced by judicial background factors, including ideological preferences.

While some express concern that political pragmatism may turn judges into "loose legislative cannons," Judge Posner suggests that judges "are less likely to be drunk with power if they realize they are exercising discretion than if they think they are just a transmission belt for decisions made elsewhere and so they bear no responsibility for any ugly consequences of those decisions" (Posner 2008, 252). Pragmatism does not disregard the law, but it recognizes that the law underdetermines judicial outcomes and attempts to make decisions that apply the law wisely.

Some may lament judicial pragmatism, yearning for Langdellian formalism, but those days never existed. Brian Tamanaha's extensive research has demonstrated that even prior to the discovery of "legal realism," judges understood that the law was not merely mechanically applied but instead influenced by judges' attitudes (Tamanaha 2009). As early as 1833, a century before the realist era, an American jurist wrote that "the courts in point of fact make the law, performing at the same time the office of legislators and judges" ("Written and Unwritten Systems of Law" 1833). Judges have always been part of politics, making political decisions. This is an inevitable aspect of their role in governance.

The law inevitably underdetermines many controversies. Whether because of delegation or hermeneutic ambiguity, traditional legal materials leave many questions unresolved, and those questions will arise in cases brought to the courts. This leaves judges to fall back upon some extralegal principle for resolution of the case. Pragmatism suggests that judges try to reach the "best" societal result, a decision that is inevitably political and influenced by judges' background ideology, but also influenced by the materials of the law.

The Structural Legal Value of Pragmatic Judicial Decision-making

The legal institutions of our nation bound judicial ideological decision-making, even beyond the constraints imposed by the separation of powers constraints discussed in the second section of the chapter. Because the governing law of our nations is created by the judiciary as a whole, rather than individual judges, it is a joint product. Because the judiciary is politically constituted, this joint product reflects the judgments of the president and Congress. While Graber is plain that his theory does not "celebrate" judicial political authority (Graber 1993), I will do so. I will characterize such political decision-making as pragmatism, because that represents the norm. This is political, because the method concerns itself with wise governance. The "ultimate test of the Justices' work must be goodness," and political pragmatism may advance that end (Wright 1971).

Pragmatism has been criticized "because it guts the rule of law" by basing decisions on extralegal considerations (Calabresi 2007, 26). In this view, judging becomes little more than making arbitrary judgments. This criticism reflects a great deal of naivety about both the law and judging. The law does not perfectly determine outcomes, and much is delegated to the courts as explained above. There may be no objective, determinate "law" to be gutted. Moreover, judges are humans influenced by their backgrounds and ideologies. The perfectly neutral rule of law is not achievable. But even if it were possible to make the law perfectly determinate and render neutral decisions, as if by algorithm, that would be inferior to our present judicial system. The judiciary is part of the political system and, as such, its judges should employ good judgment in rendering decisions.

While it is difficult to measure the value of pragmatic judicial decision-making, some evidence can be found in studies on the effect of the common law. The common law represents an affirmative embrace of discretionary political judicial decision-making within its sphere. Judges can create law in areas such as contracts and torts. By contrast, civil law judiciaries have no such authority and can only apply the dictates of legislation. In civil law systems, judges perform a more clerical function, with less discretion. The differences may be exaggerated, and civil law systems have at least some common law characteristics (Lasser 2001), but research has found real differences.

Considerable empirical evidence now testifies to the superiority of common law systems. Much of this research demonstrates the superiority of common law for financial systems (Beck 2003). Common law nations better enforce intellectual property rights (Pons and Garcia 2008). Common law judicial systems also associate with lower corruption throughout society, showing the system's value for the implementation of laws (Persson and Tabellini 2005). Common law systems provide better deterrence of accidents (Smith 2005). The greater success of common law systems may be attributed to its adaptability and relative judicial power, from the discretion given judges in resolving disputes, a discretion that uses the preexisting law but is not dictated by that law.

The common law is judge made and governed by a sort of "bottom up" pragmatism. It does not destroy the rule of law; it is closely associated with an effective rule of law. The common law is thus political, in the sense that it creates rules of governance for liability. However, the common law is not purely ideological or political, since judges rely heavily on precedents and general legal principles to reach their common law decisions.

I have more directly examined the effect of pragmatic doctrines in Supreme Court decisions on statutory interpretation. This research found that the tools of pragmatism tended to produce greater consensus on the Court, not the dissensus that might be expected from unleashed judicial discretion (Cross 2008b). Moreover, there was no association between use of these tools of pragmatism and ideological skewing of decisions. Judicial discretion does not lead to judicial "loose cannons" on deck. A separate study found that bankruptcy decisions made using pragmatism, rather than textualism, were more likely satisfactory to Congress (Bussell 2000).

Judge Posner contends that what "looks to the critics of the judiciary like willfulness might actually be the good-faith performance of a vital judicial role"; if judges limited themselves "to passively applying rules made elsewhere, the legal system might be worse than it is" (Posner 2008, 4). The judiciary serves as a somewhat redundant political decision-maker that has a unique capacity to consider "interests and values overlooked in other branches and with sensitivity" to unintended or harmful policy consequences" as reflected in particular cases (Peretti 1999, 243). I have suggested above that pure passive application of rules is an impossible achievement, given indeterminacy. Nevertheless, judges may be more or less committed to legalism, and maximizing this commitment is not societally beneficial.

The Measure of Pragmatic Judicial Decision-making

The existence and value of pragmatic judicial decision-making should not yield a Panglossian conclusion about all judicial decisions. While the structure of courts in the United States yields an appropriate overall legal system, individual judicial decisions may be excessively ideological and contrary to the desired law. This creates a certain injustice, especially for the parties to those cases that are wrongly decided. While the overall system may be functional, individual outcomes may be inappropriate.

While judges render extralegal decisions under constraints, they produce different decisions, and it is fair to debate the proper content of these decisions. Any "conclusions about judicial behavior may vary by court, by judge, and by case, or even by the time period in which decisions are rendered" (Friedman 2006, 271). Some judges show a much stronger ideological pattern of outcomes than do others. Judge Posner suggests a tradeoff between the strength of judges' political preferences and use of legal factors in decisions (Posner 2008, 80). Some judges have a more "minimalist" approach to their opinions than do others (Sunstein 2005). Judges vary in their devotion to pragmatism. Rather than evaluating the judiciary as following the law or not, we can assess their decisions according to the nature of their pragmatism. Lee Epstein suggests that strongly ideological justices are largely unconstrained by the preferences of other branches, but more moderate justices attend to those preferences (Epstein et al. 2001).

The truly salient question is the degree to which judges should be ideologically activist and whether that decision-making model is more pragmatic. Judge Posner has suggested that activist decisions of the Court are generally unwise. He fears that they can discourage experimentation and produce unpragmatic results for society. This generalization is highly debatable, as numerous activist decisions have proved pragmatic and been widely embraced by elected officials and future courts (Lindquist and Cross 2009).

If we do wish to limit the political role of the courts, it is important to recognize the inevitability of judicial discretion. The selection process should not defer to nominees' professions of disdain for judicial activism or promises to be but an umpire calling balls and strikes—even if these claims are sincere. Justices cannot escape the need to make decisions that go beyond the materials of the law.

If we choose to limit ideology on the courts, we must acknowledge ideology on the courts. Because judges are influenced by personal ideology, that ideology should be explored at nomination hearings, notwithstanding nominee claims of fealty to the law. Moreover, it is reasonable for Congress to take such ideology into account in voting on nominees because it will inevitably influence their subsequent decisions.

None of this necessarily follows. As the above sections indicate, a measure of judicial ideology is not a bad thing, so perhaps such action of moderation is unnecessary. A more ideological judiciary seems likely to be more independent of the influence of the elected branches and serve as a better check on their decisions, even as the justices act more politically. This is the key question, which is simply obscured by claims that justices are wholly political or apolitical in their actions.

Conclusion

The law is inescapably political, and judges correspondingly issue a number of discretionary, ideological decisions. This is not only inevitable, it is a wise process. Judges should not feel unduly constrained by the materials of the law, whether those of the Constitution, statutes, or prior judicial precedents. A measure of judicial political discretion is consistent with good governance.

Terri Jennings Peretti has observed that "political motivations transform the justices into mere politicians and the Court into just another political agency" (Peretti 1999, 158–59). This conclusion oversimplifies the judicial process. Judges are a different kind of politician than are legislators, and their decisions are subject to a different set of constraints. Judges are influenced by the law, as well as political concerns.

Finding that judging is inevitably political does not reject the important role of legal decision-making. The vast majority of judicial decisions place greater importance on legal materials than they do on judicial ideology (Cross 2007). Individual judicial politics play an important role when the law is less determinate. Although realist cynics may dispute this legal effect, it has been empirically validated. After the adoption of the Federal Sentencing Guidelines, which made sentencing more determinate, the interjudge variation in sentencing length dropped by about 40 percent (Anderson 1999). Judges thus are not untrammeled politicians but perform their role in governance by exercising their proclivities in cases where the governing legal materials are less clear.

The ideological associations in judicial voting behavior are plausibly explained by subconscious cognitive effects, such as motivated reasoning. Judges are seeking good answers within the law, but the perception of goodness is inevitably influenced by their background values. This is clearly political decision-making, of a sort, providing rules for governance. And it is an unavoidable necessity. As Steve Burbank notes in this volume, political decisions without any effect of the law would be dangerous, but the law without any judicial politics would be weak and feeble (Burbank, this volume). It is their complementary effect that is the strength of our judicial system.

References

Abraham, Henry. 1992. *Justices and Presidents*. New York: Oxford University Press.
Anderson, James M. 1999. "Measuring Interjudge Sentencing Disparity: Before and after the Federal Sentencing Guidelines." *Journal of Law and Economics* 42: 271–307.

Beck, Thorsten, et al. 2003. "Law and Finance: Why Does Legal Origin Matter?" *Journal of Comparative Economics* 31: 653–75.

Boiney, Lindsley G., et al. 1997. "Instrumental Bias in Motivated Reasoning: More when More Is Needed." *Organizational Behavior and Human Decision Processes* 71: 1–24.

Braman, Eileen, and Thomas E. Nelson. 2007. "Mechanism of Motivated Reasoning? Analogical Perception in Discrimination Disputes." *American Journal of Political Science* 51: 940–56

Bussell, Daniel J. 2000. "Textualism's Failures: A Study of Overruled Bankruptcy Decisions." *Vanderbilt Law Review* 53: 885–946.

Calabresi, Steven G. 2007. "A Critical Introduction to the Originalism Debate." In *Originalism: A Quarter-Century of Debate*. Washington, DC: Regnery.

Cross, Frank B. 2007. *Decision Making in the U.S. Courts of Appeals*. Stanford: Stanford University Press.

———. 2008a. *The Theory and Practice of Statutory Interpretation*. Stanford: Stanford University Press.

———. 2008b. "What Do Judges Want?" *Texas Law Review* 87: 183–233.

Cross, Frank B., and Blake J. Nelson. 2001. "Strategic Institutional Effects on Supreme Court Decisionmaking." *Northwestern University Law Review* 95: 1437–94.

Epstein, Lee, et al. 2001. "The Supreme Court as a Strategic National Policymaker." *Emory Law Journal* 50: 583–611.

Eskridge, William N. 1993. "The Judicial Review Game." *Northwestern Law Review* 88: 382–95.

Farber, Daniel A. 1992. "The Inevitability of Practical Reason: Statutes, Formalism, and the Rule of Law." *Vanderbilt Law Review* 45: 533–59.

Friedman, Barry. 2005. "The Politics of Judicial Review." *Texas Law Review* 84: 257–337.

———. 2006. "Taking Law Seriously." *Perspectives on Politics* 4: 261–76.

Funston, Richard. 1975. "The Supreme Court and Critical Elections." *American Political Science Review* 69: 795–811.

Graber, Mark A. 1993. "The Nonmajoritarian Difficulty: Legislative Deference to the Judiciary." *Studies in American Political Development* 7: 35–73.

Guthrie, Chris, Jeffrey J. Rachlinski, and Andrew J. Wistrich. 2007. "Blinking on the Bench: How Judges Decide Cases." *Cornell Law Review* 93: 1–43.

Harvey, Anna, and Barry Friedman. 2008. "Ducking Trouble: Congressionally-Induced Selection Bias in the Supreme Court's Agenda." Available at http://papers.ssrn.com/sol3/papers.cfm?abstract_id=913668.

Howard, J. Woodford, Jr. 1981. *Courts of Appeals in the Federal Judicial System: A Study of the Second, Fifth, and District of Columbia Circuits*. Princeton: Princeton University Press.

Howard, Robert M., and Jeffrey A. Segal. 2002. "An Original Look at Originalism." *Law and Society Review* 36: 113–37.

Hulbary, William E., and Thomas G. Walker. 1980. "The Supreme Court Selection Process: Presidential Motivations and Judicial Performance." *Western Political Quarterly* 33: 185–96.

Jain, Sahiendra Pratap, and Durairaj Maheswaran. 2000. "Motivated Reasoning: A Depth-of-Processing Perspective." *Journal of Consumer Research* 26: 358–71.

Klein, David E. 2002. *Making Law in the United States Court of Appeals*. Cambridge: Cambridge University Press.

Klein, Mitchell S. 1984. *Law Courts and Policy*. Englewood Cliffs, NJ: Prentice Hall.

Kunda, Ziva. 1990. "The Case for Motivated Reasoning." *Psychological Bulletin* 108: 480–98.

Landes, William M., and Richard A. Posner. 2008. "Rational Judicial Behavior: A Statistical Study." Chicago: John M. Olin Law and Economics Working Paper No. 404.

Lasser, Mitchel de S.-O.l'. 2001. "Do Judges Deploy Policy?" *Cardozo Law Review* 22: 863–900.

Lindquist, Stefanie A., and Frank B. Cross. 2009. *Measuring Judicial Activism*. New York: Oxford University Press.

Lindquist, Stefanie A., and David E. Klein. 2006. "The Influence of Jurisprudential Considerations on Supreme Court Decisionmaking: A Study of Conflict Cases." *Law and Society Review* 40: 135–62.

Lovell, George. 2003. *Legislative Deferrals: Statutory Ambiguity, Judicial Power, and American Democracy*. Cambridge: Cambridge University Press.

Marshall, Thomas R. 1989. *Public Opinion and the Supreme Court*. New York: Longman.

Merrill, Thomas W. 1994. "Textualism and the Future of the *Chevron* Doctrine." *Washington University Law Quarterly* 72: 351–77.

Mishler, William, and Reginald S. Sheehan. 1993. "The Supreme Court as a Countermajoritarian Institution? The Impact of Public Opinion on Supreme Court Decisions." *American Political Science Review* 87: 87–101.

Peretti, Terri Jennings. 1999. *In Defense of a Political Court*. Princeton: Princeton University Press.

Persson, Torsten, and Guido Tabellini. 2005. *The Economic Effects of Constitutions*. Cambridge, MA: MIT Press.

Pinello, Daniel R. 1999. "Linking Party to Judicial Ideology in American Courts: A Meta-Analysis." *Justice System Journal* 20: 219–54.

Planned Parenthood of Southeastern Pennsylvania v. Casey. 1992. 505 U.S. 833.

Pons, J. D., and M. C. Garcia. 2008. "Legal Origin and Intellectual Property Rights: An Empirical Study in the Prerecorded Music Sector." *European Journal of Law and Economics* 26: 153–73.

Posner, Richard A. 2008. *How Judges Think*. Cambridge, MA: Harvard University Press.

Powe, Lucas A., Jr. 2000. *The Warren Court and American Politics*. Cambridge, MA: Belknap Press.

Priest, George L., and Benjamin Klein. 1984. "The Selection of Disputes for Litigation." *Journal of Legal Studies* 13: 1–55.

Richards, Mark J., and Herbert M. Kritzer. 2002. "Jurisprudential Regimes in Supreme Court Decision Making." *American Political Science Review* 96: 305–20.

Segal, Jeffrey A. 1988. "Amicus Curiae Briefs by the Solicitor General during the Warren and Burger Courts." *Western Political Quarterly* 41: 135–44.

Segal, Jeffrey A., and Harold J. Spaeth. 2002. *The Supreme Court and the Attitudinal Model Revisited.* Cambridge: Cambridge University Press.

Smith, Michael L. 2005. "Deterrence and Origin of Legal System: Evidence from 1950–1999." *American Law and Economics Review* 7: 350–78.

Songer, Donald R., and Dana Roy. 2005. "A Critical Test of the Attitudinal Model." Presented at the annual meeting of the Midwest Political Science Association.

Stephenson, Matthew C. 2008. "Legislative Allocation of Delegated Power: Uncertainty, Risk, and the Choice between Agencies and Courts." *Harvard Law Review* 119: 1036–70.

Sundquist, James L. 1983. *Dynamics of the Party System: Alignment and Realignment of Political Parties in the United States.* Washington, DC: Brookings Institution.

Sunstein, Cass R. 2005. *Radicals in Robes: Why Extreme Right-Wing Courts Are Wrong for America.* Basic Books: New York.

Tamanaha, Brian Z. 2007. "How an Instrumental View of Law Corrodes the Rule of Law." *DePaul Law Review* 56: 469–505.

———. 2009. *Balanced Realism on Judging: Beyond the Formalist-Realist Divide.* Princeton: Princeton University Press.

Wald, Patricia M. 1985. "Some Thoughts on Judging as Gleaned from One Hundred Years of the Harvard Law Review and Other Great Books." *Harvard Law Review* 100: 887–908.

Wright, J. Skelly. 1971. "Professor Bickel, the Scholarly Tradition and the Supreme Court." *Harvard Law Review* 84: 769–805.

"Written and Unwritten Systems of Law." 1833, *American Jurist and Law Magazine* 9: 5

5 Path Dependence in Studies of Legal Decision-making

Eileen Braman

J. Mitchell Pickerill

J UDGES, LAW PROFESSORS, and yes, even political scientists are creatures of their training and professional socialization. Although we all come to the table with unique concerns, perspectives, and insights about legal decision-making, those views are inevitably shaped by how we first come to understand the endeavor and the assumptions of relevant colleagues with whom we interact each day. In this chapter we explore and attempt to understand path dependent influences on scholarly thinking about legal decision-making. Acknowledging that we are at a critical juncture in promoting understandings of legal reasoning that take into account the concerns of scholars from multiple perspectives, we ask and try to answer several important questions: How does what we "know" about legal decision-making shape current research? To what extent do the distinct trajectories of research in different disciplines, particularly law and political science, facilitate or hinder interdisciplinary exchange? How might the methods used by our disciplinary predecessors shape and confine our thinking?

We undergo this task because we believe that greater attention to the assumptions, approaches, and findings of researchers across disciplines is a positive development that has significant potential to improve our understanding of the factors influencing legal outcomes and the normative implications of such knowledge. This sort of interdisciplinary exchange is bound to fail, however, if legal and behavioral scholars do not come to the table in the spirit of mutual respect with a sincere openness and appreciation for what they have to learn from one another. At bottom, this means not only an appreciation of the methods and insights scholars might borrow across disciplinary lines to aid their own research in isolated instances but also a critical assessment of what knowledge and findings accumulated across disciplinary borders mean in terms of our own assumptions and the very questions we are asking. This involves the difficult task of acknowledging shortfalls in our own understandings that might be illuminated by the insights of others with different perspectives. As we are both political scientists who have also practiced law in former lives, many of our observations involve how research in our own discipline could be refined and improved though more attention to interdisciplinary understandings. We offer this commentary, however, with a sincere appreciation for the contribution that empirical research has provided in terms of understanding decision-making that is sometimes lacking in criticisms offered across disciplinary lines.

Using "path dependence" as our organizing framework, in the first part of this chapter we describe the division of labor that has evolved between law and political science in understanding legal decision-making phenomena. In the second part we examine how widely used operationalizations, datasets, and methods in our own discipline may impede innovative approaches to understanding decisional behavior. In the third part we point to specific instances in which there are significant issues of "translation" involving the operationalization of concepts that can influence perceptions of the usefulness of research across disciplines. We call for more careful attention to the conceptualization of concepts that takes into account, or at least acknowledges, the perspective of scholars from other disciplines concerned about legal reasoning.

Path Dependence in Disciplinary Approaches

At a very general level, path dependence means "that what happened at an earlier point in time will affect the possible outcomes of a sequence of events occurring at a later point in time" (Sewell 1996, 262–63; quoted in Pierson 2004, 20). To be more precise, "[P]ath dependence refers to dynamic processes involving positive feedback, which generate multiple possible outcomes depending on a particular sequence in which events unfold" (Pierson 2004, 20; citing Arthur 1994; David 2000). This latter understanding of path dependence focuses on "self-reinforcing or positive feedback processes . . . that reinforce the recurrence of a particular pattern into the future" (Pierson and Skocpol 2002,

699). Positive reinforcing feedback at different points of development not only pushes us further along the path chosen, but it makes "the costs of switching to some previously plausible alternative to rise" (Pierson 2004, 21); thus the "'roads not chosen' may become increasingly distant, increasingly unreachable alternatives." Timing, sequence, context, and conjunctures are all central to understanding the slow-moving causal processes that lead to certain social and political conditions or outcomes (see Pierson and Skocpol 2002, 699–704).

Political scientists typically use path dependency frameworks for understanding how certain institutional arrangements came to be and what the consequences of those arrangements are for political and policy outputs. Unfortunately, our scholarship can be prone to path dependent processes as well. Each fork in the road presents us with epistemological, theoretical, and methodological choices, and each of these choices occurs in a specific temporal context. When a particular choice enjoys positive feedback from peers, reviewers, editors, and others in the field, the path chosen is reinforced and we move further in that particular direction. Thus, scholars write about specific topics in specific ways using particular conventions because that is what they have been trained to do and that is what their peers in their particular discipline expect.

There are certainly strong intellectual arguments for proceeding in this manner. Social scientists, for example, endeavor to produce knowledge incrementally by building on what we know within an accepted research paradigm in the name of "normal science" (see, for example, Farr 1988; Kuhn 1962). The reference point for any piece of scholarship is usually going to be that which came before it in a specific disciplinary field or subfield—until or unless a paradigmatic shift occurs. But we argue here, as scholars trod along the given path, that they have a responsibility to be self-reflective, vigilant, and deliberative in making investigative choices.

There are many professional factors that can serve as positive reinforcement for pushing a line of research further along a particular path. For young scholars professional development and advancement revolve around publication of their research. Editors of prestigious journals and presses often show predilections toward research with particular theoretical, methodological, or ideological orientations. Where journals are refereed, manuscript reviewers tend toward approving work within a research tradition with which they are most familiar. To the extent that editors choose reviewers from a mainstream or favored research orientation, that work is most likely to be published. The same holds true for publishing with reputable book publishers, such as university presses, as well as the factors used in evaluation for prestigious grants and fellowships.

Criteria for success tend to be established and understood *within* disciplinary boundaries. Law professors and political scientists are perpetually immersed in the literature of their home fields; we constantly think about seminal debates and recent articles of import to frame our own research. Legal academics seek to have research placed in the most prestigious law reviews; political scientists usually do not get much credit for publishing in student-edited outlets, regardless of their prestige. They are more concerned with the acceptance rates and impact factors of peer-reviewed disciplinary journals. Thus, the reward structure of the academy may serve to stymie innovation and promote myopic attention to scholarly work receiving a good deal of attention within our respective domains.

It used to be that someone would peek over the disciplinary fence that separates legal from empirical approaches once only every so often to offer a critique, borrow an intuition, or organize a conference—but such encounters are becoming more and more frequent in recent years. Indeed, over the past decade political scientists have started annual "workshops" to train legal academics in empirical methods to encourage interdisciplinary exchange. Moreover, the number of articles where legally socialized individuals have criticized empirical studies or called for more attention to legal considerations seems to have increased exponentially. Calls of this type are not necessarily a new development—witness the series of articles by Wallace Mendelson (a political scientist with a Harvard law degree) in the early 1960s (for example, Mendelson 1963, 1964, 1966)—but the number and frequency of such commentaries seems to have spiked in the past fifteen years (see, for instance, Cross 1997; Edwards 1998; Cross, Heise, and Sisk 2002; Friedman 2006; Shapiro 2009; and Tamanaha 2009).

Ironically, although all of the more recent commentaries raise issues of their own, there are several reoccurring critiques that are quite similar to those mentioned by Mendelson more than forty years ago.[1] This is true for at least two reasons. First, after raising early concerns about the quantitative study of judicial behavior, there was no sustained interest from legal scholars in following up on such critiques. Judges and legal academics seemed to view empirical work as the product of number crunchers who did not understand legal decision processes. As such they were largely dismissive of quantitative approaches to understanding legal decision-making.[2] Second, empiricists went about their business without caring much what legal types had to say. Political scientists involved in behavioral research took pride in studies tending to demonstrate the influence of extralegal factors in decisional behavior. They pointed to findings in studies by Pritchett (1948), Schubert (1962), and Speath (1961, 1963, 1964) as evidence that doctrinal reasons judges gave for their case votes were not as useful as ideological factors in explaining such decisions. Theories of judicial behavior invoking political ideology and attitudinal factors were more parsimonious and easier to quantify and test than traditional accounts of legal reasoning. Moreover, the publication of these studies brought those studying courts into the mainstream of political science, which at the time was firmly in the throes of the behavioral revolution (see Clayton 1999; Maveety 2003).

In this manner two disciplines that are interested in similar phenomena have evolved quite distinctively in terms of theory and concepts related to legal decision-making. Perhaps inevitably a "division of labor" has developed based on what some have characterized as the "comparative advantage" of each approach (Ford 2006, citing Swisher 1946, APSA report on directions for research in Public Law). Most legal academics are interested primarily in normative questions and how distinct jurisprudential approaches converge on desirable outcomes. Text, intent, precedent, and the persuasive force of the principles that underlie them are the primary tools of their trade. The most common route to publication and career advancement in the legal academy over much of the last half-century has involved analysis rooted in a particular judicial decision or set of decisions that attacks the legitimacy or application of certain interpretive methods, or understandings of precedent.[3]

Behavioral scholars, on the other hand, deal in the currency of testable propositions. They are concerned primarily with data, hypotheses, and effective operationalization. Their comparative advantage has been the use of quantitative methods, statistical techniques, and, more recently, formal models to theorize about and empirically demonstrate factors significant in determining outcomes. After a half-century of such research, behavioral scholars have developed their own notions of how judges make decisions that are at odds with formalistic portrayals of legal reasoning and also quite distinct from how most legal scholars conceive of extralegal influence in terms of mechanism and degree (Braman 2009).

Of course such "comparative advantages" are subject to change, evolve, and diminish. This is especially true in times like this when interdisciplinary efforts are more encouraged than frowned upon (Martinek 2009). There is no reason that legal academics cannot master statistical techniques and test their own models. Indeed, there are some excellent examples of such work in recent years (Cross 2007, 2009; Lindquist and Cross 2005; Czarnezki and Ford 2006). Also, the number of behavioral scholars with formal legal training has significantly increased (see Posner 2008, citing specific examples). This means that the easiest critiques levied across interdisciplinary lines—that researchers don't "understand" statistical logic or decision-making norms—are becoming less available.

Even with the cadre of scholars in law and political science pushing traditional boundaries, openness to alternative approaches to understanding decisional behavior can be uneven within and across disciplines. The contributions to this book help to drive this point home. There are not so subtle differences in the style and tone of the chapters authored by law professors and political scientists. More nuanced distinctions occur within disciplinary boundaries. For instance, many of the chapters in this volume derive from behavioral political science approaches to legal decision-making. Indeed, Professors Cross and Friedman are legal academics that have incorporated empirical approaches into their analyses. On the other hand, there are also several authors whose chapters represent more traditional legal scholarship: Burbank and Pozen. While this volume is an effort to bridge disciplinary divides, these different chapters also highlight the disciplinary blinders scholars sometimes unwittingly wear. Legal scholarship sometimes makes normative claims based on a questionable empirical foundation, while political science scholars concerned with evidence and data often fail to address the normative implications of their findings. Unstated (and perhaps unconscious) assumptions in each discipline can lead scholars to talk past one another. As we discuss in the last section, the disagreement between Hall and Pozen poignantly illustrates this point.

This is part of the legacy of path dependence. Compounding the difficulty is the fact that conservative disciplinary tendencies are present in both fields although they are manifest in different ways. As we discuss below, the peer-review process can act to inhibit scholarly research innovation in political science. In legal academia scholarly innovation tends to be hierarchically driven; although several top-tier law schools are now touting the fact that their faculty includes scholars from multiple disciplines doing empirical research, this is less true of lower-tier and regional law schools that continue to see their primary function as training practitioners in the traditional norms of legal discourse.

Additionally, quantitative methods often involve their own esoteric language that law professors can feel ill equipped to evaluate, slowing the universal acceptance of such approaches among chronically skeptical legal types. Still, after some initial resistance, many judges and law professors seem to be coming to the realization that empirical approaches have something to contribute to our understandings of decisional behavior (for example, Posner 2008; Cross, Heise, and Sisk 2002; Friedman 2006). As a result, a good deal of the revived interdisciplinary debate about empirical research has centered on the adequacy of basic data and measures used in empirical studies. Law professors are well equipped to offer such commentary which does not generally necessitate an entirely different set of skills from the ones they employ in their own legal research and writing. As we point out above, some of this commentary is "old wine in new bottles," but that is not to say that it is wrong—or that political scientists doing empirical work would not benefit from thinking harder about how our data, measures, and techniques could better capture decision-making phenomena viewed as important by those socialized in the legal tradition.

Path Dependence and the Operationalization of Concepts Related to Decision-making

Most of the critiques levied against empirical scholars by judges and law professors involve the way behavioralists define and measure concepts related to legal decision-making. The tone of commentaries on quantitative work across the disciplines varies widely, as many of the chapters in this volume illustrate. Some scholars remain incredulous, unconvinced that empirical approaches capture anything useful or different than we could find out by asking judges how they make decisions (Edwards 1998; Tamanaha 2009); others seem sincerely interested in detailing what empirical scholars should do to make studies more relevant and/or credible in the eyes of those with legal backgrounds (Friedman 2006; Shapiro 2009); still others have made comments in the context of law review symposia or scholarly exchanges with quantitative scholars about what such approaches have to add to our knowledge about legal institutions (see, for example, Cross, Heise, and Sisk 2002 exchange with Epstein and King 2002).

All of these "perspectives from the outside" are useful. If nothing else they give empirical scholars doing work in political science an idea of how their questions, methods, and findings are perceived by those with different training and operating assumptions about how the law works. At this juncture, however, we think it may be useful to engage in this sort of critical assessment from the "inside," taking account of what judges and legal academics have said about empirical work. We do so with a full appreciation of the operating assumptions in our own discipline and a meaningful understanding of the benefits and difficulties attendant in empirical research.

At the outset we would like to clear up what is perhaps a widely held (if less widely expressed) misconception about empirical scholars: that we do not care about our operationalization of concepts related to legal decision-making beyond the fact that they are quantifiable (or can be measured) across a wide array of cases so that we can include them in our analyses. This is not true. Empirical scholars understand better than anyone that our findings are only as good as our measures. Early in our training we are introduced to the concept of "construct validity," referring to how well measures of particular variables capture phenomena of interest. Indeed, one might observe that effective operationalization is the sine qua non of excellent social science research—not significant findings. The most distinguished scholars understand this, and political scientists constantly remind one another of the importance of careful operationalization (although, as detailed further below, the peer review process can be a double-edged sword in terms of creative innovation in the conceptualization of concepts).[4]

Admittedly social scientists have not been perfect in translating concepts relevant to legal decision-making into our models, but it is not for lack of effort. Those involved in empirical research take great care in developing and improving the independent variables that we theorize are related to judicial behavior. This can be seen in numerous iterative studies aiming to refine some of our most central variables including ideology (Segal and Cover 1989; Segal, Epstein, Cameron and Spaeth 1995; Martin and Quinn 2002), case salience (Slotnick 1978; Maltzman and Wahlbeck 1996; Epstein and Knight 1998; Wahlbeck, Spriggs, and Maltzman 1998; Epstein and Segal 2000), and legitimacy (Dahl 1957; Easton 1965; Adamany 1973; Mondak 1990; Caldeira and Gibson 1992). Judicial politics scholars are also engaged in the constant assessment and reassessment of the state of our knowledge in periodic review articles and book chapters (see, for example, Dixon 1971; Tate 1983; Shapiro 1993; Whittington, Keleman, and Caldeira 2008; Segal 2008). These reviews typically include critical evaluations of how we are capturing concepts and how we may strive to improve our measures.

That said, we would also like to acknowledge that behavioral scholars have been narrow minded in thinking about concepts related to decision-making in ways that are closely related to the issue of path dependence in the discipline. For all our efforts to measure and capture the role of political "ideology" in studies of judicial behavior, there has been much less sustained attention to the operationalization of legal considerations in judges' choices. Rather the force of law is often conceived as a "constraint in the abstract." The assumption in many empirical studies is that if law is operating to constrain legal choices, we should not be able to observe systematic differences in the voting behavior of judges. One may question whether this conceptualization of law is valid and if there may not be better ways to test for its influence.

Another issue is the predominance of large N studies, themselves, in studies of judicial behavior. In these studies political scientists typically utilize widely available datasets (such as Spaeth's Supreme Court dataset or Songer's Court of Appeals dataset) to investigate the influence of their variable of choice on the expression of ideology in judges' case votes. While we fully acknowledge the significant contribution of the scholars who provide such data, we are concerned by the hegemonic status of this sort of research in the discipline for several reasons.[5]

First, case votes may not be the optimal variable to use for understanding how judges make decisions. There are many choices judges make in the process of thinking about cases that may reflect particular aspects of legal reasoning. For instance, one might ask how judges conclude a particular issue is determinative in cases involving multiple lines of doctrine, or why a specific case or statute is deemed authoritative in regard to a litigant or set of case facts. Yet the easy availability of data makes case votes the primary dependent variable of choice in quantitative studies. This is true even though case facts often differ substantially across cases used in empirical analyses. Such differences are *assumed* to "cancel out" in the aggregate. Although many legal scholars discount empirical work for exactly this reason, we note that this is not a fatally unrealistic assumption. The cumulative weight of studies tending to show the influence of extralegal factors in judges' decision-making should not be ignored.

For instance, the strong and constant influence of ideology in judicial voting behavior cannot be summarily dismissed; clearly, ideology "matters" in judges' outcome choices. Still, we know very little about *why it matters*. Looking at decisions other than case votes may help to shed light on how judges are able to reach conclusions consistent with their preferences in the context of thinking through legal authority. Moreover, this sort of inquiry could lead us to a more sophisticated understanding of where the law can act as a meaningful constraint on legal decision-makers and where attitudinal factors are most likely to hold sway. There are variables in large datasets that could be utilized to start investigating these questions, such as those indicating the number and types of issues raised in litigation, and which lines of authority particular judges deemed determinative in opinions they wrote or endorsed. But these variables are largely underutilized—and hardly ever explored as *dependent* variables.

Perhaps more problematic are the subtle ways in which reliance on available large datasets confines our thinking and hypothesis testing. For instance, we have all read studies in which researchers confine their analyses to periods for which data are "available," without sufficient attention to the theoretical justifications for limiting studies at seemingly arbitrary points in time because the scholars providing such data are not as current as ideas motivating the scholarship.[6] Usually it would be better for scholars to *think about reasons* to limit their studies to a subset of dates rather than utilizing cutoffs without sufficient theoretical justification. Of course, researchers *could* code variables of interest in cases to include more recent court decisions in their analyses where it is justified, but in practice most do not, further illustrating the problem of such heavy reliance on these datasets.

The prevalence of large N statistical studies and widely accepted operationalizations may also inhibit scholars from thinking creatively about other ways to capture phenomena related to legal decision-making. There are other empirical techniques that could advance our understanding of factors relevant in legal decision-making behavior. Experimental methods seem an especially promising avenue to investigate biases and constraint in normative decision-making, though they have not been widely utilized except by a handful of scholars doing work at the intersection of law and psychology (see, for example, Guthrie, Rachlinski, and Wistrich 2001; Wistrich, Guthrie, and Rachlinski 2005; Holyoak and Simon 1999; Braman 2009; and Ferguson, Babcock, and Shane 2008). There are also examples of scholars using content analyses techniques that significantly shed light on group and individual decision-making processes on collegial bodies like the U.S. Supreme Court (Tetlock, Bernzweig, and Gallant 1985; Gruenfeld 1995). Each of these alternative approaches has its own difficulties attendant to data collection, the operationalization of concepts related to legal reasoning, and the extent to which findings can be generalized to different contexts. But the significant effort entailed in using and justifying alternative methods of inquiry may be warranted to help get us "closer" to phenomena of interest in understanding legal decision-making. Obviously theoretical considerations should drive scholars' choices regarding their methods of inquiry; still, we think as a general rule that behavioral scholars should be more creative in thinking about the data and methodology appropriate for particular questions.

We also believe that there is an over-reliance on the specific operationalization of variables related to decision-making that are often developed by prominent figures in the discipline. Fundamentally, a large part of this problem is driven by the difficulties of getting scholarly work through peer review.[7] In reality, it is *hard* to get new or different conceptualizations through the process. Once particular measures are used in studies that have been published, they take on a degree of "validity" that is more or less warranted across distinct operationalizations. We understand that there are benefits to using common measures across studies. The availability of such variables cuts down on the work of empirical scholars because it reduces the need for primary coding and data collection. Moreover, it is often useful to have common measures used across studies because it allows for the effective comparison of concepts across different courts and/or decision-making contexts. In these respects scholars who take the time to develop and test such operationalizations are performing a service to the discipline that we in no way mean to diminish.

Our larger concern involves the use of existing variables in empirical research. No matter how widely utilized a particular measure is, it is *always* important to consider how the variable captures the construct of interest and whether or not there may be more appropriate ways to do so in the context of the particular questions empirical scholars are investigating. In essence we are concerned that the availability of such measures fosters a degree of "thoughtlessness" in our own discipline, much like the thoughtlessness that Daniel Lazare (1996) and Sanford Levinson (2008) have identified with respect to citizens' blind reverence for the Constitution. They may inhibit us from thinking about how to do things more appropriately, especially as our ability to capture phenomena of interest develops and the questions we are asking related to legal decision-making evolve and change (see our discussion of "case salience" in the next section for a specific example).

Compounding this difficulty is the defensive stance empirical scholars, particularly those early in their training, often take in presenting their research and submitting it for publication. The tendency is to control for every possible factor discussants and/or anonymous reviewers might be concerned about. There is much less attention to how variables are captured than the fact that they are included in a model. Researchers often use available measures as controls without sufficient theoretical justification or any attention to how these concepts are conceptualized other than parenthetical cites to published studies in which they have been used as a "proof" of their validity. This is a problem. Somewhat ironically, the best hope we have of correcting these tendencies is through the sort rigorous peer review that gives rise to them in the first place. But admittedly scholars have different tolerance for this sort of behavior, and for many reviewers such parenthetical cites might serve as heuristic cues that measures are adequate, even where they would take issue with these variables if they were given more information about how they were captured.

Given these myopic *intra*disciplinary tendencies in developing our measures, we believe that political scientists could benefit from more sustained attention to interdisciplinary understandings of forces that act upon legal decision-makers. One area where we need thought and innovation, for instance, is in tightening our conceptualizations *and* operationalizations of how legal text affects decision-making. The so-called legal model has most commonly been conceptualized and operationalized by quantitative-minded political scientists in terms of stare decisis and precedent (Spaeth and Segal 1999). This has led to more sophisticated empirical explorations of citation patterns (Fowler et al. 2007). While we do not question the sincerity of the researchers or the importance of understanding the role of precedent, the focus on precedent and citation seems to us one borne partially out of the convenience of available variables in large-N datsets and other electronic resources, such as *Shepards citations*.

It seems to us that a more central concept and analytical starting point for understanding "law" in legal decision-making involves legal text. The battle in the courts, especially appellate courts, is almost always over what a particular text means. And this seems a fruitful endeavor for interdisciplinary collaboration between law professors, who believe and write about how legal text matters (or should matter) in particular cases, and political scientists trained to test such propositions systematically. Scholars could identify similar statutes from different jurisdictions the text of which varies, and analyze the impact of textual variation on judicial decision-making. A very simple example would be to identify statutes that have been the subject of litigation that declare an executive official *may* take a certain action and others that direct that an executive official *shall* take a particular action. One could easily code for these types of differences in semantics and then analyze judicial behavior in adjudication involving these different statutes. Moreover, we should be able to devise ways to determine legal clarity beyond the rather crude conceptualization that complex cases are those with multiple legal provisions. One might anticipate that the clearer the text of a statute, the less ideology or preferences would matter and the more unified judges on a collegial bench would be. Researchers could conduct experiments or quasi experiments with carefully chosen subjects who are proficient in the English language to determine their views on the clarity of the meaning of particular statutory language and compare the results with judges' votes in cases applying those statutory provisions; if the clarity of legal text matters, we would expect judges to be more unified in the application of statutes the clearer the text of the law (see, for example, Pickerill 2009).

There are most certainly many other ways in which researchers could think about the role of law in judicial decision-making (see Friedman and Martin, this volume; Braman 2010a). Recent efforts that show promise seem to be coming primarily from a new generation of scholars involved in attempts to operationalize and measure the influence of legislative history (for example, Law and Zaring 2009) and the use of plagiarism detection software to explain the influence of lower court opinions on Supreme Court opinions (for example, Calvin, Collins, and Corley 2009).

We believe that these contributions, where researchers think outside of the proverbial box, have significant potential to promote interdisciplinary research. We must also be mindful, however, that there are differences in our understandings that can impede such progress. In the next section we discuss issues of "translation" that can arise across disciplines based on established conceptualizations of decision-making phenomena.

Path Dependence and Issues of Translation: Case Salience and Legitimacy

Sometimes the way particular measures are developed can influence their broader use and theoretical relevance for scholars interested in legal decision-making from different disciplinary perspectives. This can also be seen as a consequence of path dependence. Mertz (2008) specifically discusses the task of "translation" between law and social science, which is closely related to the notion that researchers need to be attentive to how well concepts "travel" across different contexts (Goertz and Mazur 2008, 19–20). We think this is useful, as sometimes scholars across our disciplines talk about similar concepts in very different ways.

As we begin this sort of exchange it is important to consider how concepts that pass in our own field may "play" across disciplinary lines. This is especially true as empiricists interested in measurement and operationalization can fail to capture the "essence" of what legal scholars see as relevant and/or important in our analyses. In developing our measures related to decisional behavior empirical scholars can sometimes "miss the forest for the trees." To make this point we specifically point to the trajectory of thinking with regard to two of the iteratively developed, well worn concepts mentioned above, "case salience" and "legitimacy."

Case Salience

Judicial scholars have measured "case salience" in a number of ways. Sometimes scholars presume that cases involving broad issue areas like "civil rights" are salient (see, for example, Flemming and Wood 1997); in other instances they use more objective case-specific indicators of the concept. Slotnick (1978), for instance, considers whether cases decided by the Supreme Court were subsequently included in Constitutional law case books signifying their importance, Maltzman and Wahlbeck (1996) use the number of amicus briefs filed in a case. Most recently, Epstein and Segal (2000) offer a measure indicating whether the Supreme Court decisions appear on the front page of the *New York Times*. All of these measures conceptualize salience by whether some relevant external audience (law professors, interest groups, or the general public) is "paying attention" to what the Court is doing. While this conceptualization is justifiable, and may have been appropriate where researchers were considering internal institutional practices like opinion assignment, it is far from perfect. Most significantly, because existing measures of case salience are assumed to operate the same way across judges, they fail to capture an aspect of personal relevance inherent to the concept that is arguably most important (and interesting) with regard to decisional behavior.

The term "salience" comes from cognitive psychology; it is used to describe characteristics of objects that stand out in the perceptual field. In this respect it is correct to assume that there are salient cases that receive disproportional attention across decision-makers. But there are also individual factors that may make cases stand out in the minds of some decision-makers but not others. For instance, a judge might have particular experience litigating, writing, or teaching in an area of law making cases involving that issue particularly important to her in ways that do not apply to colleagues. Consider, for instance, Justice Souter's experience writing on copyright issues. Moreover, psychological research shows that individual responses to salient stimuli often differ depending on traits and cognitions of the perceiver (Johnson, Jackson, and Smith 1989). Along these lines, one might hypothesize that the experiences of Justice Ginsberg litigating on behalf of minority interests causes her to think differently about cases involving these matters than the other justices on the Court because of her prior personal involvement with such issues. Extant measures fail entirely to capture these differences.

We note that in other subfields of political science concerned with decision-making salience is treated as an individual characteristic. Consider public opinion studies that measure issue salience by probing what respondents see as the "most important" problem or issue facing the nation (see, for instance, Lavine et al. 1996). The assumption in such studies is that these considerations will have disproportional influence in the way citizens make decisions.

Moreover, the concept of salience is most useful when there is some relevance to the relationship between perceived objects in terms of the decision task. For instance, just knowing that the economy is "salient" in today's political climate tells us *nothing in and of itself* about how individual citizens think about policy related to the issue. But knowing that a particular person lost his job, making the economy salient in his mind vis-à-vis other political issues such as the environment or global warming, gives us a pretty good guess about the relative importance that individual might place on such considerations in evaluating candidates or the president's performance (Rabinowitz et al. 1982).

In a similar vein, we wonder how much just knowing that a case is salient or that "people are watching" tells us about legal decision-making phenomena, especially where cases are decided in *seriatim*. It seems akin to knowing that the economy is important to everyone these days. It tells us *nothing at all* about how the justices think about authority in the confines of particular salient cases, or how individual justices might express differential reasoning styles with respect to issues that are most relevant to them.[8] As such, much of the *promise of the construct* for explaining decisional behavior gets lost in operationalizations now prevalent in the discipline.

Moreover, empirical scholars talk about the measure "as if" it captures some aspect of personal relevance where one could argue that existing operationalizations are, at once, over- and underinclusive. We do not know, for instance, whether all the justices are concerned about the public attention given to cases that is assumed to make cases salient in their minds. And there are surely cases our operationalizations miss that are salient to one or more of the justices for other reasons. Because we are empirical scholars, and sincerely sympathetic to the difficulty of measuring psychological constructs of this sort "from a distance," we understand how the trajectory of thinking about case salience has evolved. But at this point we think it is time to take a step back from subfield specific debates about things like relevant compendiums in developing such measures (Epstein and Knight 1998; Wahlbeck, Spriggs, and Maltzman 1998) so that we may notice the forest for the trees.

The question is: are there alternative measures that we could use that may capture the construct of salience in our empirical studies. Yes—one may see how some aspects of the justices' experience mentioned above interact with case characteristics, or, as alluded to by Epstein and Segal (2000), the number and types of questions the justices ask in oral arguments may be used as a proxy that the justice see the issues involved in particular cases as important; alternatively, one could use the proportion of time justices speak in oral arguments as a measure.[9] Are these measures perfect? No—it could be that in using such measures we behavioral scholars have to limit ourselves to cases in particular issue areas and may lose information with respect to some decision-makers. Justice Thomas, for instance, is notoriously silent in oral arguments, so any measure used to track salience using such data would fail to capture issues that may "stand out" in his perceptual field. Is it worth the effort and cost to consider these alternative operationalizations? Of course, it depends on the questions researchers are interested in—but we would guess that in many instances the answer will be yes. The fact that personal relevance can differ across justices seems as though it could be fundamentally important in how they think about cases.

That said, behavioral scholars need to think harder about *how* salience should make a difference in decisional behavior and *why it matters*. In studies looking at opinion assignment in cases where relevant audiences are watching, the logic seems obvious. For other aspects of decision-making the normative connection is less clear. It might be useful to look beyond how salience moderates the expression of ideology in case votes. One obvious hypothesis involves the role of salience in cert decisions. An inquiry along these lines may tell us something about the interaction between personal and normative considerations in decisional behavior. Where conference notes are available one might look at whether justices make more, or different kinds of arguments in the cases that are of particular relevance to them. Also one might be able to discern if they are more persuasive in the decision process by looking at vote coalitions and/or intracourt memoranda. We should be able to draw upon insights from psychology on group decision-making and opinion leadership in formulating theory and hypotheses with regard to these questions.

For as long as behavioral scholars have been trying to measure salience in judicial decision-making there has been an interest in seeing how judges might think differently in cases that "stand out" in their minds. Our only point is that we could, and in many instances should, be thinking differently about theory and measures related to the concept in ways that are less path dependent to improve our understanding of decision-making phenomena.

Legitimacy

Gibson and Caldeira, together, individually, and with the help of other colleagues have produced a truly impressive body of work on judicial "legitimacy" looking at public support for courts. They have amassed evidence involving the U.S. Supreme Court (Caldeira 1986; Caldeira and Gibson 1992; Gibson and Caldeira 1992), the European Court of Justice (Gibson and Caldeira 1998), and other high national courts (Gibson, Caldeira, and Baird 1998). They have addressed how highly visible decisions (Gibson, Caldeira, and Spence 2003) and judicial selection practices (Gibson 2008a, 2008b) can influence the esteem in which citizens hold judicial institutions. Obviously this is interesting and important work. Moreover, in developing their measures of public support for judicial institutions Gibson and Caldeira have been careful to distinguish between aspects of "specific" and "diffuse" support that have helped all of us think about these issues more carefully (Caldeira and Gibson 1992).

Looking at such research, however, one could question whether scholars in political science have gone "too far" in equating legitimacy with public opinion. Surely there is more to the construct—a normative aspect that our measures of public support fail to capture—that is part and parcel of how judges and legal scholars think about the concept. Again the issue of translation is relevant here. For legal scholars the concept of legitimacy evokes a host of democratic values important to the administration of justice including fairness, equality, adherence to procedural rules, and attention to normative aspects of legal reasoning. Just as extant measures of "case salience" fail to capture aspects of personal relevance across decision-makers, our measures of legitimacy fail to capture these important normative considerations that are inherent in the way judges and legal academics think about the concept. Certainly public support is an important aspect of legitimacy, and may be taken as some evidence of legitimacy, but it is not, and cannot be, legitimacy itself.[10]

This does not mean that the substantial effort that has been invested in developing such measures is without value. It just means that we have to be very careful in the way we discuss our findings across disciplinary boundaries acknowledging that aspects of the concept empirical scholars have been able to quantify and measure may not fully encompass the way legal scholars think about the construct. Of course this is something empirical scholars should be doing anyway—we just want to point out that it is particularly important to be explicit about what our measures capture and what they do not at this point in our collective knowledge.

The real danger with issues of "translation" across disciplinary boundaries is that scholars in one field (who may already be disinclined to accept alternative conceptualizations of concepts) may be too quick to dismiss research that could actually augment their understandings because they perceive researchers from other disciplines as trying to over-reach or mischaracterize their findings. Such misunderstandings are often based in long-entrenched differences in assumptions, methods, and conceptualizations rather than any conscious effort to distort evidence or overplay one's hand. Only through the candid discussion of such differences can promise of interdisciplinary exchange be realized.

The Hall/Pozen debate on judicial elections in this volume effectively illustrates how different disciplinary assumptions about the role of the American people in bestowing "legitimate" judicial authority can lead scholars to speak past one another. Coming from the political science tradition where scholars "accept the intrinsically political nature of appellate court decision making," (Hall, this volume) the primary (unstated) normative question Hall deals with is how to legitimate judge-made law given that decisional norms do not always work to constrain judges as well as classic democratic theory requires. Simply stated, if we know from our studies of "what *is*" that judges are making decisions according to their personal and/or political preferences, how can we justify those choices in our democratic system?

The answer for Hall is to ground judicial selection in majoritarian elections as we do for other public officials. As long as judicial elections do not *actually* suffer from long suspected deficiencies like low turnout, low information, and high roll-off (as her research tends to demonstrate), and as long as judges make

decisions that are (more or less) consistent with their party identification, giving voters a meaningful basis for choice, then partisan judicial elections can
serve as a "legitimacy bestowing" institution for state high court judges.

Coming from the legal tradition, the question for Pozen is fundamentally
different. Assuming, *arguendo*,[11] that judicial elections could be engineered to
be "highly efficacious without doing too much damage to the quality, integrity
or impartiality of the courts," he asks, is electing judges compatible with the
"kind of democracy to which we aspire" (Pozen, this volume)? The first thing
to notice in comparing these chapters is that looking through her lens of "what
is," Hall does not really ask this question. She asks how we can legitimate judicial choices given what we know about how judges make decisions. For her,
as long as judicial elections are demonstrably effective—her main empirical
focus—having judicial decisions grounded in publicly endorsed preferences is
better than a system in which judicial decisions are based on the idiosyncratic
beliefs of individuals who may never be held accountable to the citizenry.

Looking for a democratic ideal, Pozen is less sure. He points to issues of
capacity and access, arguing that "a court will never be as broadly accessible as
the legislature, nor will it possess the latter's representative structures, information gathering resources, or proactive lawmaking capacities." As such, the best
judges can do is "guess at" public sentiment on legal issues—an amorphous
sentiment that is, itself, unlikely to exist in particular instances involving nuanced or complicated legal matters (Pozen, this volume). He also laments the
potential loss of what he portrays as democracy-promoting functions in elective judicial systems. He is particularly concerned about judges' ability to protect minority rights against majority encroachment (Pozen, this volume) and
the value of public "backlash" against seminal decisions like *Roe v. Wade* (1973)
and *Brown v. Board of Education* (1954) for promoting meaningful political discourse in our democracy (Pozen, this volume). These arguments are grounded
in the idea that, as referenced above, legal academics have a basic understanding of judicial legitimacy that encompasses values *other than* majoritarian will.
Moreover, they are more likely to question the very assumption that elections
are the best way for judges to understand and be guided by such public sentiment in their decisional behavior.

Finally, it would be grossly mistaken to suggest that the difference in these
perspectives is merely one of degree, that Hall is concerned with improving
the status quo while Pozen wants to perfect it. Indeed, as noted above, Pozen's
assumption that judicial elections could be structured to work effectively puts

these authors on identical normative footing; both are essentially considering the desirability of electing judges to enhance judicial authority. Rather, the difference in these outlooks is essentially the product of interdisciplinary emphasis and omission in discussing constructs like legitimacy. Following years of scholarly tradition, Hall focuses on evidence regarding the effective expression of public sentiment in judicial elections in addressing the concept; she does not really address Pozen's normative points on access, capacity, and the democracy-enhancing functions of judging including the protection of minority rights. Similarly, Pozen, looking at the problem through an entirely normative lens, neglects to deal with the problem that hard evidence of unconstrained decision-making raises for justifications of judicial authority and state enforcement of court distributions in our democratic system (see Braman 2010b for a more detailed discussion of these issues). This is a real shame, because each of these authors makes incredibly interesting and important points. Indeed, we would be hard pressed to say that one perspective is "more valuable" than the other. The truth is that both empirical and normative approaches are critical to understand the role elections can and should play in the selection of judges. We are hopeful that pointing out path dependent differences in the conceptualization of concepts like legitimacy will help scholars from distinct disciplines to speak to, rather than across, each other.

Conclusion

Obviously, we are believers in diverse approaches to understanding legal phenomena, which is probably attributable to the fact that we both have legal and political science training. But we are also mindful of the difficulties attendant to interdisciplinary research and exchange.[12] Recognizing that distinct disciplinary traditions have their advantages and disadvantages is part of moving our scholarly discourse forward. Path dependent processes serve to shape and confine our thinking in subtle ways. They can inhibit innovation and interaction between scholars from different research traditions. But these paths define who we are; so it is important that we proceed respectfully, honoring the contributions of our disciplinary predecessors *at the same time* that we remain open to the possibility that we have much to gain from the careful incorporation of alternative approaches into our own understandings and research agendas.

   This sort of interdisciplinary interaction is not only important because it is currently "en vogue"—fundamentally, it is the best chance we have of getting things "right." Empirical scholars in political science need to take the *content of law* and how the decision-makers they are studying *actually think about cases* more seriously. Legal academics cannot exist in the heady domain of normative theory and "doctrine in the abstract" without greater attention to the political considerations and extralegal factors that influence judges in real-world cases. The worlds of "how things are" and how they "should be" need to converge if we are to have a well-rounded understanding of this institution of law we all purport to care so much about.

An important corollary is that just offering criticism across disciplinary lines is not enough to advance our understandings of normative and empirical phenomena related to legal decision-making. Indeed, at this point in our collective knowledge one could argue that raw criticism without constructive suggestions as to how to do things "better" is somewhat counterproductive. For interdisciplinary exchange to *move forward* concrete suggestions about how to conceptualize empirical findings in the context of existing normative theory are fundamentally important. On the other side, legal scholars need to advise behavioral researchers about how to empirically capture aspects of legal approaches they see as missing from our models.

At its best interdisciplinary work should not look like "business as usual" in law or political science. Scholars that work at the intersection of these fields need to take findings and assumptions from each domain seriously to develop projects that contribute significantly to knowledge in both disciplines. We understand that this may seem to some like a tall order, but we think scholars on both sides of the disciplinary fence are up to the challenge. Clearly, with the help of thoughtful colleagues to guide, direct, and potentially refocus our efforts, we have much to gain from wondering a bit off the beaten path.

Notes

1. Commonly occurring critiques include the fact that empirical studies fail to take the complexity of legal decision-making into account by focusing on case outcomes (Mendelson 1963; Friedman 2006, 266–68) and assuming cases involve a single "dominant" issue in scaling analysis (Mendelson 1963; Tanenhaus 1966). Closely related are concerns that have been raised about subjectivity in data collection and the classification of cases into one issues area or another in order to perform quantitative analyses (Mendelson 1963; Tanenhaus 1966; Cross, Sisk, and Heise 2002; Friedman 2005, 270–72, Shapiro 2009).

2. In an attempt to "raise discussion to a higher level than . . . prevail[ed]" in 1964, Tanenhaus anecdotally noted "broadside attacks on [the] quantitative investigation"

of legal decision-making. Some of the more colorful sentiments he attributed to law-yers' characterizations of empirical work at the time include, "[T]hinkers don't count and counters don't think," and "[F]igures don't lie, but liars do figure" (1964, 505).

3. This is not to say that legal scholars are not concerned about external influenc-es in legal decision-making. Indeed, legal and constitutional theorists were grappling with their own brand of thinking about extralegal influence in the guise of "legal real-ism" (Frank 1931a, 1931b) well before behavioral scholars had a fully developed "attitu-dinal model" (Segal and Spaeth 1993, 2002).

4. Goertz has provided the most careful guide to concept construction, arguing that we must understand that concepts are "causal, ontological and realist" (2006, 5). Goertz and Mazur provide ten guidelines for "creating, evaluating and modifying concepts that are applicable to concepts in general" (2008, 15). While a complete review of those guide-lines is unnecessary here, we highlight just a few that are particularly relevant for our inquiry. One important consideration in developing and using concepts is that of causal relationships within and between concepts. Another involves the accepted name of the concept and whether that name is used in a consistent manner semantically among those in the field. Moreover, researchers must ask whether the concept necessarily con-sists of multiple dimensions, and if so, they need to explicate the interdependence be-tween dimensions. And lastly, it is crucial to consider whether the concept "travels" well across time or other contexts. This last point is particularly important when considering the path-dependent nature of research, as scholars attempt to extend and expand previ-ously formulated concepts to new aspects of a research agenda. The further we progress down a path, and the more difficult it is to reverse course, the more dangerous it is to rely on concepts that might have been faulty to begin with or which have been extended in questionable ways. Therefore, the importance of evaluating how we conceptualize concepts cannot be understated.

5. Note: we leave aside the issue about whether such heavy reliance on case cod-ing by a single scholar or research team is a good idea, although the question has been raised with respect to the Spaeth dataset. See, specifically, Shapiro (2009), arguing that variables of particular interest to legal scholars may be miscoded, undervalued, and/or ignored in existing coding schemes; and Harvey (2009), arguing there may be bias in coding schemes.

6. There is inevitably going to be a lag between when cases are decided and when variables are coded. Moreover, updated datasets need to be checked for errors before they are made available for mass consumption. Unfortunately the tendency of many empirical scholars is to provide their analyses for "all" available data or cases that are most current.

7. We are by no means arguing that we should do away with the peer review. We see it as an (often painful but) essential part of the accumulation of knowledge in our discipline. But there are certain "externalities" attendant in the practice that are worthwhile to make clear, and to which we think reviewers should be mindful when reviewing pieces that offer innovative operationalizations or conceptualizations.

8. In many behavioral studies case salience is used as an independent variable to see whether it moderates the expression of ideology in the justices' case votes as

compared to cases that are not salient. Arguably there is some useful information in knowing whether judges are being more or less ideological in cases likely to get attention from outside audiences. We note, however, that findings have been mixed on this question depending on the specific operationalization of the concept. Moreover, empirical scholars "spin" conflicting findings in different ways. Where judges are not ideological in salient cases they are portrayed as caring about the institutional legitimacy of the Court and adherence to legal norms; where ideology is significant it is taken as evidence of the prevalence of attitudes in the justices' decisions. Our larger point is that the construct has greater potential to explain decisional behavior in ways that would be more interesting and perhaps relevant to scholars in other disciplines such as law or psychology.

9. Indeed, Johnson and Black (2009) are in the process of developing a particularly promising measure of salience based on oral arguments. Although they are starting with a court-based measure, we are hopeful an individual measure is not far behind.

10. To illustrate, the tension between the legitimate function that judicial institutions play in protecting fundamental rights and public opinion is as old as our nation's history. Consider the following hypothetical: if one thousand randomly surveyed individuals were asked whether Congress should limit the Supreme Court's jurisdiction to make decisions on school prayer and 60 percent (or even 90 percent) of respondents agreed that it should, would it mean that it would be "illegitimate" for the Court to make such decisions? We are going to go out on a limb and say no. One could go even further to argue that if a majority of those respondents agreed that the Court should be abolished tomorrow it would *still* have legitimate authority to make those decisions under our constitutional structure. Quite simply, the majority's momentary willingness to do away with judicial institutions does not vitiate citizen's legitimate interest in having them or judges' legitimate authority to make pronouncements that might be contrary to what a majority of citizens want.

11. This is another fundamental difference between political scientists and legal types illustrating the difference in approaches. Political scientists do not commonly make arguments *arguendo*—another consequence of our deep concern with the domain of "what is." Perhaps more importantly, it is critical to note that this assumption puts Hall and Pozen on identical normative footing, although they get there in very different ways: Hall through her evaluation of evidence regarding the adequacy of judicial elections, and Pozen by sheer (perhaps incredulous) supposition.

12. Although we have focused on the path dependent consequences for political science scholarship, it is undoubtedly true that much legal scholarship has been prone to the same processes. For instance, most constitutional law and constitutional theory scholarship from the legal academy has remained fixated and premised on the so-called counter-majoritarian problem associated with judicial review for many decades, despite a body of research primarily from political scientists raising serious questions about the validity of that concept (see Friedman 2001, 2002). There are other examples as well, but we leave a more in depth examination of path dependence in legal scholarship for another day.

References

Adamany, David W. 1973. "Legitimacy. Realigning Elections and the Supreme Court." *Wisconsin Law Review* 3: 790–846.

Arthur, W. Brian. 1994. *Increasing Returns and Path Dependence in the Economy*. Ann Arbor: University of Michigan Press.

Baum, Lawrence. 1977. "Policy Goals in Judicial Gate Keeping: A Proximity Model of Discretionary Jurisdiction." *American Journal of Political Science* 21, no. 1: 13–35.

Brace, Paul, Melinda Gann Hall, and Laura Langer. 1999. "Judicial Choice and the Politics of Abortion: Institutions, Context and the Autonomy of Courts." *Albany Law Review* 62: 1265.

Braman, Eileen. 2009. *Law, Politics and Perception: How Policy Preferences Influence Legal Reasoning*. Charlottesville: University of Virginia Press.

———. 2010a. "Searching for Constraint in Legal Decision Making." In David Klein and Greg Mitchell, eds., *The Psychology of Judicial Decision Making*. Oxford: Oxford University Press.

———. 2010b. "Democratic Crisis and Constraint: Considering the Normative Implications of Empirical Research on Legal Decision Making." Paper presented at the Annual Conference of the Midwest Political Science Association, April 2010.

Burgess, Susan R. 1992. *Contest for Constitutional Authority: The Abortion and War Power Debates*. Lawrence: University Press of Kansas.

Caldeira, Gregory A. 1986. "Neither Purse nor Sword: Dynamics of Public Confidence for the Supreme Court." *American Political Science Review* 80, no. 4: 1209–26.

Caldeira, Gregory A., and James Gibson. 1992. "The Etiology of Public Support for the Supreme Court." *American Political Science Review* 36, no. 3: 635–64.

Calvin, Bryan, Paul M. Collins, Jr., and Pamela C. Corley. 2009. "Lower Court Influence on U.S. Supreme Court Opinion Content." Paper prepared for presentation at the Midwest Political Science Association Conference, Thursday, April 2, 2009, Chicago.

Clayton, Cornell W. 1999. "The Supreme Court and Political Jurisprudence: New and Old Institutionalisms." In Cornell W. Clayton and Howard Gillman, eds., *Supreme Court Decision Making: New Institutionalist Approaches*. Chicago: University of Chicago Press, 14–41.

Cross, Frank B. 1997. "Political Science and the New Legal Realism: A Case of Unfortunate Interdisciplinary Ignorance." *Northwestern University Law Review* 92: 251–326.

———. 2007. *Decision Making on the U.S. Court of Appeals*. Stanford: Stanford University Press.

———. 2009. *Theory and Practice of Statutory Interpretation*. Stanford: Stanford University Press.

Cross, Frank B., Michael Heise, and Gregory C. Sisk. 2002. "Exchange: Empirical Research and the Goals of Legal Scholarship: Above the Rules—A Response to Epstein and King." *University of Chicago Law Review* 69: 135–51.

Czarnezki, Jason J., and William K. Ford. 2006. "The Phantom Philosophy? An Empirical Investigation of Legal Interpretation." *Maryland Law Review* 65: 841.

Dahl, Robert A. 1957. "Decision Making in a Democracy: Supreme Court as National Policy Maker." *Journal of Public Law* 6: 279–95.

David, Paul. 2000. "Path Dependence, Its Critics, and the Quest for 'Historic Economics.'" In P. Garouste and S. Ioannides, eds., *Evolution and Path Dependence in Economic Ideas: Past and Present*. Cheltenham, UK: Edward Elgar.

Dixon, Robert G. 1971. "Who Is Listening? Political Science Research in Public Law." *PS* 4, no. 1: 19–26.

Easton, David. 1965. "A Systems Analysis of Political Life." New York: Wiley.

Edwards, Harry T. 1998. "Collegiality and Decision Making on the DC Circuit Court." *Virginia Law Review* 84: 1335–71.

Epstein, Lee, and Gary King. 2002. "Exchange: Empirical Research and the Goals of Legal Scholarship: The Rules of Inference." *University of Chicago Law Review* 69: 1 et seq.

Epstein, Lee, and Jack Knight. 1998. *The Choices Justices Make*. Washington DC: CQ Press

Epstein, Lee, and Jeffrey A. Segal. 2000. "Measuring Issue Salience." *American Journal of Political Science* 44, no. 1: 66–83.

Epstein, Lee, and Thomas G. Walker. 1995. "The Role of the Supreme Court in American Society: Playing the Reconstruction Game." In Lee Epstein, ed., *Contemplating Courts*. Washington DC; CQ Press.

Farr, James. 1988. "Political Science and the Enlightenment of Enthusiasm." *American Political Science Review* 82, no. 1: 51–69.

Fenno, Richard. 1977. "U.S. Members in Their Constituencies: An Exploration." *American Political Science Review* 71: 883–917.

Ferguson, Joshua, Linda Babcock, and Peter M. Shane. 2008. "Do a Law's Policy Implications Affect Beliefs about Its Constitutionality?" *Law and Human Behavior* 32: 219–27.

Flemming, Roy B. and B. Dan Wood. 1997. "The Publiv and the Supreme Court: Individual Justice Responsiveness to American Public Moods." American Journal of Political Science. 41: 468–98.

Fowler, James H., Timothy R. Johnson, James F. Spriggs II, Sanjick Jeon, and Pahl J. Wahlbeck. 2007. "Network Analysis and the Law: Measuring the Legal Importance of Supreme Court Precedents." *Political Analysis* 15: 324–46.

Frank, Jerome. 1931a. "Are Judges Human? Part One: The Effect on Legal Thinking of the Assumption That Judges Behave Like Human Beings." *University of Pennsylvania Law Review* 80: 17–53.

———. 1931b. "Are Judges Human? Part Two: As Through a Class Darkly." *University of Pennsylvania Law Review* 80: 233–67.

Friedman, Barry. 2001. "The Countermajoritarian Problem and the Pathology of Constitutional Scholarship." *Northwestern University Law Review* 95: 933–54.

———. 2002. "The History of the Countermajoritarian Difficulty, Part II: Reconstruction's Political Court." *Georgetown Law Journal* 91: 1–66.

———. 2006. "Taking Law Seriously." *Perspectives on Politics* 4, no. 2: 261–76.

Ford, William. 2006. "Legal Realism, Hermann Pritchett and the Great Divide." Post to Empirical Legal Studies Blog (www.elsblog.org), June, 22, 2006.

Gibson, James. 2008a. "Campaigning for the Bench: The Corrosive Effects of Campaign Speech?" *Law and Society Review* 42, no. 4: 899–928.

———. 2008b. "Challenges to the Impartiality of State Supreme Courts: Legitimacy Theory and 'New Style' Judicial Campaigns." *American Journal of Political Science* 102, no. 1: 59–75.

Gibson, James, and Gregory A. Caldeira. 1992. "Blacks and the US Supreme Court: Models of Diffuse Support." *Journal of Politics* 54, no. 4: 1120–45.

———. 1995. "The Legitimacy of Transnational Institutions: Compliance, Support and the European Court of Justice." *American Journal of Political Science* 39, no. 2: 459–89.

Gibson, James, Gregory A. Caldeira, and Vanessa Baird. 1998. "On the Legitimacy of National High Courts." *American Political Science Review* 92: 343–58.

Gibson, James, Gregory A. Caldeira, and Lester K. Spence. 2003. "The Supreme Court and the US Presidential Election of 2000: Wounds Self-Inflicted or Otherwise." *British Journal of Political Science* 33 (October): 535–56.

Goertz, Gary. 2006. *Social Science Concepts: A User's Guide*. Princeton and Oxford: Princeton University Press.

Goertz, Gary, and Amy G. Mazur. 2008. "Mapping Gender and Politics Concepts: Ten Guidelines." In Gary Goertz and Amy G. Mazur, eds., *Politics, Gender, and Concepts: Theory and Methodology*. Cambridge: Cambridge University Press.

Gruenfeld, Deborah. 1995. "Status, Ideology and Integrative Complexity on the U.S. Supreme Court: Rethinking the Politics of Political Decision-Making." *Journal of Personality and Social Psychology* 68: 5–20.

Guthrie, Chris, Jeffery J. Rachlinski, and Andrew J. Wistrich. 2001. "Inside the Judicial Mind." *Cornell Law Review* 86: 777–830.

Harvey, Ana. 2008. "What Makes a Judgment 'Liberal'—Coding Bias in the US Supreme Court Judicial Database." Working paper available on author's website.

Holyoak, Keith J., and Dan Simon. 1999. "Bidirectional Reasoning in Decision Making by Constraint Satisfaction." *Journal of Experimental Psychology* 128: 3–31.

Johnson, James D., Lee A. Jackson, and Garry J. Smith. 1989. "The Role of Ambiguity and Gender in Mediating the Effects of Salient Cognitions." *Personality and Social Psychology Bulletin* 15, no. 1: 52–60.

Johnson, Timothy R. and Ryan C. Black. 2009. "Supreme Court Oral Arguments as a Heresthetical Tool: Threshold Questions from the Bench." Paper presented at the 2009 meetings of the Southern Political Science Association.

King, Gary, Robert Koehane, and Sydney Verba. 1994. *Designing Social Inquiry: Scientific in Qualitative Research*. Princeton: Princeton University Press.

Kuhn, Thomas S. 1962. *The Structure of Scientific Revolutions*. Chicago: University of Chicago Press.

Lavine, Howard, John L. Sullivan, Eugene Borgida, and Cynthia J. Thomsen. 1996. "The Relationship of National and Personal Issue Salience on Foreign and Domestic Policy Issues." *Political Psychology* 17, no. 2: 293–313.

Law, David S., and David T. Zaring. 2009. "Why Supreme Court Justices Cite Legislative History." Paper prepared for presentation at the Midwest Political Science Association Conference, April 2, 2009, Chicago.

Lazare, Daniel. 1996. *The Frozen Republic: How the Constitution Is Paralyzing Democracy*. New York: Harcourt Brace and Co.

Levinson, Sanford. 2008. *Our Undemocratic Constitution: Where the Constitution Goes Wrong (and We The People Can Correct It)*. Oxford: Oxford University Press.

Lindquist, Stephanie A., and Frank B. Cross. 2005. "Empirically Testing Dworkin's Chain Novel Theory: Studying the Path of Precedent." *New York University Law Review* 80: 1156–1206.

Maltzman, Forrest, and Paul J. Wahlbeck. 1996. "May It Please the Chief: Opinion Assignments on the Rehnquist Court." *American Journal of Political Science* 40: 421–43.

Martin, Andrew, and Kevin Quinn. 2002. "Dynamic Ideal Point Estimation via Marcov Chain Monte Carlo for the U.S. Supreme Court 1953–1999." *Political Analysis* 10: 134–53.

Martinek, Wendy. 2009. "Interdisciplinarity in Legal Scholarship." *Law and Courts* 19, no. 1: 16–18.

Maveety, Nancy. 2003. "The Study of Judicial Behavior in the Discipline of Political Science." In Nancy Maveety, ed., *The Pioneers of Judicial Behavior*. Ann Arbor: University of Michigan Press, 1–51.

Mendelson, Wallace. 1963. "The Neo-behavioral Approach to the Judicial Process." *American Political Science Review* 57, no. 3: 593–603.

———. 1964. "The Untroubled World of Jurimetrics." *Journal of Politics* 26, no. 4: 914–22.

———. 1966. "An Open Letter to Professor Spaeth and His Jurimetrical Colleagues." *Journal of Politics* 28, no. 2: 429–32.

Mertz, Elizabeth. 2008. "Introduction." In Mertz, ed., *The Role of Social Science in Law*, edited by Elizabeth Mertz. Burlington, VT: Ashgate.

Mondak, Jeffery. J. 1990. "Perceived Legitimacy of Supreme Court Decisions: Three Functions of Source Credibility." *Political Behavior* 12: 363–84.

Pickerill, J. Mitchell. 2004. *Constitutional Deliberation in Congress: The Impact of Judicial Review in Congress*. Durham: Duke University Press.

Pickerill, J. Mitchell. 2009. "Testing Textualism in Supreme Court Decision Making." Paper presented at the annual meeting of the Midwest Political Science Association, April 4–7, 2009.

Pierson, Paul. 2004. *Politics in Time: History, Institutions and Social Analysis*. Princeton and Oxford: Princeton University Press.

Pierson, Paul, and Theda Skocpol. 2002. "Historical Institutionalism in Contemporary Political Science." In Ira Katznelson and Helen V. Milner, eds., *Political Science: State of the Discipline*. New York: W.W. Norton and Company, 693–721.

Posner, Richard. 2008. *How Judges Think*. Cambridge, MA: Harvard University Press.

Pritchett, C. Herman. 1941. Division of Opinion Among Justices of the U.S. Supreme Court, 1939–1941. *American Political Science Review* 35:890–98.

Pritchett, C. Herman. 1948. "The Roosevelt Court: A Study in Judicial Politics and Values." New York: Macmillan.

Rabinowitz, George, James W. Prothro, and William Jacoby. 1982. "Salience as a Factor in the Impact of Issues on Candidate Evaluation." *Journal of Politics* 44: 41–63.

Reyes, R. M., W. C. Thompson, and G. H. Bower. 1980. "Judgmental Biases Resulting from Different Availability of Arguments." *Journal of Personality and Social Psychology* 39, no. 1: 2–12.

Sartori, Giavaonni. 1970. "Concept Misinformation in Comparative Politics." *American Political Science Review* 64: 1033–53.

Schubert, Glendon. 1962. "The 1960 Term of the Supreme Court: A Psychological Analysis." *American Political Science Review* 56: 90–107.

Segal, Jeffrey A. 1984. "Predicting Supreme Court Decisions Probabilistically: The Search and Seizure Cases (1962–1981)." *American Political Science Review* 78: 891–900.

———. 2008. "Judicial Behavior." In Keith Whittington, R. Daniel Keleman, and Gregory A. Caldeira, eds., *The Oxford Handbook of Law and Politics.* Oxford: Oxford University Press.

Segal, Jeffrey A., and Albert D. Cover. 1989. "Ideological Values and the Votes of U.S. Supreme Court Justices." *American Political Science Review* 83: 557–65.

Segal, Jeffrey A., Lee Epstein, Charles M. Cameron, and Harold Spaeth. 1995. "Ideological Values and the Votes of U.S. Supreme Court Justices Revisited." *Journal of Politics* 57, no. 3: 812–23.

Segal, Jeffrey A., and Harold J. Spaeth. 1993. *The Supreme Court and the Attitudinal Model.* New York: Cambridge University Press.

———. 2002. *The Supreme Court and the Attitudinal Model Revisited.* New York: Cambridge University Press.

Sewell, William H. 1996. "Three Temporalities: Toward an Eventful Sociology." In Terrence MacDonald, ed., *The Historic Turn in the Social Sciences.* Ann Arbor: University of Michigan Press, 245–80.

Shapiro, Carolyn. 2009. "Bringing Law to the Empirical Analysis of the Supreme Court." *Hastings Law Journal* 60: 477–537.

Shapiro, Martin M. 1993. "Public Law and Judicial Politics." In Ada W. Finifter, ed., *Political Science: The State of the Discipline.* Washington, DC: American Political Science Association.

Slotnick, Eliot. 1978. "The Chief Justice and Self Assignment of Majority Opinions." *Western Political Quarterly* 12: 318–32.

Spaeth, Harold J. 1961. "An Approach to the Study of Attitudinal Differences as an Aspect of Judicial Behavior." *American Journal of Political Science* 5: 165–80.

———. 1963. "An Analysis of Judicial Attitudes in Labor Relations Cases on the Warren Court." *Journal of Politics* 25, no. 2: 290–311.

———. 1964. "The Judicial Restraint of Mr. Justice Frankfurter—Myth or Reality?" *Midwest Journal of Political Science* 8, no. 1: 22–38.

———. 1965. "Jurimetrics and Professor Mendelson: A Troubled Relationship." *Journal of Politics* 27, no. 4: 875–80.

Spaeth, Harold J., and Jeffrey A. Segal. 1999. *Majority Rule or Minority Will: Adherence to Precedent on the U.S. Supreme Court.* New York: Cambridge University Press.

Sunstein, Cass R. 1996. *Legal Reasoning and Political Conflict.* New York: Oxford University Press.

Swisher, Carl. B. 1946. "Research in Public Law: Report on the Panel on Public Law." *American Political Science Review* 40: 552–62.

Tamanaha, Brian Z. 2009. "The Distorting Slant of Quantitative Studies of Judging." *Boston Law Review* 50: 685–755.

Tanenhaus, Joseph. 1960. "The Supreme Court's Attitudes toward Legislative Agencies." *Journal of Politics* 22, no. 3: 502–24.

———. 1966. "The Cumulative Scaling of Judicial Decisions." *Harvard Law Review* 79: 1583–94.

Tate, C. Neal. 1983. "The Methodology of Judicial Behavior Research: A Review and Critique." *Political Behavior* 5, no. 1: 51–82.

Tetlock, Philip E., Jane Bernzweig, and Jack L. Gallant. 1985. "Supreme Court Decision-Making: Cognitive Style as a Predictor of Ideological Consistency of Voting." *Journal of Personality and Social Psychology* 48: 1227–39.

Wahlbeck, Paul J., James F. Spriggs II, and Forrest Malzman. 1998. "Marshalling the Court: Bargaining and Accommodation on the Supreme Court." *American Journal of Political Science* 43: 294–315.

Whittington, Keith. 2005. "James Madison Has Left the Building." *University of Chicago Law Review* 72: 1137–58.

Whittington, Keith, R. Daniel Keleman, and Gregory A. Caldeira. 2008. "The Study of Law and Politics." In Keith Whittington, R. Daniel Keleman, and Gregory A. Caldeira, eds., *The Oxford Handbook of Law and Politics*. Oxford: Oxford University Press.

Wistrich, Andrew J., Chris Guthrie, and Jeffery J. Rachlinski. 2005. "Can Judges Ignore Inadmissible Information? The Difficulty of Deliberately Disregarding." *University of Pennsylvania Law Review* 153, no. 4: 1251–1345.

6 Looking for Law in All the Wrong Places

Some Suggestions for Modeling Legal Decision-making

Barry Friedman

Andrew D. Martin

T HE UNITED STATES prides itself on its adherence to the rule of law. Although the phrase itself is mushy and susceptible to many definitions, surely one interpretation is that disputes are resolved on the basis of the facts and pre-existing legal rules. Law implies a certain regularity of process; it rests on the notion that like cases will be treated alike. As thus defined, the law plays prominent in countless litigated disputes every day, and transactions of all sorts occur in the law's shadow.

Yet many political scientists are deeply skeptical that law does, or even can, play the role claimed for it. Studies of judicial decision-making often seek to prove that forces beyond the legal doctrine control case outcomes. At the extreme, some political scientists seem prepared to state that law does not and cannot constrain judges, and that as a result legal disputes are resolved by such things as the ideological preferences of judges, or the pressures exerted on them by other political actors. Winning and losing in a court of law, to believe much of what one reads in political science, often depends primarily if not solely on whether the judge personally or ideologically favors your cause, on whether she worries how other governmental officials will respond to her decision, on whether she fears reversal, or perhaps even hopes for a promotion. One way to evaluate the disagreement between political scientists and those who believe in the efficacy of law and legal process is to model the process of legal decision-making. What follows is an effort at clarification and specification. Our goal is to guide those who are interested in modeling law, as well as to offer some gentle critique to some who think they have been, but have not. Many of our points are hardly earth-shattering ones, yet they often seem to go unrealized or misunderstood. For the most part they are derived from observations made by those in the legal profession. Here, we agree with Frank Cross that an "internal perspective can amplify the understanding provided by external observation" (Cross 1997, 284).

We begin by discussing why one might want to model law. This is an important starting point because the apparent motivation of much of the political science literature is to establish that law cannot possibly constrain judges. Yet to come at the problem in this way is already to betray a conception of what judges *do* that differs substantially from the view held by those *in* law. In the world of law, what typically is referred to as legal doctrine performs a number of functions. One is to guide and channel judicial decision-making so that judges, even if they have discretion, exercise it in a cabined way. Another function of law is to permit prediction about how disputes might be resolved, so that society can operate. Constraint plays some role in both of these functions, to be sure, but it is a far more modest and nuanced one than discussed in much of the literature of politics.

Next we argue that most of what claims to be a legal model in the political science literature (a) is not a model or (b) does not model law. Here we specify what it means to have a model of law, and we acknowledge the work of those scholars who have attempted to do so. There have been some recent promising steps toward modeling law, often as collaborative efforts among political scientists and legal academics. We distinguish these recent tentative steps from the "legal model" that has been long discussed among some scholars of judicial behavior in political science.

We then seek to move forward the modeling of law in a modest way by drawing some distinctions that are prominent in internal understandings of the law. Although the concept of law is elusive, and precise definition is best left to scholars of jurisprudence, we believe these simple distinctions can offer guidance to those who seek to model law, or to test such a model empirically. In large part these distinctions serve to narrow the domain in which a simple descriptive or explanatory model of law might operate successfully.

We conclude by explaining that political scientists have been looking for law in (mostly) all the wrong places. The vast majority of political science studies of judicial behavior use as their domain constitutional or public law cases, where law is least determinate. They tend to bypass common law or statutory regimes, such as those involving contract or commercial law, where law's mechanisms seem to operate most effectively. By the same token, there is a tendency to study the decisions of the Supreme Court, or other high appellate courts, when intermediate appellate courts and trial courts—if not disputes that never make it to court—are the places in which one is most likely to find the regularity of law. Finally, although this is changing, most political science studies also look only at votes on the resolution of cases, rather than the opinions of the judges themselves, which may be appropriate to the study of judicial behavior, but not to law itself.

Constraint and Channeling

In much of the political science literature, the question—sometimes overt, more often implicit—is whether law constrains judges. In one form or another, law is conceived of as a vise upon the discretion of the judges (Spaeth and Segal 1999; Wahlbeck 1997; Knight and Epstein 1996). There are various theories as to why judges might adhere to this constraint voluntarily. For example, it might be because of the need to legitimize decisions (Hansford and Spriggs 2006, 22; Rasmussen 1994; Spaeth and Segal 1999). Or, judges might follow legal rules out of a fear of reversal by a higher court or a legislature (Cass 2003, 50; McNollgast 1995, 1643). Studies of judicial constraint many times seem to come up empty—in other words, these studies conclude that law does not constrain judges in the way political scientists would predict it should. This is a problem, some argue, because it means "other factors" (often deemed subtly or not so subtly illegitimate) are deciding cases.

The ability of law to constrain judges certainly is a reasonable concern. In a system dedicated to the rule of law, it seems critical that doctrine operates to decide cases, preventing other extraneous influences (Braman and Pickerill 2009; Braman 2010). Although constraint undeniably matters, there still is much nuance to the question that gets lost in the approach of political scientists. As we will discuss at greater length, courts and cases are not all alike. In some instances, we both need and expect a fair amount of constraint from judges. In others, we do not. Thus, for example, lawyers would not really expect to find precedent exercising much constraint in Supreme Court decisions in constitutional matters—and would not be particularly troubled by the fact. Yet, curiously, these are the cases most often plumbed by political scientists.

There is an entirely different way of looking at the role of law in judging, which presents many of the same sort of questions political scientists pose, but with a somewhat different focus. In this alternative conception, law serves what we might call a "channeling" function rather than a "constraining" one. Legal doctrine organizes the decision of future cases, rather than mandating specific resolutions. The standards and multipart tests of legal doctrine do not necessarily predetermine case outcomes, but they do rule in and rule out what it is appropriate for a judge to consider.

In part this difference in approaches reflects differing assessments of the motives of judges. A distinction between the entirely willful and the rule-abiding judge is important. Political science studies often see the judge as intent on avoiding the bonds of law (Clayton 1999). In the alternative conception, however, judges actually *want* to do a good job at judging. They are rule-abiding and want the system to work (Gibson 1978).

Introspective judges, even those who are realists about the determinacy of legal doctrine, regularly point to this affirmative channeling function of law, just as they acknowledge its imperfections. Henry Friendly said that the goal was to avoid decision by "hunch," meaning an "intuitive sense of what is right or wrong," and rather to be concerned with what legal criteria mandated (1961, 230).

This channeling function of law is precisely the quality that allows people and businesses to order their affairs. One might skeptically reply to all the above that the constraint and channeling functions are two sides of a coin. If law channels in any meaningful way, it must constrain. However, the metaphor is problematic. If constraint is the issue, judicial discretion represents a failing. But if channeling is the issue, some judicial discretion may not be quite so devastating. There still may be enough cabining of discretion to allow the channeling function to operate among judges who wish to follow rules, thereby allowing a social system to operate.

There is manifold evidence that people can and do order their affairs in reliance on this modest understanding of the rule of law (Chiappori and Salanié 2003). For example, a party who wants to seal a contractual deal can know the basic principles: that "acceptance" of an "offer" forms a contract, so long as there is "consideration." Indeterminacy surely plagues each of those terms, but still there is a rule by which one can plan to avoid trouble. Similarly, the police officer who wants to avoid the risk of seized goods being excluded by a judge before trial can obtain a warrant in advance. True, ex post even some "warranted" searches prove invalid, but as a predictive matter, following the warrant procedure greatly increases the odds against suppression.

Prediction, as Oliver Wendell Holmes explained so fittingly in "The Path of the Law" (1897), is what the endeavor is about. Holmes endeavored to strip the normative romanticism from law, and he steadfastly denied the notion that law students and lawyers were charged (or should be) with finding out what was "right" or "wrong" in the law. Rather, they should imagine their client as a "Bad Man" who wants to get away with all he can (459). Still, even such a "Bad Man" might want to avoid legal liability for his acts. The channeling function of law allows the Bad Man (along with others with better motives) to order his affairs. The channeling function of law permits people to predict what will be the consequences of their actions.

The possibility of making firm predictions is complicated by the fact that the law also must be able to evolve. Holmes understood this as well as anyone (ibid.). As we explain at some length below, the common law has a Janus-faced quality, because it must in order to function effectively. It has to provide sufficiently clear rules to allow society to order its affairs. By the same token, it has to take account of the felt necessities of the times.

"Modeling" "Law"

Here we examine the various models of judging "tested" by political scientists (the reason for our use of scare quotes will be readily apparent in a moment). We constrain our discussion to studies of the U.S. Supreme Court—certainly the court most studied by political scientists. Although we only review literature looking at this court, the arguments we make below are equally—if not more so—applicable to studies of lower courts as well.

The abstract of just about any empirical study of the Supreme Court published in a political science journal, and increasingly so in the law reviews, would read something like this:

> Decisions made by the justices on the U.S. Supreme Court in issue area X are very important for reasons Y. These decisions can be explained by the attitudinal, strategic, or legal model of decisionmaking. Using data collected under conditions Z, we find no evidence whatsoever for the legal model; thus, we conclude that the justices behave politically. (And that they are, therefore, nothing more than legislators in robes.)

Taken collectively, the literature suggests the existence of three distinct models that one can invoke to explain the behavior of Supreme Court justices: the "legal," the attitudinal, and the strategic. These models are tested, and believed to apply, to votes on the merits, decisions on certiorari, opinion assignment practices, and so on. The goal of the statistical analysis in this empirical scholarship of judging is to determine which of these models is best supported by the data. Not surprisingly, the political models of judging—the attitudinal and so-called strategic model—enjoy the greatest empirical support. The substantive take-home message is that the jurists acting at the top of the judicial hierarchy are, *gasp*, politicians.

But do existing studies actually model law in a meaningful way? Before critically reviewing the literature, we must first determine what a model is and how to distinguish between effective and ineffective models.

What Are Models and How Should One Judge Them?

Models—whether used by social scientists to study courts or by children to entertain themselves—are objects. One example of a model is a map, a two-dimensional physical object that incompletely represents a small piece of the surface of the earth. Another example is a toy car, which represents on a far smaller scale a fully functional automobile. So, too, is a model of judging, such as the "attitudinal model," which reduces decision-making on the merits to the interplay between the judge's attitudes and the stimulus provided by cases.

In broad terms, Clarke and Primo define models as "a kind of system whose characteristics are specified by an explicit (and sometimes elaborate) definition" (2007, 742). In political science, the purpose of modeling is to explain some observed political phenomena of interest. We use models to offer those explanations because they are internally logically consistent and let us abstract away features of the object of study that are not of interest. Models are important because they force us to be explicit about all of our assumptions (Epstein 2008, 13). Because models are objects, we would never claim that they are true or false (King, Keohane, and Verba 1994, 49), just as we would never say a pipe wrench is true or false. Objects do not carry truth value, they just exist.

Political scientists sometimes distinguish between theoretical models and empirical models. Theoretical models, whether stated using language or represented mathematically, contain statements about how observable and unobservable characteristics of the object of study are related to one another. The relationships might be as simple as when X goes up we would expect Y to go down. Or the relationships might be quite complicated, with various conditions. Many theoretical models are developed from axioms or assumptions that are known to be false—for example, rational choice models that make Herculean assumptions about the computing capacity of humans. Empirical models, on the other hand, are used to "evaluate a hypothesis or set of hypotheses about the real world" (Morton 1999, 61). These models allow us to simplify an often-times enormous amount of data and draw inferences about the existence or nonexistence of particular patterns. Many good empirical models allow us to establish the efficacy of different theoretical models. The so-called legal model of judging is a theoretical model, as are the attitudinal and strategic models. Ideally, our empirical models would distinguish among them.

How should one go about evaluating the efficacy of a model? For nearly fifty years social scientists have viewed prediction as the sine qua non of modeling. Milton Friedman wrote that "[t]he ultimate goal of a positive science is the development of a 'theory' or 'hypothesis' that yields valid and meaningful ... predictions about phenomena not yet observed" (1953, 7). Friedman was correct about not focusing on axioms when judging model quality, but his view of the purpose of modeling is too narrow. In their attempt to reconcile current practice in political science with contemporary philosophy of science, Clarke and Primo (2007) argue that a model can be judged only in the context of its purpose. For example, a map would be judged by the ability of the tourist to transport herself successfully from Battery Park to Grand Central Station, while a toy car would be judged by how much it looks like its full-size analogue. The responsibility of the modeler is to ascertain the ways in which the models are similar "*and dissimilar* to the real-world systems they seek to explain" (743).

Different types of models require different means to assess those similarities. The purposes of the models used in empirical studies of the Supreme Court are either *explanatory*, where the goal is to account for observed phenomena of all sorts; or *predictive*, where future decisions or cases are to be forecast (see the Clarke and Primo [2007] typology for other purposes). A model can be explanatory and thus useful without any predictive capacity; Epstein (2008) highlights plate tectonics as an example of a model that accounts for the dynamics of an earthquake but has no predictive power. A useful explanatory model is one that makes the most sense out of the observed data, while a useful predictive one would perform best in out-of-sample forecasting.

When faced with a scientific choice of model, Clarke and Primo argue for "usefulness" as the metric by which to judge model quality. A model is useful if it furthers an intellectual goal. This is similar to the notion of model adequacy discussed in the statistical literature (Gelman et al. 2004), where models are judged as to whether and to what extent they could support the observed data. An important implication of this method of judging model quality is the explicit rejection of the hypothetico-deductive model that permeates most political science scholarship. The theoretical models offered in political science, such as the attitudinal model, typically do offer hypotheses about observables—for example, votes on the merits cast by a Supreme Court justice. But no empirical analysis can ever "falsify" a theoretical model because models are simply objects. Nor does any empirical analysis ever show that a model is correct. Rather, empirical analysis informs the conditions under which one model is more or less useful at understanding the phenomena of interest.

Modeling is at the heart of the scientific study of judging. Models provide logically consistent ways to understand the world. Ideally, empirical studies of judging would gauge how useful a particular model of judging is to understanding a particular behavior. But this begs the question as to whether the "models" so often referred to in the political science literature are, in fact, models at all.

Attitudinal and Strategic Models of Judicial Behavior

The field of judicial behavior has been shaped by two predominant explanatory models: the attitudinal and strategic models. The attitudinal model has its intellectual roots in Pritchett's *The Roosevelt Court* (1948) and Schubert's profound methodological contributions over the following twenty years (see Schubert 1965 as an example). The attitudinal model is best articulated in the work of Segal and Spaeth (2002). Segal and Spaeth provide an explanatory model that has two components: the attitudes of the justices and the stimulus presented by each case they confront. Their model suggests that the interaction of these attitudes and the case stimuli will produce a vote on the merits. The attitudinal model "holds that the Supreme Court decides disputes in light of the facts of the case vis-à-vis the ideological attitudes and values of the justices. Simply put, Rehnquist votes the way he does because he is extremely conservative; Marshall voted the way he did because he was extremely liberal" (86). Segal and Spaeth clearly note that the domain of the attitudinal model is the Supreme Court, or courts in similar institutional positions (which in the United States would only include state courts of last resort on matters of state law).

As an explanatory model of merits votes and case outcomes the model performs quite well when tested empirically. The major methodological difficulty was in finding an exogenous measure of attitudes that could be used to model votes—that is, something other than votes in prior cases. Segal and Cover (1989) solved this problem by providing measures created only from newspaper editorials at the time of confirmation.

The attitudinal model does a good job of explaining past decisions, but does not predict future ones. Even if we knew the justices' attitudes with certainty, many coalition structures in actual decided cases would be consistent with the predictions of the model (including a unanimous Court, a 5–4 Court in one direction, or a 7–2 Court in another). At best, the attitudinal model gives us a sense of where the justices stand compared to one another in policy space: it tells us nothing about where they would divide on the merits of any given case. Indeed, the attitudinal model is only a partial explanatory model because it does not touch at all upon the process by which the justices decide which cases to hear in the first place, let alone why those cases even reach the Court.

The strategic analysis of judging spawned another class of models, which recently entered the study of judicial politics. It is important to note at the outset that there is no *single* strategic model of judicial decision-making. Strategic models are a *class* of models that share common axioms. As an empirical matter, one can only judge the usefulness of a particular strategic model rather than the entire class of models.

Strategic models are part of the rational choice tradition in political science, and were first discussed in the judicial politics field by Walter Murphy in *Elements of Judicial Strategy* (1964). Strategic models begin with the explicit assumption that actors are motivated by preferences. These preferences might be over policy—similar to the attitudinal model—but in principle can be over anything. Actors are assumed to act instrumentally to pursue their preferences in an interdependent choice context. Various equilibrium concepts are used to generate predictions about observed behavior. Much of the strategic literature is reviewed by Spiller and Gely (2008).

Some strategic models, the separation of powers models in particular, are geared toward explaining votes on the merits. In variants of this model, judges wish to influence policy consistent with their preferences, but most take into account the possible reactions of actors in the legislative or executive branches (see Epstein et al. 2001; Harvey and Friedman 2006; Segal 1997). Other strategic models examine bargaining among the justices, opinion assignment practices, and the like (see Maltzman et al. 2000). The empirical support for various strategic models is mixed. While there are several well-known cases, such as that involving the Supreme Court's decision in *Grove City College v. Bell*, 465 U.S. 555 (1984), where strategic explanations seem persuasive, systematic empirical studies on merits votes show little support for one separation of powers model (Segal 1997) and limited support for another (Epstein et al. 2001; Harvey and Friedman 2006) Other models of intracourt bargaining and decision-making have more convincing support (for example, Epstein and Knight 1997; Maltzman et al. 2000).

At one level, the attitudinal model can be thought of as a strategic model where the justices are motivated solely by policy and because of institutional independence can simply vote their policy preferences. That is to say, because Supreme Court justices seem unconstrained by other forces, they need not consider strategic considerations. Both the attitudinal model and various strategic models are powerful, useful models of judicial behavior. However, because they only explain votes on the merits or other discrete choices made by the justices, these models are not necessarily models of law.

The Legal "Model"

In contrast to the attitudinal or strategic models of decision-making, political scientists oftentimes invoke the "legal model" as a competing explanation. The legal model in political science finds its roots in late-nineteenth- and early-twentieth-century formalist explanations of mechanical jurisprudence (Tamanaha 2009). The term "legal model" was first mentioned by Beverly Cook in the *American Journal of Political Science* in 1977. She defines the model as follows:

> In the traditional legal model, judges use as their guidelines the standards set in constitution, statute, precedent, or court rule. Inputs are carefully screened to avoid the personal and subjective in favor of the neutral and objective. (Cook 1977, 571)

In addition to relying on the guidelines described by Cook, a number of other legal factors are included in common understandings of the legal model. Brenner and Spaeth (1995) refer to particular interpretive methods: "According to the legal model, Supreme Court justices decide cases based on the facts of the case in light of the plain meaning of the relevant legal provision, the intent of the people who framed the provision, *stare decisis*, and the balancing of social interests" (73). Knight and Epstein (1996) explicitly add past precedent to the list of factors included in the legal model, arguing that precedent is mechanically used to further policy goals when those goals are in accordance with existing precedent, and serve as constraints otherwise.

Taken together, the legal model as referenced in the political science literature has some commonalities. The model begins with an internalist perspective on law (Cross 1997, 225), and judicial behavior is explained presumably as a result of the nature of legal education. Brisbin (1996) asserts that the model "assumes that judicial votes result from the application of use of professional interpretive techniques, or modes of reasoning from legal principles as taught in law schools, to the interpretations of various sorts of legal texts" (1004). While particulars vary, the legal model includes precedent, intent, plain meaning, and neutral rules as explanatory variables. At its base, the model suggests that various neutral principles are used to account for behavior.

While it may be the case that each of these factors affect judging in particular ways, for the most part the "legal model" discussed in much of the literature—and in contrast to attitudinal and strategic approaches—does not constitute a model. Asserting that condition X *matters* to an outcome is an incomplete explanation. *How* condition X should matter, and under what *circumstances* and with what *limitations*, are important components of positing an explanatory model. Without rigorously sorting out these expectations, what is described as the legal model is not an explanatory object but rather is a collection of indeterminate factors. As Canon (1993) persuasively argues:

> The legal "model" is not scientific. . . . It is not a model at all in the research sense of the term. It is merely a list of things such as textual meaning, drafters' intent and precedent that judges are said to consider when making decisions. Because no one can say what weight each of the legal components should contribute or how a judge should select the most relevant precedent (or the most relevant evidence of intent, etc.) from among those urged upon him or her, it is impossible to assess the strength of the legal model. (99)

Significantly, in most if not all Supreme Court cases none of the factors or conditions mentioned as a part of the legal model are likely to be determinative—that is, condition X could just as easily account for an affirmance as a reversal. As such, even a wholly specified legal model of votes on the merits would not be useful at all.

The legal model has been severely criticized even by those working within the political science paradigm. In his critique of Segal and Spaeth's *The Supreme Court and the Attitudinal Model*, Rosenberg (1994) argues that the legal model highlighted in the book is a straw. In its stead he offers the "Legal Model Properly Understood," which "draws a bright line distinction between an a priori commitment to policy preferences or outcomes, as the Attitudinal Model postulates, and an a priori commitment to a set of interpretive principles" (7). Of course, the justice's politics might influence the interpretive methodology any given justice uses to reach decisions. Rosenberg's model could show how politics and the nomination process affect case outcomes, but it has not been tested empirically. Smith (1994) agrees that the legal model is an unconvincing construct, and argues that no jurisprudential scholar would articulate such a model. Cross (1997) finds the legal model to be ill defined and contradictory, both features that lead us to not consider it a model at all. Cross further argues that the written word and legal opinions are important for a whole host of reasons, and as such, looking solely at the merits votes is problematic. He also suggests that politics and a variety of legal factors are strongly related to one another, making empirical comparisons quite difficult.

Perhaps the most damning criticism of the legal model comes from Harold Spaeth, who claims that the legal model is not falsifiable (Benesh 2003)—that is, any outcome can be explained using the model. Although we differ substantially from Spaeth on what to take away from this, on the central point we could not agree more. The legal model is not falsifiable because it is not a model at all. Indeed, as we discuss above, models can never be confirmed or disconfirmed, because they are objects. All one can say is that a model does a better or less good job at explaining or predicting what it set out to explain or predict. Thus, what is important is to judge the usefulness of a model to some scholarly goal. A model that produces predictions that are consistent with everything is not useful at all. With some notable exceptions, the so-called legal model is wholly useless theoretically and empirically, a point to which we turn next.

The Usefulness of the Legal Model
Taken collectively there is little support for the legal model in the empirical scholarship on the U.S. Supreme Court. We reviewed every published large-N empirical study in which the legal model was invoked, and only in a small handful are the findings consistent with a legal model. Again, we differ from what many political scientists believe this means. A common conclusion is that because the legal model cannot predict outcomes, something else—typically politics—must. We, however, believe the lack of empirical support is a function of the fact that the legal model is not a model at all.

On the other hand, we can identify three empirical studies that show some promise in using legal variables to model votes on the merits or case outcomes. The first study, ironically, was published by Jeffrey Segal (1984), who today is most associated with the attitudinal model and profound legal skepticism. In his 1984 study, however, Segal tested an explicit "legal" model of Supreme Court decisions in search and seizure cases from 1962 to 1981. The key independent variables in the study are legal factors: the nature of the intrusion, the extent of the intrusion, prior justification for the intrusion, whether the intrusion was related to a lawful or unlawful arrest, and exceptions such as whether the search and seizure were after a hot pursuit. The model also takes into account the changing composition of the Court. Segal's empirical model performs quite well in classifying outcomes within the sample. Thus Segal used these legal factors in his systematic empirical model to offer some insight into the workings of a confusing area of law.[1]

Similarly, George and Epstein (1992) published an important study of Supreme Court death penalty cases from the 1971 though 1988 terms. They modeled the justices' decisions on whether or not to uphold a judgment imposing death. The authors hypothesize that case outcomes will be influenced by a number of doctrinal factors: whether the killing was intentional, whether the jury was selected to be biased in favor of the death penalty, whether results of state-initiated psychiatric examinations were considered, and whether the mitigating or aggravating circumstances of a particular case had been considered. George and Epstein found that the Court reacted consistently to doctrinal cues as hypothesized, indicating that in this area, using the variables they identified, over some of the cases in their domain, a legal model is effective in explaining outcomes.

The final study, by Richards and Kritzer (2002), offers an alternative to the standard legal model. They argue that "the central role of law in Supreme Court decision making is not to be found in precedents that predict how justices will vote in future cases. Rather, law at the Supreme Court level is to be found in the structures the justices create to guide future decision making" (306). This is precisely akin to the channeling function we describe above. Richards and Kritzer offer the concept of a jurisprudential regime, which refers to "a key precedent, or a set of related precedents, that structures the way in which the Supreme Court justices evaluate key elements of cases in arriving at decisions in a particular legal area" (ibid., 308). Based on their reading of the freedom of expression law, they suggest that two 1972 cases—*Chicago Police Department v. Mosley* (408 U.S. 92, 1972), and *Grayned v. City of Rockford* (408 U.S. 104, 1972)—established the speech-protective content-neutrality regime. Using a handful of political variables and jurisprudential variables, with interactions at the time of the regime shift, their empirical models show that these two cases fundamentally shifted the jurisprudential approach in this area of law. A companion study shows that *Lemon v. Kurtzman* (403 U.S. 602, 1971) established a new jurisprudential regime in Establishment Clause jurisprudence.

In all three of the studies the authors carefully develop a tailored legal model that provides precise hypotheses in a particular area of the law. Although much of what the authors find would not be surprising to lawyers working in these doctrinal areas, the point is that these authors used legal factors to explain case outcomes in empirical models. Not coincidentally, all of these studies were published in the *American Political Science Review*, the leading journal of the discipline. None of these studies rely on the general notion of precedent or canons of interpretation to predict case outcomes. These are explanatory models, all of which show that an interaction of what we would consider law and politics affects outcomes. None of these models are predictive, although Segal (1984) does use the model to forecast cases in the 1981 term. These studies do not offer a global legal model that accounts for all decision-making, but rather a specific model in a single area of the law. Of course there is much more to modeling law than what is done in these studies, and we offer some suggestions below.

Further support for a legal model in the empirical literature is quite slim. The only exceptions we could find are the work of: Sheehan (1990), which argues that the legal model is supported because social and economic administrative agencies enjoy the same success rate in cases before the Supreme Court; Kearney and Merrill (2000), who show that amicus briefs and the arguments therein affect case outcomes; and Lim (2000), who finds evidence of what he calls individual stare decisis in cases when it applies, and general stare decisis in cases when it does not, ultimately concluding that both the legal and attitudinal model are complementary. None of these studies offer a fully formed legal model that could be judged for its adequacy.

Ultimately, the debate among the three "models"—attitudinal, strategic, and legal—is about the scholarly burden of proof. Segal and Spaeth (2002) argue strongly that the attitudinal model is important because it disproves the legal model. We agree that the attitudinal model is important, not only because it is a model with clear predictions but also because it enjoys such strong empirical support. At the same time, we think they err—as many political scientists err—in concluding that this or a strategic model disproves a legal model. We concede that we possess an intuitive bias. We believe that it is simply implausible that, in a culture steeped in law, politics and only politics affects what Supreme Court justices—let alone lower court judges—do. Rather than framing studies as politics vs. all else—which is the norm in political science—scholars should be seeking models with superior explanatory or predictive power. Sorting out how to model law systematically and empirically remains the grand challenge, which is where we next turn.

Finding Law

In sum, we have observed two things. First, although discussions of a "legal model" are common, for the most part those seeking to gain purchase on the law have no model for doing so. Models must be logically consistent, systematic, and clear, and must be able to map observables (sometimes called independent variables—that is, those doing the explaining) to other observables (sometimes called dependent variables—the thing we wish to explain). The collection of varied factors commonly referred to as the legal model do not reach this standard. Second, there assuredly are political science studies that contain perfectly good models, such as the basic attitudinal model. But none of those models is actually modeling anything remotely close to law. At best they are predicting the *outcome* of a certain set of cases or a *vote* by a justice on the merits, without controlling for law in any way. Were these studies perfectly predictive, and were we confident that the independent variable in those studies was not collinear with law, we could safely say law played no role. However, neither of those things is true. We plainly have learned that in some courts it is possible to predict the outcomes of disputes in some number of cases. This tells us something about the forces that operate in that subset of disputes. None of what we have learned brings us any closer to knowing how law operates, or precisely what role it plays when it is playing a role.

There is a reason for such modest progress: law and the legal process are by their nature extremely difficult to model. With so many moving parts, it is no surprise that a successful model has yet to emerge. Here, we try to offer some insight into what law is (and is not), and where law can be expected to have impact (and where not). We reason primarily by distinction. Our reasoning helps to explain why most studies of the legal model are looking for law in all the wrong places.

Types of Law

The first point is that there is no one unified thing we might call "law," at least as some political science studies seem to envision it. Rather, law is a practice (Gillman 2001, 485) in which there are many differing substantive bodies of rules, as well as various procedures and processes, each of which might be called "law," and each of which might independently be modeled. Choosing among these will depend, naturally, on what one is trying to achieve or explain with any given model.

More specifically, there are different types of law. At one pass, there is constitutional law, statutory law, administrative law, and the common law. Yet it is also possible to divide the types of law differently. It is common, for example, to distinguish between public law (the rules as between the government and private entities or individuals) and private law (the rules governing relationships between private entities or individuals). These are the sorts of distinctions that models sometimes elide, which leads to further criticisms that "[p]olitical scientists often have an unduly cramped vision of the legal model" (Cross 1997, 291).

While the foregoing point is trivial at one level, it is utterly consequential at another. Each of these types of law is expected to (and we suspect that each does) operate somewhat differently than the others. The kinds of tests or tools used to find the law or interpret the law in one area may bear little relationship to another (Levi 1949). The Constitution often is "interpreted" by looking to the text and framing era intentions. There is some commonality here with statutory interpretation, which also cares about texts and intentions. Yet constitutional tests are quite varied and also include balancing, means-end analysis, least restrictive alternatives, and the like. Common law decision-making (to which we devote a great deal of attention below) is an entirely different creature altogether (Newman 1984, 200). Any discussion of modeling "law" necessarily must take into account the heterogeneity of law itself.

We suspect that for the most part when political scientists talk about a legal model what they have in mind is common law decision-making. In other words, they are focused on the process by which courts read from one case to the next, and on the constraint imposed (or not imposed) on these judges by prior precedents. In the U.S. context, there is almost always a body of common law that develops, even around statutes and constitutions, in all courts including the Supreme Court.

A superficial commonality in interpretive methodology across areas of the law can give rise to confusion in the political science literature regarding the "legal model." Yet the various categories of law have their own norms and practices, typically driven by some underlying theory regarding what each area of law is trying to accomplish. Take, for example, the contrasting role of stare decisis in constitutional and statutory cases. Political scientists interested in the role of constraint often look in constitutional cases of various sorts for judicial adherence to prior precedents (Romero 2000, 298; Laird 1994; Segal and Spaeth 2002; Brenner and Stier 1996; Segal 1984). But this is an exceedingly peculiar place to look. An explicit part of the interpretive background in the constitutional context is that prior precedents should carry less force, that the doctrine of stare decisis should be ameliorated, precisely because constitutional rules cannot easily be altered in any way other than by overturning precedent. This point was noted by Justice Brandeis in a dissent he authored in *Burnet v. Coronado Oil & Gas Company* (1932), in which he famously wrote that stare decisis was not a "universal inexorable command." What is sometimes overlooked was that Brandeis specifically focused on "cases involving the Federal Constitution, where correction through legislative action is practically impossible" (285 U.S. 393, 407–10). Brandeis's insight into stare decisis was picked up almost sixty years later in the Supreme Court's *Payne v. Tennessee* (1991) decision. Referring to Brandeis's "inexorable command" language, the *Payne* majority elaborated: "This is particularly true in constitutional cases, because in such cases correction through legislative action is practically impossible" (501 U.S. 808, 828).

Statutory precedents, on the other hand, are thought to be more durable. Again, the Supreme Court gives us guidance. In *Illinois Brick Co. v. Illinois* (1977), the majority noted that "[in] considering whether to cut back or abandon [the established] rule, we must bear in mind that considerations of stare decisis weigh heavily in the area of statutory construction, where Congress is free to change this Court's interpretation of its legislation" (431 U.S. 720, 736).[2] In interpreting statutes, courts can adhere to them, even if seemingly illogical, because such precedents are open to legislative revision. The same consideration applies to common law cases, where statutory "corrections" can alter judge-made law. Some have cast this point in terms of democratic ideals, arguing that we want a particularly strong rule of stare decisis in statutory cases in order to foster democratic participation from the other branches. Clear and stable judicial interpretations of statutes provide a clear background against which legislative bodies can operate (Sunstein 1999).

When it comes to the relative force of prior precedents and the stability of the doctrine, a similar dichotomy exists as between public law and private law. Public law decisions are often thought to be somewhat less obdurate than private law decisions precisely because the government requires a certain amount of flexibility in its actions, and perhaps because fewer reliance interests are likely to be at stake. In contrast, in private law, particularly with regard to commercial transactions, much greater stability of the law is required (Greene 2005, 1404). Even within public law, there are differences. Because of the seriousness of criminal penalties, and the concomitant need for "notice" to potential criminal defendants, one might expect more precedential stability in criminal law cases than other public law cases. Similarly, Jon Newman, a prominent U.S.

Court of Appeals judge, noted that some statutes, such as the tax code, are revisited by Congress every year, whereas others remained untouched for decades; Newman argued that this likelihood that Congress would attend to the work of courts also influenced his decision-making (Newman 1984, 209).

Once again, whether these theoretical distinctions actually hold up in the doctrine is an empirical question. There might be plenty of projects here for the willing. But if one is looking to model law—or, in particular, if one is looking for constraint in law—private law cases would be the place to look, not constitutional cases. Alas, that has not been the practice.

Hierarchies of Precedent
As the foregoing suggests, there are different types of precedents. One way to think of this, as demonstrated in the prior section, is as across substantive categories or types of law. Another way to think of it is structurally—that is, to look at the binding force of precedents within and across differing court systems.

In modeling common law decision-making, one of the most important distinctions may be that between vertical and horizontal stare decisis. Horizontal stare decisis refers to the binding effect that is given to a prior decision when the court applying a precedent case is the same as the one that rendered it. In a sense, horizontal stare decisis is about decision-making over time. Many political science studies look for constraint along this horizontal axis (Hurwitz and Stefko 2004; Segal and Spaeth 1996; Spriggs and Hansford 2002). Vertical stare decisis, in contrast, refers to the influence of a precedent case when that case is being applied by a court below the court that rendered a precedent case in a judicial hierarchy (Kornhauser 1995). Thus, when the Supreme Court of the United States considers the binding effect of its own precedents in a later case, that is horizontal stare decisis; when a federal court of appeals considers the effect of a Supreme Court decision, that is vertical stare decisis.

In law, it is a commonplace that vertical stare decisis is supposed to be much greater than horizontal. The Supreme Court has recognized this difference explicitly. In a 1989 case, *Rodriguez de Quijas v. Shearson/American Export*, the Court took the opportunity to castigate a lower court that had ignored a Supreme Court precedent. While the Court ultimately affirmed the lower court decision, the Court noted:

> We do not suggest that the Court of Appeals on its own authority should have taken the step of renouncing [the Supreme Court precedent]. If a precedent of this Court has direct application in a case, yet appears to rest on reasons

rejected in some other line of decisions, the Court of Appeals should follow the case which directly controls, leaving to this Court the prerogative of overruling its own decisions. (490 U.S. 477, 484)

By contrast, as we saw above, the Supreme Court takes varying approaches to how bound it is by its own precedents.

Even this straightforward distinction masks significant subtleties. Horizontal stare decisis is not the same on every court. On the Supreme Court it is quite weak (Posner 2008, 14; Edwards 1985, 621). It is puzzling, then, why so many studies invoke the importance of precedent when modeling Supreme Court decisions (see Baum 2006, 4–5). On the federal Court of Appeals it varies depending upon whether a precedent is from within the same circuit or not (Kim 2007; Caminker 1994a; Caminker 1994b). As for vertical stare decisis, there is reason to imagine that the precedential effect might be stronger as between intermediate appellate courts and trial courts, than as between high courts and intermediate appellate courts (Caminker 1994a, 843). That is because the trial courts are thought to be charged primarily with applying precedents to sets of facts, not formulating broad rules of general application. They are resolving disputes. On the other hand, intermediate appellate courts do develop broad rules, and may be delegated authority by high courts to flesh out general rules (ibid., 846).

These nuances become greater yet when one considers the federal system in the United States. First, state courts have their own rules of stare decisis, which may operate differently from those of the federal courts (Lindquist 2009, 11; Lindquist and Pybas 1998). Second, there are special intersystem rules as well. State courts are not bound by federal circuit court precedents (Posner 2008; Hiscock 1924); they are bound by Supreme Court decisions. Federal trial courts sitting in diversity cases do consider themselves bound by the decisions of state high courts. Some modelers have suggested that cases in which states decline to follow the decisions of the Supreme Court in interpreting their own constitutions undermine claims of precedential effect (McClurg and Comparato 2004, 3). Jumping to this conclusion fails to recall that the system is purposely designed to be, in the words of Judge Posner, "a decentralized, quasi-competitive system of lawmaking" (Posner 2008, 277).

Even where the rules are seemingly rigid, there still may be divergence—and principled divergence at that. Court systems function to resolve ordinary disputes, but they also are part of a political system of governance. Thus, breakdowns in what look to be structured rules of stare decisis may reflect inter-systemic struggles, or reflect a means of moderating them short of outright conflict. Although the ostensible purpose of a tiered system of appellate review is to develop a coherent body of law (Kornhauser 1995; Rogers 1995), the Supreme Court sometimes permits divergence precisely so that it can observe the range of possibilities for resolution of an issue. This is the frequently documented technique of "percolation" (Kornhauser 1995, 1625; Caminker 1994b, 57; Estreicher and Sexton 1984, 732).

The Norms of Different Courts

It should be readily apparent at this point that all courts are not the same, and yet this point deserves a moment of attention. When conducting studies of judicial behavior, political scientists often focus on the Supreme Court (Kim 2007). This is understandable, as the Supreme Court is of a higher profile than other courts and its work seems both more interesting and more important. A similar bias can be found in work of the legal academy as well (Baum 2006, 4–5).

Nonetheless, given the purposes of studies of judicial behavior and the endeavor of modeling law, the Supreme Court may prove to be the least promising body to study. A large part of its workload is constitutional, which is—as we have seen—already the most indeterminate or flexible area of the law. The Court takes very few cases a year. At the risk of grievous overstatement, the cases can be divided into those with open legal questions in need of resolution, high-profile public cases, and a small set of cases in which the lower courts have gone badly astray and require correction. The nature of the Court's caseload, as at least two of these categories indicate, is such that there will be strong legal (and perhaps other) arguments on both sides. Open questions are, by definition, those in which the precedents do not constrain.

By contrast, the federal circuit courts see a steady fare of common law, criminal, statutory, and administrative cases. As federal appellate judge Harry Edwards notes, the type of law before the court also varies between the appeals courts and the highest courts in the land; the "staple business of the courts of appeals is not constitutional adjudication, but statutory interpretation, review of administrative action, and oversight of the federal district courts" (Edwards 1985, 621). Many of these are far more ordinary than the cases that make their way to the Supreme Court, and often the doctrine appears far more settled.

The state courts receive relatively little attention when it comes to modeling law, but there are many advantages to using them as grounds for study. State courts see a great variance in types of cases: matters of criminal law, state and federal statutory and administrative, and state constitutional law (Friedman 2004; Hershkoff 2001). In addition, the state courts hear a much higher percentage of common law matters, including ordinary commercial disputes. Finally, they also have different selection procedures for their judges, providing the possibility of natural experiments.

The Dynamic Nature of Precedent

A foundational difficulty exists with modeling law, which relates to its dynamism. The dynamism of the common law is most likely the reason that some of the studies we identify as truly modeling law see the predictive ability of their models decline over time (see George and Epstein 1992; Richards and Kritzer 2002). Not only do many political science studies overlook the dynamism of the common law, they also seem to affirmatively believe case law is stable. Understandably, it seems in the nature of rules that they should remain relatively stable. The nature of the common law, however, is that subsequent cases alter prior precedential cases, yielding a new rule. That is because, as we explained above, the common law must mediate two things at once: the stability needed for ordering of affairs, and the ability for the law to change so that it accommodates the needs of the times.

A famous example of the evolutionary face of the law comes from the doctrine of privity, particularly with respect to products liability. Privity refers to the relationship between tortfeasor and victim required for the law to allow liability. When privity was applied strictly, for example, a seller could be held liable only for a product defect if the buyer had bought directly from the seller. This worked fine in a market without middlemen, but the doctrine strained as the national economy shifted to mass production and the stream of commerce lengthened such that buyers rarely dealt with the manufacturer.[3] As a result of this strain, the privity doctrine began to shift, first using legal fictions about who exactly was party to the contract and what the terms were. The pressures of the mass market continued, however, until, in a series of important cases starting with *MacPherson v. Buick Motors* (1916), state courts abandoned the privity restriction and opened the doors to modern-day products liability (111 N.E. 1050, 1053). *MacPherson* was written by Benjamin Cardozo, who later sat on the Supreme Court of the United States and was considered one of the masters at managing this tension between stability and change. In Cardozo's opinions the law could change mightily, and yet the decision effecting the change would be neatly woven into prior law so that the rate of change was barely evident.

A "rule" in the common law is not some abstract principle of law, but the interaction of an abstract principle with the facts of the present case. Later cases necessarily refashion the prior rule, in part by their application of new facts, but in part as well by the way later cases describe the prior one. What may seem dicta in a prior case becomes rule later, and vice versa.

Edward Levi called this process "the indispensable dynamic quality of law," and acknowledged how puzzling it might seem to those fixated on rules (Levi 1949, 2). Levi, a well-respected University of Chicago law professor, was tapped by Gerald Ford to be attorney general at a period when the country—following the Watergate scandal—needed to restore its faith in law. Many years before his time of government service, he wrote a well-known and admired text for law students endeavoring to learn this aspect of the legal process. "[It] cannot be said," wrote Levi, "that the legal process is the application of known rules to diverse facts." Rather, he explained, "the rules are discovered in the process of determining similarity or difference." He acknowledged—indeed, emphasized—that "the classification changes as the classification is made. The rules change as the rules are applied" (ibid., 3).

It is the process of defining similarity and difference that allows the common law to move with the times. Analogy is what makes the common law go, but the appropriate analogies between and among cases do not exist in some absolute, preordained sense. They emerge only through the reasoning of many judges looking at the same problem. "If the society has begun to see certain significant similarities or differences, the comparison emerges with a word. When the word is finally accepted, it becomes a legal concept. Its meaning continues to change" (ibid., 8).

Despite the evidence to support the dynamic nature of common law, the research design of even those studies of judicial behavior that truly manage to model the law tends to be static, which explains some difficulties in the studies' explanatory capacity. This is true, for example, of the George and Epstein (1992) and Richards and Kritzer (2002) studies. These authors identify the variables that seem to count in resolving the cases. In the short term, their studies show some explanatory power, and yet this deteriorates over time. What these authors are seeing is that the dynamic nature of the common law renders certain aspects of a case less crucial as one moves away from the time of the case. Thus, George and Epstein look at various factors present in death penalty cases that seem determinative in the early cases but eventually faded in explanatory value, such as particularized circumstances and aggravating factors (George and Epstein 1992, 329). But no wonder; given the dynamic nature of the common law, this is to be expected. The factors that spelled success in early cases, factors that were both necessary and sufficient, become merely necessary over time as further refinement of the law introduced new variables that were determinative.

Outcomes v. Opinions/Rule

Finally, we mention the distinction between the *outcome* of a case, and the *opinion* drafted by the court in that case. This is a distinction that has drawn attention in the literature (see Carrubba et al. 2008; Maltzman et al. 2000; Friedman 2006). Yet many studies—hampered no doubt by coding problems—continue to focus only on outcomes, as though that is all there is to law.

When a court decides a case, it does two things. First, it awards a judgment. Second, it explains how or why it reached that judgment, often in a written opinion. As we have explained above, much work in political science seems devoted to the proposition that the opinions themselves are disguises to cover up a decision reached in a different way. Opinions *are* justifications, but they also provide rules for the future. Whether an opinion is persuasive or not in explaining why a court did what it did, it nonetheless provides a rule for the decision in future cases.

One might doubt that opinions ever are truly rules for the future. One might suspect that the judge in a subsequent case will decide on factors other than the rule in the prior case. Of course, for this to be true—that is, for the precedents to have *no* weight—one would have to argue that this always happens. This is an empirical proposition, and one might properly be skeptical that it will ever prove out. But no study of which we are aware has come remotely close to doing so.

Moreover, even if judges regularly departed from precedents in some cases, those precedents still might be ordering the affairs of many actors outside courts. As we indicated earlier, judicial opinions contain tests and standards that govern the application of the law. They tell observers what counts. Out of the set of all possible disputes, many never occur because of general agreement that the tests in opinions were appropriate and govern (Priest and Klein 1984). Court decisions are a subset of these possible disputes, the subset in which something broke down.

What is important to point out for present purposes is that to the best of our knowledge, *no* study has ever even attempted to predict what the content of the *opinion* in a subsequent case will be. In other words, studies regularly try to predict outcomes in later cases from prior precedents. But if one is trying to model how the law operates, then outcomes may be the wrong dependent variable. What one might want to attempt to do is predict when and how *rules* will be changed.

Conclusion: What One Might Model

There are many reasons one might seek to model law. What should be clear by now is that whatever the reason, the types of studies most commonly conducted are likely to be the least promising ones. In a sense, students of judicial behavior have been looking for "law" where one is least likely to find it.

The Supreme Court is the realm for a huge proportion of political science studies of judicial behavior. The Court's decisions in constitutional law or civil rights play a particularly big role. There are famous studies that look mostly to the Supreme Court's Fourth Amendment or "civil rights" jurisprudence (Segal 1984; Segal and Spaeth 1996; Romero 2000; Hensley and Smith 1995; Murphy 1958). (We use scare quotes because modern studies typically are conducted using the Spaeth database, and the coding of cases as such, yet the category itself is quite broad and suffers from some serious difficulties [see Harvey and Woodruff 2011; Shapiro 2009].)

Yet there has been remarkably little attention given to areas that might prove quite profitable. If one wanted to guess in which cases precedent was most determinate, and where tacit and explicit overruling would be least likely—that would be in the mill run commercial cases. One might study these in the federal courts (in diversity cases), though state courts undoubtedly are the predominant forum for these kinds of cases.

Indeed, if one really wanted to know how law operates, one might not study cases at all. There is a very real problem of selection bias in this obsession with litigated disputes. After all, countless contracts are formed every day and do not make their way to litigation. Numerous actors in the public and private arena daily make decisions based on a prediction of how courts would resolve disputes should those decisions ultimately find their way into a court. It is possible that in reaching these predictions regarding dispute resolution, those making them take into account the ideology or attitudes of judges, and the strategic milieu in which they operate. It is more likely, however, they look simply to the law.

There is something to the law that works. Precisely what this is has eluded many political science studies over time. There may be many reasons for this, but the most obvious is that for the most part, those studies are simply not modeling law at all.

Notes

1. Only later did Segal deem these legal factors case stimuli (Segal and Spaeth 2002, 312; Segal, Spaeth, and Benesh 2005, 38), and thus consistent with the attitudinal model. But in the culture of law, Segal was right (in 1984) and wrong thereafter: his variables are indeed legal factors (Friedman 2006).

2. See also *Patterson v. McLean Credit Union* (1989), in which the Court noted that "[c]onsiderations of stare decisis have special force in the area of statutory interpretation, for here, unlike in the context of constitutional interpretation, the legislative power is implicated, and Congress remains free to alter what we have done" (491 U.S. 164, 172).

3. The effect of the Industrial Revolution on privity contracts is best captured in *Henningsen v. Bloomfield Motors* (161 A.2d 80–81, 83–84, 1960).

References

Baum, Lawrence. 2006. *Judges and Their Audiences: A Perspective on Judicial Behavior*. Princeton: Princeton University Press.

Benesh, Sara. 2003. "Chapter 5: Harold J. Spaeth: The Supreme Court Computer." In Nancy Maveety, ed., *The Pioneers of Judicial Behavior*. Ann Arbor: University of Michigan Press.

Brady, Henry E., and David Collier, eds. 2004. *Rethinking Social Inquiry: Diverse Tools, Shared Standards*. Lanham, MD: Rowman and Littlefield.

Braman, Eileen. 2010. "Searching for Constraint in Legal Decision Making." In David Klein and Greg Mitchell, eds., *The Psychology of Judicial Decision Making*. Oxford: Oxford University Press.

Braman, Eileen, and Mitchell Pickerill. 2009. "Path Dependence in Studies of Legal Decision Making." Conference on Legal Decision Making at Maurer Law School, Indiana University.

Brenner, Saul, and Harold J. Spaeth. 1995. *Stare Indecisis: The Alteration of Precedent on the Supreme Court, 1946–1992*. Cambridge: Cambridge University Press.

Brenner, Saul, and Marc Stier. 1996. "Retesting Segal and Spaeth's Stare Decisis Model." *American Journal of Political Science*: 40: 1036–48.

Brisbin, Richard A. 1996. "Slaying the Dragon: Segal, Spaeth and the Function of Law in Supreme Court Decision Making." *American Journal of Political Science* 40: 1004–17.

Caminker, Evan H. 1994a. "Must Inferior Courts Obey Superior Court Precedents?" *Stanford Law Review* 46: 817–73.

———. 1994b. "Precedent and Prediction: The Forward-Looking Aspects of Inferior Court Decisionmaking." *Texas Law Review* 73: 1–82.

Canon, Bradley C. 1993. "Review of *The Supreme Court and the Attitudinal Model,* by Jeffery A. Segal and Harold J. Spaeth." *Law and Politics Book Review* 3: 98.

Carrubba, Cliff, Barry Friedman, Andrew D. Martin, and Georg Vanberg. 2008. "Does the Median Justice Control the Content of Supreme Court Opinions?" Working paper.

Cass, Ronald A. 2003. *The Rule of Law in America.* Baltimore, MD: Johns Hopkins Press.

Chiappori, Pierre-Andre, and Bernard Salanié. 2003. "Testing Contract Theory: A Survey of Some Recent Work." In M. Dewatripont, L. Hansen, and P. Turnovsky, eds., *Advances in Economics and Econometrics—Theory and Applications.* Cambridge: Cambridge University Press.

Clarke, Kevin A., and David M. Primo. 2007. "Modernizing Political Science: A Model-based Approach." *Perspectives on Politics* 5: 741–53.

Clayton, Cornell W. 1999. "The Supreme Court and Political Jurisprudence: New and Old Institutionalisms." In Cornell W. Clayton and Howard Gillman, eds., *Supreme Court Decision-Making: New Institutional Approaches.* Chicago: University of Chicago Press.

Cook, Beverly B. 1977. "Public Opinion and Federal Judicial Policy." *American Journal of Political Science* 21: 567–600.

Cross, Frank B. 1997. "Political Science and the New Legal Realism: A Case of Unfortunate Interdisciplinary Ignorance." *Northwestern University Law Review* 92: 251–326.

Crowley, Donald W. 1987. "Judicial Review of Administrative Agencies: Does the Type of Agency Matter?" *Political Research Quarterly* 40: 285–303.

Dworkin, Ronald. 1986. *Law's Empire.* Cambridge, MA: Harvard University Press.

Edwards, Harry T. 1985. "Public Misperceptions Concerning the 'Politics' of Judging: Dispelling Some Myths about the D.C. Circuit." *University of Colorado Law Review* 56: 619–46.

Epstein, Joshua M. 2008. "Why Model?" *Journal of Artificial Societies and Social Simulation* 11: 12–17.

Epstein, Lee, and Jack Knight. 1997. *The Choices Justices Make.* Washington, DC: CQ Press.

Epstein, Lee, Jack Knight, and Andrew D. Martin. 2001. "Dahl Symposium: The Supreme Court as a Strategic National Policymaker." *Emory Law Journal* 50: 583–611.

Estreicher, Samuel, and John E. Sexton. 1984. "A Managerial Theory of the Supreme Court's Responsibilities: An Empirical Study." *New York University Law Review* 59: 681–822.

Friedman, Barry. 2004. "Under the Law of Federal Jurisdiction: Allocating Cases between Federal and State Courts." *Columbia Law Review* 104: 1211–79.

———. 2005. "The Politics of Judicial Review." *Texas Law Review* 84: 257–338.

———. 2006. "Taking Law Seriously." *Perspectives on Politics* 4: 261–76.

Friedman, Milton. 1953. *Essays in Positive Economics.* Chicago: University of Chicago Press.

Friendly, Henry J. 1961. "Reactions of a Lawyer-Newly Become Judge." *Yale Law Journal* 71: 218–38.

Gelman, Andrew, John B. Carlin, Hal S. Stern, and Donald B. Rubin. 2004. *Bayesian Data Analysis*. 2d ed. Boca Raton, FL: CRC Press.

George, Tracy E., and Lee Epstein. 1992. "On the Nature of Supreme Court Decision Making." *American Political Science Review* 86: 323–37.

Gibson, James L. 1978. "Judges' Role Orientations, Attitudes, and Decisions: An Interactive Model." *American Political Science Review* 72: 911–24.

Gillman, Howard. 2001. "What's Law Got to Do with It? Judicial Behavioralists Test the 'Legal Model' of Judicial Decision Making." *Law and Social Inquiry* 26: 465–504.

Greene, Abner S. 2005. "Can We Be Legal Positivists without Being Constitutional Positivists?" *Fordham Law Review* 73: 1401–14.

Hansford, Thomas G., and James F. Spriggs, II. 2006. *The Politics of Precedent on the U.S. Supreme Court*. Princeton: Princeton University Press.

Harvey, Anna, and Michael J. Woodruff 2011. "Confirmation Bias in the United States Supreme Court Judicial Database." *Journal of Law, Economics, and Organization*, forthcoming.

Harvey, Anna, and Barry Friedman. 2006. "Pulling Punches: Congressional Constraints on the Supreme Court's Constitutional Rulings, 1987–2000." *Legislative Studies Quarterly* 31: 533–62.

Hensley, Thomas R., and Christopher E. Smith. 1995. "Membership Change and Voting Change: An Analysis of the Rehnquist Court's 1986–1991 Terms." *Political Research Quarterly* 48: 837–56.

Hershkoff, Helen. 2001. "State Courts and the 'Passive Virtues': Rethinking the Judicial Function." *Harvard Law Review* 114: 1833–1942.

Hinich, Melvin J., and Michael C. Munger. 1997. *Analytical Politics*. Cambridge: Cambridge University Press.

Hiscock, Frank Harris. 1924. "Progressiveness of New York Law." *Cornell Law Review* 9: 371–87.

Holmes, Oliver Wendell. 1897. "The Path of the Law." *Harvard Law Review* 10: 457–78.

Hurwitz, Mark S., and Joseph V. Stefko. 2004. "Acclimation and Attitudes: 'Newcomer' Justices and Precedent Conformance on the Supreme Court." *Political Research Quarterly* 57: 121–29.

Kearney, Joseph D., and Thomas W. Merrill. 2000. "The Influence of Amicus Curiae Briefs on the Supreme Court." *University of Pennsylvania Law Review* 148: 743–855.

Kim, Pauline T. 2007. "Lower Court Discretion." *New York University Law Review* 84: 383–442.

King, Gary, Robert O. Keohane, and Sidney Verba. 1994. *Designing Social Inquiry*. Princeton: Princeton University Press.

Knight, Jack, and Lee Epstein. 1996. "The Norm of Stare Decisis." *American Journal of Political Science* 40: 1018.

Kornhauser, Lewis A. 1995. "Adjudication by a Resource-Constrained Team: Hierarchy and Precedent in a Judicial System." *Southern California Law Review* 68: 1605–30.

Kritzer, Herbert M., and Mark J. Richards. 2003. "Jurisprudential Regimes and Supreme Court Decisionmaking: The Lemon Regime and Establishment Clause Cases." *Law and Society Review* 37: 827–40.

Laird, Vanessa. 1994. "Planned Parenthood v. Casey: The Role of Stare Decisis." *Modern Law Review* 57: 461–67.

Levi, Edward H. 1949. *An Introduction to Legal Reasoning.* Chicago: University of Chicago Press.

Lim, Youngsik. 2000. "An Empirical Analysis of Supreme Court Justices' Decision Making." *Journal of Legal Studies* 29: 721–52.

Lindquist, Stephanie A. 2009. "*Stare Decisis* as Reciprocity Norm." Conference on Legal Decision Making at Maurer Law School, Indiana University.

Lindquist, Stefanie A., and Frank B. Cross. 2005. "Empirically Testing Dworkin's Chain Novel Theory: Studying the Path of Precedent." *New York University Law Review* 80: 1156–1206.

Lindquist, Stephanie A., and Kevin Pybas. 1998. "State Supreme Court Decisions to Overrule Precedent, 1965–1996." *Justice System Journal* 20: 17–37.

Maltzman, Forest, James F. Spriggs, and Paul J. Wahlbeck. 2000. *Crafting Law on the Supreme Court: The Collegial Game.* Cambridge: Cambridge University Press.

McClurg, Scott, and Scott Comparato. 2004. "Rebellious or Just Misunderstood: Assessing Measures of Lower Court Compliance with U.S. Supreme Court Precedent." Paper presented at the annual meeting of the Midwest Political Science Association, Chicago, IL.

McNollgast. 1995. "Politics and the Courts: A Positive Theory of Judicial Doctrine and the Rule of Law." *Southern California Law Review* 68: 1631–82.

Morton, Rebecca B. 1999. *Methods & Models: A Guide to the Empirical Analysis of Formal Models in Political Science.* New York: Cambridge University Press.

Murphy, Richard W. 2003. "Separation of Powers and the Horizontal Force of Precedent." *Notre Dame Law Review* 78: 1075–1163.

Murphy, Walter F. 1958. "Civil Liberties and the Japanese American Cases: A Study in the Uses of Stare Decisis." *Western Political Quarterly* 11: 3–13.

———. 1964. *Elements of Judicial Strategy.* Chicago: University of Chicago Press.

Newman, Jon O. 1984. "Between Legal Realism and Neutral Principles: The Legitimacy of Institutional Values." *California Law Review* 72: 200–216.

Posner, Richard A. 1993. *Cardozo: A Study in Reputation.* Chicago: University of Chicago Press.

———. 2008. *How Judges Think.* Cambridge, MA: Harvard University Press.

Priest, George L., and Benjamin Klein. 1984. "The Selection of Disputes for Litigation." *Journal of Legal Studies* 13: 1–55.

Pritchett, C. Herman. 1948. *The Roosevelt Court: A Study in Judicial Politics and Values, 1937–1947.* New York: Macmillan.

Rasmussen, Eric. 1994. "Judicial Legitimacy as a Repeated Game." *Journal of Law, Economics and Organization* 10: 63–83.

Richards, Mark J., and Herbert M. Kritzer. 2002. "Jurisprudential Regimes in Supreme Court Decision Making." *American Political Science Review* 96: 305.

Rogers, John M. 1995. "Lower Court Application of the 'Overruling Law' of Higher Courts." *Legal Theory* 1: 179–204.

Romero, Francine Sanders. 2000. "The Supreme Court and the Protection of Minority Rights: An Empirical Examination of Racial Discrimination Cases." *Law and Society Review* 34: 291–313.

Rosenberg, Gerald N. 1994. "Remarks, Symposium on *Supreme Court and the Attitudinal Model*." *Law and Courts: Newsletter of the Law and Courts Section of the American Political Science Association* 4: 6–8.

Schaefer, Walter V. 1966. "Precedent and Policy." *University of Chicago Law Review* 34: 3–25.

Schapiro, David L. 1995. *Federalism: A Dialogue.* Evanston, IL: Northwestern University Press.

Scheb, John M., II, and William Lyons. 2001. "Judicial Behavior and Public Opinion: Popular Expectations Regarding the Factors That Influence Supreme Court Decisions." *Political Behavior* 23: 181–94.

Schubert, Glendon. 1965. *The Judicial Mind: The Attitudes and Ideologies of Supreme Court Justices, 1946–1963.* Evanston, IL: Northwestern University Press.

Segal, Jeffery A. 1984. "Predicting Supreme Court Cases Probabilistically: The Search and Seizure Cases, 1962–1981." *American Political Science Review* 78: 891–900.

———. 1989. "Ideological Values and the Votes of U.S. Supreme Court Justices." *American Political Science Review* 83: 557–65.

———. 1997. "Separation-of-Powers Games in the Positive Theory of Congress and Courts." *American Political Science Review* 91: 28–45.

Segal, Jeffrey A., and Albert D. Cover. 1989. "Ideological Values and Votes of US Supreme Court Justices." *American Political Science Review* 83: 557–65.

Segal, Jeffery A., and Harold J. Spaeth. 1996. "The Influence of Stare Decisis on the Votes of United States Supreme Court Justices." *American Journal of Political Science* 40: 971–1003.

———. 2001. *Majority Rule or Minority Will: Adherence to Precedent on the U.S. Supreme Court.* Cambridge: Cambridge University Press.

———. 2002. *The Supreme Court and the Attitudinal Model Revisited.* New York: Cambridge University Press.

Segal, Jeffrey Allan, Harold J. Spaeth, and Sara Benesh. 2005. *The Supreme Court in the American Legal System.* Cambridge, UK: Cambridge University Press.

Shapiro, Carolyn. 2009. "Bringing Law to the Empirical Analysis of the Supreme Court." *Hastings Law Journal* 60: 477–540.

Sheehan, Reginald S. 1990. "Administrative Agencies and the Court: A Reexamination of the Impact of Agency Type of Decisional Outcomes." *Western Political Quarterly* 43: 875–85.

Smith, Gordon. 1996. *Reforming the Russian Legal System.* Cambridge, UK: Cambridge University Press.

Smith, Rogers M. 1994. "Remarks, Symposium on *Supreme Court and the Attitudinal Model*." *Law and Courts: Newsletter of the Law and Courts Section of the American Political Science Association* 4: 8–9.

Songer, Donald R., and Stefanie A. Lindquist. 1996. "Not the Whole Story: The Impact of

Justices' Values on Supreme Court Decision Making." *American Journal of Political Science:* 40: 1049–63.

Spaeth, Harold J., and Jeffery A. Segal. 1999. *Majority Rule or Minority Will: Adherence to Precedent on the U.S. Supreme Court.* New York: Cambridge University Press.

Spiller, Pablo T., and Rafael Gely. 2008. "Strategic Judicial Decision-Making." In Keith E. Whittington, R. Daniel Kelemen, and Gregory A. Caldeira, eds., *The Oxford Handbook of Law and Politics.* Oxford: Oxford University Press.

Spriggs, James F., II, and Thomas G. Hansford. 2002. "The U.S. Supreme Court's Incorporation and Interpretation of Precedent." *Law and Society Review* 36: 139–60.

Sunstein, Cass R. 1999. *One Case at a Time: Judicial Minimalism on the Supreme Court.* Cambridge, MA: Harvard University Press.

Tamanaha, Brian Z. 2009. "The Distorting Slant in Quantitative Studies of Judging." *Boston College Law Review* 50: 685–758.

Wahlbeck, Paul J. 1997. "The Life of the Law: Judicial Politics and Legal Change." *Journal of Politics* 59: 778–802.

7   Stare Decisis as Reciprocity Norm

Stefanie A. Lindquist

L IKE ACTORS in other governmental institutions, judges within appellate courts are subject to their own unique set of governing norms and practices. Many of these norms are formal in nature, involving specific statutory, constitutional, or procedural rules that regulate or proscribe jurisdiction, appellate procedure, and judicial tenure and selection. In addition to these formal norms, however, courts also develop informal norms that similarly constrain judicial actors to the extent that they produce shared expectations about appropriate behavior. Examples of such informal norms at the U.S. Supreme Court include secrecy during deliberations, the Rule of Four, and opinion assignment procedures (O'Brien 1999; Epstein and Knight 1998). These informal norms do not require governmental or other external enforcement to ensure cooperation because other mechanisms often exist that allow participants to monitor and sanction defectors and thus to maintain the norm at some level. In that sense, they constitute an equilibrium outcome among participants (Knight 1992).

Among the most important informal norms within collegial courts are those that involve consensual decision-making. Such consensual norms govern judges' propensity to write dissenting or concurring opinions that publicize their disagreements (see Caldeira and Zorn 1998; Narayan and Smyth 2005), as well as their willingness to adhere to existing precedent (Rasmusen 1994; Spaeth and Segal 1999; Hansford and Spriggs 2006). These norms may emerge because of a shared commitment to the rule of law or to institutional legitimacy. They may also exist, however, because policy-oriented judges, motivated to ensure that their own precedents are respected, are able to promote the norm by encouraging certain shared expectations and by creating incentives regarding adherence to those expectations.

The extent to which judges adhere to the consensual norm of stare decisis has particularly important implications for institutional legitimacy and authority. According to the norm, judges must follow principles of law enunciated in prior court decisions and apply them in all future cases that involve substantially similar facts.[1] Occasional departures from precedent are justified when they allow judges to alter unsound or unjust legal doctrines that are no longer consistent with prevailing social or economic conditions, even in the absence of legislative intervention (Cardozo 1921; Levi 1949). As with dissent, however, frequent departures from the norm may have detrimental consequences for the judiciary and for the public good. The norm of stare decisis promotes private ordering of citizens' affairs by enabling them to plan their social and economic transactions with confidence that they act in compliance with existing law (Eskridge and Frickey 1994, 568; Hanssen 1999). Stare decisis also encourages private settlement of disputes by discouraging individuals from forum and judge shopping, furthers fair and efficient adjudication by sparing litigants the need to relitigate (and judges the need to reconsider) every issue in every case, and discourages a rush of litigation whenever a change of personnel occurs on the bench. Thus, stare decisis serves important functions that bolster institutional legitimacy. Where judges frequently reject existing precedent, the potential adverse institutional and social consequences are great. As Epstein and Knight observe in the context of the U.S. Supreme Court:

> To the extent that members of a community base their future expectations on the belief that others will follow existing laws, the Court has an interest in minimizing the disruptive effects of overturning existing rules of behavior. If the Court makes a radical change, the community may not be able to adapt, resulting in a decision that does not produce an efficacious rule (1998, 164).

Because consensual norms within courts therefore have significant ramifications for the effective operation of judicial institutions and the rule of law, it is important that we understand the manner in which these norms develop and the institutional structures that are likely to sustain them.[2] To do so, however, requires a theory that convincingly explains why cooperative norms emerge in judiciaries and that enables researchers to generate falsifiable hypotheses regarding the development and maintenance of those norms such that empirical evaluation is possible. This objective also requires research within a comparative institutional context because institutional rules and structures are likely to have a significant impact on the evolution and stability of cooperative norms.[3] Since the state supreme courts vary significantly on a wide variety of institutional characteristics, they offer an ideal natural laboratory to evaluate how institutions affect the development of consensual norms such as stare decisis. In ways that will become clear, the varied institutional structures that characterize these courts have the potential to shape the development and strength of cooperative norms within them. Their study could thus result in observations that shed light on the evolution and stability of cooperation within alternative governmental institutions, which has been described as "an issue of foremost importance for the science of politics" (Bendor and Swistak 1997, 290).

A Theory of Precedent as Consensual Norm

Strategic models of judging provide a promising starting point for researchers interested in understanding how individual preferences interact with institutional constraints to promote the development of consensual norms (Axelrod 1984). Cooperative norms often play an important role in solving social dilemmas, which "occur whenever individuals in interdependent situations face choices in which the maximization of short-term self interest yields outcomes leaving all participants worse off than feasible alternatives" (Ostrom 1998, 1; see also Posner 1993). Such a dilemma may arise in the context of judicial decision-making on collegial appellate courts. Assuming that judges are primarily motivated by their personal policy preferences (see Schauer 1997; Epstein and Knight 1998), each judge on a collegial court thus wishes to vote in accordance with her own policy preferences regardless of existing precedent. A completely sincere judge, motivated by her own preferences, will therefore choose the outcome she prefers ideologically, even if doing so would require the invalidation of a conflicting precedent. If all judges choose to follow their own policy preferences in this way, however, then any existing precedents, including those produced by judges serving on the court, are vulnerable to similar invalidation. Judges are thus faced with a social dilemma of the kind described by Ostrom. If judges maximize their own self-interest by sincerely voting to further their own policy preferences in the short term regardless of conflicting precedent, they create an environment in which their own precedential opinions are similarly vulnerable to invalidation in the long run. Or, in game theoretic terms, individual rationality drives each judge to defect in the short term, thus achieving an equilibrium that would substantially undermine, if not eliminate, individual adherence to stare decisis. This equilibrium is suboptimal for all players/judges in the long run, however, who ultimately desire to have their preferences preserved and followed as precedent in the future.[4]

Reciprocity norms develop as one means people can develop to cope with social dilemmas that result in suboptimal benefits for the group. One mechanism to sustain cooperation, for example, is repeated play. Iterated interactions allow the players to establish strategies that achieve cooperation to the extent that the value of long-term cooperation is sufficiently large for each player. "If the value of future cooperation is large and exceeds what can be gained in the short term by cheating, then the long-term individual interests of the players can automatically and tacitly keep them from cheating, without the need for any additional punishments or enforcements by third parties" (Dixit and Skeath 1999, 257). When the game is infinitely repeated or where it extends for indeterminate duration, players who defect in early rounds can be "punished" with defection in subsequent rounds, while players who cooperate can be "rewarded" with cooperation. On the other hand, where the relationship between the players is of a fixed and known length, the rational strategic move in the last round is to defect (as no benefit from cooperation can accrue in future rounds)—this will create a rollback or unraveling effect that produces cheating to the very first round of play.

In appellate courts, the probability of rollback may depend on the institutional arrangements that structure judges' interactions over time. Under some institutional arrangements, judges may not know for certain how long their interaction will continue, such that the game is likely to continue only with some probability. Where the game is likely to continue with low probability (that is, where judges hold their seats for shorter periods because they are vulnerable to electoral constraints), judges are more likely to discount the benefits of future cooperation in comparison to the contemporary payoffs associated with votes that conform to their own personal preferences rather than to precedent. This simple model highlights the importance of judges' perception of the endpoint to the game they are playing with their colleagues on the bench, which may be shaped by institutional rules regarding judicial selection and tenure length. Other institutional factors are also relevant to the norm's development in appellate courts, including court size: collegial courts involve the potential cooperation or defection of up to nine players (for courts in the United States).

Drawing on the literature explaining cartel behavior, O'Hara (1993) suggests that cartels are commonly understood to have an optimal membership size because it is harder to monitor the decision-making behavior of cartel members that form a larger group. In the case of judicial decision-making, judges who sit on a large collegial court may have more difficulty "keeping track" of the cooperative or defecting behavior of all court members, which would make it more difficult for them to punish or reward defectors over the long term. Even if monitoring difficulties are not the problem, Posner (1993) argues that judges on larger courts will experience greater incentives to "free-ride" on their fellow judges' adherence to stare decisis because they are more likely to believe that their own individual behavior will have little effect on the practice of stare decisis followed by court members generally.

These parameters offer a basis upon which to evaluate adherence to precedent empirically by isolating variables that reflect their values in the real world. In that sense, the model provides a useful theoretical tool for evaluating stare decisis and may be used to generate hypotheses concerning judges' decisions to defy stare decisis by overruling precedent. The hypotheses developed below specifically concern the propensity of courts to overrule precedent, an event that reflects a clear deviation from the norm of stare decisis.[5] They also focus on adherence to precedent in state supreme courts, where institutional variation allows for the testing of the hypothesized relationships between institutional characteristics and overruling behavior.

First, the repeated game theoretic model highlights the idea that justices will cooperate and respect other colleagues' prior doctrinal pronouncements when they expect to engage in repeated interactions with those colleagues. The model points out the potential unraveling effect when judges on the same court have knowledge of a specific or probable endpoint to their service with other judges. In those situations, judges are less likely to cooperate with their colleagues' decisions because they will discount the benefits of future cooperation more severely. On the other hand, where judges serve in longer terms, have life tenure, or where the probability of retirement is less certain, this unraveling effect should be less pronounced. Thus judges may make calculations regarding their willingness to adhere to the norm in light of the average tenure length of justices sitting on the court. More specifically, the theory leads to the expectation that average tenure on a court will be inversely related to the frequency of overruling behavior in state supreme courts because longer judicial tenure will promote consensus and cooperation, rather than dissensus and defection.

This proposition is supported by an early study of the Rhode Island Supreme Court (Beiser 1974), where justices serve for life. Beiser found that Rhode Island justices followed a strong norm of acquiescence to their brethren's opinions. Similarly, Skeel (1999) found that the opinions of the Delaware Supreme Court, where justices serve relatively long twelve-year terms, are characterized by strong unanimity. The U.S. Supreme Court obviously provides a clear counterpoint to these examples, however, since over time, consensual norms on that court have become increasingly lax even as the justices enjoy lifetime tenure (see Caldeira and Zorn 1998).

An additional hypothesis stems from the idea that while judge tenure length may be important, even in states with legally mandated shorter terms, justices may have little expectation that their colleagues will leave the bench because the seats are not subject to electoral competition. In these states, risks to tenure are lessened and the unraveling effect should be less pronounced, promoting cooperation rather than dissensus. Brace and Hall (1993) have shown that when state justices are selected by partisan ballot in states with high levels of electoral competition, the justices may dissent more frequently in certain contexts. Of course, elected judges also face countervailing pressures that do not affect appointed judges. Judges subject to electoral constraints must attend to constituency preferences that may strain their commitment to precedent when existing precedent is inconsistent with constituent expectations. For these reasons, it is expected that elected, as opposed to appointive, systems will more likely promote the overruling of court precedents.

Finally, the model implicitly predicts that court size may have an impact on the strength of stare decisis among judges on any given court. Since state supreme courts do vary from a minimum of five authorized seats to a maximum of nine seats, the theory predicts that justices on state supreme courts with nine seats will overrule precedent more often than those serving on courts with seven or five seats.[6]

Evaluating a Strategic Account of Adherence to Precedent

To test the hypotheses set forth above, data were gathered to measure the frequency of state supreme court decisions overruling existing case law in each year over the period from 1975 to 2004.[7] The data include only those decisions that reflect violations of intertemporal stare decisis; overruling actions by the state legislature (that is, superseding by statute) or by the U.S. Supreme Court are excluded.

From a descriptive standpoint, the data reveal considerable variation across the state courts in terms of their propensity to overrule precedent. Figures 7.1a–1d on pages 180–81 enable comparison of the mean and median values on the frequency of overruling decisions across the states, by region. Over the thirty-year period presented in the dot plots, it appears that some states overruled existing precedent very infrequently, while others were quite active. In the Midwest, the Illinois Supreme Court almost never overruled precedent; its mean and median counts are both close to zero. Nebraska and Ohio, on the other hand, overruled more than six precedents per year on average. Northeastern states demonstrate less variation, with values clustering between zero and three for all states. Means and medians for the Western states reflect greater dispersion. Montana and Washington are particularly distinguished in terms of their propensity to overrule; in the case of Montana, this proclivity to overrule precedent has been recognized and criticized in the literature (Renz 2004). Southern states are also remarkably varied, with Texas (Criminal) and Alabama leading the pack with the largest median overrulings over the period (close to ten for Alabama, almost fifteen for Texas). These findings comport with existing research demonstrating a high rate of overruling behavior in Alabama (Lindquist and Pybas 1998).

What explains these variations? The theoretical model and research hypotheses presented above directed attention to several variables of particular interest, including tenure length, selection method, and court size. To test whether these variables were related to a court's propensity to overrule precedent, the number of overrulings in each state court in each year from 1975 to 2004 was regressed on the following measures: (1) Tenure Length, measured as the average number of years served by sitting justices on each supreme court per year; (2) Selection Method, measured as a dummy variable reflecting whether the state's formal selection mechanism involves (a) legislative or gubernatorial appointment (the reference category), (b) merit selection, (c) nonpartisan election, or (d) partisan election; and (3) Court Size, measured as the number of authorized seats on each court per year. These variables are the primary focus of the analysis in this chapter.

Of course, a number of important alternative explanations may exist for relatively high or low rates of overruling decisions. Primary among them is ideological change on the court; ample evidence exists at the U.S. Supreme Court that ideological change on the Court drives overruling behavior (Brenner and Spaeth 1995). Thus, the model includes a measure of absolute value of the ideo-

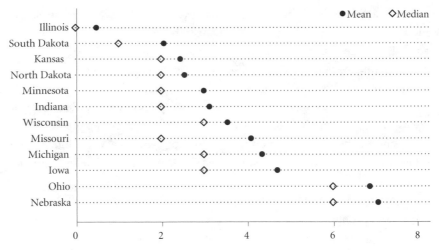

A. Midwestern States

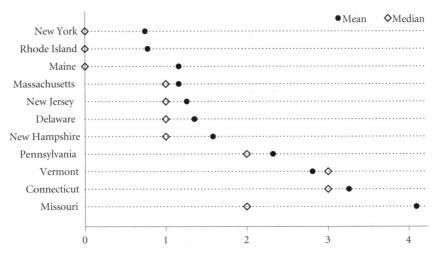

B. Northeastern States

FIG. 7.1. Mean/Median Frequency of Overrulings in Midwestern, Northeastern, Western, and Southern States, 1975–2004

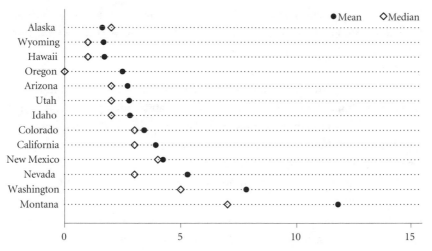

C. Western States

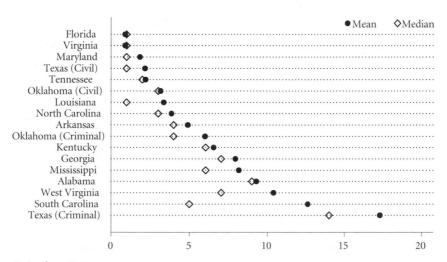

D. Southern States

logical change in each court's median ("PAJID") Scores[8] over the previous year.[9] In addition, the chief justice may be in a position to apply rewards and sanctions to individual members that promote adherence to precedent (compare Brace and Hall 1993). To account for this potential influence, the model incorporates a variable reflecting the extent to which the chief justice exercises discretion over opinion assignment, measured as a dummy variable coded as one if the chief justice has exclusive authority to assign the majority opinion and 0 otherwise.

Further variables must also be controlled. First, court dockets differ in terms of the mixture of cases on their agenda and their caseloads. To control for these differences, a dummy variable was added to the model reflecting the presence or absence of an intermediate appellate court. Where an intermediate court exists, supreme court justices typically exercise greater discretion to choose the cases on their dockets. This discretionary docket may lead to increased overruling behavior controlling for other factors, as justices in states with intermediate appellate courts may exercise their certiorari jurisdiction to identify cases as vehicles for legal change. Professionalization of the judiciary may also affect overruling behavior if professionalization carries with it an increased concern for institutional legitimacy. As a proxy for professionalization, therefore, the model includes a measure of the number of law clerks assigned to each associate justice. Increasing assistance by law clerks may cut both ways, of course, if these newly minted lawyers press their justices to innovate or provide justices with the necessary leisure time to craft opinions that change the legal status quo. As for caseload itself, a direct measure of the number of cases on each court's docket per year would be ideal. Unfortunately, comparable data across courts for the years analyzed here is extremely difficult to acquire.[10] For that reason, the model includes a control for state population, which is highly correlated with total supreme court filings ($r = .75$) for the years and states in which caseload date is available and reliable. Caseload mix may also be affected by the demographic characteristics of the states; a variable was therefore included in the model to reflect the level of urbanization in each state. Finally, the opportunity to overrule precedents may depend on the available pool of precedents in each state. To account for differences in the number of precedents available for review and invalidation, a measure reflecting the age of the state was incorporated into the model as well.

Furthermore, state supreme court justices' responsiveness to precedent may be affected by the state's political environment. Where the state legislature is highly professional and active, for example, obsolete judicial decisions may be

superseded by statute, obviating the need for the court to overrule its own decisions. For that reason, the model controls for legislative professionalism in each
state based on a measure developed by Squire (2007). Other institutional constraints may affect the justices' behavior as well. Where constitutional amendments are easily obtained, it may affect the justices' adherence to precedent,
either because it narrows their policy-making authority or because they must
overturn precedent to bring judicial doctrines into conformity with changing
constitutional principles. For that reason, a measure of the rate of constitutional amendment in each state since 1975, created by Donald Lutz (1994), was
included in the model. Finally, regional effects were controlled with dummy
variables reflecting the state's geographic location, with the South omitted as
the reference category.

In the model of overruled decisions per year, the dependent variable constitutes a count of the number of such decisions truncated at zero; as such,
it conforms to a poisson distribution. Given overdispersion in the data, the
model was fitted using negative binomial regression (NBMR), with fixed effects
for each state. Although a number of the control variables achieved statistical
significance, only the variables of interest (court size, tenure length, and selection method) are discussed below.[11]

Results

Tenure Length, Court Size, Selection Method
The model provides preliminary support for the hypothesis that longer tenure
lengths promote more stable precedent. This measure evaluates the notion that
justices may structure their behavior in relation to the likelihood of continued
interaction with their colleagues currently on the bench. Note that this measure
is superior to one based solely on formal term length, since even in states with
short terms, competition for seats may be minimal. In contrast, the tenure variable measures the *actual average tenure* experienced by justices in each court.
As tenure length increases, the number of cases overruled decreases.

In addition to tenure length, court size is also significantly associated with
overruling behavior, suggesting a free rider effect on the cooperative norm.
Richard Posner noted this possibility in 1993. In discussing adherence to precedent, he observed that a serious free rider problem exists but that members
of higher courts "are few enough to be concerned about the impact of their
behavior with respect to precedent on the survival of the practice of decision

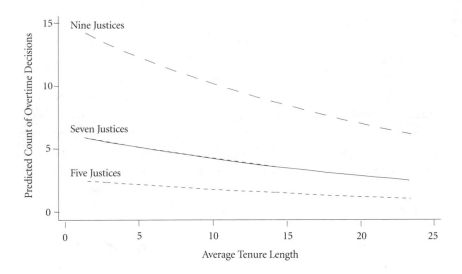

FIG. 7.2. Court Size by Tenure Length

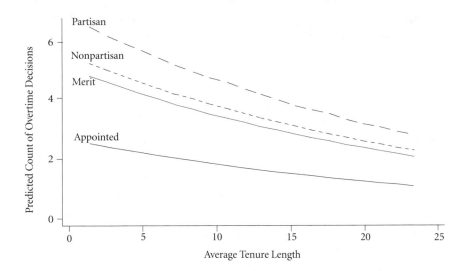

FIG. 7.3. Selection Method by Tenure Length

according to precedent in their jurisdiction" (1993, 18 n. 30). He added a caveat, however: "We might expect, therefore, that a comparison of the different state supreme courts (which differ in size) would show that the smaller the court, the less frequently it overrules its previous decisions" (ibid.). In fact, this hypothesis is strongly supported in the data. Larger courts overrule precedent more frequently.

Figure 7.2 provides a graphical depiction of the impact of court size on overruling frequency, controlling for tenure length. To create the figure, all other variables were held at their means. Note the substantively large impact of moving from a court with five or seven justices to one with nine justices. It appears that the addition of two judges to a seven-member court has the potential to significantly alter justices' willingness to adhere to existing precedent. In addition, the graph illustrates that tenure length has the more pronounced influence on these larger courts; justices' overruling behavior on smaller courts seems impervious to considerations regarding the time horizon on service with fellow judges on the bench.

Selection method also plays an important role in terms of the stability of precedent. Partisan elected courts are far more likely to overturn existing precedent than courts selected by other methods. This finding stands in interesting contrast to Hanssen's conclusions based on appeal rates in state supreme courts. Hanssen (1999) concluded that appeal rates in elected states are significantly lower than in other states because litigants are able to predict case outcomes based on ideological or partisan cues created by these selection mechanisms. The findings in this study support Hanssen's conclusions to the extent that they show that elected judges are less willing to allow precedent to bind their decisions. In this sense, their behavior may be quite predictable on ideological grounds. Figure 7.3 graphically illustrates the relationship between selection method, tenure length, and overruling behavior, holding all other variables constant at their means, and demonstrates the profound influence selection method exercises over adherence to precedent.

Discussion

These findings provide some empirical support for the strategic model of overruling behavior. The data support the hypothesis that court size, tenure length, and selection method, in particular, will influence courts' adherence to the norm of stare decisis. At this point, however, it is important to pause and consider alternative explanations for these results. With respect to judges selected by partisan election, it is very possible that selection effects explain the results found here. Posner has observed that adherence to judicial norms is part of the judicial "game": "[If] you don't obey them, you're not playing the judicial 'game.'" According to Judge Posner, the rules of the game are imparted in law school, and "judicial selection procedures select for persons who *want* to play the judicial game rather than some other game, such as partisan politics" (1997, 365). Yet judges elected via partisan ballot may indeed be playing the game of partisan politics and may be less willing to adhere to precedent as a result. In their study of elected and appointed courts, Choi, Gulati, and E. Posner find that elected judges make more campaign contributions and are more likely to have gone to law school in a lower-ranked law school in the state in which they sit (2010, 327). According to these authors, elected judges "are more like politicians and less like professionals" (ibid.). Perhaps we should not be surprised that they overturn precedent more often. The influence of selection method, therefore, may itself be due to selection bias in that *certain types of judges* are more likely to participate in judicial elections.

As for the influence of tenure length, one explanation is that cooperative norms are more likely to form when judges expect to serve longer terms with each other, thus providing the sanctioning opportunities for those judges seeking to enforce the norm. At the same time, however, the impact of this variable may have a simpler explanation: where judges serve for longer periods with each other, they are more likely to have participated in the production of precedent with which they continue to agree over time. Courts with stable judiciaries are more likely to produce stable precedent. This latter explanation is undermined to some extent, however, by the model's control for ideological change on the court.

The variable reflecting court size is less amenable to alternative explanations. It is difficult to conceptualize why court size should be related to overruling behavior except through reference to free rider considerations. Controlling for other factors, court size is positively related to the propensity to overrule. This result is most easily explained in reference to the collective action problems experienced by larger groups.

In total, the model provides some preliminary support for the strategic model of precedent, but it is not dispositive. Adherence to the norm of stare decisis may depend in part on institutional mechanisms or structures that enable judges to promote cooperation and sanction defectors, as suggested by

the theory. Nevertheless, reasonable alternative explanations exist for the influence of at least some of the variables in the model. Yet the results do indicate
clearly that the strength of stare decisis is affected by a number of institutional
and contextual factors, whether or not their influence is specifically related to
strategic behavior by individual judges. In that sense, the model highlights the
importance of institutional structures to the development of consensual behaviors within courts.

From a normative perspective, interpretation of these results may depend
on one's perspective regarding the value of stare decisis. Social science cannot
assist observers in drawing conclusions about optimal levels of adherence to
the norm. Stability and predictability in the rule of law are certainly valuable,
but so is the law's adaptation to changing circumstances. To the extent that one
values strong adherence to precedent, institutional structures that favor that
result include judicial appointment with longer tenure lengths and a smaller
court. On the other hand, for those who prefer legal rules that reflect the preferences of constituents and that are more easily adapted to change, different
institutional structures are preferable.

That having been said, this research provides only a starting point for considering the influence of institutional structures on adherence to stare decisis. Because the available data is limited at this point to aggregate measures of
court performance, the study's results must be interpreted as provisional only.
Judge-level and case-level data is likely to shed additional light on the influences that shape the development of this important reciprocity norm in appellate courts. Strategic accounts of human behavior begin with clearly specified assumptions about the content and ordering of personal preferences and
generate empirical predictions derived from those axiomatic principles. These
models of rational behavior typically focus on the probability of cooperation
among strategic actors given certain contextual constraints, thus making them
uniquely promising for the analysis of consensual norms on collegial courts. In
particular, strategic models assume that rational decision-makers (1) have and
are aware of their own preferences, and (2) understand any limitations on their
ability to realize their preferred outcome, including formal institutional rules
and the anticipated actions of other participants in the decision-making process. Game theorists in political science have highlighted the extent to which
formal institutional constraints or rules and the anticipated actions of other
participants structure strategic interactions among political actors. Indeed, the
notion that institutional constraints structure the strategic interactions among

judicial actors has gained a strong foothold in political science studies of the courts (see Epstein and Knight 1998; Rogers, Flemming and Bond 2006).[12] This study contributes additional evidence to the discussion over the relationship between strategic decision making and institutional norms within courts.

Notes

Funding for this research was provided by the National Science Foundation, SES #0550618. For their helpful comments on this chapter, I thank Mitu Gulati, Eric Posner, Eric Rasmusen, Neil Siegel, Lee Epstein, Emerson Tiller and the participants in a Law and Economics Workshop at Northwestern University. Thanks also go to John Hudak, Jenna Lukasik, Travis Shrout and Marina Ghulyan for their research assistance.

1. Stare decisis may take several forms. For example, "hierarchical" stare decisis refers to the obligation of lower courts to follow the decisions of courts situated at a higher level in the court hierarchy (Songer, Segal, and Cameron 1994). Stare decisis may also refer to the self-imposed obligation of judges on a single court to adhere to the earlier precedents of that same court, which has been labeled "intertemporal *stare decisis*" (Stearns 1995, 789 n. 8). Intertemporal stare decisis describes the adherence to precedent practiced by the U.S. Supreme Court and by state supreme courts, which occupy the highest positions within the federal and state judicial systems.

2. What constitutes "optimal" levels of dissent or overruling is beyond the scope of this chapter. Correlations between trust in the courts and consensus levels, however, can be measured empirically and would be a worthy topic for future research. For an assessment of institutional variables (judicial selection methods) on appeal rates, which implicates these ideas, see Hanssen (1999).

3. Formal institutional structures serve to shape or produce certain equilibria within collective decision-making arrangements (Greif 1998; Knight 1992; Shepsle 1979).

4. For an extended game theoretic account of precedent based on prisoners' dilemma, see Rasmusen (1994) and O'Hara (1993).

5. Some may object that overruling is not the only means to invalidate or undermine a precedent; precedent may be undermined with consistent negative treatment, for example. This observation is correct and would be problematic to the current study if the states differed systematically in terms of such implicit deviations from precedent. At this point, no evidence exists that the states do differ systematically on this dimension; future research might focus on this question.

6. Studies of dissenting behavior have drawn conflicting results when assessing the impact of court size on the development of consensual decision-making. Hall and Brace (1989) found that court size was unrelated to rates of dissent, while Glick and Vines (1973) found that court size was related to patterns of dissent. More recent studies have found a positive correlation between dissenting behavior and court size on U.S. courts of appeals (Lindquist 2007).

7. These data were collected from Westlaw by (1) downloading all citations (in excess of 2 million cites) to decisions rendered by the (fifty-two) state supreme courts over the entire course of their histories, (2) reformatting those citations using Perl programming language to create efficient input files for Westcheck, (3) submitting the files to Westcheck, (4) parsing the Westcheck output to identify all red flagged cases and the decisions overruling those case in whole or in part, and (5) generating a comprehensive database of all overruled and overruling decisions for all states across all years. I am grateful to Charles Keckler for the prototype of the programs that enabled this data collection process.

8. PAJID scores were created by Paul Brace, Laura Langer, and Melinda Hall (2000) based on elite and citizen ideology in the judges' state at the time of appointment or election, adjusted for party identification. The scores range from 0 to 100, with larger values associated with increased liberalism.

9. In addition to average tenure length, a variable was incorporated in the model measuring the standard deviation of the tenure length of the individual justices sitting on the court.

10. The National Center for State Courts compiles such data, but the states report the information in different formats and occasionally fail to report it altogether.

11. Model results and descriptive statistics are available on request from the author.

12. As Epstein and Knight have described the rational choice perspective, strategic justices "realize that their ability to achieve their goals depends on a consideration of the preferences of others, of the choices they expect others to make, and of the institutional context in which they act" (1998, xiii).

References

Axelrod, Robert. 1984. *The Evolution of Cooperation*. New York: Basic Books.

Beiser, Edward N. 1974. "The Rhode Island Supreme Court: A Well-Integrated Political System." *Law and Society Review* 8: 167–86.

Bendor, Jonathan, and Piotr Swistak. 1997. "The Evolutionary Stability of Cooperation." *American Political Science Review* 91: 290–307.

Brace, Paul, and Melinda Gann Hall. 1990. "Neo-Institutionalism and Dissent in State Supreme Courts." *Journal of Politics* 53: 54–70.

———. 1993. "Integrated Models of Judicial Dissent." *Journal of Politics* 55: 914–35.

Brace, Paul, Laura Langer, and Melinda Gann Hall. 2000. "Measuring the Preferences of State Supreme Court Justices." *Journal of Politics* 62: 387–413.

Brenner, Saul, and Harold Spaeth. 1995. *Stare Indecisis: The Alteration of Precedent on the Supreme Court, 1946–1992*. Cambridge: Cambridge University Press.

Caldeira, Gregory, and Christopher C. W. Zorn. 1998. "Of Time and Consensual Norms in the Supreme Court." *American Journal of Political Science* 42: 874–902.

Cardozo, Benjamin. 1921. *The Nature of the Judicial Process*. New Haven: Yale University Press.

Choi, Stephen J., Mitu Gulati, and Eric A. Posner. 2010. "Professionals or Politicians: The Uncertain Empirical Case for an Elected Rather than Appointed Judiciary." *Journal of Law, Economics and Organization* 27(1): 290–336.

Dixit, Avinash, and Susan Skeath. 1999. *Games of Strategy*. New York, NY: W. W. Norton and Co.

Epstein, Lee, and Jack Knight. 1998. *The Choices Justices Make*. Washington DC: Congressional Quarterly Press.

Eskridge, William N., Jr., and Philip P. Frickey, eds. 1994. *Hart and Sack's The Legal Process: Basic Problems in the Making and Application of Law*. Westbury, NY: Foundation Press.

Glick, Henry R., and Kenneth N. Vines. 1973. *State Court Systems*. Englewood Cliffs NJ: Prentice-Hall.

Greif, Avner. 1998. "Historical and Comparative Institutional Analysis." *American Economic Review* 88(2):80–84.

Hall, Melinda Gann, and Paul Brace. 1989. "Order in the Courts: A Neo-Institutional Approach to Judicial Consensus." *Western Political Quarterly* 42: 391–407.

———. 1992. "Toward an Integrated Model of Judicial Voting Behavior." *American Politics Quarterly* 20: 147–68.

———. 1999. "State Supreme Courts and Their Environments: Avenues to General Theories of Judicial Choice," in Cornell Clayton and Howard Gillman, eds., *Supreme Court Decision Making: New Institutionalist Approaches*. Chicago: University of Chicago Press.

Hansford, Thomas, and James F. Spriggs II. 2006. *The Politics of Precedent on the United States Supreme Court*. Princeton: Princeton University Press.

Hanssen, F. Andrew. 1999. "The Effect of Judicial Institutions on Uncertainty and the Rate of Litigation: The Election versus Appointment of State Judges." *Journal of Legal Studies* 28: 205–32.

Knight, Jack. 1992. *Institutions and Social Conflict*. Cambridge: Cambridge University Press.

Levi, Edward H. 1949. *An Introduction to Legal Reasoning*. Chicago: University of Chicago Press.

Lindquist, Stefanie A. 2007. "Bureaucratization and Balkanization on the United States Courts of Appeals: The Origins and Effects of Decision Making Norms in the Federal Appellate Courts." *University of Richmond Law Review* 41: 659–705.

Lindquist, Stefanie, and Kevin Pybas. 1998. "State Supreme Court Decisions to Overrule Precedent, 1965–1996." *Justice System Journal* 20: 17–27.

Lutz, Donald. 1994. "Toward a Theory of Constitutional Amendment." *American Political Science Review* 88: 355–70.

Narayan, Paresh Kumar, and Russell Smyth. 2005. "The Consensual Norm on the High Court of Australia." *International Political Science Review* 26, no. 2: 147–68.

O'Brien, David. 1999. "Institutional Norms and Supreme Court Opinions: On Reconsidering the Rise of Individual Opinions," in Cornell W. Clayton and Howard Gillman, eds., *Supreme Court Decision Making: New Institutionalist Approaches*. Chicago: University of Chicago Press.

O'Hara, Erin. 1993. "Social Constraint or Implicit Collusion?: Toward a Game Theoretic Analysis of Stare Decisis." Reprinted in Maxwell Stearn, ed. 1997. *Public Choice and Public Law: Readings and Commentary.* Cincinnati, OH: Anderson Publishing Co.

Ostrom, Elinor. 1998. "A Behavioral Approach to the Rational Choice Theory of Collective Action." *American Political Science Review* 92: 1–22.

Posner, Richard A. 1997. "Social Norms and the Law: An Economic Approach." *The American Economic Review* 87(2): 365–69.

Posner, Richard A. 1993. "What Do Judges Maximize (The Same Thing That Everyone Else Does)?" *Supreme Court Economic Review* 3: 18–42.

Rasmusen, Eric. 1994. "Judicial Legitimacy as a Repeated Game." *Journal of Law, Economics and Organization* 10: 63–83.

Renz, Jeffrey. 2004. "Stare Decisis in Montana." *Montana Law Review* 65: 41–92.

Schauer, Frederick. 1997. "Judicial Incentives and the Design of Legal Institutions." Paper presented at the annual meeting of the American Political Science Association, Washington, DC.

Shepsle, Ken. 1979. "Institutional Arrangements and Equilibrium in Multidimensional Voting Models." *American Political Science Review* 23: 27–60.

Sickels, Robert. 1965. "Illusion of Judicial Consensus: Zoning Decisions in the Maryland Court of Appeals." *American Political Science Review* 59: 100–104.

Skeel, David A., Jr. 1999. "The Unanimity Norm in Delaware Corporate Law." *University of Virginia Law Review* 83: 127–74.

Spaeth, Harold, and Jeffrey Segal. 1999. *Majority Rule or Minority Will?* Cambridge: Cambridge University Press.

Squire, Peverill. 2007. "Measuring Legislative Professionalism: The Squire Index Revisited." *State Politics and Policy Quarterly* 7: 211–27.

Songer, Donald R., Jeffrey A. Segal and Charles M. Cameron. 1994. "The Hierarchy of Justice: Testing a Principal-Agent Model of Supreme Court-Circuit Court Interactions." *American Journal of Political Science* 38(3): 673–96.

Stearns, Maxwell L. 1997. *Public Choice and Public Law: Readings and Commentary.* Cincinnati: Anderson Publishing Co.

III WHAT LAW HAS TO DO WITH WHAT JUDGES DO AND ITS IMPLICATIONS FOR JUDICIAL SELECTION

8 How Judicial Elections Are Like Other Elections and What That Means for the Rule of Law

Matthew J. Streb

GEORGETOWN UNIVERSITY law professor Roy Schotland (1985, 78) famously quipped that judicial elections were becoming "noisier, nastier, and costlier." Schotland was ahead of the curve, because the conventional wisdom at the time of his writing was that judicial elections were primarily sleepy affairs that looked little like elections for other offices.[1] Almost twenty years after Schotland's writing, the Brennan Center for Justice, with the Justice at Stake Campaign and the National Institute on Money in State Politics, issued a report documenting a "new politics of judicial elections" (Goldberg et al. 2002). Observers of the courts were alarmed by this report (and four subsequent reports), precisely because judicial elections seemed to have many of the same characteristics as other elected contests, especially regarding the costs and tone of the elections. To reform organizations like the Brennan Center, the fact that judicial elections were "noisier, nastier, and costlier" threatened to undermine judicial independence and the integrity of the courts.

Although many works have documented the politicization of judicial elections in recent years, few have thoroughly compared the characteristics of judicial elections to elections for other offices—namely, the U.S. Congress and state legislatures. From a public law perspective this relationship is important, because it provides a better understanding of the selection method to the state courts used in part by thirty-nine states. This comparison may be even more interesting to scholars of political behavior, because of the low-information nature of most judicial elections. It is possible that scholars' findings regarding legislative elections, especially those for Congress, do not hold for judicial elections. Because of the low visibility of most judicial elections, candidates, campaigns, and voters may not look or act the same as in races for higher profile offices.

Beginning largely with the work of Hall (2001a), scholars started to analyze judicial elections more systematically on a variety of subjects. As a result, there is a much better understanding today regarding the characteristics of judicial elections and how they compare to elections for other offices. In this chapter, I tie this research together to present a comprehensive view of what scholars know about judicial elections and how those findings are similar or dissimilar to elections for other offices. In other words, what is the conventional wisdom concerning election to other offices, and does it hold for judicial elections? Topics covered include contestation, competition, and electoral success; campaign spending and the effects of money; the involvement of interest groups and political parties; and who votes and how they make their voting decisions.

The traditional view that judicial elections, especially those for the states' high courts, are mostly sleepy affairs has been debunked. Indeed, judicial elections do share many of the same characteristics as elections for other offices. The parallels go far beyond the well-documented findings of the costs and negativity of judicial elections, but extend into other areas such as challenger quality, partisan involvement, and participation as well. The chapter concludes with a discussion of what these similarities mean for the legitimacy of the courts and the rule of law. Although the concerns about the increasing political nature of judicial elections affecting court legitimacy are mostly exaggerated, the fact that judges must face voters can undermine the rule of law and due process by forcing them to behave as strategic actors whose decisions may rest on a pending election. Therefore, states should consider alternatives to electing judges. However, given the popular support for electing judges, eliminating an electoral component to the state judicial selection process is unlikely. As a result, professional and reform organizations, such as the American Bar Association (ABA) and Justice at Stake, advocate "improving" judicial elections by making them nonpartisan. Yet the trend toward nonpartisan elections does not eliminate the worst aspects of judicial elections and creates additional problems. In short, if states are going to elect judges, they should be elected in partisan contests.

Contestation, Competition, and Electoral Success

Perhaps nothing is more crucial in a representative democracy than contested and competitive elections. As political theorist Dennis Thompson (2002, 6) writes, "A competitive struggle for the people's vote is for many political scientists and political theorists the very definition of democracy."[2] Competition promotes accountability (Griffin 2006), which increases the probability that citizens' voices will be heard. It should come as no surprise, then, that scholars have written numerous articles examining the conditions for contestation and competition in congressional and state legislative elections (for example, Jacobson 1989; Mondak 1995; Stone, Maisel, and Maestas 2004; Van Dunk 1997; Hogan 2004a).

Although volumes have been written on contestation and competition in legislative elections, few studies on the subject exist for judicial elections. As noted, the conventional wisdom regarding judicial elections was that judges were rarely challenged, and those who were rarely faced stiff competition (see Dubois 1980). To opponents of judicial elections, this result was to be celebrated, not bemoaned, because of the nature of the judiciary. If the probability of a judge's being challenged (or even defeated) was great, then judicial independence would be threatened. Judges would feel more pressure to rule with regard to public opinion than based on the facts of the case. Judges are different than legislators, and, while some accountability of judges is needed, electoral accountability should not trump independence.

The view that judicial elections, at least at the Supreme Court level, are largely uncontested and uncompetitive has been discredited largely because of the work of Hall (2001a; 2007a). Examining state Supreme Court elections from 1980 to 1995 (Hall 2001a) and in a later analysis through 2000 (Hall 2007a), she found that levels of contestation and competition were remarkably similar to those for the U.S. House of Representatives. Although House incumbents were more likely to face challengers than Supreme Court justices (84.9 percent to 58.1 percent), the results depend somewhat on whether the judicial election is partisan or nonpartisan. From 1996 to 2000, judges running in partisan elections were actually *more* likely to be challenged than House incumbents (Hall 2007a).

It is possible, however, that the old conventional wisdom regarding contestation at the Supreme Court level remains true for lower-level courts. After all, the Supreme Court is "the court of last resort," and may be viewed as more important and prestigious than trial or intermediate appellate courts (IAC). As a result, perhaps contestation rates in Supreme Court races are not representative of all judicial elections. To test for this possibility, Streb, Frederick, and LaFrance (2007) probe contestation rates for IAC elections from 2000 to 2006 and compare the results to elections for the U.S. House or state supreme courts. They find that the traditional view of judges running unopposed holds at the IAC level. Roughly 90 percent of House incumbents and 64.7 percent of Supreme Court justices were challenged over the course of the study, but only 26.6 percent of IAC judges faced an opponent.[3] Open seat IAC races were more likely to be contested than those that had an incumbent, but they still did not reach the levels of contestation for House or Supreme Court elections. Roughly 97 percent of House and 90 percent of Supreme Court open seat elections were contested, compared with only 64 percent of the IAC contests.

These descriptive analyses show similarities between Supreme Court and House elections regarding contestation, although not so when one considers IAC elections.[4] More rigorous analysis also indicates a significant degree of similarity between Supreme Court and legislative elections. One consistent finding of studies of legislative elections is that challengers are strategic actors; in other words, they assess the situation and determine when the probability of success is greatest (for example, Jacobson 1989; Van Dunk 1997). Normally, this time would be when an incumbent is not running for re-election (that is, open seats). However, incumbents who barely won their previous election may also be vulnerable and, as a result, strategic candidates should challenge them.

Constructing a model of contestation for Supreme Court elections, Hall and Bonneau (2006) find that Supreme Court challengers act strategically. Candidates who were in a difficult election the last time they ran—defined by Hall and Bonneau as receiving less than 60 percent of the vote—were significantly more likely to be challenged than those whose previous election was not competitive. Moreover, judges who had yet to be elected but obtained office by appointment because of death, resignation, or retirement—something that is quite common—were also significantly more likely to have an opponent. Streb and Frederick (2009) essentially replicate Hall and Bonneau's model at the IAC level and uncover analogous results.

Regarding contestation, then, legislative and judicial elections, especially at the Supreme Court level, are related. However, contestation is only half of the story. Simply because an incumbent is challenged does not mean that she will face a difficult re-election. The questions that remain are whether levels of competition in judicial elections are similar to those in legislative elections, and if the conditions that lead to competitive elections are the same.

In a nutshell, the answer is yes. In fact, contested judicial elections are actually slightly more competitive than contested elections to the U.S. House of Representatives. According to Hall's (2007a) data, the average incumbent representative in contested elections received 64.8 percent of the vote, a percentage higher than the 60 percent that is normally considered to be the mark of a competitive election. At the Supreme Court level, the average incumbent in a contested election garnered only 56.9 percent of the vote, an indication that the average contested Supreme Court election is competitive.

When contested, elections at the IAC level are remarkably competitive as well. Although incumbent IAC judges are not frequently challenged, those who are can expect a battle. IAC judges who are challenged face greater competition than their counterparts in U.S. House or Supreme Court elections (Streb, Frederick, and LaFrance 2007). While the average incumbent member of Congress and Supreme Court justice received 66.7 percent and 59.0 percent of the vote, respectively, from 2000 to 2006, the average IAC judge obtained only 54.6 percent of the vote over the same period.

Not only are levels of competition in contested appellate court and congressional elections similar, but the conditions that lead to competitive elections are comparable. As in legislative elections, the most vulnerable incumbents are more likely to be challenged and, not surprisingly, those elections are more likely to be competitive (Hall and Bonneau 2006; Streb and Frederick 2009).

Additionally, at least at the Supreme Court level, the quality of the challenger appears to matter as well. One of the most heavily documented empirical relationships regarding both elections to the U.S. Congress (Abramowitz 1988, 1991; Carson, Engstrom, and Roberts 2007; Jacobson 1989, 2004; Krasno 1994; Krasno and Green 1988) and the state legislatures (Van Dunk 1997) is that the quality of the challenger faced by the incumbent acts as a major determinant of his or her electoral fate.[5] The relationship between challenger quality and incumbent vote share also exists, to an extent, in judicial elections. Hall and Bonneau (2006) use the traditional measure of challenger quality (whether the candidate held prior office) and find that challengers in Supreme Court elections with experience on the bench perform almost 5 percentage points better than inexperienced candidates. However, no such relationship occurs at the IAC level (Streb and Frederick 2009). It is unclear why a variable that is so consistently significant for other offices does not have the same effect in lower appellate court elections. One possibility could be the even lower-information nature of these elections. IAC elections may fly so far below the public's radar that even the strongest challengers are virtually unknown. Without individual-level data, it is impossible to know if this is indeed the case.

Finally, contested and competitive elections are one thing, but whether a judge actually loses is another. Again, similarities exist between the defeat rates of incumbent legislators and judges. From 1980 to 2000, only 5.6 percent of all U.S. representatives were defeated. During the same time, roughly 9 percent of Supreme Court incumbents lost their seats. An astonishing 22.9 percent of justices running in partisan races were not re-elected (Hall 2007a). Similar defeat rates occurred at the IAC level between 2000 and 2006, as 7.8 percent of IAC judges lost re-election (Streb, Frederick, and LaFrance 2007).

The vulnerability of judges allows for another comparison of judicial and congressional elections. Although more work is needed on the subject, the incumbency advantage that exists in congressional elections appears to be slightly different in judicial elections. Congressional incumbents may benefit from their ability to bring home earmarks (Alvarez and Saving 1997; although, see Feldman and Jondrow 1984), perform casework (Fiorina 1977; Yiannakis 1981; although, see Johannes and McAdams 1981), and build a positive "home style" (Fenno 1978). Judges are not capable of providing such perks. Moreover, congressional incumbents may benefit from simple name recognition (Jacobson 2009), something that judges even at the Supreme Court level may not possess. However, one area in which the incumbency advantage seems similar is regarding candidate spending. As in legislative elections, incumbent judges spend substantially more than challengers (Bonneau 2007b).

In sum, legislative and Supreme Court elections share many of the same characteristics regarding questions of contestation, competition, and electoral success. Less overlap exists between IAC elections and legislative contests. As I explain in the concluding section, the levels of contestation and competition in judicial elections may force some judges to act strategically, which has implications for due process and the rule of law.

Campaign Spending and the Effects of Money

Perhaps the most controversial aspect of any election is the role of money. For some time, election reformers have worried about the influence of money in campaigns because of the fear that a representative's vote is for sale. In fact, in

Buckley v. Valeo (1976) the Supreme Court upheld individual contribution limits to candidates because of the concern over corruption, or at least the "appearance of corruption." The apprehension over the role of money is heightened
even further in judicial elections. Legislators have constituencies, and lobbying
elected officials, even indirectly through campaign contributions, is an important component of a representative democracy. However, judges have no constituency and are expected to be neutral observers. Lobbying of representatives
is expected, but lobbying of judges is not (and, indeed, is prohibited by ex parte
communication rules). Moreover, the ability of an interest group to influence
a legislature is somewhat limited because of the size of the body; controlling
the bench is far easier. Indeed, interest groups have realized this fact and have
contributed substantial amounts of money to judicial candidates.[6] As Bonneau
(2007a) illustrates, average total campaign spending in state Supreme Court
elections rose markedly between 1990 and 2004, even when controlling for inflation.[7] In 2004, combined candidate spending averaged roughly $900,000.

Today's Supreme Court elections now rival, and in several cases exceed,
congressional elections in terms of candidate spending. As a point of comparison, the average winner in House elections in 2004 spent approximately $1 mil-
lion and the average loser spent roughly $270,000.[8] Added together, these num-
bers are slightly higher than spending in the average Supreme Court race from
that same year. In more extreme cases, spending in Supreme Court elections
easily surpasses most races for the U.S. House and even some contests for the
U.S. Senate. For example, candidates in the controversial 2004 Illinois Supreme
Court election combined to spend approximately $10 million. The contest was
more expensive than nineteen of the thirty-four U.S. Senate races held that
year.

Not only is significant money being raised and spent by judicial candidates
at levels that compete with elections for the legislature, but the effect of money
on candidate success is similar as well. Numerous scholars have studied campaign spending in legislative elections, and a few constant results emerge. First,
open seat elections generally tend to be more expensive than races matching
an incumbent against a challenger (Abramowitz and Segal 1992; Hogan 2000).
This result is not surprising, since no candidate has the incumbency advantage in open seat races. From a strategic politician standpoint the probability
of winning for a nonincumbent is best without an incumbent on the ballot,
which increases the cost of the race (Jacobson 2004). Second, challenger spending affects how well challengers do in U.S. House, Senate, and state legislative

elections; the more a challenger spends, the more successful he or she is likely to be (Jacobson 1978; Green and Krasno 1988; Abramowitz 1991; Squire 1989; Ansolabehere and Gerber 1994; Gierzynski and Breaux 1991). Challengers get more "bang for their buck" than incumbents, because they do not have the name recognition of incumbents (Jacobson 2009). Moreover, money helps get the challenger's message to the people and may win over copartisans who originally sided with the incumbent.

The facts that open seats are more expensive than races involving incumbents and that challengers increase their probability of winning the more they spend are relatively uncontroversial. Less clear is the effect of campaign spending by incumbents. Jacobson (1978, 1990) has long held that spending in congressional elections is largely challenger driven. If incumbents face a well-funded challenger, then they must spend more money to fend off that challenger. Conversely, a poorly funded challenger will not threaten the incumbent, lessening the incumbent's need to spend significant sums of money. "Spending money does not cost [incumbents] votes, to be sure," writes Jacobson (2009, 48); "rather, incumbents raise and spend more money the more strongly they feel themselves challenged." However, not everyone agrees with Jacobson's argument. Green and Krasno (1988, 1990) attack Jacobson's findings largely on methodological grounds and claim that his analysis suffers from a problem of endogeneity (see also Gerber 1998). Contrary to Jacobson, they argue that more spending can improve an incumbent's vote share.

The conclusions regarding the role of money in congressional races hold at the state Supreme Court level as well. Bonneau has conducted the most extensive analyses of campaign spending in judicial races. He finds that, like congressional races, open seat contests tend to be the most expensive (Bonneau 2004, 2005). In terms of aggregate spending, open seat IAC contests are also generally more expensive than incumbent/challenger races (Frederick and Streb 2008). However, when other variables are taken into consideration, open seat IAC elections are actually *less* expensive than contests involving an incumbent. This finding is puzzling given the results of numerous other studies. It may be related to the fact that IAC incumbents are challenged significantly less frequently than incumbents running in races for the Supreme Court or Congress (Streb, Frederick, and LaFrance 2007), making those IAC races when incumbents are challenged more special, hence more expensive.

Additionally, as in the other elections, challenger spending in Supreme Court races has a significant effect on vote shares. Bonneau (2007b, 496) notes that "for every 1 percent increase in challenger spending, the incumbent's level of electoral support decreases by almost 1.8 percentage points." Regarding incumbent spending, Bonneau's findings are more in line with Jacobson's (1978, 1990) than Green and Krasno's (1988, 1990). Supreme court justices did not increase their vote shares the more money they spent. Similar to Jacobson, Bonneau (2007b, 496) argues that this insignificant result "is likely due to strategic behavior by the incumbent. Incumbents only raise (and spend) money when they are electorally vulnerable. The more electorally secure the incumbent is, the less money he or she will need to raise and spend." At the IAC level, Streb and Frederick (2009) report that, with the exception of incumbent judges who were first appointed to the bench, sitting judges who increase the difference in spending with their challengers do not increase their vote share or probability of winning.[9] Again, challengers appear to get more bang for their electoral buck than incumbents.

Political Party and Interest Group Involvement

Another point of comparison between legislative and judicial elections is the role played by political parties and interest groups. This subject is especially interesting given the nature of the judiciary. Judicial reform groups such as the Brennan Center and the Justice at Stake Campaign question the involvement of both groups in judicial elections, because of the fear that judges will resemble politicians instead of being impartial interpreters of the law. Indeed, few states hold partisan judicial elections for this reason. In most states that elect judges, candidates' party affiliations are not listed on the ballot and the activities of parties may be limited as well.[10] However, the use of nonpartisan elections does not mean that parties have remained on the sidelines. In fact, the little that is known about party involvement in judicial elections indicates that they play a role equivalent to that in elections for other offices.

Political scientists have long believed that parties are an essential part of the electoral process, because they help the public make sense of a complex political world (for example, Aldrich 1995). Yet with the collapse of the party machines, the decline in party identification in the 1960s and 1970s, the rise of candidate-centered elections, and the increasing importance of television, some believed that parties lost their relevance (Broder 1972; Wattenberg 1998). Indeed, party organizations moved from a "textbook paradigm," where they controlled all aspects of candidates' campaigns, to an "accommodationist paradigm," where they essentially became "parties in service" (Menefee-Libey 2000; Aldrich 1995). Nevertheless, not everyone bought into the death of the party organization. Gibson et al. (1985) found that parties were resurging at the local level. Moreover, Frendreis and Gitelson (1999) argued that parties were the "spokes of a candidate-centered wheel."

In terms of legislative elections, parties may no longer control all aspects of the campaign, but they still take an important part. For example, parties are heavily active in the recruitment of congressional and state legislative candidates (Frendreis et al. 1994). Furthermore, a survey conducted by Frendreis and Gitelson (1999) found that roughly 75 percent of county party chairs arranged fund-raisers for or contributed to state legislative candidates. Additionally, more than half of the county parties distributed mailings, prepared press releases, or bought newspaper ads. Virtually every county party distributed posters or lawn signs for its legislative candidates. Finally, a substantial majority of county parties organized get-out-the-vote (GOTV) events for their candidates (ibid.).[11]

Far less work has examined the role of parties in judicial elections, and much of it is more anecdotal than systematic (for example, Champagne 2001) or focused on one state rather than generalizable (for example, Cheek and Champagne 2005; Eisenstein 2000). However, Streb (2007) conducted a survey of 783 county party chairs regarding their participation in trial court elections. Not surprisingly, parties reported being more involved in every activity including candidate recruitment, campaign contributions, fund-raising, candidate advertising, campaign strategy, candidate endorsements, and GOTV efforts when their judges were elected in partisan elections as opposed to nonpartisan contests. The level of activity in these efforts paralleled, and in some cases surpassed, party activity in legislative elections. For instance, while roughly 75 percent of party chairs arranged fund-raising events or contributed to candidates in state legislative elections (Frendreis and Gitelson 1999), roughly 67 percent did so in partisan judicial elections. Additionally, 60 percent of Republican chairs and 70 percent of Democratic chairs reported conducting GOTV efforts in behalf of legislative candidates (ibid.), yet more than 80 percent of county chairs involved in partisan trial court elections did so. Party chairs reported being more active in coordinating with the candidates' campaigns in partisan judicial elections than in county-level campaigns.[12]

Perhaps more surprising than the role that parties take in partisan judicial elections is the part they play in nonpartisan contests. Although parties were always significantly more active in partisan contests, roughly half of the county parties reported being involved in the recruitment of judicial candidates, distributing posters or lawn signs, coordinating with the candidate's campaign organization, endorsing candidates, conducting GOTV efforts, and organizing campaign events in nonpartisan elections (Streb 2007). The fact that parties appear to be a central component to judicial campaigns even in nonpartisan contests is not positive news for people hoping to keep the activities of parties in judicial elections to a minimum.

If party activity in judicial elections is a worry to the judicial reform and professional organizations mentioned previously, then interest group involvement may be even more alarming. Interest groups have long played a role in elections for other offices, everything from contributing money to candidates, independent spending in behalf of candidates, endorsing candidates, and mobilizing voters. Concern about the influence of interest groups can be traced back to Madison's writing of *Federalist 10* in which he warned about the "mischiefs of faction." In more recent times, the influence of interest groups has been problematic to some, especially as it relates to campaign contributions and independent spending. Interest groups are prohibited from contributing money directly to candidates; they can do so only by establishing Political Action Committees (PACs). The number of PACs has grown enormously since the 1970s and with that growth came an explosion of PAC contributions (Herrnson 2008). PAC contributions to congressional candidates totaled about $12.5 million in 1974, compared with more than $348 million in 2006. This figure does not include the substantial sum of money that PACs spend independently of candidates. In the 2006 congressional midterm elections, PACs exhausted more than $35 million on independent expenditures, a record at the time for a midterm election (ibid.).

The Bipartisan Campaign Reform Act (BCRA), signed into law in 2002, was designed to limit the influence of interest groups by outlawing soft money—unlimited and unregulated donations to political parties that could be used for grassroots party building activities. However, as the 2004 and 2008 presidential elections illustrate, groups simply found other loopholes that allowed them to put significant amounts of money into the system. Most notably, "527 organizations"—tax-exempt groups that can raise and spend unlimited sums on campaigns as long as they do not expressly call for the election or defeat of specific candidates and do not coordinate their activities with federal candidates or parties—spent millions of dollars independently of the presidential candidates. Swift Boat Vets and POWs for Truth may have been the best known of these organizations, but that organization's spending paled in comparison to groups like Americans Coming Together and the Media Fund, which expended $78 million and $54 million in 2004, respectively.[13] In 2008, 527s were less visible but still combined to spend roughly $200 million (Hershey 2010).

It has been well documented that interest groups are increasingly active in judicial elections as well (see, for example, Sample, Jones, and Weiss 2007; Goldberg 2007). Specifically, interest groups have contributed to candidates and spent independently substantial sums of money, in some cases equaling the money expended in congressional races. The increase in interest group spending is particularly controversial in judicial elections, primarily because of the source of the majority of the money. Not surprisingly given their likelihood of appearing before the court, business interests and trial lawyers are the two largest donors to judicial campaigns. From 2000 to 2009, business groups contributed to Supreme Court candidates more than $62.5 million, and trial lawyers donated $59.2 million (or 30.2 percent and 28.6 percent, respectively, of all money raised) (Sample, Skaggs, Blitzer, and Casey 2010). In the 2004 Illinois Supreme Court race mentioned previously, one group estimates that national tort reform groups contributed more than $1 million to one candidate, while the other received money primarily from trial lawyers (Heller 2004). The U.S. Chamber of Commerce, which spent $20 million on TV ads, direct mail, and phone calls in the 2006 congressional elections (Herrnson 2008), expended more than $700,000 in *one* 2006 Michigan Supreme Court election (Sample, Jones, and Weiss 2007).

Perhaps nowhere is the activity of interest groups more apparent (or controversial) than in a 2004 West Virginia election in which Chief Justice Warren McGraw was challenged by a relatively unknown lawyer named Brent Benjamin. McGraw was targeted by the 527 organization "And for the Sake of the Kids," which was funded mostly by Don Blankenship, the CEO of Massey Coal. Blakenship spent roughly $3 million independently during the campaign running advertisements primarily against McGraw, accusing him of being lenient on child molesters. Benjamin defeated McGraw and soon after found himself hearing a case on appeal by Blankenship and Massey Coal. Benjamin was one of three justices (in a 3–2 decision) voting to overturn a $50 million verdict against Massey Coal. His vote sent outrage throughout much of the legal community and forced the Supreme Court to hear a case, *Caperton et al. v. A. T. Massey Coal Co.* (2009), regarding recusal standards for judges. The Supreme

Court ruled that the Due Process Clause required Benjamin to have recused himself, "given the serious risk of actual bias."[14]

However, the influence of interest groups in judicial elections extends far beyond money. Because of the Supreme Court's ruling in *Republican Party of Minnesota v. White* (2002) that declared the "announce clause"—a canon that prohibited judicial candidates from announcing their views on disputed political or legal issues—to be unconstitutional, interest groups started sending questionnaires, similar to the kind that legislative candidates are frequently asked to complete, to judicial candidates. For example, in 2006 right to life groups in Kentucky and North Carolina asked judicial candidates whether they agreed or disagreed with the statement "I believe that *Roe v. Wade* was wrongly decided." In an Alabama Supreme Court race, a socially conservative group asked candidates whether they agreed or disagreed with phrases such as "Unborn Child Is Fellow Human Being," "The State Can Acknowledge God," and "Alabama 'Lawsuit Abuse' Harms Economic Development" (Sample, Jones, and Weiss 2007).

Even with the low visibility of most judicial elections, political parties and interest groups appear to be just as active in races for judge as they are in higher profile elections, including those for Congress. On the one hand, this occurrence could be positive. The more money that parties and interest groups spend, the more likely voters are to encounter information about judicial candidates. Likewise, if parties and interest groups are endorsing candidates or engaging in GOTV efforts, the information costs for voters decline. On the other hand, it is exactly the kind of information that parties and interest groups are likely to supply that concerns those worried about a politicized judiciary. Parties and interest groups are less apt to focus on issues such as qualifications and bench temperament, issues on which scholars concerned with the integrity of the courts would like to see people casting votes, and instead raise the kinds of ideological issues in the questionnaires discussed in the preceding paragraph.

Participation and Voting

Although the ruling in *White* may make it more likely that candidates will discuss political issues on the campaign trail, the question remains whether voters will actually use that information in the voting booth. In fact, for scholars of political behavior, perhaps no subject is more interesting regarding judicial elections than who participates in those elections and what influences voters' decisions when casting their ballots.

First, few people vote in judicial elections. In his article "Why Judicial Elections Stink," Geyh (2003) puts forth the "Axiom of 80"; one part of that axiom is that roughly 80 percent of people do not vote in contests for judge. Indeed, ballot roll-off in judicial elections—the percentage of people who cast a ballot but failed to vote for judge—can be quite high. Hall (2007b) has provided the most comprehensive study of ballot roll-off in state Supreme Court elections. Examining Supreme Court elections from 1980 to 2000, she finds that average ballot roll-off is roughly 25 percent. Streb, Frederick, and LaFrance (2009) note that the average ballot roll-off in IAC races from 2000 to 2007 was slightly higher (just below 30 percent). Roll-off for both types of appellate court elections is greater than for most other offices or propositions for which people vote. Although admittedly the study looks only at roll-off in one election year in one state, Wattenberg, McAllister, and Salvanto (2000) report that average roll-off for House and state legislative elections is 4 percent and 8 percent, respectively. Even for low-information partisan statewide contests, such as controller or insurance commissioner, roll-off is around 5 percent. In his study of statewide propositions, Magleby (1984) finds that roll-off averages between 15 and 18 percent, still substantially lower than roll-off in appellate court elections.

Although voter roll-off is generally greater in judicial elections than in elections for other offices, the conditions that promote participation are quite similar. Voter roll-off in judicial elections is not random; certain factors increase or decrease the number of people casting ballots. For example, competitive elections normally lessen ballot roll-off (Wattenberg, McAllister, and Salvanto 2000; Bullock and Dunn 1996). The same is true for judicial elections (Hall 2007b; Streb, Frederick, and LaFrance 2009). As with elections for mayor, state legislature, or statewide offices (Schaffner, Streb, and Wright 2001; Schaffner and Streb 2002), roll-off is greater in nonpartisan elections (Hall 2007b; Streb, Frederick, and LaFrance 2009). As they do for other offices, cues such as the gender or ethnicity of the candidate also lessen roll-off in judicial elections (McDermott 1997, 1998; Streb, Frederick, and LaFrance 2009). Finally, as in legislative elections, campaign spending influences participation in judicial elections; the more money spent by campaigns either increases turnout or decreases voter roll-off (Caldeira and Patterson 1982; Cox and Munger 1989; Hall and Bonneau 2008).

It is clear that the conditions that promote or hinder roll-off in judicial elections are similar to those in other elections. However, less obvious is who exactly is participating in judicial elections. Part of the reason that this question is so difficult to answer is because of the scarcity of individual survey data on voting in judicial elections (Streb 2009). Studies of political participation for offices such as the presidency or Congress, in which a plethora of survey data exists, find that some people are more likely to vote than others. In particular, socioeconomic status often determines whether someone participates; those with higher incomes and more formal education are more likely to vote (see, for example, Wolfinger and Rosenstone 1980; Verba, Schlozman and Brady, 1995). Furthermore, the older a person is the more likely she is to vote (Wattenberg 2008).

Some scholars have examined who participates in races for judge, but more work is needed to determine whether the results for other offices hold for judicial elections. Using aggregate data, Hall (2007b) finds that roll-off is less in jurisdictions with greater education levels (although, see Streb, Frederick, and LaFrance 2009). Still, because of the use of aggregate level data, Hall is limited in what she can say about who specifically is voting in judicial elections. Baum and Klein (2007) are able to provide some insight into the question of who participates by analyzing surveys of voters in Ohio state Supreme Court elections in 1998 (what they consider a low-visibility year for judicial elections in the state) and 2002 (considered high-visibility elections). Five variables are included in their model of participation: strength of partisanship, strength of ideological leanings, income, education, and political knowledge. They find that the partisan, ideology, and income variables have little effect on a person's decision to vote in the contests. On the other hand, political knowledge and education did matter, especially in the low-visibility contests. As useful as Baum and Klein's study is, it barely scratches the surface regarding individual-level participation in judicial elections. They examine only one state and a few demographic variables. Scholars should continue pursuing this line of research to get a better grasp on who is voting for judge.

As important as understanding who participates is answering what influences people's vote choices in judicial elections. Again, a substantial body of literature exists examining this question for other offices. Perhaps more so than any other variable, party identification is the driving force behind people's votes (for example, Campbell et al. 1960; Brody and Page 1972; Jackson 1975; Markus and Converse 1979; Bartels 2000; Green, Palmquist, and Schickler 2002). The effect of party on vote choice has ebbed and flowed, but it has generally remained the central determinant, especially for down-ballot offices. One variable that has often rivaled party identification is incumbency; this is especially true in congressional elections (Jacobson 2009). Part of the reason partisans defect to incumbents of the opposing party may simply be name recognition; incumbents are better known than challengers. However, with a candidate's party identification on the ballot, something else must be driving partisan defection. Voters may engage in retrospective evaluations of incumbents, rewarding incumbents when times are good and punishing them when they are bad (Fiorina, 1981). Moreover, as mentioned previously, incumbents have advantages such as bringing home pork, performing casework, and building home style. All of these aspects could lead to voters crossing partisan lines.

The determinants of vote choice in judicial elections are not as clear. First, most judicial elections are nonpartisan, so the partisan cue is not readily available. Second, as noted earlier, the incumbency advantage that judges have may not be as strong as the one that exists for legislators. What is known about voting in judicial elections does not show the public in a particularly positive light. Survey after survey finds an apathetic and ill-informed public (see, for example, Dubois 1980; Johnson, Schaefer, and McKnight 1978; Baum 1989; Lovrich and Sheldon 1983). According to Geyh (2003, 63), "[V]oter ignorance, apathy, and incapacity" are the norm in judicial elections. People not only have trouble recalling for whom they voted, they do not even recognize the candidates. In one study, only 14.5 percent of people interviewed immediately after voting could identify a single candidate on the ballot (Johnson, Schaefer, McKnight 1978). The lack of information has led to some downright embarrassing elections. Perhaps most infamously, in a 1997 Texas Supreme Court election a man named Gene Kelly beat an intermediate appellate court judge who was supported in the primary by both the plaintiffs' bar and the defense bar. Kelly then spent less than $8,000 in the general election against an opponent who exhausted more than $1 million, mostly on ads reminding voters "He's Not That Gene Kelly." Kelly still captured 44 percent of the vote. Even with the increased visibility of some Supreme Court elections, at least one study finds that more visible campaigns do not change the determinants of voting (Baum and Klein 2007). Without partisan affiliation often available on the ballot, voters rely on other less reliable cues such as a candidate's ethnicity or gender (Squire and Smith 1988; Dubois 1984).

However, not everyone holds the view that voters in judicial elections are ill informed. Hall and Bonneau (2006, 2009) have made the most spirited defense of the public's participation in these elections. As mentioned previously, using aggregate data the two authors find that quality challengers perform better than nonquality challengers. They argue this indicates that the public is able to distinguish between stronger and weaker challengers. Moreover, more voters cast ballots in competitive judicial elections than uncompetitive contests, likely because they are exposed to more information. Additionally, Hall (2001a) finds possible evidence of retrospective voting in judicial elections. Her aggregate analysis indicates that a state's lagged murder rate is negatively related to the incumbent's electoral performance (see also Streb and Frederick 2009; but see Hall and Bonneau 2006). There is a disconnect then between the aggregate- and individual-level data. Hall and Bonneau's findings are intriguing and their arguments should be taken seriously. However, it is not clear that people are really distinguishing between challenger quality based on the aggregate-level data. It simply could be that stronger challengers have more name recognition, and it is this aspect on which people are casting votes, not the characteristics of the candidate. More and better individual-level data is needed to know which of these claims is most accurate.

Conflicts of Interest, Strategic Judges, and the Rule of Law

If judicial elections now share many of the same characteristics as elections for other offices, then what does that mean for the legitimacy of the courts and the rule of law? Since Gibson has written extensively on the topic of court legitimacy in this volume, I will only say a brief word about the subject here. Many observers of the judiciary, including some judges, argue that the fact that judicial elections now mirror elections for other offices threatens the public's perception of the courts as an impartial body. Former Texas Supreme Court chief justice Thomas R. Phillips went so far as to state that increasingly political judicial elections have created "a crisis" in the courts (Rutledge 2002). Such hyperbolic statements simply are not supported by empirical evidence.

The argument of those who are concerned with court legitimacy is that the judiciary is held in high regard by the public, more so than the legislature. Empirical evidence does exist on that account (for example, Hibbing and Theiss-Morse 1995). If judicial elections take on the same characteristics as other elections, especially regarding negativity, party and interest group involvement, and money, then public perception of the courts could be influenced. Because judges are supposed to uphold the law instead of acting politically, perhaps the public backlash will be even greater for the judiciary.

Yet the empirical evidence to date indicates that the reform groups mentioned previously at best got it only part right. As Gibson's work (2008a, 2008b, 2009) illustrates, the public neither is turned off by judicial candidates making policy statements on the campaign trail, nor are they particularly upset by negative advertising. Gibson does uncover evidence that campaign contributions can detract from a court's legitimacy, but it is difficult to argue that the decline borders on a "crisis." The empirical evidence—at this point anyway—that the public is outraged by the increasingly political nature of judicial elections simply is not there. Concerns over the legitimacy of the courts because of the changes in judicial elections seem to be driven more by elites than the rank-and-file.

That being said, the fact that the public continues to have confidence in the state courts does not mean that there is no reason to be concerned that judicial elections have taken on the characteristics of other elections. Judicial elections may not have influenced public perception of the courts in any meaningful way, but they have threatened due process and the rule of law. The increasing money spent in judicial elections and the activity of interest groups have created a conflict of interest that, at the very least, is disconcerting. This is not to say that judges are so unethical that they simply rule with the side that donated the most money to the campaign. To go back to the *Caperton* example, even Benjamin ruled against the interests of Massey Coal in other cases. And, quite frankly, the empirical evidence regarding the influence of campaign contributions on rulings is unclear. However, some evidence—limited as it may be—exists indicating that contributions could influence judicial decisions (Cann 2007; Bonneau and Cann 2009).[15] Moreover, it is difficult to believe that even the most ethical judge can completely discount the fact that an individual or organization donated money directly to the campaign or spent significant money independently in support of the judge. Certainly the same issues exist regarding the relationship between representatives and donors, but the difference between a congressperson who cannot wield much influence without the help of a couple hundred of her colleagues and a judge who simply has the power in many instances to rule on a case, or significantly influence the outcome of a case because of her rulings, is enormous. Furthermore, the job of representatives is to be responsive to their constituents in pursuing policies they feel are in the best interest of the country or jurisdiction they serve; the job of the judge is to uphold the law. In some cases public opinion and the law may be similar, but at times significant differences could exist between what the public wants and what the law actually is.

Proponents of judicial elections might agree with the statements made in the preceding paragraph but would likely argue that stricter campaign finance or recusal rules would alleviate the conflict of interest. Additionally, public financing of judicial elections would improve the process. I am not convinced that these ideas lessen the concern about money in judicial elections. Public financing of judicial elections may be better than the status quo, but it would not alleviate the conflict of interest. The controversy surrounding the *Caperton* case, for example, would not have changed even if West Virginia had publicly financed judicial elections. Stricter disclosure laws also might be an improvement, and could provide valuable information to voters, but they, too, would do little to lessen a conflict of interest. Finally, clear recusal laws that are enforced would be better than the status quo, but it is not entirely clear what would happen if each justice on the high court received contributions from a party appearing before the court. With the size of most courts of last resort and the amount of money that is being spent in these races, this occurrence is not unlikely.[16]

The cost of judicial elections is not the only way in which they mirror elections for other offices and, as a result, threaten the rule of law. Judges may take their job of interpreting the law seriously, but they also want to remain on the bench. If judicial challengers act strategically by challenging judges who are most electorally vulnerable—and as I have shown, they do—then, like any politician, the judge may try to avoid putting herself in a vulnerable electoral position in the first place. Moreover, if voters make retrospective evaluations of judges the same way they do legislators—again, there is some evidence that they do—then judges may anticipate those evaluations and rule accordingly. Finally, if a judge sees a colleague face a difficult election—something that contestation and competition rates in Supreme Court elections indicate is not uncommon—this may influence the judge's behavior on the bench. In each case, the rule of law may take a backseat to judicial survival.[17]

In Chapter 1, Segal discusses three models developed by political scientists regarding judicial decision-making. One such model, the strategic model, portrays justices as rational actors whose decisions are influenced by their goals. Normally, the strategic model applies to judges' perceptions of how their colleagues, the legislature, or the executive will react to their decisions. For example, a judge may strategically position herself in the majority even though she does not agree with the majority if there is the potential to write a watered-down opinion. Yet strong empirical evidence exists that public opinion also encourages elected judges to act strategically (Hall 1992; Shepherd 2009).[18] Like U.S. Senators, judges serve longer terms that allow them to discount public opinion earlier in the term. However, as re-election approaches, judges (just like senators) may alter their decisions to be more in line with public opinion (Kuklinski 1978; Elling 1982; Thomas 1985). For instance, judges are less likely to overturn death penalty cases in the year of their re-election than in the year prior to or following an election (Brace and Boyea 2007). Moreover, a study of Pennsylvania trial court judges finds that judges become more punitive in criminal cases as their elections approach (Huber and Gordon 2004). The fact that whether a person's death sentence is upheld or what a person's punishment may be depends on when a judge is up for re-election raises serious questions about due process.

It is possible that elections actually promote the rule of law, because they force judges to be more in line with what the law is. The fact that judges are less likely to overturn a death penalty sentence the closer they are to re-election may not be a problem if the law of the state allows for the death penalty and judges use their personal opposition to such a law to overturn death sentences, as Rose Bird did in California. Not wanting to enrage the public, as the election approaches the judge may be less likely to overturn a death penalty sentence, hence be consistent with the law. Yet, even if true, the fact that two people convicted of the same crime may get different verdicts simply based on when a judge is up for re-election is a grave injustice. Moreover, there are likely to be times when public pressure pushes judges away from the law.

That being said, even with the problems of judicial elections, the public strongly supports electing judges (Geyh 2003); in other words, judicial elections are here to stay. Since that is the case, observers of the courts need to find ways to improve the process. Here, again, one can look to what is known about other elections to guide reform efforts. As noted, one reform that is often pushed by groups like the Justice at Stake Campaign is to replace partisan elections with nonpartisan contests. As Hall notes in this volume, such an effort is misguided (see also Bonneau and Hall 2009). Again, partisan involvement is not absent from nonpartisan contests. Moreover, nonpartisan elections actually heighten the need for money because the costs of voter mobilization increase (ibid.). In partisan elections, partisans can make their decisions once in the voting booth by simply relying on the party cue provided by the ballot; in other words, the candidate had to spend no money to get a vote. That is not the case in nonpartisan contests.

If elections are to be held, then the interests of the voter must be considered. Nonpartisan elections place an unnecessary burden on the voter by removing a cheap, reliable cue. As a result, like elections for other offices, voter roll-off is significantly higher in nonpartisan contests than in partisan races. Additionally, even if the average judge strives to uphold the law the majority of the time, compelling evidence exists that Democratic and Republican judges rule differently (for example, Brace and Hall 1993; Hall and Brace 1992); there is something to be said for the attitudinal model articulated by Segal in Chapter 1. It matters if a judge is a Democrat or Republican and voters should be aware of this information. If this information exists, voters will use it—and use it effectively—as they do for other offices (Lewis-Beck et al. 2008). Finally, Gibson's research (2008a, 2008b, 2009) indicates that voters are not surprised—or particularly offended—by partisan involvement in judicial races.

In sum, understanding how judicial elections are like—or dislike—elections for other offices can help guide the debate over judicial selection. There are reasons to be concerned that judicial elections are taking on the characteristics of other elections. As a result, states should consider eliminating electoral components to judicial selection. On the other hand, many of the electoral reforms advocated by groups like the American Bar Association or the Justice at Stake Campaign will do little to alleviate the problems of judicial elections and, instead, create new issues that could have negative consequences.

Notes

1. When I refer to "elections for other offices," I generally mean legislative elections (federal or state), unless otherwise noted.

2. Although, see Brunell (2008).

3. As in Supreme Court races, partisan elections were slightly more likely to be contested than nonpartisan contests.

4. It is important to note that these studies ignore trial court elections. Although I know of no systematic analysis of contestation at the trial court level, given their lack of visibility it is likely that contestation rates are more similar to IAC elections than Supreme Court contests.

5. Although there has been some debate over how to operationalize a quality challenger variable (for example, Krasno and Green 1988; Jacobson 1989), it is generally coded as whether a challenger has held previous elected office (Jacobson 1989; Van Dunk 1997).

6. Additionally, they have spent even more money independently of candidates' campaigns.

7. However, Frederick and Streb (2008) find that spending has not increased substantially in IAC elections after controlling for inflation.

8. These numbers were obtained from http://www.opensecrets.org/bigpicture/elec_stats.php?cycle=2004 (accessed March 4, 2009).

9. Streb and Frederick (2009) speculate that judges who are new appointees benefit from more spending for reasons similar to those affecting challengers. Appointed judges are more vulnerable than previously elected judges (Hall and Bonneau 2006; Streb and Frederick 2009), but also may suffer from less name recognition.

10. Yet these limits on party involvement in campaigns and judicial candidates' activities with parties have been under attack in the courts. A U.S. district court ruled recently that judges can join political parties, solicit campaign contributions, and endorse partisan candidates (Rohde 2009).

11. For additional studies on party involvement in legislative elections, see Herrnson (1986); Francia et al. (2003); and Hogan (2004b).

12. It is important to note that the timeframes of the Frendreis and Gitelson survey and the Streb survey are different, so a perfect comparison cannot be made.

13. These figures were obtained from the Federal Elections Commission website (www.fec.gov), accessed March 6, 2009.

14. *Caperton et al. v A. T. Massey Coal Co.* 129 S. Ct. 2252 (2009).

15. Yet even here one must be cautious not to make too much of these findings. First, they apply only to a small number of states (Georgia, Michigan, and Texas) and do not indicate that "justice is for sale" in every case.

16. Additionally, it is possible that a group will donate or spend strategically in hopes of removing an unfriendly judge from a case because she received campaign support from that group.

17. And, as Hall (2001b) illustrates, when faced with the prospect of a difficult election some judges may choose to retire.

18. Public opinion may influence appointed judges as well. Appointed judges may be hesitant to make an unpopular ruling to uphold the legitimacy of their institution.

References

Abramowitz, Alan I. 1988. "Explaining Senate Election Outcomes." *American Political Science Review* 82: 385–403.

———. 1991. "Incumbency, Campaign Spending, and the Decline of Competition in U.S. House Elections." *Journal of Politics* 53: 34–57.

Abramowitz, Alan I., and Jeffrey A. Segal. 1992. *Senate Elections*. Ann Arbor: University of Michigan Press.

Aldrich, John H. 1995. *Why Parties? The Origin and Transformation of Political Parties in America*. Chicago: University of Chicago Press.

Alvarez, R. Michael, and Jason L. Saving. 1997. "Deficits, Democrats, and Distributive Benefits: Congressional Elections and Pork Barrel Politics in the 1980s." *Political Research Quarterly* 50: 809–831.

Ansolabehere, Stephen, and Alan Gerber. 1994. "The Mismeasure of Campaign Spending: Evidence from the 1990 U.S. House Elections." *Journal of Politics* 56: 1106–18.

Bartels, Larry M. 2000. "Partisanship and Voting Behavior, 1952–1996." *American Journal of Political Science* 44: 35–50.

Baum, Lawrence. 1989. "Voters' Information in Judicial Elections: The 1986 Contests for the Ohio Supreme Court." *Kentucky Law Journal* 77: 645–65.

Baum, Lawrence, and David Klein. 2007. "Voter Responses to High-Visibility Judicial Campaigns." In Matthew J. Streb, ed., *Running for Judge: The Rising Political, Financial, and Legal Stakes of Judicial Elections*. New York: New York University Press.

Bonneau, Chris W. 2004. "Patterns of Campaign Spending and Electoral Competition in State Supreme Court Elections." *Justice System Journal* 25: 21–38.

———. 2005. "What Price Justice(s)? Understanding Campaign Spending in State Supreme Court Elections." *State Politics and Policy Quarterly* 5: 107–25.

———. 2007a. "The Dynamics of Campaign Spending in State Supreme Court Elections." In Matthew J. Streb, ed., *Running for Judge: The Rising Political, Financial, and Legal Stakes of Judicial Elections*. New York: New York University Press.

———. 2007b. "The Effects of Campaign Spending in State Supreme Court Elections." *Political Research Quarterly* 60: 489–99.

Bonneau, Chris W., and Damon M. Cann. 2009. "The Effect of Campaign Contributions on Judicial Decisionmaking." Unpublished manuscript. Available at http://ssrn.com/abstract=1337668.

Bonneau, Chris W., and Melinda Gann Hall. 2009. *In Defense of Judicial Elections*. New York: Routledge.

Brace, Paul, and Brent D. Boyea. 2007. "Judicial Selection Methods and Capital Punishment in the American States." In Matthew J. Streb, ed., *Running for Judge: The Rising Political, Financial, and Legal Stakes of Judicial Elections*. New York: New York University Press.

Brace, Paul, and Melinda Gann Hall. 1993. "Integrated Models of Judicial Dissent." *Journal of Politics* 54: 914–35.

Broder, David. 1972. *The Party's Over*. New York: Harper and Row.

Brody, Richard A., and Benjamin I. Page. 1972. "The Assessment of Policy Voting." *American Political Science Review* 66: 450–58.

Brunell, Thomas L. 2008. *Redistricting and Representation: Why Competitive Elections Are Bad for America*. New York: Routledge.

Buckley v. Valeo, 424 U.S. 1 (1976).

Bullock, Charles S., III, and R. E. Dunn. 1996. "Election Roll-Off: A Test of Three Explanations." *Urban Affairs Review* 32: 71–86.

Caldeira, Gregory A., and Samuel C. Patterson. 1982. "Contextual Influences on Participation in U.S. State Legislative Elections." *Legislative Studies Quarterly* 7: 359–81.

Campbell, Angus, Philip E. Converse, Warren E. Miller, and Donald E. Stokes. 1960. *The American Voter*. New York: Wiley.

Cann, Damon M. 2007. "Justice for Sale? Campaign Contributions and Judicial Decisionmaking." *State Politics and Policy Quarterly* 7: 281–97.

Carson, Jamie L., Erik J. Engstrom, and Jason M. Roberts. 2007. "Candidate Quality, the Personal Vote and the Incumbency Advantage in Congress." *American Political Science Review* 101: 289–303.

Champagne, Anthony. 2001. "Political Parties and Judicial Elections." *Loyola of Los Angeles Law Review* 34: 1411–27.

Cheek, Kyle, and Anthony Champagne. 2005. *Judicial Politics in Texas: Partisanship, Money, and Politics in State Supreme Courts.* New York: Peter Lang.

Cox, Gary W., and Michael C. Munger. 1989. "Closeness, Expenditures, and Turnout in the 1982 U.S. House Elections." *American Political Science Review* 83: 217–31.

Dubois, Philip L. 1980. *From Ballot to Bench: Judicial Elections and the Quest for Accountability.* Austin: University of Texas Press.

———. 1984. "Voting Cues in Nonpartisan Trial Court Elections: A Multivariate Assessment." *Law and Society Review* 18: 395–436.

Eisenstein, James. 2000. "Financing Pennsylvania's Supreme Court Candidates." *Judicature* 84: 10–19.

Elling, Richard. 1982. "Ideological Change in the United States Senate: Time and Electoral Responsiveness." *Legislative Studies Quarterly* 7: 75–92.

Feldman, Paul, and James Jondrow. 1984. "Congressional Elections and Local Federal Spending." *American Journal of Political Science* 28: 147–64.

Fenno, Richard F., Jr. 1978. *Home Style: House Members in Their Districts.* New York: Longman.

Fiorina, Morris P. 1977. "The Case of the Vanishing Marginals: The Bureaucracy Did It." *American Political Science Review* 71: 177–81.

———. 1981. *Retrospective Voting in American National Elections.* New Haven: Yale University Press.

Francia, Peter L., Paul S. Herrnson, John P. Frendreis, and Alan R. Gitelson. 2003. "The Battle for the Legislature: Party Campaigning in State House and State Senate Elections." In John C. Green and Rick Farmer, eds., *The State of the Parties: The Changing Role of Contemporary American Parties.* 4th ed. Lanham, MD: Rowman and Littlefield.

Frederick, Brian, and Matthew J. Streb. 2008. "Paying the Price for a Seat on the Bench: Campaign Spending in State Intermediate Appellate Court Elections." *State Politics and Policy Quarterly* 8: 410–29.

Frendreis, John, and Alan R. Gitelson. 1999. "Local Parties in the 1990s: Spokes in a Candidate-Centered Wheel." In John C. Green and Daniel M. Shea, eds., *The State of the Parties.* 3d ed. Lanham, MD: Rowman and Littlefield.

Frendreis, John, Alan R. Gitelson, Gregory Flemming, and Anne Layzell. 1994. "Local Political Parties and Legislative Races in 1992." In John C. Green and Daniel M. Shea, eds., *The State of the Parties: The Changing Role of Contemporary American Parties.* Lanham, MD: Rowman and Littlefield.

Gerber, Alan. 1998. "Estimating the Effects of Campaign Spending on Senate Outcomes Using Instrumental Variables." *American Political Science Review* 92: 401–11.

Geyh, Charles Gardner. 2003. "Why Judicial Elections Stink." *Ohio State Law Journal* 64: 43–79.

Gibson, James L. 2008a. "Campaigning for the Bench: The Corrosive Effects of Campaign Speech?" *Law and Society Review* 42: 899–927.

————. 2008b. "Challenges to the Impartiality of State Supreme Courts: Legitimacy Theory and 'New-Style' Judicial Campaigns." *American Political Science Review* 102: 59–75.

————. 2009. "'New Style' Judicial Campaigns and the Legitimacy of State High Courts." *Journal of Politics* 71: 1285–1304.

Gibson, James L., Cornelius P. Cotter, John F. Bibby, and Robert J. Huckshorn. 1985. "Whither the Local Parties? A Cross-Sectional and Longitudinal Analysis of the Strength of Party Organizations." *American Journal of Political Science* 29: 139–60.

Gierzynski, Anthony, and David A. Breaux. 1991. "Money and Votes in State Legislative Elections." *Legislative Studies Quarterly* 16: 203–17.

Goldberg, Deborah. "Interest Group Participation in Judicial Elections." In *Running for Judge: The Rising Political, Financial, and Legal Stakes of Judicial Elections*, Matthew J. Streb (ed.). New York: New York University Press, 2007.

Goldberg, Deborah, Craig Holman, and Samantha Sanchez. 2002. *The New Politics of Judicial Elections: How 2000 Was a Watershed Year for Big Money, Special Interest Pressure, and TV Advertising in State Supreme Court Campaigns*. Washington, DC: Justice at Stake.

Gordon, Sandford C., and Gregory A. Huber. 2007. "The Effect of Electoral Competitiveness on Incumbent Behavior." *Quarterly Journal of Political Science* 2: 107–38.

Green, Donald Phillip, and Jonathan Krasno. 1988. "Salvation for the Spendthrift Incumbent: Reestimating the Effects of Campaign Spending in House Elections." *American Journal of Political Science* 32: 884–907.

————. 1990. "Rebuttal to Jacobson's 'New Evidence for Old Arguments.'" *American Journal of Political Science* 34: 363–72.

Green, Donald, Bradley Palmquist, and Eric Schickler. 2002. *Partisan Hearts and Minds: Political Parties and the Social Identities of Voters*. New Haven: Yale University Press.

Griffin, John D. 2006. "Electoral Competition and Democratic Responsiveness: A Defense of the Marginality Hypothesis." *Journal of Politics* 68: 894–910.

Hall, Melinda Gann. 1992. "Electoral Politics and Strategic Voting in State Supreme Courts." *Journal of Politics* 54: 427–46.

————. 2001a. "State Supreme Courts in American Democracy: Probing the Myths of Judicial Reform." *American Political Science Review* 95: 315–30.

————. 2001b. "Voluntary Retirements from State Supreme Courts: Assessing Democratic Pressures to Relinquish the Bench." *Journal of Politics* 63: 1112–40.

————. 2007a. "Competition as Accountability in State Supreme Court Elections." In Matthew J. Streb, ed., *Running for Judge: The Rising Political, Financial, and Legal Stakes of Judicial Elections*. New York: New York University Press.

————. 2007b. "Voting in State Supreme Court Elections: Competition and Context as Democratic Incentives." *Journal of Politics* 69: 1147–59.

Hall, Melinda Gann, and Chris W. Bonneau. 2006. "Does Quality Matter? Challengers in State Supreme Court Elections." *American Journal of Political Science* 50: 20–33.

————. 2008. "Mobilizing Interest: The Effects of Money on Citizen Participation in Supreme Court Elections." *American Journal of Political Science* 52: 457–70.

————. 2009. *In Defense of Judicial Elections*. New York: Routledge.

Hall, Melinda Gann, and Paul Brace. 1992. "Toward an Integrated Model of Judicial Voting Behavior." *American Politics Quarterly* 20: 147–68.

Heller, Emily. 2004. "Judicial Races Get Meaner." *National Law Journal*, October 25. Available at http://www.law.com/jsp/article.jsp?id=1098217051328 (accessed August 6, 2007).

Herrnson, Paul. 1986. "Do Parties Make a Difference? The Role of Party Organizations in Congressional Elections." *Journal of Politics* 48: 589–615.

————. 2008. *Congressional Elections: Campaigning at Home and in Washington*. 5th ed. Washington, DC: CQ Press.

Hershey, Marjorie Randon. *Party Politics in America*, 14th edition. New York: Longman, 2010.

Hibbing, John R., and Elizabeth Theiss-Morse. 1995. *Congress as Public Enemy: Public Attitudes toward American Political Institutions*. New York: Cambridge University Press.

Hogan, Robert E. 2000. "The Costs of Representation in State Legislatures: Explaining Variations in Campaign Spending." *Social Science Quarterly* 81: 941–56.

————. 2004a. "Challenger Emergence and Electoral Accountability in State Legislative Elections." *Journal of Politics* 66: 543–60.

————. 2004b. "Party Activists in Elections Campaigns." In John A. Clark and Charles L. Prysby, eds., *Southern Political Party Activists: Patterns of Conflict and Change, 1991–2001*. Lexington: University Press of Kentucky.

Huber, Gregory A., and Sanford Gordan. 2004. "Accountability and Coercion: Is Justice Blind When It Runs for Office?" *American Journal of Political Science* 48: 247–63.

Jackson, John. 1975. "Issues, Party Choices, and Presidential Votes." *American Journal of Political Science* 19: 161–85.

Jacobson, Gary C. 1978. "The Effects of Campaign Spending on Congressional Elections." *American Political Science Review* 72: 469–91.

————. 1989. "Strategic Politicians and the Dynamics of U.S. House Elections, 1946–1986." *American Political Science Review* 83: 773–93.

————. 1990. "The Effects of Campaign Spending in House Elections: New Evidence for Old Arguments." *American Journal of Political Science* 34: 334–62.

————. 2004. *The Politics of Congressional Elections*. 6th ed. New York: Pearson Longman.

————. 2009. *The Politics of Congressional Elections*. 7th ed. New York: Pearson Longman.

Johannes, John R., and John C. McAdams. 1981. "The Congressional Incumbency Effect: Is It Casework, Policy Compatibility, or Something Else?" *American Journal of Political Science* 25: 512–42.

Johnson, Charles A., Roger C. Schaefer, and R. Neal McKnight. 1978. "The Salience of Judicial Candidates and Elections." *Social Science Quarterly,* 49: 371–78.

Krasno, Jonathan S. 1994. *Challengers, Competition, and Reelection: Comparing Senate and House Elections*. New Haven: Yale University Press.

Krasno, Jonathan S., and Donald Phillip Green. 1988. "Preempting Quality Challengers in House Elections." *Journal of Politics* 50: 920–36.

Kuklinski, James. 1978. "Representatives and Elections: A Policy Analysis." *American Political Science Review* 72: 165–77.

Lewis-Beck, Michael S., William G. Jacoby, Helmut Norpoth, and Herbert F. Weissberg. 2008. *The American Voter Revisited*. Ann Arbor: University of Michigan Press.

Lovrich, Nicholas P., Jr., and Charles H. Sheldon. 1983. "Voters in Contested, Nonpartisan Judicial Elections: A Responsible Electorate or a Problematic Public." *Western Political Quarterly* 36: 241–56.

Magleby, David B. 1984. *Direct Legislation: Voting on Ballot Propositions in the United States*. Baltimore, MD: Johns Hopkins University Press.

Markus, Gregory B., and Philip E. Converse. 1979. "A Dynamic Simultaneous Equation Model of Electoral Choice." *American Political Science Review* 73: 1055–70.

McDermott, Monika L. 1997. "Voting Cues in Low-Information Elections: Candidate Gender as a Social Information Variable in Contemporary United States Elections." *American Journal of Political Science* 41: 270–83.

———. 1998. "Race and Gender Cues in Low-Information Elections." *Political Research Quarterly* 51: 895–918.

Menefee-Libey, David. 2000. *The Triumph of Campaign-Centered Politics*. New York: Chatham House.

Mondak, Jeffrey J. 1995. "Competence, Integrity, and the Electoral Success of Congressional Incumbents." *Journal of Politics* 57: 1043–69.

Republican Party of Minnesota v. White, 536 U.S. 765 (2002).

Rohde, Marie. 2009. "Federal Judge Rules State Judges Can Join Political Parties." *Milwaukee Journal-Sentinel*, February 18. Available at http://www.jsonline.com/news/milwaukee/39793162.html (accessed March 7, 2009).

Rutledge, Jesse. "Texas Chief Justice Urges Reform of N.C. Judicial Election System." July 3, 2002. Available at http://www.ncjudges.org/media/news_releases/7_3_02.html (accessed April 10, 2009).

Sample, James, Lauren Jones, and Rachel Weiss. 2007. *The New Politics of Judicial Elections, 2006: How 2006 Was the Most Threatening Year Yet to the Fairness and Impartiality of Our Courts—And How Americans Are Fighting Back*. Washington, DC: Justice at Stake.

Sample, James, Adam Skaggs, Jonathan Blitzer, and Linda Casey. 2010. *The New Politics of Judicial Elections, 2000–2009: Decade of Change*. Washington, DC: Justice at Stake.

Schaffner, Brian F., and Jennifer Segal Diascro. 2007. "Judicial Elections in the News." In *Running for Judge: The Rising Political, Financial, and Legal Stakes of Judicial Elections*, ed. Matthew J. Streb. New York: New York University Press.

Schaffner, Brian F., and Matthew J. Streb. 2002. "The Partisan Heuristic in Low-Information Elections." *Public Opinion Quarterly* 66: 559–81.

Schaffner, Brian F., Matthew J. Streb, and Gerald C. Wright. 2001. "Teams without Uniforms: The Nonpartisan Ballot in State and Local Elections." *Political Research Quarterly* 54: 7–30.

Schotland, Roy. 1985. "Elective Judges' Campaign Financing: Are State Judges' Robes the Emperor's Clothes of American Democracy?" *Journal of Law and Politics* 2: 57–167.

Sheldon, Charles H., and Linda S. Maule. 1997. *Choosing Justice: The Recruitment of State and Federal Judges*. Pullman: Washington State University Press.

Shepherd, Joanne. 2009. "The Influence of Retention Politics on Judges' Voting." *Journal of Legal Studies* 38: 169–203.

Squire, Peverill. 1989. "Challengers in U.S. Senate Elections." *Legislative Studies Quarterly* 14: 531–47.

Squire, Peverill, and Eric R. A. N. Smith. 1988. "The Effect of Partisan Information on Voters in Nonpartisan Elections." *Journal of Politics* 50: 169–79.

Stone, Walter J., L. Sandy Maisel, and Cherie Maestas. 2004. "Quality Counts: Extending the Strategic Politician Model of Incumbent Deterrence." *American Journal of Political Science* 48: 479–95.

Streb, Matthew J. 2007. "Partisan Involvement in Partisan and Nonpartisan Trial Court Elections." In Matthew J. Streb, ed., *Running for Judge: The Rising Political, Financial, and Legal Stakes of Judicial Elections*. New York: New York University Press.

———. 2009. "The Need for More Individual-Level Judicial Election Data." *Justice System Journal* 30: 123–30.

Streb, Matthew J., and Brian Frederick. 2009. "Conditions for Competition in Low-Information Judicial Elections." *Political Research Quarterly* 62: 523–37.

Streb, Matthew J., Brian Frederick, and Casey LaFrance. 2007. "Competition, Contestation, and the Potential for Accountability in Intermediate Appellate Court Elections." *Judicature* 91: 70–78.

———. 2009. "Voter Roll-off in a Low-Information Context: Evidence from Intermediate Appellate Court Elections." *American Politics Research* 37: 644–69.

Thomas, Martin. 1985. "Electoral Proximity and Senatorial Roll-Call Voting." *American Journal of Political Science* 29: 96–111.

Thompson, Dennis F. 2002. *Just Elections: Creating a Fair Electoral Process in the United States*. Chicago: University of Chicago Press.

Van Dunk, Emily. 1997. "Challenger Quality in State Legislative Elections." *Political Research Quarterly* 50: 793–907.

Verba, Sidney, Kay Lehman Schlozman, and Henry E. Brady. 1995. *Voice and Equality: Civic Voluntarism in American Politics*, Cambridge, MA: Harvard University Press.

Wattenberg, Martin P. 1998. *The Decline of American Political Parties, 1952–1996*. Cambridge, MA: Harvard University Press.

———. 2008. *Is Voting for Young People?* New York: Pearson Longman.

Wattenberg, Martin P., Ian McAllister, and Anthony Salvanto. 2000. "How Voting Is Like Taking an SAT Test: An Analysis of American Voter Rolloff." *American Politics Quarterly* 28: 234–50.

Wolfinger, Raymond E., and Steven J. Rosenstone. 1980. *Who Votes?* New Haven: Yale University Press.

Yiannakis, Diana Evans. 1981. "The Grateful Electorate: Casework and Congressional Elections." *American Journal of Political Science* 25: 568–80.

9 On the Cataclysm of Judicial Elections and Other Popular Antidemocratic Myths

Melinda Gann Hall

A perfect storm of hardball TV ads, millions in campaign contributions and bare-knuckled special interest politics is descending on a growing number of Supreme Court campaigns. The stakes involve nothing less than the fairness and independence of courts in the 38 states that elect their high court judges.

—Goldberg, Samis, Bender, and Weiss (2005, vi).

A CATACLYSM IN American state judiciaries is imminent, according to some of the nation's most prominent court reform organizations and legal scholars, in the guise of competitive elections for the high court bench and the campaigns that accompany them. But are expensive, hard-fought elections really signaling the demise of the integrity of state judiciaries and the public's acceptance of state judicial power?

In sharp contradistinction to the menacing characterizations of the democratic process dominating public advocacy on this subject and the attacks designed to end judicial elections altogether or to impair their effectiveness, I argue that there is no compelling evidence to suggest the need to replace democratic processes with selection schemes divorced from meaningful citizen participation. There are, however, significant issues meriting attention where viewpoints grounded in empirical reality would balance doomsday rhetoric and promote a more measured dialogue about how best to staff the state court bench.

Most critical is the need to examine the scientific record, or facts that should already be in evidence but instead have been obfuscated or ignored. Remarkably, empirical scholarship supports the case for electing judges and effectively challenges the wisdom of replacing partisan elections with nonpartisan elections and the Missouri Plan. These studies also provide tentative evidence that several of the dire predictions about the prevailing political climate are likely overdrawn.

Consider the astonishing "flip-flop" that has occurred in the framing of the judicial elections controversy. In the 1960s, partisan elections were harshly criticized for failing to fulfill their raison d'être of promoting accountability. The most serious charges were that incumbents rarely were challenged or defeated and that citizens were uninterested and uninformed (e.g., Caufield 2007; Dubois 1980; Rottman and Schotland 2001). Today, attacks against judicial elections have intensified because incumbents are facing stiff competition and because voters are taking a keen interest in these races. Underlying these renewed attacks is the fundamental belief that campaign politics has deleterious effects on judges and courts.

In other words, the modern court reform movement initially criticized judicial elections for failing to resemble elections to other important offices but now condemns them because they do. And underlying this "damned if they do, damned if they don't" approach is an unflattering view of voters. In fact, voters now are being cast as too unsophisticated to view judges through any kind of political lens without losing trust in state judiciaries. In essence, judicial reform advocates are relegating the legitimacy of state courts to the widespread acceptance of discredited myths about the apolitical nature of judging and the selection process.

At the same time, as political scientists evaluate the basic assumptions underlying criticisms of judicial elections (e.g., Baum 1987; Baum and Klein 2007; Bonneau and Hall 2009; Hall 2001, 2007), many of these contentions are proving to be overdrawn or incorrect. This is not surprising given the disjuncture in methods of analysis that persists between the legal academy and political scientists, which in turn perpetuates markedly different perceptions of judging. Political scientists, who embrace empiricism, accept the intrinsically political nature of appellate court decision-making (i.e., what *is*). Legal academicians, who use logical reasoning and normative theories as primary tools, emphasize what *should be*: judicial choices governed entirely by law.

Without question, legal scholars excel in conceptual clarity and logical modes of reasoning. Unfortunately in the case of judicial elections, logic has produced conclusions that are inaccurate or unsubstantiated. For example, while it makes perfect sense to posit that public officials might favor their most generous contributors or that citizens will react negatively to appearances of impropriety, these hypotheses are not evidence that any bias or adverse public reactions actually occur. Nonetheless, because vituperative assumptions about the corrosive effects of money were accepted as fact, advocacy from the legal community now falls just short of zealotry in its condemnation of democratic politics.[1]

On the other side of the aisle, political scientists are skilled in testing theoretically robust hypotheses under stringent standards of scientific validity. With state judicial selection, however, political scientists have bungled concepts, accepted at face value the same unverified and highly debatable assumptions as the legal community, and steadfastly ignored the normative implications of their work. Moreover, these shortcomings have been exacerbated by the discipline's almost single-minded obsession with the U.S. Supreme Court, leaving the study of state courts to a small though capable handful of scholars who have produced crucial evidence fairly late in the game.

Bridging the chasm between legal scholars and political scientists while addressing the shortcomings of both camps will facilitate a more careful dialogue about the politics of judicial selection. Indeed, the striking disregard of empirical facts on the part of the legal community, combined with conceptual chaos and the absence of much of a research or advocacy role by political scientists, has contributed mightily to an unchecked assault on judicial elections.

Empirical Studies of State Supreme Court Elections[2]

There now is a rapidly developing body of empirical work on state supreme court elections,[3] and the story is exciting from the perspective of democratic politics. Moreover, these races differ dramatically on multiple dimensions, suggesting that anecdotal evidence and case studies will not be sufficient for understanding complex processes across the great diversity of American states.

An excellent illustration is voter turnout, measured as ballot roll-off. From 1990 through 2004, roll-off in supreme court elections averaged 22.9 percent, which certainly explains why many would question the efficacy of judicial elections (Bonneau and Hall 2009). However, comparisons across elections, states, and election systems reveal a more complicated reality. Ballot roll-off ranged from 1.6 percent to 65.1 percent across elections and averaged from 12.5

percent to 59.2 percent across states. Partisan, nonpartisan, and retention elections[4] averaged 14, 27, and 26 percent, respectively.[5]

These variations in ballot roll-off are vivid reflections of the ways in which state supreme court elections differ on a variety of dimensions. Political scientists attempting to explain these and other intriguing patterns have moved beyond descriptions of a select set of races to nationwide studies using theoretically derived multivariate models in which the wide range of factors influencing these elections are controlled and alternative explanations are tested. Overall, these studies have produced notable results that support the case for electing judges.

Challengers in Supreme Court Elections

Far from being idiosyncratic, the decisions of challengers to take on incumbents reflect strategic thinking about the probability of winning and sensitivity to the political climate (Bonneau and Hall 2003; Hall and Bonneau 2006, 2008). Particularly vulnerable are unpopular incumbents who barely won their previous races or are appearing before voters for the first time after having been appointed. In fact, justices who never were elected in the first place are highly likely to be challenged (Bonneau and Hall 2009) and defeated (Dubois 1980). Judicial elections are not de facto appointment systems.

Also, challengers are drawn into the electoral arena by a variety of contextual factors, including ballot type (partisan versus nonpartisan), electoral constituency (statewide versus district), and state partisan competition (Bonneau and Hall 2003; Hall and Bonneau 2006, 2008). Statewide partisan elections, district-based nonpartisan elections, and political climates characterized by lively two-party competition significantly increase the probability of challengers. In fact, when designing the basic rules of the game, states play a resounding role in deciding the nature of supreme court elections—the very premise driving judicial reform.

Citizen Participation and Vote Choice

Voter apathy is not inherent in state supreme court elections (Baum and Klein 2007; Hall 2007, Hall and Bonneau 2008). Instead, citizen participation is driven primarily by factors that increase the salience of these races and provide information to voters (Baum and Klein 2007; Hall 2007; Hojnacki and Baum 1992). Particularly effective are partisan elections, qualified challengers, tight margins of victory, and big spending (Baum and Klein 2007; Hall 2007; Hall and Bonneau 2008). Rather than being alienated by expensive rough-and-tumble campaigns or partisan elections, greater proportions of the electorate participate in these kinds of contests than in less exciting races. There do not appear to be any behavioral manifestations of a disaffected electorate stemming from these controversial elections.[6]

Of course, voting serves little purpose if citizens are incapable of making reasoned choices. However, studies of state supreme courts consistently conclude that the electorate is fairly sophisticated. Voters prefer challengers who have experience on the bench over challengers who do not, and challengers from appellate courts over trial courts (Hall and Bonneau 2006). Otherwise, state electorates vote retrospectively on issues relevant to judges (Hall 2001) and make issue-based choices when sufficient information is provided in campaigns (Baum 1987; Baum and Klein 2007; Hojnacki and Baum 1992).

Beyond these findings, two core principles of American politics illuminate this issue: (1) partisanship is an effective heuristic, and (2) partisanship is an excellent predictor of judicial behavior. Thus, even if the electorate merely responds to partisan labels apart from candidate- or issue-based evaluations, these choices still are rational. By effectively summarizing ideological orientations toward politics, partisanship allows voters to choose as though fully informed.

The most recent affirmation of this principle in a nonjudicial context is *The American Voter Revisited*, which analyzes the 2000 and 2004 presidential elections. Even for the most powerful and politically visible office in the nation, most Americans vote on the basis of partisanship. In fact, Lewis-Beck et al. (2008, 415) reiterate that "the typical American voter . . . shows little political involvement, limited grasp of the issues, and not much ability to think in coherent, ideological terms." However, "American voters are far from fools," because of the power of the partisan choice (ibid., 425).

Money, Money, Money

Rising campaign costs are widely regarded as one of the most pressing threats to American state judiciaries. Although the cost of seeking office is escalating for the state high court bench and for other important political offices (Bonneau 2007), supreme court campaign costs are not increasing uniformly for all candidates or in all states. Instead, campaign costs reflect a variety of electoral contingencies: the strength of the challenger, the value of the seat, and the overall political and institutional context (Bonneau and Hall 2009). Critical among these is whether partisan labels are on the ballot. Contrary to conventional wisdom, nonpartisan elections substantially increase the costs of seeking office, ceteris paribus, thereby exacerbating pressures on judges to generate campaign war chests (ibid.).[7]

Moreover, there is no systematic evidence that state supreme court justices are at the mercy of special interests and other high-rollers when their electoral fates are being determined. Supreme court elections resemble elections to nonjudicial offices: spending is important but is only one of many factors affecting how well candidates perform (Bonneau 2007; Bonneau and Hall 2009; Hall and Bonneau 2006). Above all, campaign fundraising and spending favor incumbents (Bonneau 2007).

From a different perspective, money is essential for educating and mobilizing voters. Without advertising and other forms of information dissemination, candidates (including sitting judges) cannot present their credentials or discuss their opponents' shortcomings, and voters will not engage in the races.

Supreme Court Elections in Historical Perspective

Many of the derisive depictions of elections proffered by judicial reform activists have proven to be exaggerated if not patently incorrect. One of the best examples is the widely accepted myth that, until recently, supreme court elections were sleepy affairs with an extraordinary incumbency advantage.

Consider Dubois' study of twenty-five non-Southern states from 1948 through 1974. In this epic work, Dubois (1980, 50) classified *the majority* (51.3 percent) of partisan supreme court elections as competitive by the stringent standard of having been won by 55 percent of the vote or less, compared with 14.8 percent of nonpartisan elections. Likewise, only a small minority (13.3 percent) of partisan races failed to draw challengers, compared with 50.7 percent of nonpartisan elections (ibid.).[8] Finally, as a percentage of all partisan and nonpartisan elections, defeat rates were, respectively, 19.0 and 7.5 percent. Among incumbents serving during that period, defeat rates were 15.7 and 11.4 percent, respectively (ibid., 109).[9] The corresponding defeat rate (from 1954 to 1974) in the U.S. House of Representatives, the quintessential democratic institution, was 8.2 percent (Abramson, Aldrich, and Rohde 2008).

These incredible and certainly overlooked statistics are comparable to those for 1980 through 1995 (Hall 2001, 317–19), during which partisan and nonpartisan elections were won by 55 percent of the vote or less in, respectively, 35.6 and 25.4 percent of the races. Likewise, incumbents in partisan elections were challenged 61.1 percent of the time, reaching a high of 81.8 percent in 1994, compared with 44.2 percent in nonpartisan elections (but up to 60 percent in 1982). With defeats, partisan elections averaged 18.8 percent, compared with nonpartisan elections at 8.6 percent.[10] The defeat rate for the House during this period was 6.5 percent.

These facts were not unfamiliar to an astute group of political observers in the 1980s. Schotland's (1985, 78) iconic characterization of judicial elections as "noisier, nastier, and costlier" was published over twenty-five years ago and referred to elections in the late 1970s and early 1980s. Indeed, after the 1986 and 1988 Ohio Supreme Court races, Hojnacki and Baum (1992, 944) described as "increasingly common" those "new style" campaigns that make "candidates and issues far more visible than in the average judicial contest." Interestingly, Hojnacki and Baum (ibid., 945) appeared to welcome this development by noting that "it is not just the most emotional and dramatic issues in new-style campaigns that can reach voters effectively. Under the right conditions, voters can respond to more prosaic issues such as tort law."

Even in the popular press, a *Los Angeles Times* editorial (Chen 1988, 1) written in the aftermath of the 1986 defeats of three California Supreme Court justices observed:

> The intense public focus on [the California] high-stakes battle has all but obscured a trend that, some now say, threatens the independence and the moral foundations of the nation's judiciary. Throughout the country, judges increasingly are being forced to hit the campaign trail—to raise huge sums of money, often from special interest groups that have a tangible stake in the outcome of the cases before the courts, . . . generating countless free-spending judicial campaigns all over the country.

The article specifically mentioned thirteen states in which these campaigns were taking place, or 34 percent of all states electing judges in 1988.

In sum, supreme court elections have been competitive by the standards of American politics for at least six decades. Although we lack systematic data on campaigns from earlier years, it seems unlikely that these elections went unnoticed by voters or were devoid of electioneering by judges, challengers, political parties, or organized interests. In fact, Brandenburg and Schotland (2008, 1236) report that "at least back into the 1980s, ads run in judicial campaigns have been so disturbing that they are presented as horror cases when legislators and others consider changes in judicial selection methods."

Remarkably, there is no convincing evidence whatsoever that states historically experiencing highly competitive supreme court elections are suffering crises in their judiciaries. Stated well in *Siefert v. Wisconsin* (2009, 40), "One would think that if partisan behavior in judicial elections were . . . detrimental to the integrity of the judiciary . . . so many states could not continue to maintain that system for so long, sometimes more than 150 years." Even worse, the purported fixes to partisan elections—removing partisan labels (nonpartisan elections) and precluding challengers (retention elections)—rendered into self-fulfilling prophecies many of the most negative aspects of judicial elections, including reluctant challengers, lack of voter interest, expensive campaigns, and interest group involvement (Hall 2001, 2007; Hall and Bonneau 2006, 2008).

The Shaky Record of the Judicial Reform Movement

Unfortunately, inaccuracy has plagued the modern court reform movement. In addition to mischaracterizing supreme court elections historically, reformers insisted, among other things, that nonpartisan and retention elections would enhance the quality of the bench, provide a better basis for selecting judges than partisanship, and remove the stains of partisan politics. None of these promises has been fulfilled. Judges do not vary in tangible qualifications across selection systems (e.g., Glick and Emmert 1987; Hurwitz and Lanier 2008); removing partisan labels suppresses voting, produces idiosyncratic outcomes, and raises the cost of seeking office (Hall 2001, 2007; Hall and Bonneau 2008); and partisanship persists in nonpartisan and retention elections (e.g., Hall 2001; Squire and Smith 1988).

In fact, elected supreme court justices perform as well as, or better than, justices selected by other methods in opinion writing, opinion quality, and following federal precedent (Choi, Gulati, and Posner 2007). Regarding their decisions, justices chosen in partisan elections are the most independent of all when independence is measured as voting less often with partisan colleagues (ibid.).

Of course, some of the latest predictions concern the purportedly catastrophic consequences of attack advertising and *Republican Party of Minnesota* v *White* (2002). The basic claim is that campaigns are becoming rancorous free-for-alls in which qualified incumbents are imperiled by various forms of gutter politics, which in turn undermines public trust and judicial legitimacy. Indeed, *White* is widely regarded as a watershed that "significantly altered the landscape of judicial elections" (Caufield 2007, 39).

The White Decision and Electoral Competition

The latest predictions about *White* are testable hypotheses. To assess whether *White* has reduced the incumbency advantage or otherwise intensified competition, we need only examine recent elections. Figure 9.1 provides a graphical

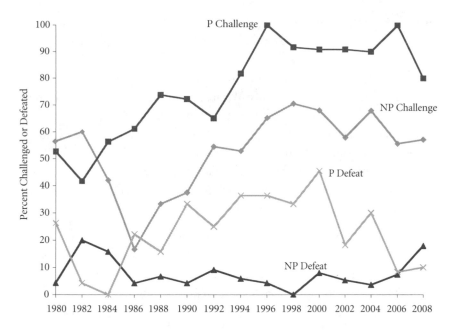

FIG. 9.1. Incumbents Challenged or Defeated

depiction of contestation and defeat rates for incumbents in partisan and non-partisan supreme court elections from 1980 through 2008.[11]

As Figure 9.1 clearly indicates, except for the nonpartisan defeat rate in 2008, contestation and defeats show a downward trend in recent years. While each reader can decide whether 2002 is pre- or post-*White*, given that the decision was issued in June after the primaries but before the general election, the fact remains that *White* has not changed the most outward traits of state supreme court elections.

Regarding contestation, challengers in partisan elections have been a near certainty since 1996. However, partisan contestation in 2008 was the lowest in eight election cycles. In nonpartisan elections, where contestation has been less prevalent but has risen fairly steadily since 1986, the challenge rate in 2004 was even with 2000 but dipped to the lowest level in six election cycles in 2006, rising only slightly in 2008.

As for defeats, partisan elections have become safer for incumbents, a trend that began in 2002. In fact, defeat rates in 2006 and 2008 were at their lowest since 1984. Nonpartisan elections display a different trajectory. While nonpartisan defeat rates in 2004 and 2006 declined or matched the 2000 level, defeats increased in 2008 to the highest level since 1984.[12] Whether this trend will continue is unclear, but this is the only evidence that *White* has negated the incumbency advantage.

In short, except for nonpartisan defeats in a single year, supreme court seats have become less competitive since *White*, a trend confirmed by multivariate analyses (Hall and Bonneau 2008; Peters 2009). At the same time, research shows that interest group activity in supreme court campaigns has declined (Hale, McNeal, and Pierceson 2008). *White* simply has not caused challengers or interest groups to flood into the electoral arena or produced any diminution of the incumbency advantage except for nonpartisan defeats in 2008, a trend offset by steep declines in partisan defeats.

White, Attack Advertising, and Public Perceptions of Courts

Even if *White* has had no immediate electoral consequences for incumbents, the decision may be eroding citizen support for courts by altering the campaigns themselves, though no behavioral manifestations of this are apparent in the election returns. But how prevalent are attack ads, and are they "metastasizing" (Sample, Jones, and Weiss 2007, vi) across the nation?

Consider Figure 9.2, which displays televised attack advertising by race in 2002, 2004, and 2006.[13] In fact, attacks occur only in a minority of supreme court elections and declined by 5.7 percentage points from 2004 to 2006. The proportion of races with attack ads in 2002, 2004, and 2006 was, respectively, 11.1, 16.3, and 10.6 percent. Collectively, these ads have been broadcast in only eleven of the twenty-two states (50 percent) using partisan or nonpartisan elections. Importantly, seven of these eleven states (Georgia, Illinois, Louisiana, Michigan, Mississippi, Nevada, and West Virginia) hosted only a single race with attack ads during all three election cycles. Only four states (Alabama, Kentucky, Ohio, and Washington) have had more than one race with attack ads from 2002 through 2006.

Thus, televised attack advertising has not reached epic proportions in supreme court elections or spread across the United States but instead remains relatively unusual.[14] It also bears repeating that we lack information about the kinds of campaigns that were conducted in the past and thus cannot ascertain whether negativity is indeed new or how extensively television and other media were used in previous decades by candidates, parties, or organized interests. Finally, television advertising per se is nothing to lament. One scarcely can imagine being concerned about the mere presence of television ads in any other American election.[15]

Even so, if attack advertising diminishes judicial legitimacy or other posi-

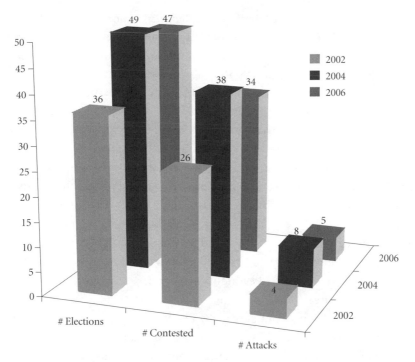

FIG. 9.2. Attack Advertising in State Supreme Court Elections. Source: The Brennan Center for Justice

tive perceptions of courts, small doses could be serious. On this issue, Gibson (2009) has produced intriguing evidence: neither policy talk nor attack advertising has adverse effects on the public's perception of judicial impartiality. Gibson's conclusions (ibid.) are consistent with Kelleher and Wolak's (2007) study of public confidence, which failed to detect any differences in confidence in "community" courts between states using partisan or nonpartisan elections and states using other methods of judicial selection. Likewise, Cann and Yates (2008) show that only the most politically uninformed in partisan elections lack confidence in courts, suggesting that information is a powerful antidote to negativity and pointing to causes other than elections of disaffection.

These various conclusions are consistent with extant research on legislative and executive elections. In studies evaluating the effects of negative congressional campaigns on institutional approval and political efficacy, "the search for evidence against negative advertisements has yielded nothing" (Jackson, Mondak, and Huckfeldt 2009, 63). Indeed, Geer (2006) argues that negativity in presidential elections is indispensable to democracy.

Finally, some reform activists (e.g., Rutledge 2009) assert that public opinion polls reveal the harmful effects of campaigning and show public support for ending competitive elections. However, when viewed in their entirety these polls actually substantiate the opposite. Justice at Stake's (2008) survey in Minnesota is an excellent case in point. This poll shows that voters agree that the following terms describe Minnesota courts: impartial (78 percent), fair (82 percent), and honest and trustworthy (80 percent). At the same time, sizable proportions believe that courts are swayed by public opinion (47 percent), controlled by special interests (41 percent), favor contributors (47 percent), and are political (69 percent). Similarly, the majority (59 percent) thinks that campaign contributors influence decisions a great deal or some of the time, and only a small fraction (5 percent) believes not at all.[16] Otherwise, Minnesota voters overwhelmingly consider voting on judges to be important (92 percent) and view the governor's power to appoint judges as a threat to impartiality (55 percent). Yet they view contested elections (49 percent) and campaign advertising (74 percent) as threats.

Obvious questions about potentially biased question wording aside, these interesting juxtapositions illustrate the cognitive dissonance often present in public opinion but hardly support the case against elections. Even when voters recognize the possible pitfalls of elections, they express strongly positive views of courts and the importance of electing judges while also viewing gubernatorial appointment as a greater threat than contested elections. In short, there is no popular groundswell to eradicate contestable elections,[17] and maintaining respect for courts does not appear to be dependent upon legal myths about judging.[18]

In this regard, one wonders if court reform advocates follow the news. For decades, the popular media have described the federal judicial appointment process in political terms and regularly characterize the ideological makeup of the U.S. Supreme Court. CNN's treatment of Justice Souter's retirement is a prime example. Upon the announcement of Justice Souter's retirement, legal correspondent Jeffrey Toobin described the Court's membership as four liberals (Stevens, Ginsburg, Breyer, Souter), four conservatives (Roberts, Scalia, Thomas, Alito), and one swing voter (Kennedy). Mr. Toobin also emphasized that President Obama would nominate a like-minded replacement and fellow Democrat, and then speculated about what a membership change would mean for the future direction of the Court.[19] Similar dialogue on this subject appeared on every news network and across radio, print media, and the Internet.

Thus, even with federal judges who are not elected, Americans are sensitized to the fact that judging is a political art as well as legal science and that partisanship plays a definitive role in the selection process and in judicial decisions. In this regard, it does not appear that citizens must see judges or the selection process as apolitical in order to view them positively. Indeed, the U.S. Supreme Court ranks among the most highly respected political institutions in the world.

Another Perspective on Electing Judges

With the current revisionist perspective recognizing the efficacy of judicial elections, the disagreement really has become a dispute over the projected impact of competitive elections on the American judiciary. According to prevailing wisdom, challengers are bad, campaigning is bad, and electoral defeats are bad, all because they impair the independence and legitimacy of courts.

But consider an alternative view. Supreme court elections are almost the prototype of what elections should be in the United States. These races are competitive, interesting, and reflect a series of reasonable choices by challengers and voters. Also, to the extent that electoral pressures force judges to abandon their own agendas in favor of the rule of law, courts are strengthened and the public good is enhanced. Finally, there is little evidence that voters must view judges as above the political fray, particularly in states hosting decades of hotly contested races. The assumption that judges must not engage in electioneering without disastrous consequences is quite likely another ivory tower myth.

Judicial politics scholarship offers a basic set of propositions that informs this discussion. First and foremost, American courts are powerful institutions charged with resolving some of the most important issues on the political agenda. Second, in deciding these questions, judges often have substantial discretion and personal preferences that influence their choices.[20] Third, like other political actors, judges are constrained in their ability to make decisions solely on the basis of their preferences. Among these constraints are state and federal law, their own ambitions, and the political environment (e.g., Brace and Hall 1997; Hall 1987, 1992, 1995; Langer 2002; Peters 2009; Savchak and Barghothi 2007). Thus, the very precepts of judicial politics scholarship discard traditional notions that state supreme court justices are tightly constrained by law and lack a meaningful policy-making role.

Accordingly, it is not unreasonable to expect that judges, like other public officials, should have their discretionary choices scrutinized. In order to know the empirical literature but still reach an inapposite conclusion, one must argue that judges and courts simply are different. The argument would go something like this: the incumbency advantage is sacred (i.e., judges are entitled among public officials and should never have their decisions evaluated), judges should act without constraint (i.e., individual preferences, including sharp deviations from law, should prevail), and the American people must never be exposed to information that might cause them to conclude that judges are political actors (i.e., ignorance is bliss, or perhaps voters are stupid). There is an additional assumption: that popular preferences are incompatible with the rule of law.

Conceptual Clarity as a Starting Point

Somehow we have gotten lost in a rhetorical muddle about independence and accountability while losing sight of the rule of law. Accountability can be defined in many ways but in its most basic form is a formal arrangement by which citizens control who holds office. Unfortunately, in modern parlance, independence has been reduced to the state of not having to seek voter approval. This simplistic formula is lodged in contemporary rhetoric: defining independence as freedom from elections and then decrying that the integrity of the judiciary is being jeopardized when any form of electoral politics is present. Even worse, this tautological loop tells us little without providing evidence that these negative effects actually occur and how any proposed solutions will correct the problem without introducing others.

A more complex view relates to judicial decisions, particularly whether judges should adjust their behavior to constituency preferences in matters where they have discretion. Of course, case facts and relevant law can be unambiguous and, in these circumstances, judges should apply law objectively. The extent to which judges have opportunities to exercise discretion depends on a number of factors, including the type of court, facts of the case, and the issues being litigated.

But when law is not a definitive guide, the accountable judge would follow constituency preferences when those preferences are known, while the independent judge would vote her own preferences. In this way, the accountable judge would be practicing a form of what the legal academy labels "popular constitutionalism." Alternatively, the independent judge would be constrained by no other actor.

On this issue, a critical point is this: the extent to which a judge surrenders to partisan pressures, political ambition, or any other force is entirely within her own control. While there may be unique pressures on judges who are elected rather than appointed, it nonetheless is the case that each judge must decide which constituencies she represents, even if that choice is at her own electoral peril. In this manner, independence and accountability are not antithetical to each other.

Moreover, whether these strategic calculations are desirable or not depends on the relationship between the justices' preferences, public sentiment, and the rule of law. When public sentiment and the rule of law coincide, curbing the blatant display of personal preferences should enhance judicial legitimacy. Evidence on this score is limited, but studies of the death penalty and abortion in state supreme courts support the conclusion that public sentiment forced compliance with law rather than deviation from it. Strategic voting in accordance with public preferences is evidenced by liberal justices in states with the death penalty (e.g., Hall 1987, 1992, 1995) and by conservative justices in states with liberal abortion laws (Brace, Hall, and Langer 1999). Stated differently, we cannot always accurately assume that public preferences represent fiat or that judges' unchecked preferences are any less dangerous than the threat of majority tyranny. Also, public pressures do not always take an anti–civil rights or anti–civil liberties form.[21]

The same arguments can be offered about impartiality. Advocates and scholars rightfully are concerned that judges will be swayed to support the interests of wealthy contributors. But again, whether a judge engages in political favoritism or more serious breaches of ethics is entirely within her control, at the same time that existing laws already govern these situations. Importantly, there are alternatives for handling conflicts of interest that do not require eliminating judicial elections.

Fundamentally, accountability and independence are now seen as mutually exclusive goals rather than means to an end. Further, independence and impartiality frequently are used interchangeably. Thus, one of the consequences of conceptual imprecision is the tendency to equate the absence of electoral pressures not only with independence but also with impartiality. An otherwise excellent article illustrates this point. Savchak and Barghothi (2007, 408) opine that "to the extent that merit system judges become more responsive to the public as they face impending retention elections, their impartiality is compromised while accountability is enhanced."

As discussed, electoral pressures producing decisions consistent with public opinion do not necessarily imply a lack of impartiality, especially if public opinion causes a judge to follow the law. Similarly, the absence of public pressure does not guarantee that judges are, by default, impartial or independent. Geyh (2008, 86) expertly makes this point by identifying two primary aspects of independence: (1) the ability of courts to act without encroachments from the legislative and executive branches, and (2) the ability of courts to be free from "threats or intimidation that could interfere with their ability to uphold the rule of law." Thus, the absence of an electoral connection hardly guarantees that other, perhaps more serious pressures will not befall judges, or that their own personal preferences left unfettered will produce desirable results. Indeed, there must be a delicate balance "to ensure that judges are independent enough to follow the facts and law without fear or favor, but not so independent as to disregard the facts or law to the detriment of the rule of law and public confidence in the courts" (ibid.). Removing democratic processes will not guarantee independence or impartiality but merely provides judges and courts with independence from the electorate.

Of course, there are other definitions of independence. But as aptly expressed, "Independence is only a useful term if it allows observers to objectively determine whether it is present or not" (Tiede 2006: 133). This precept applies equally well to accountability and impartiality. Thus, conceptual clarity is paramount.

Alternative Selection Schemes

For decades, judicial reform advocates have campaigned to replace partisan elections with nonpartisan elections or the Missouri Plan. The new goal of the nation's largest and most powerful legal advocacy organization is to end judicial elections altogether.[22] As the American Bar Association (2003, viii) contends:

> Whatever its historic rationale there can no longer be justification for contested judicial elections accompanied by "attack" media advertising that require infusions of substantial sums of money. These contested elections threaten to poison public trust and confidence in the courts by fostering the perception that judges are less than independent and impartial, that justice is for sale, and that justice is available only to the wealthy, the powerful, or those with partisan influence.

Specifically, the American Bar Association (ABA) now recommends that judges be appointed by governors from lists prepared by nonpartisan selection commissions for a single term of office or to a mandatory retirement age. Remarkably, the ABA Plan explicitly rejects legislative confirmation (ibid., 70–71), which is deemed in the same manner as judicial elections to be so unacceptably wracked with politics as to threaten judicial legitimacy. The ABA plan is unlike any other currently operating in the United States and certainly is the least democratic.[23]

Presently twelve states (Connecticut, Delaware, Hawaii, Maine, Massachusetts, New Hampshire, New Jersey, New York, Rhode Island, South Carolina, Vermont, and Virginia) appoint their high court benches.[24] Governors make these nominations except in South Carolina and Virginia, where state legislatures choose judges. Similarly, appointments must be confirmed by one or both houses of the state legislature except in Massachusetts and New Hampshire, where appointments are approved by an elected Executive Council. Only Massachusetts, New Hampshire, and Rhode Island provide lifetime tenure. In the remaining nine states, justices are appointed for terms ranging from six years (Vermont) to fourteen years (New York), with any subsequent terms subject to the approval of a judicial commission (Hawaii), governor, or state legislature.

In sum, nine states currently use appointment systems in which supreme court justices must seek approval from the executive or legislative branch to continue in office. Needless to say, these courts are far from independent. In fact, evidence suggests that justices subject to reappointment by other political elites act strategically to avoid retaliation (Brace, Hall, and Langer 1999; Langer 2002). These justices infrequently docket cases presenting constitutional challenges to state law and rarely invalidate legislation, ceteris paribus. In other words, appointment systems with fixed terms impair judicial review and undermine the system of separation of powers.

Despite a deep commitment to judicial independence, neither the ABA nor any other court reform organization has denounced these appointment schemes or is seeking to replace them with the ABA model. These major players appear to be concerned only about independence from the electorate.

Historically, the ABA plan brings us full circle. Initially, judicial elections were a reform to appointment systems, to guard against encroachment from the legislative and executive branches and to give citizens a voice against arrogant and incompetent judges (Hall 1983; Sheldon and Maule 1997). The ABA plan corrects the problems associated with judicial elections albeit in an extreme way and avoids separation-of-powers issues, but the plan does little to guarantee the rule of law. Stated well in *Siefert v. Alexander* (2009, 80), "Although many in the legal community demonize judicial elections and exalt a system of appointment, a 'merit' selection process has its own flaws and is no guarantee that the judiciary will be free from partisan bias or the perception of it." Moreover, the ABA plan precludes broad citizen representation even indirectly through legislative confirmation. There also are no effective mechanisms for removing judges who implement their own political agendas or are incompetent. While judges would be subject to removal for obvious misconduct or criminal behavior, they would not be eligible for sanction for making unprincipled, biased, or foolish decisions. In short, the ABA plan is not a miracle cure for the ills of judicial elections and may create more devastating crises of legitimacy than competitive elections ever could.

Why Judicial Elections Are Uniquely American

Reform advocates often point to the fact that electing judges is unique to the United States. This is because few nations in the world manifest such a distinct confluence of institutional arrangements: constitutional democracy, separation of powers with checks and balances, federalism, judicial review, and common law.[25] Judges who act within this unusual configuration have extraordinary power and discretion that judges in other nations do not share. Critical among these is federalism, which guarantees fundamental rights and freedoms at the national level while promoting "laboratories of democracy" in the states. Given the carefully engineered nexus between state governments and citizen preferences at the local level, and the stringent guarantees of civil rights and liberties at the national level, the practice of electing judges emerged as a mechanism for insulating state judiciaries from legislative and executive encroachment while giving citizens a voice in the exercise of judicial power.

A New Road Ahead

Political scientists and legal scholars are in an excellent position to work together to provide balance to the public dialogue. Even if the case for electing judges is not convincing to some, there still is a need to integrate any proposed solutions with an overall assessment of what the pitfalls of each alternative might be. In other words, advocacy should focus on the advantages and disadvantages of each selection scheme and not just on the negative aspects of elections.

Moreover, redesigning judicial elections should be part of the nation's attention to elections generally. Concerns about the corrosive effects of money and negative campaigns are not limited to judicial elections, yet condemning legislative or executive elections is unthinkable. We should match solutions to problems and stop the hyperbolic tendency to insist that judicial elections end when complications arise. Campaign reforms in many shapes are being considered and may prove to be effective antidotes to some of the prevailing ills of American elections.

Of critical concern is the seeming conflict of interest created when generous contributors appear as counsel or direct parties in litigation—the appearance of impropriety difficulty. In fact, this is perhaps the most valid point of legal scholars and public advocates today. Recently, Gibson (2009) presented some tentative evidence that perceptions of impropriety stemming from campaign contributions may negate citizens' perceptions of impartiality in courts and legislatures.[26] Deciding how best to mitigate this will require careful thought and creativity, but there are options short of ending elections altogether. *Caperton v. A. T. Massey Coal Company* (2009) is a start. However, much more work is needed to devise meaningful recusal standards, effective campaign finance and disclosure laws, and other appropriate reforms.

A sharper empirical focus on the causes and consequences of state judicial legitimacy also is essential. While we might reasonably posit that perceptions of political neutrality are fundamental to state judicial legitimacy, these assertions are largely untested. As a scientific matter, we simply do not know what determines state court legitimacy and whether brief events like campaigns, which occur within a complicated political context, can have a direct impact, for what duration, and with what consequences. We also must remind ourselves that *elections are perhaps the most powerful legitimacy-conferring institutions in the world.*

Finally, we must acknowledge that there is no perfect system for staffing the bench. Appointive systems (including the Missouri Plan) can be plagued by elitism, cronyism, and intense partisanship (e.g. Dimino 2004, 2005); and legislative selection systems can manifest these same deficiencies and inhibit judicial review (Brace, Hall, and Langer 1999; Langer 2002). Each selection system has advantages and disadvantages and, in large measure, reflects core beliefs about who should control access to the bench and monitor judicial performance. These issues are enormously complex and challenging, but the nation deserves a more careful and balanced discussion of these alternatives than what currently is being offered.

Notes

This chapter was developed through roundtable presentations at the 2008 Midwest Political Science Association Meeting and the 2008 American Political Science Association Meeting, and was presented as a paper in March 2009 at the "What's Law Got to Do with It" Conference at Indiana University School of Law. For their comments on this chapter and ongoing dialogue about the politics of electing judges, I am grateful to Chris Bonneau, Charles Geyh, and Matthew Streb. Of course, the views expressed in this chapter are entirely my own.

1. For an exception, see Dimino (2004, 2005).

2. This chapter cannot effectively summarize all of the empirical work on state supreme court elections or alternative selection plans. I focus instead on significant works supporting the case for partisan elections. For a more comprehensive review, see Bonneau and Hall (2009).

3. This discussion is limited to state supreme courts for two primary reasons: (1) few empirical studies exist of other state courts, and (2) state supreme courts are where expensive, highly competitive races regularly occur.

4. Retention elections are not really elections in most respects. No incumbents were defeated from 1996 to 2005, only 7 of 434 (1.6 percent) incumbents were defeated from 1980 to 2008, and the average vote from 1980 through 2006 to retain incumbents was 72.1 percent. Importantly, this extraordinary incumbency advantage cannot be explained by judicial competence. As studies show (e.g., Hurwitz and Lanier 2008), there are no observable differences in the quality of judges across selection systems.

5. All of the ballot roll-off figures are derived from Bonneau and Hall (2009).

6. Neither the ABA nor any other group has expressed the concern that nasty campaigns will inhibit voter participation. However, the fundamental premise of their case is that campaigning negates positive citizen attitudes, including trust and confidence. As extensive empirical research on executive and legislative elections documents, the most pronounced symptom of such distrust and disillusionment is voter disaffection.

7. Multivariate analysis shows that nonpartisan elections are more expensive than partisan elections when other factors influencing expenditures also are measured. These factors include the size of the electorate, whether the seat is open or involves an incumbent, whether the incumbent has a strong or weak challenger, and whether the incumbent is a seasoned campaigner or is seeking voter approval for the first time. If these various traits were immutable to partisan or nonpartisan elections, there would

be no need to control for their effects. However, because these factors vary considerably over time and by selection system, a more robust approach is necessary for valid inference. Simply adding columns of numbers will lead to erroneous conclusions.

8. These statistics were calculated using Table 3 in Dubois (1980, 50).

9. These statistics were calculated using Tables 3 and 13 in Dubois (1980, 50 and 109).

10. Open seat elections are intensely competitive, whether partisan or nonpartisan. These races consistently draw challengers and are won by narrow margins (e.g., Hall 2001).

11. I collected these data from official reports of Secretaries of State.

12. Arkansas and North Carolina changed from partisan to nonpartisan elections effective 2002 and 2004, respectively. These changes are unrelated to the nonpartisan defeat rate in 2008. None of the 2008 defeats were in Arkansas or North Carolina.

13. The data in Figure 9.2 were assembled from various reports of the Brennan Center (http://www.brennancenter.org) that categorize television ads by tone: attack, promote, or contrast. The ads are counted exactly as coded by the Brennan Center.

14. At the time of writing and revision, the Brennan Center had not reported summary statistics or categorized ads in the 2008 elections. Thus, these figures are not included in Figure 9.2.

15. Justice at Stake criticizes the rise of television advertising, charging that "television advertising is often used to misrepresent or distort facts, and mislead or scare voters" (Sample, Jones, and Weiss 2007, 1). However, there is little to substantiate this serious assertion. Only a small proportion of races involve campaign negativity, and even when attack ads are aired these messages are a small proportion of total advertising Caufield (2007).

16. These figures were derived by combining the top two categories for each response, such as "very well" and "well," "strongly agree" and "agree," "very important" and "important."

17. Question 30 of the Minnesota poll described the selection plan currently in operation (nonpartisan elections) and then asked respondents to agree or disagree that the method is a good way to choose judges. Some 52 percent responded with "strongly yes" or "yes." Moreover, in an open-ended follow-up about why voters who responded negatively would not rate the system favorably, 13 percent responded that there was insufficient information to vote and 19 percent answered that there are never challengers or choice in the races.

18. Respondents expressing confidence in courts, judges, governor, and state legislature were, respectively, 84, 76, 56, and 58 percent. Minnesotans have considerably higher confidence in their judiciary than in the other branches of government, despite any issues with elections or campaign politics.

19. The CNN interview with Jeffrey Toobin aired on May 26, 2009, at about 9:53 A.M. EST.

20. Beginning with the legal realists and path-breaking scholars like C. Herman Pritchett and Glendon Schubert, political scientists have challenged the validity of

normative accounts of judging as closely bound by law. In studies of the U.S. Supreme Court, several generations of scholars have established the primacy of the justices' preferences in voting. Although critics assert that arguments are overdrawn, evidence is overwhelming that "private attitudes . . . become public law" in the nation's highest court. Studies of other federal and state courts also have documented the impact of preferences, as well as the political and legal context, on judicial choice.

21. The 2008 defeat of Elliot Maynard, Chief Justice of the West Virginia Supreme Court of Appeals, illustrates well how voters have managed judicial impropriety. Voters ousted Chief Justice Maynard after photographs emerged of him on the French Riviera with Don Blankenship, CEO of Massey Energy. At the time, Massey Energy had an appeal pending before the Court, which later was decided in the company's favor, overturning a verdict of $76.3 million (http://judgepedia.org/index.php/Elliott_Mayard). In a closely divided decision, Chief Justice Maynard voted in favor of Massey Energy.

22. While the ABA seeks to end judicial elections, retired Supreme Court Justice Sandra Day O'Connor and her newly formed Judicial Selection Initiative are lobbying for the Missouri Plan revised to include performance evaluations. However, acceptance of the Missouri Plan on a statewide basis has stalled for almost two decades. Tennessee was the last state to adopt the Missouri Plan, starting with the 1994 elections. Interestingly, Tennessee has just revised its system after intense controversy over lawyers dominating the process and the lack of transparency.

23. The American Bar Association Commission on the 21st Century Judiciary's report *Justice in Jeopardy* was adopted by the House of Delegates at their 2003 Annual Meeting in San Francisco (http://www.abanet.org/judind/jeopardy/). Accessed May 13, 2009.

24. I collected this information in January 2009 from each state's webpage.

25. The United Kingdom, which many Americans view as politically similar to the United States, exemplifies how differently courts are organized and judicial power accorded in other constitutional democracies. Until 2009, the highest court in the UK was the Appellate Committee of the House of Lords, one of two legislative chambers composing the Parliament. In 2009, a Supreme Court was created by moving the Appellate Committee to a new building and prohibiting the justices (also Lords) from sitting in the House during their Supreme Court service. However, Parliamentary supremacy prevails. No court in the UK has the power of judicial review, or the power to overrule Parliament.

26. Gibson (2009) generated these intriguing findings using experimental vignettes embedded in a survey. However, as with all positive findings in experiments, caution is essential. Experiments lack "real world" validity. Campaign contributions may have an impact under highly controlled conditions, but we now must ascertain whether these effects occur under normal circumstances, for what duration, and with what consequences.

References

Abramson, Paul R., John H. Aldrich, and David W. Rohde. 2008. *Change and Continuity in the 2006 Elections.* Washington, DC: Congressional Quarterly Press.

American Bar Association Commission on the 21st Century Judiciary. 2003. *Justice in Jeopardy.* Chicago: American Bar Association.

Baum, Lawrence. 1987. "Explaining the Vote in Judicial Elections: The 1984 Ohio Supreme Court Elections." *Western Political Quarterly* 40 (June): 361–71.

Baum, Lawrence, and David Klein. 2007. "Voter Responses to High-Visibility Judicial Campaigns." In Matthew Streb, ed., *Running for Judge: The Rising Political, Financial, and Legal Stakes of Judicial Elections.* New York: New York University Press.

Bonneau, Chris W. 2007. "Campaign Fundraising in State Supreme Court Elections." *Social Science Quarterly* 88 (March): 68–85.

Bonneau, Chris W., and Melinda Gann Hall. 2003. "Predicting Challengers in State Supreme Court Elections: Context and the Politics of Institutional Design." *Political Research Quarterly* 56 (September): 337–49.

———. 2009. *In Defense of Judicial Elections.* New York: Routledge.

Brace, Paul, and Melinda Gann Hall. 1997. "The Interplay of Preferences, Case Facts, Context, and Structure in the Politics of Judicial Choice." *Journal of Politics* 59 (November): 1206–31.

Brace, Paul, Melinda Gann Hall, and Laura Langer. 1999. "Judicial Choice and the Politics of Abortion: Institutions, Context, and the Autonomy of Courts." *Albany Law Review* 62 (4): 1265–1303.

Brandenburg, Bert, and Roy A. Schotland. 2008. "Justice in Peril: The Endangered Balance Between Impartial Courts and Judicial Election Campaigns." *Georgetown Journal of Legal Ethics* 21 (Fall): 1229–58.

Cann, Damon M., and Jeffrey L. Yates. 2008. "Homegrown Institutional Legitimacy: Assessing Citizens' Diffuse Support for State Courts." *American Politics Research* 36 (March): 297–329.

Caperton v. A. T. Massey Coal Company. 2009. 173 L.Ed.2d 1208.

Caufield, Rachel P. 2007. "The Changing Tone of Judicial Election Campaigns as a Result of *White.*" In Matthew Streb, ed., *Running for Judge: The Rising Political, Financial, and Legal Stakes of Judicial Elections.* New York: New York University Press.

Chen, Edwin. 1988. "Fund-Raising Ills: For Judges, the Stakes Are Rising." *Los Angeles Times,* March 4, Metro Desk Section, Home Edition.

Choi, Stephen J., G. Mitu Gulati, and Eric A. Posner. 2007. "Professionals or Politicians: The Uncertain Empirical Case for an Elected Rather than Appointed Judiciary." John M. Olin Law and Economics Working Paper No. 357 (2d Series), University of Chicago.

Dimino, Michael R. 2004. "Judicial Elections versus Merit Selection: The Futile Quest for a System of 'Merit' Selection." *Albany Law Review* 67: 803–19.

———. 2005. "The Worst Way of Selecting Judges—Except All the Others That Have Been Tried." *Northern Kentucky Law Review* 32 (2): 267–304.

Dubois, Philip L. 1980. *From Ballot to Bench: Judicial Elections and the Quest for Account-ability.* Austin: University of Texas Press.

Geer, John G. 2006. *In Defense of Negativity: Attack Ads in Presidential Campaigns.* Chicago: University of Chicago Press.

Geyh, Charles Gardner. 2008. "Methods of Judicial Selection and Their Impact on Judicial Independence." *Daedalus* 137 (Fall): 86–102.

Gibson, James L. 2009. "'New Style' Judicial Campaigns and the Legitimacy of State High Courts," *Journal of Politics* 71 (October): 1285–1304.

Glick, Henry R., and Craig Emmert. 1987. "Selection Systems and Judicial Characteristics: The Recruitment of State Supreme Court Justices." *Judicature* (December–January): 228–35.

Goldberg, Deborah, Sarah Samis, Edwin Bender, and Rachel Weiss. 2005. *The New Politics of Judicial Elections, 2004.* Washington, DC: Justice at Stake.

Hale, Kathleen, Ramona McNeal, and Jason Pierceson. 2008. "New Judicial Politics? Interest Groups in State Supreme Court Races." Paper presented at the annual meeting of the Midwest Political Science Association, Chicago, April 3–6, 2008.

Hall, Kermit L. 1983. "The Judiciary on Trial: State Constitutional Reform and the Rise of the Elected Judiciary, 1846–1860." *The Historian* 44 (May): 337–54.

Hall, Melinda Gann. 1987. "Constituent Influence in State Supreme Courts: Conceptual Notes and a Case Study." *Journal of Politics* 49 (November): 1117–24.

———. 1992. "Electoral Politics and Strategic Voting in State Supreme Courts." *Journal of Politics* 54 (May): 427–46.

———. 1995. "Justices as Representatives: Elections and Judicial Politics in the American States." *American Politics Quarterly* 23 (October): 485–503.

———. 2001. "State Supreme Courts in American Democracy: Probing the Myths of Judicial Reform." *American Political Science Review* 95 (June): 315–30.

———. 2007. "Voting in State Supreme Court Elections: Competition and Context as Democratic Incentives." *Journal of Politics* 69 (November): 1147–59.

Hall, Melinda Gann, and Chris W. Bonneau. 2006. "Does Quality Matter? Challengers in State Supreme Court Elections." *American Journal of Political Science* 50 (January): 20–33.

———. 2008. "Mobilizing Interest: The Effects of Money on Citizen Participation in State Supreme Court Elections." *American Journal of Political Science* 52 (July): 457–70.

Hojnacki, Marie, and Lawrence Baum. 1992. "'New Style' Judicial Campaigns and Voters: Economic Issues and Union Members in Ohio." *Western Political Quarterly* 45 (December): 921–48.

Hurwitz, Mark S., and Drew Noble Lanier. 2008. "Diversity in State and Federal Appellate Courts: Change and Continuity Across 20 Years." *Justice System Journal* 29 (1): 47–70.

Jackson, Robert A., Jeffrey J. Mondak, and Robert Huckfeldt. 2009. "Examining the Possible Corrosive Impact of Negative Advertising on Citizens' Attitudes toward Politics." *Political Research Quarterly* 62 (March): 55–69.

Justice at Stake. 2008. *Minnesota Public Opinion Poll on Judicial Selection.* See http:// www.gavelgrab.org/wp-content/resources/polls/MinnesotaJusticeatStakesurvey.pdf. Accessed March 3, 2009.

Kelleher, Christine A., and Jennifer Wolak. 2007. "Explaining Public Confidence in the Branches of State Government." *Political Research Quarterly* 60 (December): 707–21.

Langer, Laura. 2002. *Judicial Review in State Supreme Courts: A Comparative Study.* Albany: SUNY Press.

Lewis-Beck, Michael S., William C. Jacoby, Helmut Norpoth, and Herbert F. Weisburg. 2008. *The American Voter Revisited.* Ann Arbor: University of Michigan Press.

Peters, C. Scott. 2009. "Canons of Ethics and Accountability in State Supreme Court Elections." *State Politics and Policy Quarterly* 9 (Spring): 24–55.

Republican Party of Minnesota v. White. 2002. 536 *U.S.* 765.

Rottman, David B., and Roy A. Schotland. 2001. "What Makes Judicial Elections Unique?" *Loyola of Los Angeles Law Review* 34 (June): 1369–73.

Rutledge, Jesse. 2009. *The New Politics of Judicial Elections in the Great Lakes States, 2000–2008.* Washington, DC: Justice at Stake.

Sample, James, Lauren Jones, and Rachel Weiss. 2007. *The New Politics of Judicial Elections, 2006.* Washington, DC: Justice at Stake.

Savchak, Elisha Carol, and A. J. Barghothi. 2007. "The Influence of Appointment and Retention Constituencies: Testing Strategies of Judicial Decisionmaking." *State Politics and Policy Quarterly* 7 (Winter): 394–415.

Schotland, Roy. 1985. "Elective Judges' Campaign Financing: Are State Judges' Robes the Emperor's Clothes of American Democracy?" *Journal of Law and Politics* 2: 57–167.

Sheldon, Charles H., and Linda S. Maule. (1997). *Choosing Justice: The Recruitment of State and Federal Judges.* Pullman: Washington State University Press.

Siefert v. Alexander. 2009 *U.S. Dist.* LEXIS 11999.

Squire, Peverill, and Erin R. A. N. Smith. 1988. "The Effect of Partisan Information on Voters in Nonpartisan Elections." *Journal of Politics* 50 (February): 169–79.

Tiede, Lydia Brashear. 2006. "Judicial Independence: Often Cited, Rarely Understood." *Journal of Contemporary Legal Issues* 15 (1): 129–61.

10 Are Judicial Elections Democracy-Enhancing?

David Pozen

I N HER CONTRIBUTION to this volume and in a recent book, Melinda
Gann Hall charges the opponents of judicial elections with being "antidemocratic" (Hall, this volume). Blinded by their "unflattering view of voters"
(ibid.) and in thrall to the Article III model of life-tenured executive appointment, these naysayers have, in her telling, ignored the empirical evidence. Hall's
own work has shown that campaigns for state high court judgeships now feature significant amounts of spending and competition, as well as fairly robust
forms of political speech and participation (for example, Hall 2001). Yet at the
same time as judicial elections have been going up and up on these standard
legitimacy-conferring dimensions, the opposition has only doubled down,
launching "a full-scale war" against the institution (Bonneau and Hall 2009, 1,
128).[1] The legal community's advocacy in this regard, Hall says, "falls just short
of zealotry in its condemnation of democratic politics" (Hall, this volume).

By framing the debate over state judicial selection as one between those
who would privilege democratic values and those who would privilege other
(unnamed) values in the method they favor, Hall reprises a classic dichotomy that has defined this literature. On the one hand, it is assumed, choosing
judges by election facilitates self-government by empowering the people to
hold accountable these important officials. Whatever else they might be, elections are "democracy-enhancing institutions" (Bonneau and Hall 2009, 2). On
the other hand, it is argued, choosing judges by election undermines their
independence and therefore threatens values such as professionalism, legality,

and impartiality. There is posited an inescapable tradeoff between the democratic benefits that judicial elections offer and the extrinsic costs they impose. Whether one supports or rejects their usage depends upon how one weighs this tradeoff.

But is it so clear that judicial elections are, or could realistically ever be, democracy-enhancing institutions? As far as I can tell, none of the many fine scholars to have participated in the debate has taken care to explicate this presupposition or to subject it to critical scrutiny. This omission looks particularly odd in light of the prodigious body of work that seeks to reconcile judicial review by the unelected federal courts with democratic imperatives.

Responding to Hall's charge, this short essay aims, first, to put the conventional wisdom on firmer conceptual ground, and then to show how it might be upended. Even an efficacious, abuse-free system of judicial elections, I will argue, does not necessarily advance the cause of self-government—at least, not unless one takes a highly controversial view of the judicial function and of democracy itself. The opponents of judicial elections need not cede the democratic high ground. Beyond any of the specific arguments that I make in the space I have here, my larger aim is to suggest how the "endless" debate over judicial selection (Geyh 2008) might be shifted onto more productive terrain.

The Democratic Case for Electing Judges

When a supporter of judicial elections asserts that they are "more democratic" than alternative selection methods such as executive appointment or merit selection, what exactly might she mean? More generally, what would a democratic case for electing judges look like? In this part, I offer a sympathetic reconstruction of the arguments I take to be motivating these sorts of claims.

Judicial Elections outside the Courthouse
Let us consider first what competitive, multicandidate judicial elections, including re-elections, may entail for the world beyond the courthouse. We can posit a variety of interrelated mechanisms through which they might advance democratic values.

Elections as Acts of Popular Sovereignty. The most basic democratic argument for judicial elections focuses on their procedural and expressive dimensions. Its premise is enticingly straightforward: as government officials who wield significant discretionary authority to "make" and apply law, judges should be selected by those over whom they hold power. Elections provide a mechanism—the paradigmatic mechanism—for enshrining popular control over the institution in question. A system of majoritarian selection may lead to any number of harms, yet by weighting each voter's judgment identically and explicitly, it is often thought to be consistent with both political equality and procedural fairness (Waldron 1999, 113–14). It is our default means of choosing and constraining those who would speak for us.

In the commitment to popular rule they signify, as well as the equivalence they draw between judges and other officials chosen at the ballot box, elections can undercut the ethic of "judicial supremacy" that some critics see as pervading our national legal culture (Kramer 2004, 125). Elections demonstrate that the courts serve "the actual people of the here and now" (Bickel 1986, 17), and not just some antiquated legal text or esoteric professional code. They make it clear that ordinary citizens are entitled and expected to disagree with their judges.

Judicial elections are special moments, then, for affirming our collective commitment to popular sovereignty over the administration of law. To be sure, the "popular" nature of any given election may be marred by interest group capture, incumbent advantages, low turnout, or other pathologies. And gubernatorial and legislative appointments of judges can be seen as popular acts, too, in that the selecting officials are themselves selected by the public. But in an appointive system the connection to the demos is mediated, attenuated. The people have no necessary role to play. However imperfectly, elections can help clarify the democratic basis of judicial authority and legitimate that authority by grounding it in repeated popular consent.

Elections as Accountability Mechanisms. Elections are not merely symbolic vehicles for affirming the people's active, ongoing sovereignty over their laws and the officials who interpret and apply those laws. They are also practical tools for translating that sovereignty into desired outcomes, for ensuring that judicial doctrine remains tethered to community views. If voters disapprove of the decisions that judges have been rendering, they can throw the bums out. Elections give ordinary citizens a means to register dissent, if not also to elicit campaign pledges, and thereby to shape the trajectory of adjudicated law.

Elections are special in this regard as well. Every judicial selection and retention system incorporates various forms of popular accountability. When the governor or the legislature controls reappointments, judges are judged by the people's representatives. Life-tenured federal jurists are checked by their desire for approbation and compliance, commitments elicited during the appointment process, the potential for promotion, and Congress's ability to control jurisdiction, remedies, and salaries. Although causation remains obscure, these sorts of factors have consistently prevented the outputs of the federal courts from straying beyond the mainstream of opinion (Friedman 2009). Yet while no American judge is insulated entirely from popular influence, only elected judges stake their jobs on it. Elections entail the crudest and most potent form of public discipline of all the selection methods; they effectuate the people's will most directly.

It should not be surprising to learn, then, that states that use elections have granted their judges significantly shorter terms than states that use appointments (Pozen 2008, 284–85), for the choice to hold elections reflects a commitment to public accountability that demands continual satisfaction. Nor should it be surprising that the empirical evidence increasingly shows that, compared with state judges in appointive and merit-selection jurisdictions, judges facing re-elections, particularly partisan re-elections, are more likely to decide cases in a manner consistent with majority opinion.[2] Elections can force faster and fuller correspondence between judicial outputs and popular preferences.

Elections as Dialogue. Judicial elections are also comparatively noisy. Merit-selection panels labor in obscurity before proffering their slate of candidates to the appointing authority. Governors and presidents vet potential nominees behind closed doors before introducing the selections as a fait accompli. Although confirmation hearings can generate public discussion about the candidates and their views, they do so in a highly structured, performative, and time-bounded way. In practice, confirmation hearings at the federal level have rarely achieved any significant level of debate. I have not seen any research on confirmation hearings at the state level, but I have to imagine that they tend to be even more devoid of substantive content.

Judicial election campaigns, by contrast, increasingly generate political speech on the order of a legislative or executive contest. Candidates develop distinctive positions and seek to communicate them through the media and through direct appeals. This is the defining feature of the "new era": as campaign conduct codes have been weakened and attack ads, interest groups, and big money have flooded the market, judicial races have become "nastier, noisier, and costlier" (Schotland 1998, 150).

Despised by critics, these same attributes of judicial elections can serve democratic ends. Competitive races can render the work of the courts more salient and comprehensible. They facilitate public discourse about previous judicial decisions and potential future decisions. They encourage judges to communicate with the people, and the people to communicate with each other, about the methods and consequences of legal interpretation. They encourage ordinary citizens to try to become judges. They serve as agenda setters and focal points that help citizens coordinate opposition to or support for government policy. They create a kind of marketplace of legal ideas. They reward active political participation and persuasive norm contestation at the expense of passivity. They have, in short, the potential to transform a legal culture from one that is apathetic, sterile, and professional into one that is active, vibrant, and popular. The nastier, noisier, and costlier they are, the greater their transformative potential.

Elections as Teaching Moments. Finally, elections can serve democratic ends by educating members of the public about the content of their laws, as written and as interpreted, and about the work of the courts. This "teaching" function of judicial elections is made explicit whenever the supervising authorities publish voter information guides. It is made even more pointed when these guides incorporate measures of "judicial performance," as they increasingly do (Kourlis and Singer 2007). Any time that a judicial candidate takes to the airwaves, puts up a billboard, or mails out a flyer, an opportunity arises for her to address legal questions, and to do so in a format and register accessible to the lay citizen. Some candidates may decline to take this opportunity. Some may transmit misleading or sensationalistic messages. But others will do so in earnest. Mobilized groups of citizens can likewise try to inform and persuade the masses.

If U.S. Supreme Court rulings still have the capacity to provide a "vital national seminar" on important legal issues (Rostow 1952, 208), state court races have the capacity to distribute the CliffsNotes to the millions of Americans not enrolled. While confirmation hearings can serve a teaching function as well, the lessons are filtered through representatives and ignored by most citizens. As dialogue, judicial elections can prime and stimulate a democratic debate about the legal system. As teaching moments, they can clarify and vivify the stakes.

Judicial Elections inside the Courthouse

We have seen that judicial elections might claim a special normative legitimacy on account of the popular empowerment, evaluative accountability, civic discourse, and legal education they promise. Whether or not they have come—and ever could come—anywhere close to fulfilling this promise is hotly debated, with political scientists like Hall taking a far more optimistic view than most lawyers. We will return to this question later. But Hall also suggests another line of democratic argument for judicial elections: that they are desirable because of their capacity to influence the substantive content of judicial decisions. How might elections do this in democracy-enhancing ways?

Judicial Restraint. For those court-watchers who worry about the countermajoritarian difficulty and who see popular control over the content of law as an intrinsic (or at least presumptive) democratic good, the central recommendation has long been judicial restraint. In the service of democracy, these theorists have called on federal judges to give greater deference to the considered judgments of "the people" and their representatives. Such deference could take many forms. It might involve relaxed scrutiny of the decisions made by the other branches, liberal use of the political question doctrine and the constitutional avoidance canon, a minimalist approach that seeks common moral ground and narrow legal holdings, special solicitude for legislative achievements borne of mass popular mobilization, or simply a less grandiose self-presentation.

Will an elective system be more or less likely than alternative selection systems to produce judges who are restrained in these ways? The answer is far from clear. It depends upon, among other things, what the reselecting authority wants and what the judges think that authority wants. Although we can posit mechanisms through which elective systems will conduce to greater restraint than life tenure or merit selection, a system of gubernatorial or legislative reappointment may be superior to all of these.

First, restraint may be forced upon the judiciary at the voting booth, through the types of jurisprudes favored by the electorate. If a stable majority of voters in any given state desires judges who will grant legislation the highest presumption of constitutionality, the composition of that state's judiciary will, assuming minimal voter competence, come over time to reflect this jurisprudential trait. In political cultures that brand less deferential judges "activists" or "legislators in robes," judicial elections may likewise tend to produce and reward candidates who already believe, in advance of being selected, that courts should have a modest footprint. Still, it may be unrealistic to think that the average electorate will value such restraint as much as the average legislature or executive, the bodies that will most often be its direct beneficiaries.

Second, elected judges may be induced to practice restraint because they anticipate that this is what the voters and opinion-makers desire, and they wish to preserve their jobs. The empirical literature has largely corroborated the rational-choice assumption that a key strategic objective of elected judges, like all other elected officials, is to get selected and reselected: "Judges want to secure the job and keep it" (Burbank and Friedman 2002, 26). The literature has further indicated that, "[w]hile voters in judicial elections generally are uninformed, . . . judges nonetheless perceive their positions to be at risk, and therefore adjust their behavior when deciding controversial cases" (Brace, Hall, and Langer 1999, 1271 n. 34). Members of the public do not actually need to say or do anything to curb what election supporters like Hall see as "the blatant display of judicial preferences" permeating our courts (Hall 2009, 286).

Elected judges might reasonably assume, for example, that any statute passed by the legislature and signed by the governor commands the support of a majority of voters, and that striking it down will incur a political cost. They might therefore be loath to do so. Although systems of legislative or gubernatorial retention create even more obvious incentives to avoid statutory invalidations, the relative force of these incentives has been dimmed by the long judicial terms and strong norms of reappointment that prevail in most states that use such a system (Pozen 2008, 283–85, 319), as well as by the close connections that many elected judges have to political parties. Using a remarkably rich dataset, Joanna Shepherd recently found no statistically significant difference among retention methods in state justices' likelihood of overturning statutes (2009a).[3]

Elected judges might further assume that recognizing new constitutional rights that benefit a minority group, and deciding novel or nonessential legal questions more generally, risks generating popular backlash. Consciously or subconsciously, on account of both ex post incentives and ex ante selection effects, it is plausible that elected judges will aim to steer clear of such outcomes.

Judicial Populism. It is not obvious why someone who wants the judiciary to satisfy "constituency preferences" (Hall 2009, 286) should prize only restraint in jurisprudence, especially when the judges are selected in the same basic manner as the officeholders to whom they are meant to be deferring. Consider this passage from Richard Posner's latest book on judging:

[A]s long as the populist element in adjudication does not swell to the point where unpopular though innocent people are convicted of crimes, or other gross departures from legality occur, conforming judicial policies to democratic preferences can be regarded as a good thing in a society that prides itself on being the world's leading democracy. (2008, 136–37)

What, exactly, would it mean for a judge to conform her policies to constituency or democratic preferences? Hall and Posner do not elaborate. One possibility is that the judge ought to practice the deference techniques described above and cede as much ground as possible to the coordinate branches. This is the standard prescription of those who worry about appointed courts' democratic credentials. Lurking in their theory, however, is another possibility: that the judge ought to incorporate into her decision-making calculus the beliefs of the citizenry, to the extent she can perceive them, irrespective of what the legislature or executive has done. Bonneau and Hall make the point explicit. The democracy-respecting judge, they write, ought to "draw upon public perceptions and the prevailing state political climate when resolving difficult disputes" (2009, 15). Let us call this approach—the manipulation of interpretive outcomes to promote what the voting public appears to desire—*majoritarian judicial review.*[4]

Majoritarian review can (at least in theory) promote popular-sovereignty values without being lawless, unprincipled, or perverse. First, it is important to bear in mind that, at the state level, many judges already have extensive experience as policy-makers. These judges are common-law generalists, and their constitutional structures frequently contemplate that they will issue advisory opinions, engage political questions, perform administrative functions, and participate in decisions on budgetary matters and access to government services (Hershkoff 2001). In light of these background characteristics, the idea that a state judge would possess the competence and legitimacy to advance popular preferences might sound less far-fetched. Second, judges who adopt this approach need not be mere ciphers for public opinion. As in many respectable theories of political representation, they could lead as well as follow—within limits—when they believe their constituents lack relevant information or ought to take a different tack. Third, these judges need not run roughshod over the other branches. If the legislature and executive have settled on a view, that will often serve as a good proxy for what the people want.

Fourth, and most important, these judges need not act wantonly or extra-legally. They can confine their populism to cases in which public sentiment seems clear and widespread, however that is gauged, and in which the legal answer seems unclear. Public opinion could be used to supplement or gloss the traditional interpretive aids; it could be reserved for when the orthodox legal materials are in equipoise; it could be given more or less weight depending on context; and so forth. Just as there are many different types of judicial restraint, there are many different types of majoritarian review, and for purposes of this essay we may be agnostic as among them. As used here, majoritarian review entails only that the judge assigns public opinion some meaningful role in the decisional calculus, either as an external source of value (like justice or welfare) or as an independent source of legal meaning. At the least, the majoritarian jurist can aim to avoid the least popular options within the range of plausible alternatives, within what Judge Posner calls the "zone of reasonableness" (2006, 1053, 1065–66).

Elective judiciaries have a special relationship to majoritarian review, not only in their expected outputs but also in their structural logic. To see this, we need to consider a more general, and surprisingly undertheorized, normative question: should the fact that a judge is selected by any particular method have any bearing on how he or she decides cases? The traditional view of lawyers has been an emphatic no. Regardless of how they came to hold office, judges should decide cases solely on the basis of their own legal judgment. For as Justice Scalia warned in *Cheney v. United States District Court*, 541 U.S. 913, 920 (2004), "[T]o expect judges to take account of political consequences . . . is to ask judges to do precisely what they should not do." This kind of interpretive independence, Kathleen Sullivan observes, "ensures the rule of law by ensuring that courts decide cases in accord with the law and facts, uninfluenced by judges' political affiliations, financial debts, or other improper skewing factors" (2008, 1334).

There is, however, a plausible alternative to this traditional understanding, and it is one that complements the theory of majoritarian review. It is the idea that jurisprudential norms *should* change when the selection and retention methods change, that there is no global ideal of judicial craft that exists independent of judicial structure. Whereas an appointive system with life tenure implicitly asks its judges to follow the law and the law alone, an elective system might legitimize a different conception of the judicial role. It might "send a signal to judges that sensitivity to public opinion is part of the job description" (Pozen 2008, 277). Jed Shugerman has recently described this idea under the rubric of "role fidelity" (2010). The advent of judicial elections created a new personal narrative for the judge, Shugerman hypothesizes, in which the judge came to see it as her duty to incorporate considerations of "constituency and conscience" into the panoply of legal materials used to decide cases (ibid., 1399). She came to see herself, that is, more like a legislator.

On this view, even if an elected judge is about to retire and will never face another vote, role fidelity demands that she nevertheless attend to constituent preferences in each and every case of public concern. When critics such as Kathleen Sullivan decry the "improper skewing factors" that prey upon elected judges, they are impliedly equating these judges with federal judges. They are overlooking the possibility that what would be an improper skewing factor in the federal context might be an appropriate factor in a state context.

It seems safe to assume that majoritarian review is already pervasive (though perhaps often subconscious) among our elected state judges. In addition to the evidence that these judges tend to decide cases in more voter-friendly ways, we already know, for example, that they become significantly more punitive in criminal sentencing as their re-election date approaches (Huber and Gordon 2004; Berdejó and Yuchtman 2010). This research is particularly notable because it deals with what Brian Tamanaha has dubbed the "rule of law baseline" problem (2009, 751, 757): the problem, which cripples empirical analysis of the determinants of judicial decision-making, that it can be virtually impossible to confirm the "correct" legal answer in any given case, and consequently to measure deviations therefrom. The sentencing evidence is so powerful because it suggests that elected judges systematically deviate from their *own* views of what the correct legal answer is.

They do this, one assumes, because they understand that voters tend to favor harsh criminal sentences and that the availability heuristic renders recent decisions more salient than older ones. They are afraid that their next opponent will accuse them of being soft on crime. In the vernacular of political scientists, judges who are facing re-election make sentencing decisions "strategically" rather than "sincerely." It does not follow that elected judges are more likely than other types of judges to deviate from the guidelines or to make objective errors in sentencing determinations. Sentencing is an area in which legislatures have given courts discretion to choose among a range of outcomes. Elected judges appear to be guided in those choices by popular preferences, at least in the years preceding re-election.

There are plenty of reasons why one might condemn this result. Proponents of judicial elections must find a way to accommodate these findings, however, and it is not available to them to pretend that majoritarian review is not occurring or that it is equally likely to occur in appointive and merit-selection jurisdictions. Elective systems create demonstrably superior incentives to reach popular outcomes. The proponents' strongest move, I submit, is to accept this charge and then seek to flip it—to draw on the concepts of majoritarian review and role fidelity and to praise, rather than discount, the possibility of judges who will *not* resist public clamor and criticism. Taken together, these concepts can collapse much of the distinction between deciding cases strategically and deciding them sincerely, as the vindication of public opinion becomes part of the elected judge's professional duty.

The Democratic Case against Electing Judges

Do the arguments outlined above justify Hall's thesis that judicial elections are democracy-enhancing institutions? On numerous grounds, the balance of this chapter will argue, the answer is no. Hall's empirical research confounds some widely held intuitions about the defects of judicial elections. But her thesis is ultimately a normative one, and to evaluate it we must consider the relationship between judicial selection method and the role of a judge in a democracy. Without having done so, it is hard to take seriously the contention that "the better choice is obvious" between partisan elections and all other systems (Bonneau and Hall 2009, 139).[5]

Efficacy and Voter Capacity

Hall is highly sensitive to one critique of the democratic case for electing judges: namely, that the case fails on its own terms because these elections are bound to be inefficacious as instruments for expressing or instantiating the popular will. "[I]f voters have no idea what they are doing when selecting among candidates for state courts or are easily manipulated by campaign advertisements," Hall acknowledges, "then what is the point of having elections at all?" (ibid., 2). She counters, however, that voters *are* interested in judicial elections and capable of assessing candidates—at least, so long as they are provided with competitive, partisan races that give them the tools with which to do so.

To corroborate this argument, Hall points to her own research on voter behavior. Her work has debunked the notion that the electorate will invariably be apathetic about judicial races. It is remarkable to learn, for example, that partisan state supreme court elections are now significantly more competitive than elections for the U.S. House of Representatives in terms of challenger and retention rates (Hall 2001).

Hall is much less convincing in her claims about voter competence. She is able to show that voters will respond to certain cues on the ballot: they are more likely to select candidates who have previous judicial experience as against candidates who lack it, and to select candidates with appellate court experience as against trial court experience (Bonneau and Hall 2009, 96–102). But this is all she is able to show. From these findings, it is a stretch to claim that voters in judicial races make "fairly sophisticated" decisions or that "reform advocates need to rethink traditional notions" about judicial elections (ibid., 6, 103). Also conspicuously absent from the political science literature is any account, even an anecdotal account, of a judicial race that came remotely close to fulfilling the deliberative and educative ideals sketched above. Nevertheless, Hall has done a valuable service in pushing back on the lawyer's conclusory charge—motivated, no doubt, by a dose of elitism and guild pride—that ordinary folks are incapable of choosing rationally in this context.

A more sophisticated version of the lawyer's charge appears in a recent article by political theorist Mariah Zeisberg (2009). Zeisberg argues that because of the special nature of the judicial role, political parties and campaigns cannot supply the galvanizing messages, structured cleavages, and information shortcuts needed to enable voters to register discernible policy choice. The reason for this, Zeisberg asserts, is that the work of judges is too complex factually and methodologically to be reduced to digestible chunks; partisan cues, biographical information, and campaign slogans will tend to "mask . . . instead of illuminate" many of the central dynamics of judicial decision-making (787). The only way in which judicial elections could achieve "the imperative of communicative transparency," Zeisberg concludes, is if judges were to be wholly results-oriented in their approach to deciding cases, with results evaluated according to the political commitments of the parties structuring the elections (794). Yet this approach would violate basic principles of legality that lead us to use judges in the first place.

Zeisberg raises important and challenging questions, but a defender of judicial elections has the resources to mount a colorable rebuttal. To begin with, it might be argued, political parties and interest groups can supply relevant deliberative and motivational goods in judicial elections. They can do this because it *is* possible to distinguish among judicial candidates on the basis of their substantive and methodological views, and because the Democratic and

Republican parties in America today *do* represent distinctive visions of the judicial function (Post and Siegel 2006).[6] Avowing an "originalist" jurisprudence, running on the Republican ticket, belonging to the Federalist Society, securing endorsements from various advocacy organizations or prominent individuals—each of these may provide a valuable heuristic for the otherwise clueless voter. Zeisberg overlooks the extent to which the work of legislatures and executives is similarly opaque to the average citizen. As compared with, say, the legislative appropriations process, there is nothing so complex about the adjudicative process as to disable meaningful public comprehension. There is no need for judges to be even partially results-oriented to reach systematically different interpretive conclusions in certain types of cases and thereby to attract or repel systematically different types of voters.

Zeisberg also overlooks the extent to which a few high-salience issues can determine a judicial race. Judges usually agree. When justices Ruth Bader Ginsburg and Antonin Scalia were colleagues on the DC Circuit, they voted with each other 95 percent of the time they sat on a panel together during the 1983 term (Edwards 1985, 645). Yet everyone knew that Ginsburg was the "liberal" and Scalia the "conservative" jurist; it would have been unthinkable for President Reagan to have nominated Ginsburg for the Supreme Court or for President Clinton to have nominated Scalia. All of the action is in the remaining 5 percent. Voters, pundits, and other groups might reasonably focus on that domain of disagreement in comparing the two as candidates for the bench.[7]

Furthermore, Zeisberg's argument is, as she acknowledges, contingent on low levels of information in the judicial election environment, which leads to "the overwhelming significance of accurate cues for structuring voter choice" (2009, 797). If campaigns for the bench could be engineered to generate robust information about the candidates and their views, it would become increasingly untenable to insist that voters nonetheless lack the ability to make rational selections. After all, legislative and executive races in America today are hardly paragons of reasoned discourse, republican virtue, or informed decision-making, yet most of us accept without reservation that these officials ought to be selected at the ballot box.

The contingency of Zeisberg's argument highlights a potential circularity problem facing those who criticize judicial elections on grounds of efficacy or competence: to a significant extent, the failure of voters to pay attention or to make intelligent choices in prior elections may have been a product of flaws in the prior campaign structures. Candidates for the bench have started to discuss their views on legal and political questions much more openly in recent years. If the worry is that levels of popular interest and participation are still too low, states might pursue reforms aimed at increasing voter turnout. For instance, they could permit judicial candidates to affiliate with political parties and liberalize conduct codes so that they can issue pledges on how they will approach certain types of cases. Few states have yet to take either step. If, to borrow from Thomas Jefferson, the people are not yet "enlightened enough" to choose judges wisely, states might seek "to inform their discretion by education" (1820, 161). States could augment the foregoing reforms by disseminating voter information guides, linking judicial campaigns to broader educational outreach programs, or, more ambitiously, holding public debates or assemblies.

I do not mean to claim that reforms such as these would likely be successful or worth the cost. My claim, rather, is that many of the traditional concerns about voter ignorance and apathy might be seen to reflect bugs in the traditional model of judicial elections, rather than inescapable features of an elective system. On this score, at least, I am inclined to think that Hall has successfully shifted the burden to the other side to explain why these races are destined to be meaningless or quixotic affairs.

Institutional Quality and Integrity

Hall is also sensitive to a second line of attack on judicial elections, which stresses their potential to generate judiciaries that are lower in quality or captured by donors or special interests. A related line of attack emphasizes the loss in public confidence that "new-style" races, featuring policy-oriented campaigning and high information content, may entail.

These criticisms raise not only lawyerly concerns, it is important to appreciate, but also democratic ones. For if elections really do tend to degrade the technical merits, basic fairness, or perceived legitimacy of judicial processes, they may also tend to decrease a society's capacity for efficient exchange, rational planning, inclusive governance, and collective action generally. Among the many other goals it is meant to serve, after all, the judiciary plays critical dispute-resolution and legal-settlement functions in our polity. The state courts also play a critical role in supervising the administration of nonjudicial elections. These points are familiar, but their implications for the judicial selection debate are easily overlooked. Inasmuch as elective judiciaries stand in tension with principles of legality, equity, and efficiency, they also—and consequently—stand in tension with the demands of self-government. Seen in a different light, many of the rule-of-law-type critiques of elective judiciaries can be recast as democratic critiques.

Hall appreciates these concerns at a theoretical level, but she downplays them as unsubstantiated in fact. I believe she is much too quick here. Although the evidence is far from dispositive, we certainly have findings to suggest that relative to their unelected counterparts, elected judges tend to underperform on metrics such as rates of disciplinary action (Schotland 2007) and citations by out-of-state courts (Choi, Gulati, and Posner 2010); engage in more pronounced cyclical behavior in sentencing (for example, Huber and Gordon 2004; Berdejó and Yuchtman 2010); and side with in-state litigants more frequently (Helland and Tabarrok 2002; Tabarrok and Helland 1999). A growing body of research shows that elected judges also tend to rule in favor of campaign contributors (for example, Shepherd 2009c), and some survey evidence suggests that new-style races can sow mistrust of the courts (Cann and Yates 2008).[8]

This research is by no means conclusive. But the findings are sufficiently robust, and their theoretical basis is sufficiently solid, that they cannot be dismissed as "myth" (Bonneau and Hall 2009, 131, 135). They suggest not only that elected judges are responding to popular preferences within the "zone of reasonableness" (Posner 2006, 1053, 1065–66)—a practice which, we saw earlier, might plausibly be claimed as a victory for democracy—but also that elected judges are playing favorites outside the zone and thereby reaching some results hardly anyone would find legally justified. On this score, I believe the burden remains on advocates like Hall to show that competitive elections can be reconciled with judicial impartiality and with public faith therein.[9]

Hall's main line of rebuttal has been to emphasize that unelected judges may also act in inappropriate ways, while their heightened independence creates a heightened risk that they will act in "arrogant" or unpredictable ways (Bonneau and Hall 2009, 139). The point is a fair one; it is to cabin these sorts of risks that all but three of the nonelective states deny their judges any form of life tenure. Yet the point does not respond to the charge that elections have been creating qualitatively more severe threats to the integrity of the judicial process. And Hall dramatically overstates the case against nonelective systems. Her repeated suggestion that these systems "promote the unfettered exercise of personal preferences" (ibid., 137) is never substantiated—and indeed seems downright bizarre in light of the judiciary's practical inability to enforce its own judgments, the relative ease and frequency with which state supreme court rulings are overturned, and the voluminous literature showing that even life-tenured federal judges rarely stray from mainstream opinion. *All* judging is fettered. The real concern with judges' facing retention decisions made by legislatures or governors, in my view, is not that they will decide cases based on personal whim but that they may skew case outcomes to please those bodies.

What about the possibility of improving judicial elections through regulation? Unable to convince states to abandon elections, reformers have been focusing for years now on more modest proposals, such as enhanced recusal rules and stricter contribution limits. Through measures such as these, it is at least conceivable that elective systems could be engineered to provide sufficiently robust competition, accountability, and debate to excite their democratic defenders, while also providing sufficiently robust protections for judicial independence and public confidence to placate their legalist foes.

Conceivable, but exceedingly unlikely. For as I have argued elsewhere, the rule-of-law-type concerns about judicial elections noted in this section interact in paradoxical ways with the efficacy and capacity concerns noted in the previous section. Many of the reforms that would be best suited to enhancing the deliberative, participatory, and representational character of judicial races—reforms such as permitting candidates to affiliate with parties, to promise to reach certain outcomes, and to debate each other in public—threaten to politicize the courts in profound new respects. The very same reforms most likely to enhance the democratic credibility of judicial elections, that is, are the ones most likely to undermine the integrity of the judiciary as a distinctively legal institution (Pozen 2008).

Take one critical example: allowing candidates to run as Democrats or Republicans arguably is essential for generating meaningful voter choice in judicial elections, just as in legislative and executive elections. Maybe more so, given that the vast majority of nonlawyer voters are unequipped to evaluate the records of judicial candidates on their own. No other heuristic is as salient or informative as the partisan label; the democratic defender of elective judiciaries is virtually compelled to support its use. However, by bringing judges into the fold of the parties, this reform also creates a powerful new set of extralegal influences on judicial behavior in any case with potential political valence. It risks subverting the perception and reality of a just legal system, increasing judges' dependence on donors (Kang and Shepherd 2011), and generating decisions "explainable only by partisanship" (Conference of Chief Justices 2005, 13). To find this an attractive state of affairs, one would have to embrace an unusual theory of the role of courts in a democracy.

Majoritarian Review Revisited

But let us put aside all of the concerns listed above. Let us grant that I was being alarmist and that, in a properly structured system, elections can be reasonably efficacious without doing too much collateral damage to the quality, integrity, or impartiality of the courts. Bracketing these issues allows us to focus on one of the most fundamental, and yet least explored, issues in the debate: the relationship between judicial selection method, jurisprudence, and the kind of democracy to which we aspire.

Hall and her coauthor Chris Bonneau, recall, seem to celebrate the fact that elective systems breed judges who are systematically more likely to practice majoritarian review, to "draw upon public perceptions and the prevailing state political climate while resolving difficult disputes" (2009, 15). In my view, the supporter of judicial elections has little choice but to take this position. Any number of regulatory reforms, such as enhanced disqualification and disclosure rules, could mitigate the risk of judicial favoritism toward discrete parties. Promajoritarian decision-making, by contrast, is not so easily rectifiable; it is, rather, the presumed point of using elections. The notion that we could manipulate an elective system so that its judges ignore the political consequences of their decisions is not only Panglossian but perverse. For if that is the goal, then there is no good reason to use elections in the first place.

Would the responsible practice of majoritarian review enhance democracy? Not necessarily. Even if judicial elections could be engineered to facilitate meaningful deliberation and voter choice, to generate high-quality judges from all walks of life, to prevent judges from being captured by particular donors or interest groups, to maintain public trust in the judiciary, and to minimize self-interested or otherwise improper rulings, their usage might *still* be criticized on democratic grounds. I have written previously about the potential for judicial elections to undermine democracy by facilitating majoritarian excesses, governmental abuses, factionalism, and electoral mischief (Pozen 2008, 317–24). Here, let us briefly consider four additional avenues of critique.

Legislative Supremacy. Perhaps the most basic democratic problem with majoritarian review concerns institutional roles and competencies: compared with executive and especially legislative efforts to advance popular values and beliefs, judicial efforts will inevitably fall short on standard procedural criteria. Even when its members are elected at regular intervals, a court will never be as broadly accessible as the legislature, nor will it possess the latter's deliberative structures, information-gathering resources, or proactive lawmaking capabilities. Judges are not actually authorized to "represent" constituents in any formal sense, nor do they engage in the sorts of dialogic interactions that help make that representation meaningful. Arguments proffered in courts are often technical and spare compared with the explicit value disagreements hashed out on a senate floor (Waldron 2006). While there is room to debate whether an elected judge ought to be susceptible to popular influence in executing her duties, legislators remain avowedly open to popular influence throughout the duration of their tenure. Elective judiciaries might legitimately be responsive to the present popular will at the margins, when the law is unclear. Legislatures unabashedly aspire to effectuate the popular will *except* at the margins.

Judges cannot even promise to decide a case in a certain way without violating standard canons of judicial ethics. Should that case then come before the judge, she would be disqualified from hearing it, since virtually every state code of conduct requires recusal any time the judge's impartiality might reasonably be questioned (Goldberg, Sample, and Pozen 2007, 518). It is a basic expectation of legislators, by contrast, that they will make and be held accountable for specific campaign promises about specific policy outcomes. Furthermore, elective judiciaries are currently more distant from their constituents in a temporal sense, as every state that selects its judges by election grants them relatively long tenure in comparison with other elected officials (Schotland 2007, 1094).[10]

However flawed a state legislature may be as a stand-in for "the people themselves," then, it will have thicker and more extensive connections to them than will the judiciary. As a vehicle for democratic representation, the legislature will always have superior bona fides.

These comparative points suggest why it might undermine democratic values for a court, even when elected, to strike down a duly promulgated law that does not clearly violate the Constitution—and therefore why the democratic case for judicial restraint could be applied to elected state courts as well as to the appointed federal ones. They likewise suggest why, if the goal is to maximize representativeness or responsiveness in government, elective systems may be inferior in some respects to appointive systems that put the courts under the thumb of the legislature. Moreover, taken to their logical endpoint, these arguments can help shift the focus of debate away from judicial selection. For why fixate on selection and retention methods when the structure of judicial review can itself be changed? Irrespective of its judicial selection and retention scheme, a jurisdiction could promote legislative supremacy more directly by instituting a supermajority voting rule for statutory invalidations or a streamlined procedure for legislative overrides, as several U.S. states and Common-wealth countries have done, or simply by doing away with judicial review of legislation altogether.

The points sketched here cannot sink the democratic defense of majoritar-ian review for a number of reasons, including legislative-process pathologies that steer statutory outcomes away from the popular will and the absence of a clear legislative position, in many situations, to which a court might defer. But at a minimum, they call into question the representative character of elective judiciaries, as well as the notion that it advances democratic values when courts override or overlook the legislature in an effort to do just that.

Coherence, Feasibility, and Direct Democracy. In advocating that judges draw upon public preferences in resolving difficult legal questions, Hall im-plicitly assumes that the public has intelligible preferences on these questions, and that judges have the ability to discern them. These assumptions are prob-lematic, to say the least, and there may be strong rule-consequentialist grounds to prefer judges who ignore the anticipated reaction to their rulings (Sunstein 2007). But under certain conditions, the assumptions are not so implausible as to defeat the theory out of hand. It seems fair to expect that a significant number of citizens will have coherent, ascertainable preferences on at least a few high-salience legal questions.

The deeper problem, I believe, is not that members of the public are un-able to develop intelligible, respect-worthy preferences on questions of law, but rather that they are unlikely to do so on the precise sorts of questions that come before a court. State judges do not address legal questions in a vacuum. They do so in the context of specific cases, laden with all manner of supplemental claims, factual particularities, procedural histories, jurisdictional complexities, and doctrinal precedents that shape and constrain the judicial task. Ordinary citizens have neither the training, nor the resources, nor the time to engage these disputes in the way that judges must engage them. They are far better equipped to develop meaningful preferences on how a controversy ought to come out in a general sense—to think aspirationally about what their laws ought to provide in a class of cases, rather than interpretively about what they already do provide in a particular case.

An election supporter like Hall can plausibly dismiss as "antidemocratic" the concern that citizens will invariably approach legal interpretation through the lens of ordinary politics, and thereby conflate their sense of the proper re-sult with their momentary desires. She cannot, in my view, plausibly dismiss the concern that citizens will invariably evaluate most controversies at a higher level of abstraction, and with less sensitivity to the demands of professional legal reason, than would be appropriate for a judge. This descriptive feature of our sociolegal order, if not many others, severely limits the coherence and utility of any jurisprudence that aspires to vindicate popular preferences. For those preferences are unlikely to be keyed to the precise issues facing any given judge, or to have been developed, tested, and refined in any manner resembling the judicial process.

We also need to consider what kind of popular preferences, exactly, majoritarian review should aspire to vindicate in the first place. Is it the prevailing will of the current citizenry, as might be reflected in a vote or a poll? The prevailing will within the motivated minority that has actually bothered to engage the issue, submit amicus briefs, write editorials, lobby the legislature, and so forth? Or would the judge better serve democracy by attending instead to the majority will that would arise under conditions of fuller information, participation, and deliberation? To the extent that majoritarian review licenses the judge to depart from the will of the present people (as best she can perceive it) in the service of some idealized or transtemporal conception thereof, it begins to license the kind of free-wheeling and paternalistic judicial role that election supporters like Hall so fear. Yet to the extent that it requires the judge to remain focused on what today's citizens want as the touchstone for negotiating interpretive ambiguity, this begs another question of institutional design: why not just ask them?

Mechanisms of direct democracy such as ballot initiatives and referenda are common in many U.S. states and would seem to hold privileged, if not paradigmatic, status as vehicles for eliciting and vindicating the public's legal views. Judicial elections might have a unique claim to satisfy a commitment to political equality with respect to the composition of the judiciary. But they do not give citizens an equal share in the elaboration of law in a remotely comparable sense. Although the mechanisms of direct democracy are sufficiently burdensome that they could never fully usurp the judicial role in determining legal meaning, they could at least be used to determine very important questions. And they are just as compatible with unelected courts as with elected ones.[11]

Constitutionalism and the Fallacy of Composition. There is nothing about the theory of majoritarian review that suggests it would or should be inapplicable to constitutional law. To the contrary, we might expect that majoritarian review will be especially prevalent in this area, given that the average question of constitutional interpretation is both politically more salient and textually less determined than the average statutory or regulatory question. And we might expect that advocates like Hall would find this an especially attractive site for their interpretive method, given the unique symbolic and instrumental significance of constitutions and the relative difficulty of revising them. State constitutions may not be as important as their federal counterpart, but they are still enormously consequential in the lives of Americans. It would take a fairly radical commitment to presentist majority rule to maintain that judges should take into account the prevailing public sentiment every time they sentence a criminal, apply a common-law doctrine, or resolve a high-profile dispute. It is less radical to think that they should do so every time they functionally amend the constitution.

The current debate over same-sex marriage can help make the point more concrete. A question such as whether the equal protection clause of a state constitution guarantees a right to same-sex marriage is precisely the kind of textually underdetermined, newly emergent, value-laden, high-salience question for which it makes the most sense, conceptually, to endorse majoritarian review. If it seems clear that the bulk of the citizenry would strongly oppose a ruling that gay couples have a right to marry, Hall's logic suggests that the judge ought to aim to avoid such a ruling. The theory of majoritarian review—and, if we take the logic one step further, the choice to elect judges—presupposes that contemporary majorities should be empowered to influence the interpretation of the many non-self-evident provisions of their constitution, as against the understandings of those provisions that would emerge from a process of judicial reasoning less responsive to public opinion.

The notion that such responsiveness enhances the democratic legitimacy of the judicial system may strike some readers versed in federal constitutional theory as odd.[12] Depending on its precise formulation, this view may conflict with the idea that a constitution embodies an intergenerational scheme of self-government that combines majoritarian and nonmajoritarian aspects in the service of something greater than "statistical" democracy (Dworkin 1996, 20). It may conflict with the idea that judicially enforced constitutional rights can themselves be democracy-enhancing, for instance because they compensate for breakdowns in the political process caused by irrational prejudice, special-interest pressures, incumbent self-entrenchment, temporal myopia, or other pathologies; because they help keep government officials within the bounds of their enabling grant of power; because they honor commitments made in more profound moments of prior populism, involving heightened political engagement and agreement; or because certain kinds of secure entitlements of person and property are necessary prerequisites to meaningful social discourse and self-determination. The view may also conflict with the idea that judicial review embodies a deontic commitment to forms of political equality that help legitimize democratic rule, such as providing all aggrieved persons an opportunity for a fair hearing on a claim that some law or practice violates their rights. If everyone knows at the outset than an elected court is less likely than an unelected court to rule in favor of same-sex marriage because its members are less willing to contravene the apparent preferences of their constituents (whether out of a high-minded commitment to role fidelity, a self-interested commitment to job preservation, or anything in between), this value may be degraded.

These sorts of arguments can easily lapse into the polemical: an enormous amount of fine-grained work would be needed to map the competing theories of judicial review, democracy, and constitutionalism onto the competing methods of judicial selection and retention. I recite this litany simply to show that a jurisprudence and a judicial selection method that privilege contemporary sentiment may be at odds with thicker conceptions of democracy that encompass ideals of political equality, liberty, and universality as essential components of self-government. Corrupted forms of majoritarian review, in which judges privilege the views of powerful interests rather than the community as a whole, deviate even further from these ideals. Selecting judges through popular election aligns the decision-making norms of the courts more closely with those of the legislature, and in so doing can undermine some of the distinct democratic benefits that the former have, in countless formulations, been thought to provide.

The case for majoritarian review, then, is potentially at odds with many classic conceptions of constitutional law and the judicial role—not only with theories that romanticize courts as guardians of light and truth, but also with ones that would assign courts a protective role over *democratic* values. Perhaps some supporters of judicial elections really do subscribe to an ideal of self-government that seeks to maximize current voters' influence over all decisions of state or that lacks any notion of higher-order law. Absent some such belief, it is a fallacy of composition to think that making the selection method or the internal ethic of each part of government more democratic, invariably makes the government as a whole more democratic (Vermeule 2009,

37–39). Even if one believes that majoritarian decision-making procedures are uniquely fair or uniquely supportive of political equality, it does not follow that every institution of government ought to be selected by them or aim to reproduce them.

Backlash. But still, isn't there a clear democratic benefit from the fact that elective judiciaries are more likely to avoid the kinds of extreme backlash we have seen at the federal level in response to a few cases, such as *Roe v. Wade*, 410 U.S. 113 (1973)? Once again, it depends upon one's conception of democracy, as well as the dynamics of backlash. Robert Post and Reva Siegel have recently argued that it is not necessarily a bad thing, democratically speaking, for courts occasionally to eschew minimalism and to render decisions that risk generating outrage (2007). The presence of backlash indicates that a segment of the population feels deeply aggrieved, it can be disruptive and inefficient, and it can come over time to undermine the goals that inspired the contested ruling. Yet backlash can also sharpen legal questions, catalyze political engagement, and ultimately invigorate the democratic responsiveness and legitimacy of the courts' work. Sometimes, moreover, backlash may be an unavoidable "consequence of vindicating constitutional rights" (ibid., 395).

Elected judges, however, will generally seek to avoid backlash at all costs. Any segment of the population angry enough about a judicial decision to protest it represents a serious threat to the judge's re-election bid. Especially in low-information election environments, the safest strategy for an incumbent, absent a clear and widely held communal desire to move the law in some particular direction, will be to preserve the legal status quo. According to a group of state judges who met recently with Judge Posner, "The goal, if you are standing for reelection, is to avoid scrutiny. The goal in getting elected is to avoid negative attention, to be invisible" (Posner 2009, 1822). Hall herself has found that elected judges are less likely to publish dissents on politically volatile issues (1987). So long as Americans continue to be skeptical of judicial innovation and to favor incumbents, majoritarian review is likely to remain a relatively conservative, and opaque, social practice.

Consider once more the same-sex marriage example. It is a remarkable feature of the evolving constitutional jurisprudence on this subject that all four of the state high courts yet to find a constitutional right to same-sex marriage (Massachusetts, California, Connecticut, and Iowa, in chronological order),[13] plus all three of the high courts to issue sympathetic rulings covering much of the same ground (Hawaii, Vermont, and New Jersey),[14] were courts selected by gubernatorial appointment or by merit selection. It a remarkable testament to constitutional theory's inattention to state judicial selection that hardly anyone has noted this connection. Each of these opinions provoked significant forms of backlash, at the national as well as state level. Yet several of them also appear to have solidified support for same-sex marriage within the jurisdiction.

In my home state of Massachusetts, where justices are appointed by the governor and hold office until age seventy, legislative efforts to recognize same-sex marriage had gone nowhere for many years, and seemed to have no immediate prospects, prior to the landmark *Goodridge* decision (Jacobi 2006). Nevertheless, polls taken just days after the opinion came down showed that a full half of the state's residents supported the court's decision (Phillips and Klein 2003), and its logic now seems solidly entrenched. *Goodridge* transformed the political culture. "[O]nce *Goodridge*'s dust had settled," researchers have consistently found, "the state's elected institutions were significantly more supportive of [same-sex marriage] than they had been at the outset" (Keck 2009, 162). Decisions such as *Goodridge* have also emboldened some politicians from other states to endorse marriage rights for same-sex couples, not through any binding legal force but through their reasoning, their mainstreaming effect, and their persuasive authority.

To be sure, the rulings in favor of same-sex marriage by appointed and merit-selected high courts did not come out of nowhere. As scholars have documented at the federal level, judges continue to care about how their decisions are received even when they have life tenure, and judicial interpretations of open-ended constitutional guarantees are invariably shaped over time by changing social mores, grassroots movements, partisan trends, and countless other extrajudicial inputs. *Goodridge* likely never would have happened, would not have been possible, if the Massachusetts polling numbers in support of same-sex marriage had been in the single digits.

However, if the capacity of any court to forge new popular understandings will always be heavily dependent on context, the first wave of pro-same-sex-marriage decisions suggests that there can be a substantial difference between elected and nonelected judges in their willingness to try. Elected judges generally lack the job security, the moral stature, and the professional self-conception to defy entrenched norms or strongly held expectations. The nonelective selection method of the courts in the first wave plainly was not a sufficient factor to account for their rulings. It may have been a necessary one.

At one level, we saw earlier, the majoritarian review facilitated by an elective system makes the law more fluid. A concern for public opinion adds to the store of permissible interpretive materials, and it invites measures designed to elicit and enforce voter preferences. At another level, though, it makes the law more rigid, by preempting courts from issuing decisions ahead of the legal zeitgeist—decisions such as *Goodridge* that might have altered *future* public opinion, whether through their agenda-setting effects, the force of their arguments, the real-life consequences they engender, the cover they give to politicians, or any number of other mechanisms. When pusillanimous judicial interpretations merely reproduce and reinforce prevailing beliefs, when judges aspire to invisibility, the complex dialectic of backlash never gets off the ground. The courts contribute nothing distinctive to the "discursive formation of popular will upon which democracy is based" (Post and Siegel 2004, 1036).

In the short term, these jurisprudential implications might seem to mark a democratic triumph, as there will be fewer instances of judicial decisions—by unelected officials, no less—that roil a significant portion of "the actual people of the here and now" (Bickel 1986, 17). Yet if we take the diachronic view and conceptualize a people through time, as all constitutions invite us to, this triumph begins to look more hollow. A system that ties judges too tightly to public opinion can usurp the achievements of previous generations by channeling interpretation toward contemporary understandings of the provisions they enacted. It can usurp the achievements of future generations by foreclosing judicial innovations that might have helped generate, consolidate, and legitimize new understandings of the law. It can leave us in a majoritarian circle.

Conclusion

Melinda Gann Hall's book begins with the claim that it "represents the most comprehensive, systematic examination of state supreme court elections . . . ever undertaken" (Bonneau and Hall 2009, xv). That this claim is accurate (to my knowledge) reflects the important contributions Hall and her coauthor Chris Bonneau have made to the empirical study of state judicial selection. That this claim is accurate of a book that fails to engage with democratic theory, constitutional theory, or jurisprudence—indeed, that makes no attempt to engage in sustained normative analysis of any kind—reflects how much more work there is to do. A good place to begin would be to recognize just how contingent and contestable, and in some ways how radical, is the notion that judicial elections enhance democracy.

Notes

I am grateful to Charles Geyh for the invitation to contribute this essay and for his suggestion that it be framed as a response to Melinda Gann Hall; to Professor Hall for her graciousness; and to Bert Brandenburg for helpful conversation. The essay draws heavily on Pozen (2010). The views expressed herein are the author's alone and do not necessarily reflect the views of the Department of State or the United States Government.

1. Bonneau and Hall repeatedly invoke military imagery to convey the nature of this threat. "Judicial reform advocates," they warn, "are not just assaulting a method for choosing judges but also are waging war on democratic processes and the rights of citizens to maintain control over government" (2009, 139).

2. Research on this question has exploded in the past decade. For summaries of the literature with citations to leading studies, see Levi and Gulati (2009, 397–99) and Shepherd (2009b, 174–76).

3. Shepherd did find, however, that justices facing gubernatorial or legislative reappointment are more likely to vote for litigants from the other branches in civil cases, and that they do so with increasing frequency as their reappointment date approaches (2009a). A decade prior, Paul Brace, Melinda Gann Hall, and Laura Langer found that judges subject to competitive re-elections are less likely to overturn abortion-related statutes than merit-selected judges and judges with life tenure; that gubernatorial and legislative retention procedures lead to the fewest invalidations; and that the latter result is driven by judges' declining to hear challenges rather than rejecting them on the merits (1999).

4. This label is concededly crude. Like politics itself, majoritarian judicial review may not reflect a purely numbers-driven calculus in practice. But in theory, at least, those such as Hall who have urged judges to draw upon public sentiment appear to agree that judges should attend primarily to the *most widely held* sentiment; there is an irreducibly majoritarian basis to the literature's populist theories of judging. It is useful, furthermore, to draw the rhetorical contrast with the so-called "countermajoritarian" theories of judicial review that predominate in academic discussions of the U.S. Supreme Court.

5. Needless to say, Bonneau and Hall favor the former option. Although their research focuses on state supreme courts, their rhetoric suggests a preference for elections at all levels of the judicial hierarchy.

6. Zeisberg acknowledges that her argument would not hold if "major party divisions [were to] occur along jurisprudential lines" (2009, 794).

7. Moreover, this domain is liable to be larger in state supreme courts than in the lower federal courts, because the former have substantial control over their dockets and so can decline to hear cases that present only clear-cut issues.

8. James Gibson, however, has found that public trust in and respect for the courts are not diminished by candidates' policy pronouncements (for example, 2008). No study, as far as I am aware, has found that public confidence in the courts *increases* in response to new-style campaigns.

9. With respect to these sorts of worries about elected judges' lack of independence, I do not understand why "a critical point is this: the extent to which a judge surrenders to partisan pressures, political ambition, or any other force is entirely within her own control" (Hall, this volume). If, on account of the incentives it created and the norms it fostered, one set of lobbying rules made it far more likely that members of Congress would take bribes, and a critic therefore recommended a different set of lobbying rules, would it be an adequate response that the choice whether to take a bribe always remains with the individual legislator? The whole debate over judicial selection method necessarily takes the institutional point of view.

10. There is nothing inevitable about this arrangement; a state could grant its elected judges shorter terms than its legislators. That every state has done the opposite suggests a widely held ambivalence about the representative function of elected judges—a concern that they not be *too* responsive to their constituents.

11. Given her apparent commitment to presentist popular control over difficult legal questions, it would be interesting to learn whether Hall would support a robust practice of direct democracy in the states.

12. Readers who reject the analogy between federal constitutional law and state constitutional law may not much care what theorists of the former have had to say. This is a complicated issue that I cannot adequately treat here. I take it, however, that most participants in the debate over state judicial selection view state constitutions as "real" constitutions and state supreme court justices as "real" constitutional judges, and so would at least be inclined to entertain the analogy.

13. *Varnum v. Brien*, 763 N.W.2d 862 (Iowa 2009); *Kerrigan v. Comm'r of Pub. Health*, 957 A.2d 407 (Conn. 2008); In re Marriage Cases, 183 P.3d 384 (Cal. 2008); *Goodridge v. Dep't of Pub. Health*, 798 N.E.2d 941 (Mass. 2003).

14. *Lewis v. Harris*, 908 A.2d 196 (N.J. 2006); *Baker v. State*, 744 A.2d 864 (Vt. 1999); *Baehr v. Lewin*, 852 P.2d 44 (Haw. 1993).

References

Berdejó, Carlos, and Noam Yuchtman. 2010. "Crime, Punishment, and Politics: An Analysis of Political Cycles in Criminal Sentencing." Working paper. Available at http://faculty.haas.berkeley.edu/yuchtman/Site/Noam_Yuchtman_files/Berdejo_Yuchtman_Sept_Complete_plus_app_1.pdf.

Bickel, Alexander M. 1986. *The Least Dangerous Branch: The Supreme Court at the Bar of Politics*. 2d ed. New Haven: Yale University Press.

Bonneau, Chris W., and Melinda Gann Hall. 2009. *In Defense of Judicial Elections*. New York: Routledge.

Brace, Paul, Melinda Gann Hall, and Laura Langer. 1999. "Judicial Choice and the Politics of Abortion: Institutions, Context, and the Autonomy of Courts." *Albany Law Review* 62: 1265–1302.

Burbank, Stephen B., and Barry Friedman. 2002. "Reconsidering Judicial Independence." In Stephen B. Burbank and Barry Friedman, eds., *Judicial Independence at the Crossroads: An Interdisciplinary Approach*. Thousand Oaks, CA: Sage.

Cann, Damon M., and Jeff Yates. 2008. "Homegrown Institutional Legitimacy: Assessing Citizens' Diffuse Support for State Courts." *American Politics Research* 36: 297–329.

Choi, Stephen J., G. Mitu Gulati, and Eric A. Posner. 2010. "Professionals or Politicians: The Uncertain Empirical Case for an Elected rather than Appointed Judiciary." *Journal of Law, Economics and Organization* 26: 290–336.

Conference of Chief Justices. 2005. "Brief in Support of Defendants/Appellees." Filed in *Republican Party of Minn. v. White*, 416 F.3d 738 (8th Cir. 2005).

Dworkin, Ronald. 1996. *Freedom's Law: The Moral Reading of the American Constitution*. Cambridge, MA: Harvard University Press.

Edwards, Harry T. 1985. "Public Misperceptions concerning the 'Politics' of Judging: Dispelling Some Myths about the D.C. Circuit." *University of Colorado Law Review* 56: 619–46.

Friedman, Barry. 2009. *The Will of the People: How Public Opinion Has Influenced the Supreme Court and Shaped the Meaning of the Constitution*. New York: Farrar, Straus and Giroux.

Geyh, Charles Gardner. 2008. "The Endless Judicial Selection Debate and Why It Matters for Judicial Independence." *Georgetown Journal of Legal Ethics* 21: 1259–82.

Gibson, James L. 2008. "Challenges to the Impartiality of State Supreme Courts: Legitimacy Theory and 'New-Style' Judicial Campaigns." *American Political Science Review* 102: 59–75.

Goldberg, Deborah, James Sample, and David E. Pozen. 2007. "The Best Defense: Why Elected Courts Should Lead Recusal Reform." *Washburn Law Journal* 46: 503–34.

Hall, Melinda Gann. 1987. "Constituent Influence in State Supreme Courts: Conceptual Notes and a Case Study." *Journal of Politics* 49: 1117–24.

———. 2001. "State Supreme Courts in American Democracy: Probing the Myths of Judicial Reform." *American Political Science Review* 95: 315–30.

———. 2009. "The Controversy over Electing Judges and Advocacy in Political Science." *Justice System Journal* 30: 284–91.

Helland, Eric, and Alexander Tabarrok. 2002. "The Effect of Electoral Institutions on Tort Awards." *American Law and Economics Review* 4: 341–70.

Hershkoff, Helen. 2001. "State Courts and the 'Passive Virtues': Rethinking the Judicial Function." *Harvard Law Review* 114: 1833–1941.

Huber, Gregory A., and Sanford C. Gordon. 2004. "Accountability and Coercion: Is Justice Blind When It Runs for Office?" *American Journal of Political Science* 48: 247–63.

Jacobi, Tonja. 2006. "How Massachusetts Got Gay Marriage: The Intersection of Popular Opinion, Legislative Action, and Judicial Power." *Journal of Contemporary Legal Issues* 15: 219–41.

Jefferson, Thomas. 1820. "Letter from Thomas Jefferson to William Charles Jarvis, Sept. 28, 1820." In Paul Leicester Ford, ed., *The Writings of Thomas Jefferson 1816–1826,* vol. 10. New York: G. P. Putnam's Sons.

Kang, Michael S., and Joanna M. Shepherd. 2011. "The Partisan Price of Justice: An Empirical Analysis of Campaign Contributions and Judicial Decisions." *New York University Law Review* 86: forthcoming.

Keck, Thomas M. 2009. "Beyond Backlash: Assessing the Impact of Judicial Decisions on LGBT Rights." *Law and Society Review* 43: 151–85.

Kourlis, Rebecca Love, and Jordan M. Singer. 2007. "Using Judicial Performance Evaluations to Promote Judicial Accountability." *Judicature* 90: 200–207.

Kramer, Larry D. 2004. *The People Themselves: Popular Constitutionalism and Judicial Review.* New York: Oxford University Press.

Levi, David F., and Mitu Gulati. 2009. "Judging Measures." *University of Missouri-Kansas City Law Review* 77: 381–413.

Phillips, Frank, and Rick Klein. 2003. "50% in Poll Back SJC Ruling on Gay Marriage." *Boston Globe,* November 23, 2003, A1.

Posner, Richard A. 2006. "The Role of the Judge in the Twenty-First Century." *Boston University Law Review* 86: 1049–68.

———. 2008. *How Judges Think.* Cambridge, MA: Harvard University Press.

———. 2009. "A Conversation with Judge Richard A. Posner." *Duke Law Journal* 58: 1807–23.

Post, Robert, and Reva Siegel. 2004. "Popular Constitutionalism, Departmentalism, and Judicial Supremacy." *California Law Review* 92: 1027–43.

———. 2006. "Originalism as a Political Practice: The Right's Living Constitution." *Fordham Law Review* 75: 545–74.

———. 2007. "*Roe* Rage: Democratic Constitutionalism and Backlash." *Harvard Civil Rights Civil Liberties Law Review* 42: 373–433.

Pozen, David E. 2008. "The Irony of Judicial Elections." *Columbia Law Review* 108: 265–330.

———. 2010. "Judicial Elections as Popular Constitutionalism." *Columbia Law Review* 110: 2047–2134.

Rostow, Eugene V. 1952. "The Democratic Character of Judicial Review." *Harvard Law Review* 66: 193–224.

Schotland, Roy A. 1998. "Comment." *Law and Contemporary Problems* (Summer): 149–55.

———. 2007. "New Challenges to States' Judicial Selection." *Georgetown Law Journal* 95: 1077–1103.

Shepherd, Joanna M. 2009a. "Are Appointed Judges Strategic Too?" *Duke Law Journal* 58: 1589–1626.

———. 2009b. "The Influence of Retention Politics on Judges' Voting." *Journal of Legal Studies* 38: 169–203.

———. 2009c. "Money, Politics, and Impartial Justice." *Duke Law Journal* 58: 623–85.

Shugerman, Jed Handelsman. 2010. "The Twist of Long Terms: Judicial Elections, Role Fidelity, and American Tort Law." *Georgetown Law Journal* 98: 1349–1413.

Sullivan, Kathleen M. 2008. "*Republican Party of Minnesota v. White*: What Are the Alternatives?" *Georgetown Journal of Legal Ethics* 21: 1327–45.

Sunstein, Cass R. 2007. "If People Would Be Outraged by Their Rulings, Should Judges Care?" *Stanford Law Review* 60: 155–212.

Tabarrok, Alexander, and Eric Helland. 1999. "Court Politics: The Political Economy of Tort Awards." *Journal of Law and Economics* 42: 157–88.

Tamanaha, Brian Z. 2009. "The Distorting Slant in Quantitative Studies of Judging." *Boston College Law Review* 50: 685–758.

Vermeule, Adrian. 2009. "The Supreme Court, 2009 Term—Foreword: System Effects and the Constitution." *Harvard Law Review* 123: 4–72.

Waldron, Jeremy. 1999. *Law and Disagreement*. New York: Oxford University Press.

———. 2006. "The Core of the Case against Judicial Review." *Yale Law Journal* 115: 1346–1406.

Zeisberg, Mariah. 2009. "Should We Elect the US Supreme Court?" *Perspectives on Politics* 7: 785–803.

IV WHAT LAW HAS TO DO WITH WHAT JUDGES DO AND ITS IMPLICATIONS FOR PUBLIC CONFIDENCE IN THE COURTS

11 Judging the Politics of Judging

Are Politicians in Robes Inevitably Illegitimate?

James L. Gibson

MANY LEGAL SCHOLARS assume that politicized processes of selecting state and federal judges in the United States contribute—and some would say contribute mightily—to the erosion of confidence in the judiciary. The assumption of this position is that anything associated with politics delegitimizes courts: politics poisons the judiciary. Campaigning for the bench in particular is commonly said to pose every manner of threat to the "nonpolitical" nature of the judiciary, the most crucial wellspring of institutional legitimacy. As one observer put it:

> The spread of negative campaigning in judicial races is likely to have adverse consequences for the court system. The motives of judicial candidates will be cast into doubt, and public esteem for the judiciary will suffer. Not only will candidates for judicial office be equated with ordinary politicians, but the impartiality, independence, and professionalism of the judiciary will also be called into question. Large-scale advertising in state judicial elections will further politicize state courts in the eyes of the public. (Iyengar 2002, 697)

Courts in the United States are at risk owing to the processes used to select judges.

Unfortunately, however, this assumption has not been subjected to much rigorous, empirical investigation. In order to assess this hypothesis with any degree of rigor, several tasks must be undertaken. First, some definitions are in order. While it is not too difficult to define "confidence"—a substantial literature on attitudes toward courts exists—more demanding is the task of deriving an agreeable definition of "politicized." And more difficult still is the unpacking of the processes by which politicization undermines confidence (if in fact it does). If the politicization/legitimacy connection is to be considered as an empirical characterization of the American judiciary today, much more effort must be put into testing each of the linkages in what is undoubtedly a fairly complex causal model of citizen attitude formation and change.

The overriding hypothesis of this paper is that the consequences of politicization cannot be apprehended without direct investigation of *what it is citizens want from their courts*. What I will refer to as the "Expectancy Model" includes two crucial elements: what citizens expect of courts, and what they perceive courts to be doing. The conventional (if often implicit) assumption seems to be that (1) nearly all citizens hold the same expectations of courts, (2) that expectations of judicial independence trump all other possible functions courts might perform, and (3) that all citizens hold similar views of how judges go about making decisions.[1] Because citizens are assumed to value judicial independence above all else, deviation from independence—as in making courts more accountable through the political process—is therefore thought to undermine judicial legitimacy. However, to the extent that citizens view courts as inherently and inevitably political in nature, then politicization is unlikely to detract from judicial legitimacy. Thus the central empirical objective of this paper is to map citizens' expectations of the judiciary and to determine whether a connection exists between these attitudes and the willingness to extend legitimacy to courts.

Even though Legitimacy Theory is widely accepted among legal scholars and social scientists, it is perhaps useful to begin this analysis with an overview of the theory and especially how it is connected to the expectations citizens hold of institutions.

Legitimacy Theory and Its Application to the Judiciary

Legitimacy Theory is widely used among scholars of the judiciary to try to explain why ordinary citizens would accept a court decision with which they disagree. The theory begins by positing that legitimacy becomes particularly relevant in the presence of an objection precondition, which is simply to assert that people will accept decisions that they find agreeable, and that issues of acceptance and acquiescence become significant only when a decision is objectionable. Why do citizens accept or obey the law? They do so because they believe the institution creating the law has the right to make such decisions and does so through a set of procedures for decision-making that are acceptable to the citizens. Legitimacy means being willing to grant the authority to an institution to make decisions; legitimacy is predicated upon a set of expectations for procedures—and in the judicial case, those expectations center around the decision-maker being fair, open-minded, and impartial. It follows as well that if an institution has a right to make decisions, that institution should not be punished for making objectionable decisions. Easton's apt phrase is that legitimacy may be thought of as a reservoir of good will, which means that the institution can get away with making decisions with which people disagree. As Martin Lipset (1981, 64) put it: legitimacy "involves the capacity of a political system to engender and maintain the belief that existing political institutions are the most appropriate and proper ones for the society."

Within the American context, examples of the Supreme Court relying upon its legitimacy to ensure compliance with its decisions are not difficult to find. For example, most scholars believe that the Court's high level of legitimacy allowed its highly controversial decision in *Bush v. Gore* to "stick." Furthermore, the Court's controversial ruling in the presidential election did not undermine the legitimacy of the institution itself (Gibson, Caldeira, and Spence 2003; Kritzer 2001; Nicholson and Howard 2003; and Yates and Whitford 2002); indeed, it may have even enhanced it (Gibson 2007). It seems that public attitudes toward the U.S. Supreme Court are remarkably resistant to alteration by the decisions of the Court. This case presents a textbook illustration of the power of institutional legitimacy.

Furthermore, in the American context, examples of failed efforts to punish the U.S. Supreme Court are also easily found (see Whittington 2003; Geyh 2006). Every year, in the U.S. Congress, a wide variety of court curbing bills are introduced.[2] The failure of those bills to pass is in no small degree a function of the unwillingness of the American people to punish the Court for its decisions. Because the U.S. Supreme Court enjoys great popular legitimacy, citizens are unwilling to support efforts to punish the institution for its decisions, even its objectionable decisions. That unwillingness is a fundamental consequence of the legitimacy of the institution.

All institutions need political capital in order to be effective, to get their decisions accepted by others and be successfully implemented. Since courts are typically thought to be weak institutions—having neither the power of the "purse" (control of the treasury) nor the "sword" (control over agents of state coercion)—their political capital must be found in resources other than finances and force. For courts, their principal political capital is institutional legitimacy.

But where do courts get their legitimacy? In a democratic society, the principal sources of legitimacy for political institutions are elections and accountability. As part of the social contract, citizens grant authority to political institutions to make public policy and therefore accept the decisions they produce. The contract is enforced by accountability. Institutional decision-makers who repeatedly make decisions with which citizens disagree are subject to replacement; institutions that fail repeatedly also can be radically restructured (for example, court packing) or even abolished. Electoral accountability is perhaps the most powerful source of legitimacy for political institutions in a democratic polity.

According to Brandenburg and Schotland (2008, 102): "More than 89 percent of America's state judges must stand for election to sit on the bench or retain office." However, courts throughout the world are not typically subject to electoral accountability (Kritzer 2007). Consequently, many courts begin with a legitimacy shortfall. This is of course particularly true of the U.S. Supreme Court, where the legitimacy shortfall is punctuated by lifetime tenure, which makes any sort of policy-making accountability virtually impossible. In the absence of an electoral connection, courts seek legitimacy through the rule of law, by which I mean courts are deemed to be legitimate to the extent that their decision-making is principled and grounded in the universalism of law—that is, to the extent that their decision-making processes are procedurally correct and acceptable. The image of the blind lady justice is most apposite for this source of legitimacy.

Connected to this view of legitimacy is expertise: that is, to the extent that judges are deemed to be experts in law who ably apply their legal training to decisions within the context of the rule of law, legitimacy attaches. Even in a democratic society, a wide variety of public-policy decisions are turned over to experts—for instance, much of the control of the economy is placed within the purview of relatively unaccountable institutions. Such experts are subject to limited accountability; they are given the freedom to "do the right thing" within the context of their expertise.

Judges seek to enshroud their decision-making with technical imagery, suggesting to their constituents that their decisions ought to be accepted because they are correct, in the same sense that decisions on the economy must be accepted because they represent the judgments of experts on technical issues. Judges tell us that they follow the law, and because they follow the law, their decisions should be accepted. In following the law, they are giving effect to the will of the majority through its support of legislation and constitutions. To package decisions as discretionless and guided only by technical expertise is to inoculate those institutions from challenges and to confer legitimacy upon them.

There can be no doubt therefore that legitimacy is one of the most highly valued forms of political capital. As I have presented the theory here, legitimacy turns on institutional decision-makers satisfying expectations regarding the procedural components of their decision-making. Citizens expect judges to make decisions in a fair and impartial way, and when they do so, that process of decision-making virtually automatically generates an obligation to comply. Thus, the satisfaction of expectations is crucial to legitimacy.

We typically think of courts as subject to some defining sets of expectations, as I have mentioned several times already, particularly the requirement that they be fair and impartial. It seems quite reasonable to assume that the vast majority of citizens in a democratic polity expect their judges to make decisions in a fair and impartial way on the basis of the rule of law.

But these are of course not the only expectations citizens might hold of judges. They might, for instance, expect judges to make decisions that are fair and just, and it may very well be that in some instances fairness and the rule of law battle with one another. In the instance of conflict between justice and legality, some may prefer that fairness trump legality; others prefer that legality be deemed superior to fairness. The expectations citizens hold matter.

Furthermore, in many instances, the technical aspects of decisions are nearly irrelevant to rendering decisions. Under such conditions—the condition under which law is not dispositive, the condition under which discretion exists on how decisions should be made—citizens may expect that judges take into account the broader values of the society in making their decisions. But not all citizens will agree with that. Some may believe that decisions ought to be made only on the basis of the intent of those creating the legislation and constitutions; others may disagree. If citizens understand decision-making to be discretionary in the sense that judges must choose their course of action rather than deduce it, then it follows that law cannot be the only legitimate basis of decision-making. But again, citizens likely differ on these issues. The essential point here is that expectations matter and that expectations vary across citizens.

Only a handful of studies have seriously considered the expectations citizens hold of judges and courts, although scholars of the legislative process have paid more attention to citizens' expectations of Congress (for example, Kimball and Patterson 1997). For example, focusing on public attitudes toward the German Federal Constitutional Court, Baird (2001) shows that the nature of the expectations citizens hold of the FCC, and especially expectations of legalistic styles of decision-making, are related to the willingness to attribute legitimacy to the institution (see also Baird and Gangl 2006).

I have presented here a simple theory of expectations. It is doubtful, however, that expectations are themselves quite so simple. Citizens may expect many things from their judicial institutions, and the things they expect may not be internally coherent or consistent. Some citizens may understand the judiciary as just another political institution, whereas others may view the judiciary as a unique institution that should act in a fashion quite distinct from other political institutions. Citizens vary on this score. In a society in which courts are very well defined, quite salient public institutions, often rendering important public-policy decisions—such as in the United States—citizens may have reasonably well developed but diverse understandings of and expectations of courts.

Thus, legitimacy is ultimately grounded in the satisfaction of the expectations of the citizenry. In the case of courts (but perhaps more broadly as well), the expectations primarily concern processes of decision-making. It is crucial, therefore, to understand the nature of these expectations.

Summary: The Research Question

Do politicized judicial selection processes undermine judicial legitimacy, and, if so, how widely? To the extent that people expect and prefer a judiciary that is well insulated from the political process, politicization of selection processes may undermine the legitimacy of courts. But to the extent that citizens instead expect political accountability for their judges, politicized campaigning is unlikely to affect legitimacy. The effect of judges' activities in their pursuit of a judgeship depends mightily on what people want from their judges, not what legal judicial elites think people should want from their judges. Thus, it is crucial to map the expectations people hold and to determine whether those expectations are connected to the willingness to extend legitimacy to judicial institutions.

Research Design

The analysis is based upon a three-wave panel survey conducted in Kentucky in 2006. A sample of residents was interviewed before the fall elections, during the election season, and well after the elections. Details on the survey can be found in the Appendix, below.

This research focuses on a state in which politicized campaigns are relatively new but not unheard of. At this point in history, states such as Ohio and Texas are not particularly revealing, since citizens of those states have long witnessed highly politicized campaigning for judicial office. At the other end of the continuum, some states have, to date, been immune to politicization. For instance, in the high court elections of 2004, all of the candidates in ten states reported raising *no contributions* as part of their campaigns for a seat on the state court of last resort (Goldberg et al. 2005, 14). Kentucky lies between the extremes on this continuum. Among the twenty-one states in which judicial candidates raised at least some contributions in 2004, Kentucky defined the median, with candidates in ten states raising less than $239,317 and candidates in ten states raising more than that figure. Moreover, also in 2004, abortion-related questionnaires were distributed by interest groups to judicial candidates in Kentucky. Some candidates refused to answer the questionnaires, which prompted a well-publicized lawsuit by the Family Trust Foundation challenging legal and ethical constraints on speech that appear to commit a candidate to a position that might come before the courts. The Family Trust Foundation was successful in its litigation.[3] Thus, in terms of the prior judicial election and the political context to which these respondents had most recently been exposed, some but perhaps not a very high degree of judicial politicization existed.

Finally, I note that an experimental vignette about the effects of campaigning on perceived impartiality that was part of the initial interview of the Kentucky respondents (Gibson 2008) has been replicated with a national sample of Americans and produced quite similar results (Gibson 2009). Nothing about Kentucky seems to be significantly aberrant when it comes to judicial elections and the legitimacy of the Supreme Court. So although statistical theory provides little basis for generalizing these findings to other state judiciaries, Kentucky satisfies a number of design criteria that make it a useful state for an inquiry such as this.[4]

Analysis

Expectations of Kentucky Judges

We asked the respondents to give us their views of the characteristics of a good Kentucky Supreme Court judge, and their replies are reported in Table

11.1. Note that some obvious attributes—for example, being fair and impartial in decision-making—were purposefully excluded from the questionnaire because I thought it safe to assume (based in part on pretest results) that virtually all Kentuckians wanted their judges to decide cases in a fair and impartial manner. So rather than being an exhaustive list of judicial traits, this question focused on areas where I expected some disagreement among Kentuckians.

Two characteristics stand out from the rest in this table: Kentuckians are strongly united in the view that their Supreme Court judges ought to "strictly follow the law no matter what people in the state may want," and "be especially concerned about protecting people without power from people and groups with power." On their face, these items seem contradictory. "Strictly following the law" seems to indicate a procedural characteristic, especially when it is juxtaposed with an outcome—what the people of the state may want. On the other hand, protecting people without power smacks of substance, not procedure. Moreover, the former seems highly legalistic (following the law); the latter item seems much more political in the sense that it addresses power differentials in the larger society, not necessarily the strength of legal arguments. Of those rating "following the law" as very important, 75.1 percent also rate "protecting people without power" as very important (even though the responses to these two items are virtually uncorrelated).

I also note from Table 11.1 that the constituency for a very explicitly political view of judging is perhaps small, but it is far from trivial. While only 18.5 percent of the respondents favor partisanship as a basis for judicial decision-making, 43.7 percent expect to have their own ideological views given weight by the judges, and nearly one-third (30.1 percent) believe in majoritarianism as a basis of judicial decision-making. Indeed, nearly one-half (46.5 percent) of the respondents agree that judges ought to be "involved in politics, since ultimately they should represent the majority." This majoritarian politics view of judging is attractive to a substantive proportion of the people of Kentucky.

These data certainly suggest complex, if not confused, views of judges (see Bybee 2009). Indeed, for some of these characteristics, it may be that the responses are not particularly high in substantive content. Considering the entire set of ten items, the squared Multiple Correlation Coefficients between the item and the set are below .07 for the following statements: strictly follow the law (.06), protect people without power (.05), respect existing decisions (.07), and refuse to accept campaign contributions (.03). These small coefficients may indicate that the responses contain a great deal of idiosyncratic variance, variance that may be random because little substance underlies the respondents'

TABLE 11.1

Expectations of the Characteristics of a Good Supreme Court Justice,
Kentucky 2006

Characteristic	% rating very important	Mean	Std. dev.	N
Protect people without power	72.9	3.64	.69	1438
Strictly follow the law	71.8	3.62	.68	1437
State policy positions during campaigns	64.2	3.49	.80	1438
Refuse to accept campaign contributions	48.2	3.17	.96	1435
Respect existing decisions	47.2	3.32	.76	1437
Represent the majority	46.5	3.07	1.05	1436
Give my ideology a voice	43.7	3.18	.88	1435
Use contributions to get issue stands out	40.9	3.06	.97	1436
Decide the way the want majority wants	30.1	2.72	1.09	1435
Base decisions on party affiliations	18.5	2.11	1.13	1433

The items read:

"Now I would like you to focus on thinking about the characteristics of a good Supreme Court judge, that is, what a good judge ought to be like. First, how important would you say it is for a good Kentucky Supreme Court judge to . . .

"Be especially concerned about protecting people without power from people and groups with power.

"Strictly follow the law no matter what people in the country may want.

"State how they stand on important legal and political issues as part of their campaigning for a position on the Kentucky Supreme Court.

"Refuse to accept any campaign contributions from anyone — individuals, groups, and political parties.

"Respect existing Kentucky Supreme Court decisions by changing the law as little as possible.

"Be involved in politics, since ultimately they should represent the majority.

"Give [conservatives/liberals] a strong voice in how the constitution is interpreted.

"Use campaign contributions to get their messages out about where they stand on important issues likely to come before the court.

"Decide cases the way the majority of the people in Kentucky prefer, even if it goes against existing laws.

"Base their decisions on whether they are a Republican or a Democrat."

The response varies from (1) Not at all important/Don't know to (4) Very important. Thus, higher mean scores indicate greater ascribed importance to the characteristic.

answers. These findings may indicate that characteristics such as following the law and protecting those without power are largely platitudes, to which nearly all subscribe, but which, at the same time, have little practical meaning in the minds of many if not most citizens. The remainder of the items are all reasonably intercorrelated.

In fact, when these six items are factor analyzed (Common Factor Analysis), a unidimensional structure is revealed.[5] All items load on the first unrotated factor at .40 or higher, with the strongest loading associated with the "represent the majority" (be involved in politics) item. Cronbach's alpha for the six-item set is .65, indicating modest reliability (mean inter-item correlation = .23). The latent dimension suggested by these factor analysis results is one that seems to indicate the degree to which the respondents favor a politicized view of judging.

Because the correlation between the factor score and a simple summation of the response to the six items is .99, I will use the former as the indicator of the expectation of a politicized judiciary. I also use for some purposes a simple count of the number of items of the six that the respondent rated as "very important." A very small percentage of respondents (2.8 percent) have entirely politicized expectations of judges. The mean of the distribution is 2.4, which is decidedly skewed toward holding less political expectations of judges. The most important finding from this analysis is that Kentuckians vary in what they expect from their judges, even if a highly politicized view of judging is rejected by a majority, but not a great majority, of the people.[6]

Summary. As I have noted, the most important conclusion of this portion of the analysis is that the expectations people hold of their judges vary. Not everyone accepts that mechanical jurisprudence constitutes the best form of judging; not everyone accepts that judicial independence is a value trumping all other considerations. Instead, people have different conceptions of judging, leading them to hold different expectations about what constitutes a good judge. The importance of this finding is that, because people have different conceptions of judging, campaign activity (and other off-the-bench judicial behavior) is unlikely to be uniformly evaluated. Most specifically, if some citizens expect the judiciary to make ideologically based decisions, then those citizens are unlikely to be offput when judges express their ideological views during the selection process. The conclusion that policy talk and other forms of politicized campaigning would cause these citizens to evaluate the judiciary as illegitimate is most likely wrong, at least for a substantial portion of the population.

Expectations and the Institutional Legitimacy of the Kentucky Supreme Court

To what degree are the expectations people hold of the judiciary connected to the willingness to extend legitimacy to courts? One might hypothesize that those with more politicized expectations of courts hold the judiciary in lesser esteem because they are less likely to subscribe to a mythical view of judging. As we have argued in the context of the U.S. Supreme Court (for example, Gibson and Caldeira 2009a), support for the Supreme Court results from exposure to the institution and its legitimizing symbols. Consequently, it is revealing to explore the interconnections of expectations and institutional legitimacy.[7]

I measured loyalty toward the Kentucky Supreme Court with reactions (collected on five-point Likert response sets) to the following conventional in-

TABLE 11.2

Loyalty Toward the Kentucky State Supreme Court, Attentive Public, 2006

Item	Level of Diffuse Support (Percentage[a])			Mean[b]	Std. dev.	N[c]
	Not Sup-portive	Unde-cided	Support-ive			
Do Away with the Court	19.7	11.2	69.1	3.61	1.09	1938
The Court can be trusted	16.1	18.0	65.9	3.54	.89	1937
Limit the Court's Jurisdiction	36.0	22.2	41.9	3.07	1.05	1933
Remove Judges Who Decide Against Majority	40.3	20.5	39.3	2.96	1.11	1937
Majority View of Constitution is Most Important	51.9	17.3	30.8	2.74	1.13	1937
Court Gets Too Mixed Up in Politics	45.7	27.6	26.7	2.75	.98	1936
Make the Court Less Independent	63.5	12.9	23.5	2.53	1.04	1939
Politics Inevitable, Must Control the Court	57.8	19.4	22.8	2.56	1.06	1938

Note: The statements read:

"If the Kentucky Supreme Court started making a lot of decisions that most people disagree with, it might be better to do away with the Supreme Court altogether. (Disagree)

"The Kentucky Supreme Court can usually be trusted to make decisions that are right for the state as a whole. (Agree)

"The right of the Kentucky Supreme Court to decide certain types of controversial issues should be reduced. (Disagree)

"Judges of the Kentucky Supreme Court who consistently make decisions at odds with what a majority of the people in the state want should be removed from their position as judge. (Disagree)

"The Kentucky Supreme Court may have its ideas about what the constitution means, but more important is what the majority of people think the constitution means. (Disagree)

"The Kentucky Supreme Court gets too mixed up in politics. (Disagree)

"The Kentucky Supreme Court ought to be made less independent so that it listens a lot more to what the people want. (Disagree)

"It is inevitable that the Kentucky Supreme Court gets mixed up in politics; therefore, we ought to have stronger means of controlling the actions of the Kentucky Supreme Court. (Disagree)"

[a]The percentages total to 100 percent across the three columns (except for rounding errors).

[b]The means and standard deviations are calculated on the uncollapsed, five-point Likert response sets. Higher mean scores indicate higher levels of institutional support.

[c]N represents the institution's attentive public – those with some awareness of the institution.

dicators (see Table 11.2). Following earlier research on attitudes toward courts, I analyze the responses to these questions only among what is termed the "attentive public"—those who claim at least some level of awareness of the institution.[8] In this case, 4.9 percent of the respondents are excluded as too ill informed for their attitudes to have much substantive meaning. Table 11.2 reports the univariate frequencies on these court support variables.

The data in Table 11.2 support a variety of conclusions. First, "don't know" responses on these propositions were issued by about one-fifth of the respondents. The percentages of respondents without an opinion on the statements vary from a low of 11.2 to a high of 27.6, but in general the proportion is about one-fifth. This finding is itself somewhat surprising in that one might have expected considerably higher rates of nonopinionation.

Across the various statements, support for the Kentucky Supreme Court varies widely from 22.8 to 69.1 percent of the respondents giving supportive replies. Only a small proportion of Kentuckians (19.7 percent) would do away with the court if it made a string of objectionable decisions, although a substantial majority (63.5 percent) would prefer a court that is *less* independent of the will of the people. If a general conclusion can be drawn from the responses to these various statements, it is that the idea of an independent institution blocking efforts of the majority of the people to have its way politically is not very attractive to a considerable number of Kentucky citizens.

When these eight items are subjected to Common Factor Analysis, a two-dimensional solution emerges.[9] However, the second factor is defined overwhelmingly by the statement about expressing trust in the Supreme Court.[10] When the seven items defining the first dimension are separately factor analyzed, a strongly unidimensional solution emerges. Consequently, I have extracted from the unrotated eight-item factor solution a single factor score as the indicator of institutional loyalty. The trust item has a low loading on this factor. However, the correlation between the factor score and a simple summated index of the replies to the eight items is .99.[11] Moreover, Cronbach's alpha for the eight-item set is .74, and alpha varies trivially with the deletion of the trust item (that is, = .75). For simplicity, I use the summated index as the measure of institutional loyalty. I also use for some descriptive purposes a variable that is a count of the number of supportive responses (mean supportive = 3.2, among the attentive public).

As expected, those holding more politicized expectations of courts are decidedly less supportive of the Kentucky Supreme Court ($r = -.38$; $p < .000$).[12] Those with politicized expectations are much less willing to extend the legitimacy to the court that it needs to be effective.

The Relationship between Institutional Support and Knowledge of the Courts

Because it is typically assumed that more knowledgeable citizens are more important to the judiciary—and that the more knowledgeable hold attitudes that differ from the less knowledgeable—the next interconnection that must be considered is that between loyalty toward the Kentucky Supreme Court and knowledge of the Kentucky judicial systems. To do so, a measure of judicial knowledge is necessary.

As I have noted, the expectations questions were asked at the opening of the t_2 interview. So as to avoid clouding the issues of causality, I have used a measure of knowledge derived from the t_1 interview, during which we asked the Kentuckians factual questions about their Supreme Court. The questions we asked and the percentages of respondents answering correctly are:

Whether the justices are elected or not—24.0 percent correct (elected)
Whether the justices serve a life or fixed term—32.9 percent correct (fixed)
Whether the justices have the "last say" on the meaning of the constitution—45.6 percent correct (they do)

Across all three items, the average number of correct answers is 1.0, with fully one-third of the respondents getting none of the test items correct and only 7.3 percent answering accurately to all three. Although these questions were asked during a period of relatively low salience of the state judiciary,[13] by no means can knowledge of the state Supreme Court be judged to be anything but dismally low.[14] Interestingly, the correlation between the general court knowledge index and awareness of the candidates in the election (measured at t_2) is only .11, which most likely reflects the fact that two different types of knowledge are being measured: general information about the institution and specific information about who is running at the moment, in the respondent's judicial district.

Extant research has uniformly revealed that greater knowledge of courts is connected to greater support for them (for example, Gibson, Caldeira, and Baird 1998; Gibson and Caldeira 2009a). Kentucky is no exception to this general rule: the correlation between the support index and knowledge is .16 ($p <$ .000), which comes as no surprise.

Connecting Expectations with Knowledge of the Courts

A few commentators acknowledge that some citizens distinguish little between courts and other political institutions, and, for those folks, finding that the politicized view of judging has a nontrivial constituency will be of little surprise. Most of these observers dismiss this model of judging as inappropriate, and they do so on normative grounds (for example, judicial independence and the rule of law trump everything). Some believe that the politicized view of judging is only embraced by the politically ignorant, and that, were they better informed, they would abandon this position. For instance, Jamieson and Hardy (2008, 12) assert: "With ignorance about the judiciary comes an increased disposition to believe that judges are biased and a reduced tendency to hold that the courts act in the public interest" (see also Jamieson and Hennessy 2007).

The degree to which views of judging are connected to knowledge and ignorance is an important empirical question. Consequently, the simple hypothesis guiding this portion of the analysis is that those more knowledgeable about the Kentucky judiciary will tend to reject the view that the courts should respond to political inputs and pressures. Knowledge and the politicized view of judging should be inversely related.

The specific hypothesis I test in this section is that those most knowledgeable about courts hold distinctive expectations of judging. Table 11.3 reports the relationships between court knowledge and the importance assigned to different judicial characteristics.

The most common finding of this table is that those with high levels of knowledge *differ little* from those with relatively low levels of knowledge (see the tau-beta column). For instance, the vast majority of Kentuckians, irrespective of the information they hold about the Kentucky judiciary, expect that judges should protect people without power from those with power. Those high and low in knowledge do not differ on whether a judge should strictly follow the law, respect existing decisions, or even give the respondent's ideology a voice. In terms of campaign activity, no knowledge differences exist on whether judges should refuse to accept campaign contributions, use contributions to get their issue stands out, or state their policy positions during their campaigns (although the difference on the last item approaches statistical significance: $p = .062$). It is noteworthy that the strongest difference between the more and less knowledgeable is on the statement about representing the majority. Empirically, those high in knowledge are a minority in Kentucky (7.9 percent). If they think of themselves as in the minority, then that might explain their reluctance to agree that courts should represent the majority.

Those with high levels of knowledge are distinctive in their expectations on three of the characteristics reported in Table 11.3. The knowledgeable are less likely to assert that judges should represent the majority, that they should base their decisions on their party affiliations, and that they should decide the way the

TABLE 11.3

The Impact of Judicial Knowledge on Expectations

	Amount of Judicial Knowledge				
Characteristic	0	1	2	3	tau-beta
Protect people without power	72.2	72.6	73.5	76.3	.02
Strictly follow the law	70.2	71.3	71.3	*82.5*	.03
State policy positions during campaigns	65.9	64.9	64.3	*53.5*	-.04
Refuse to accept campaign contributions	44.2	49.8	54.9	*39.5*	.03
Respect existing decisions	48.4	47.4	43.7	50.9	-.01
Represent the majority	54.4	40.7	53.7	*25.4*	-.11***
Give my ideology a voice	45.5	41.3	46.6	40.7	-.03
Use contributions to get issue stands out	40.2	41.2	43.2	36.0	-.02
Decide the way the want majority wants	30.7	30.7	31.2	22.8	-.07**
Base decisions on party affiliations	19.2	18.4	19.6	14.0	-.07***

Note: The entries shown are the percentages of respondents rating the characteristic as "very important," the most extreme point on the response set. The correlation shown is calculated from the full distribution of importance ratings. N ≈ 1,436.

Differences across all levels of judicial knowledge: *** $p < .001$ ** $p < .01$ * $p < .05$.

Italic entries for the highest level of knowledge indicate that the difference between those high in knowledge and all others is significant at $p < .05$.

For the full text of the items, see the note to Table 11.2.

majority wants. Using the full index of politicized expectations, a highly significant but not particularly strong relationship exists between levels of knowledge and the politicization of judicial expectations. The correlation between knowledge and holding politicized expectations is −.14, indicating that more knowledge is associated with less emphasis on political orientations for judges.[15]

Table 11.3 also reports the items upon which those highest in political knowledge (that is, who score a "3" on the knowledge index) are distinctive from the remainder of the sample. On four items, the difference is statistically significant at $p < .05$. The most knowledgeable are distinctive in their views of strictly following the law, stating policy positions during campaigns, refusing to accept campaign contributions, and representing the majority. Not all of these relationships are substantively meaningful: for example, on refusing to accept campaign contributions, those highest in knowledge hold about the same views as those lowest in knowledge. Overall, the correlation between a knowledge dichotomy (high versus all else) and the index of politicized expectations is −.15, which is the same as the relationship with the more finely tuned measure of knowledge.

These findings are decidedly mixed. One conclusion is that the more knowledgeable place less emphasis on political aspects of judging, as in their rejection of the view that courts should represent the majority. At the same time, however, those high in knowledge are little more committed to a mechanical view of judging than those low in knowledge. Furthermore, a majority of those with high knowledge assert that judges should state their policy positions during their campaigns for a seat on the bench, and a large majority believe that judges should protect the powerless. These findings seem to indicate a complex, if not confused, view of what it is judges should be doing.

Perhaps what these data indicate is something like the following. Perhaps only a small portion of the population views mechanical jurisprudence as feasible or desirable. Everyone most likely favors judges who prefer justice over legality, to the extent that the two conflict. And most people also recognize that judges make public policy and that great discretion is available within many if not most cases. Consequently, a sizable proportion of the population wants to know something about the ideologies of those who put themselves forward for a seat on the high court.

Where the more and less knowledgeable differ, however, is on the degree to which judges are little more than politicians in robes. The less knowledgeable seem to hold the view that judges should represent majority opinion, implementing the ideological views of the majority, even if not their partisanship. In this sense, low levels of knowledge seem to be associated with the view that judges are representatives, perhaps even in the mold of other elected public officials. We might even refer to this as an "instructed delegate" style of representation, in the sense that the job of the representative is to take policy instructions from her or his constituents.

The more knowledgeable do not completely eschew representation, but are perhaps more attracted to the "trustee" style of representation. Trustees are elected because they hold values similar to the majority, but at the same time, once elected, are expected to exercise their own independent judgment, and to the extent possible (that is, where law does not conflict with justice), follow extant law. In this view, judges are not mechanical jurisprudes—they are instead policy-makers with a great deal of available discretion—and their ideologies are entirely relevant to judging. At the same time, they are different from other representatives in the sense of being expected to exercise independent and principled judgment. All agree, however, that in one form or another, judges should reflect the views of their constituents; in this sense, the constituency for strict judicial independence is small.

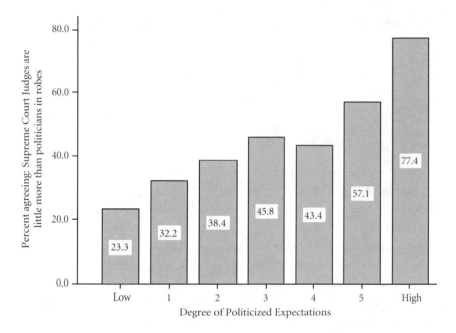

FIG. 11.1. Expectations and Beliefs About the Distinctiveness of Judges

This then leads to the question of whether those holding politicized expectations of judges also hold distinctive views of courts. Are courts then just the same as legislatures and executives? Is there anything distinctive about the judiciary when it comes to its relationships with its constituents?

We asked the respondents to agree or disagree with this statement: "Supreme Court judges are little more than politicians in robes." Fully 40 percent of the respondents (40.2 percent) agreed with this statement, and another 13.0 percent were uncertain about it. The remaining 46.7 percent of the respondents, a plurality but not a majority, reject this view of judges. Obviously, Kentuckians are quite divided in their views of their judges and politics.

Most important, the expectations one holds of the judiciary are strongly connected to the belief that judges are politicians in robes. Figure 11.1 reports this strong relationship ($r = .27$, $p < .000$). A large majority of those holding politicized views of judges believe that judges are politicians in robes; only a very small percentage of those not holding politicized expectations agree with the statement. To state the relationship in the opposite direction (since the nature of the causal connection between the two variables is ambiguous), those who believe that judges are politicians in robes are quite likely to hold politicized expectations ($r = .27$, $p < .000$), a finding that may indicate that believing that judges are politicians in robes is not necessarily a disparaging view. It seems clear that a substantial proportion of the constituents of the Kentucky Supreme Court view that institution in explicitly political terms.[16]

Discussion and Concluding Comments

Perhaps the most important conclusion of this paper is that Kentuckians vary in many of the expectations they hold of their judiciary. Many of the constituents of the Kentucky Supreme Court expect that institution to represent their views on the policy issues it decides. If directly asked to choose between the independence and accountability of judges, a substantial proportion of Kentuckians would select accountability, even if it is the accountability of the trustee, not the instructed delegate.

As a consequence of the variability in expectations, I predict that citizens also vary in how they are affected by the behaviors of judges. If citizens expect judges to make public policy, then it stands to reason that they are unlikely to be offput when judges announce their policy views in their campaigns for a judgeship. If citizens expect judges to represent the views of the majority of their constituents, then it hardly would be surprising to find that judges representing the views of the majority are viewed favorably. The simple point of this analysis has been only to suggest that citizens' views of the appropriateness of certain types of judicial activities have a great deal to do with whether those activities undermine judicial legitimacy.

This view runs deeply contrary to almost all judicial understandings of public confidence and faith in the judiciary. Legal elites typically begin with either assumptions about what citizens expect from the courts, or, more likely, presumptions about what citizens *ought to expect* from their courts. Legal elites, I conjecture, overwhelmingly support strong judicial independence with little direct accountability to the people (just as professors overwhelmingly support strong professorial independence with little direct accountability to students or administrators). They most likely also support both impartial judicial decision-making and the appearance of impartiality, and I do not doubt that most Americans support these values as well, at least at the abstract level.

But here is the rub: legal elites presume that activities such as discussion of legal ideologies during judicial campaigns are offensive to citizens, not because they are, but because they ought to be. The explorations of this paper suggest that legal elites are wrong in assuming that public expectations of judges are uniform,[17] in assuming that the constituency for a politicized model of judging is minute, and therefore in assuming that a wide variety of off-the-bench judicial behavior threatens the legitimacy of elected state courts. To the extent that popular confidence in the judiciary is a standard for evaluating the behaviors of judges, we must be aware that the sources of confidence are disparate and perhaps even contested, and that popular and elite expectations of judges may not be consonant.

Appendix: The Panel Survey Design

t_1—The Initial Interview

This survey is the initial wave in a three-wave panel survey of the residents of Kentucky. The questionnaire was subjected to a formal test, and on the basis of the results of the pretest, was significantly revised. The survey was conducted by Schulman, Ronca, and Bucuvalas, Inc. (SRBI) during the early summer of 2006. Computer Assisted Telephone Interviewing was used. Within households, the respondents were selected randomly. One adult age eighteen or older was selected as the designated respondent in each eligible household.[18] No respondent substitution was allowed. The interviews averaged just over twenty minutes. The selected respondent was offered $10 for completing the interview. A total of 20,078 telephone numbers were used in the survey, with a resulting AAPOR Cooperation Rate #3 of 38.7 percent and an AAPOR Response Rate #3 of 28.7 percent (see American Association for Public Opinion Research 2000). The final data set was subjected to some relatively minor poststratification and was also weighted by the size of the respondent's household.

t_2—The Second Interview

In the month before the general election, the survey firm attempted to reinterview all of the respondents interviewed earlier as part of the t_1 survey. Of the 2,048 respondents from the first survey, interviews were completed with 1,438 individuals. The AAPOR Response Rate #3 is 78.7 percent, and the Cooperation Rate #3 is 89.4 percent.

I have carefully investigated the t_2 sample to determine whether any evidence of unrepresentativeness can be found. One way in which the representativeness of the t_2 sample can be assessed is to determine whether those who were interviewed in the second survey differ from those who were not interviewed. The null hypothesis (H_0) is that no difference exists between the two subgroups.

With over 1,400 completed interviews at t_2 and more than 2,000 at t_1, tests of statistical significance are not very useful (that is, even trivial differences are statistically significant given this large number of cases). Therefore, I focus on the degree to which the dichotomous variable indicating a successful t_2 interview predicts responses to a number of important t_1 variables. The only interesting relationship discovered in this analysis (using as a criterion an eta of greater than or equal to .10 as an indication of a notable difference) has to do with the age of the respondent: eta = .15.[19] The average age of those interviewed at t_2 is 51.3 years; for those not interviewed, the age is 46.1. This finding is typical of panel surveys, with young people being difficult to track down for subsequent interviews.

In terms of substantive variables, however, I find virtually no interesting differences. For instance, in terms of knowledge of courts, I find statistically significant but trivial differences between those interviewed at t_2 and those not, with those interviewed having only slightly greater knowledge of courts than those not interviewed (30.5 versus 26.4 percent, respectively, with relatively high knowledge). Awareness of the Kentucky Supreme Court is similarly distributed (79.2 versus 74.1 percent with at least some awareness). In terms of support for the Court, the correlation between the feeling thermometer responses and whether a t_2 interview was conducted is .06; for the institutional loyalty factor score (measured, of course, at t_1) the correlation is .07. In general, the analysis reveals that the t_2 sample is biased in favor of higher levels of information and awareness, but the bias is slight indeed. Moreover, when poststratification weights are applied to the t_2 data, even this minimal bias becomes entirely trivial.

t_3—The Final Interview
The final interview in the three-wave panel was conducted several months after the end of the 2006 election process. Only those respondents interviewed at t_2 (N = 1,438) were eligible for the t_3 interview. Using the AAPOR standards (Response Rate #3), the t_3 response rate is .77, with a cooperation rate of .94 (#3). Of course, with such high rates of interviewing, practically no issues of representativeness emerge.

The question of how to weight the panel data is somewhat complicated. The t_1 survey was subjected to some slight poststratification so as to improve its representativeness. Weights were then developed for the t_2 and t_3 surveys to improve the representativeness of these subsamples. The target for the t_2 and t_3 weighting was the characteristics of the t_1 survey. As a consequence, when I analyze the panel data, I use the t_3 weight, but when I consider only the t_1 data, I use the original weight variable. Since virtually all of the analysis reported in this paper is based on questions asked in the third interview, the data are weighted by the t_3 weight.

Notes

This research has been supported by the Law and Social Sciences Program of the National Science Foundation (SES 0451207). Any opinions, findings, and conclusions or recommendations expressed in this material are those of the author and do not necessarily reflect the views of the National Science Foundation. I greatly value the support provided for this research by Steven S. Smith and the Weidenbaum Center on the Economy, Government, and Public Policy at Washington University in St. Louis. This is a revised version of a paper delivered at the "What's Law Got to Do with It?" conference, Indiana University School of Law, Bloomington, March 27–29, 2009. I am most appreciative of the comments on Charles Geyh and Jesse Atencio on the conference version of this paper.

1. For example, Benesh (2006, 700) argues that Americans prefer independence over accountability, citing evidence from Heagarty (2003, 1305). My reading of the evidence, however, is that this conclusion is far from solid (and certainly Heagarty's data are far from dispositive). For some research supportive of this view, see Wenzel, Bowler, and Lanoue 2003. More generally, judicial independence is most likely a multidimensional concept, with citizens supporting some types of independence (for example, from the executive) but not others (such as from the preferences of the majority of the citizenry). So when Bybee (this volume) finds that 73 percent of people believe that judges should be shielded from outside pressure and allowed to make decisions based on their own reading of the law, this should not be understood to mean that people expect judges to be independent *of every source* of accountability for their decisions. As he acknowledges, people hold ambivalent opinions about the judicial system.

2. The U.S. Supreme Court is particularly vulnerable to attempts at controlling its jurisdiction over certain types of cases (for example, flag burning) because its legal mandate is defined by ordinary legislation, not the constitution.

3. The Family Trust Foundation sued to overturn Canon 5B(1)(c) of Kentucky's Code of Judicial Conduct after failing in its effort to survey all candidates for judicial office in Kentucky in 2004 on a variety of contentious legal issues. The foundation succeeded in getting the canon declared to be in violation of the First Amendment to the U.S. Constitution *(Family Trust Foundation of Kentucky v. Wolnitzek*, 345 F. Supp. 2d 672 (E.D. Ky. 2004)). For a discussion of campaign speech by candidates for judicial office, see Bopp and Woudenberg 2007. Bopp successfully argued *Republican Party of Minnesota v. White* before the U.S. Supreme Court.

4. In some sense, no single state can ever be "representative" of some larger population or subpopulation of states, especially on matters of judicial selection and retention.

Each state has its own somewhat idiosyncratic history with judicial campaigns (especially since politicized campaigns are relatively new). And indeed, if one looks closely at the traditional five-category description of methods of selecting judges in the United States, one finds a great deal of *within-category* variability, so states we often collapse together are in fact heterogeneous (for example, Pennsylvania). Consequently, I have tried in this analysis to be cautious about overclaiming in the ability to generalize from Kentucky.

5. The eigenvalues of the first two extracted factors are 2.173 and .985.

6. I note that the correlations between the index of politicized judicial expectations and the responses to the relatively nonpolitical expectation are not quite as might be hypothesized: one might have expected them to be significantly negative in the sense that the antonym of the politicized model of judging is the legalistic model. The correlation between the index and the expectation that judges strictly follow the law is $-.04$, indicating no relationship whatsoever. The correlation of the index with the item on refusing to accept campaign contributions is .02. I understand this coefficient as suggesting that the idea of rejecting campaign contributions is a platitude, a symbolic value (like apple pie), that holds relatively little meaning for respondents. For instance, of those asserting that it is very important to refuse campaign contributions, 42.6 percent also said that it is very important for judicial candidates to use campaign contributions to get their views on important issues out to the people. Questions about campaign contributions are most likely useful only when they force people to evaluate contributions in relationship to other, perhaps conflicting, values.

At the same time, however, the correlation of the index and the item on protecting people without power is .17, while the correlation with the item on respecting existing decisions is .22. These relationships are not easy to understand; but the most important conclusion is that, in the minds of the people of Kentucky, politicized judging is compatible with respecting existing decisions and is not incompatible with strictly following the law.

7. A substantial empirical literature exists regarding citizens' attitudes toward courts. For a recent example, see Gibson and Caldeira 2009a.

8. This follows the convention established in our earlier work on institutional legitimacy. See, for example, Gibson, Caldeira, and Baird 1998.

9. The eigenvalue of the second factor is 1.07, which is only marginally greater than the conventional standard of 1.0 for assigning a substantive interpretation to a factor.

10. An obvious possible explanation for this finding is that the trust item is scored in the opposite direction compared with the other statements. Some of the "glue" that binds the responses to the seven questions together (response set) is randomized with this variable, resulting in lower inter-item correlations.

11. The correlation between the trust item and the factor score is .26.

12. This correlation is based on measuring court attitudes at t_1, prior to the measurement of expectations. The identical set of questions was put to the respondents at t_2 (after the expectations questions) and at t_3. The correlation between expectations and support at t_2 is $-.48$; for support at t_3 and expectations, the coefficient is $-.41$. Irrespective of what index is used, support and expectations are strongly intercorrelated.

13. Recall that the survey was fielded outside the normal electoral season (early summer of 2006).

14. These findings contrast strongly with those of Gibson and Caldeira (2009b) on public knowledge of the U.S. Supreme Court. For instance, more than two-thirds of Americans know that the justices of the Supreme Court are appointed, and significant majorities know that the justices are appointed to life terms.

15. When the index is regressed on court knowledge at t_1, court knowledge at t_2, and candidate knowledge at t_2, all three predictors are significantly related to rejecting the politicized view of judging, with each of the regression coefficients achieving statistical significance. The cumulative effect of the three variables is an R^2 of .04 ($p < .000$).

16. The survey did not allocate many questions to exploring differences across institutions. We did, however, use a feeling thermometer to collect opinions toward the state legislature and the state Supreme Court. The correlation between holding politicized expectations of courts and the difference in the thermometer scores (a measure of the distinctiveness of judicial attitudes) is −.16: As politicized expectations increase, the two institutions are judged more similarly.

17. Bybee (2009) is undoubtedly correct when he refers to this view as a "half-law-half-politics understanding of the courts."

18. The method is that devised by Rizzo, Brick, and Park 2004.

19. In all of this analysis, I have used unweighted data.

References

American Association for Public Opinion Research. 2000. *Standard Definitions: Final Dispositions of Case Codes and Outcome Rates for Surveys.* Ann Arbor, MI: AAPOR.

Baird, Vanessa A. 2001. "Building Institutional Legitimacy: The Role of Procedural Justice." *Political Research Quarterly* 54, no. 2 (June): 333–54.

Baird, Vanessa A., and Amy Gangl. 2006. "Shattering the Myth of Legality: The Impact of the Media's Framing of Supreme Court Procedures on Perceptions of Fairness." *Political Psychology* 27, no. 4: 597–614.

Benesh, Sara C. 2006. "Understanding Public Confidence in American Courts." *Journal of Politics* 68, no. 3 (August): 697–707.

Bopp, James, Jr., and Anita Y. Woudenberg. 2007. "To Speak or Not to Speak: Unconstitutional Regulation in the Wake of *White.*" *Justice System Journal* 28, no. 3: 329–34.

Brandenburg, Bert, and Roy A. Schotland. 2008. "Keeping Courts Impartial amid Changing Judicial Elections." *Daedalus* 137, no. 4 (Fall): 102–9.

Bybee, Keith J. 2009. "The Rule of Law Is Dead! Long Live the Rule of Law." Paper presented at the "What's Law Got to Do with It?" Conference, Indiana University School of Law, Bloomington, March 27–28, 2009.

Geyh, Charles Gardner. 2006. *When Courts & Congress Collide: The Struggle for Control of America's Judicial System.* Ann Arbor: University of Michigan Press.

Gibson, James L. 2007. "The Legitimacy of the U.S. Supreme Court in a Polarized Polity." *Journal of Empirical Legal Studies* 4, no. 3 (November): 507–38.

———. 2008. "Challenges to the Impartiality of State Supreme Courts: Legitimacy Theory and 'New-Style' Judicial Campaigns." *American Political Science Review* 102, no. 1 (February): 59–75.

———. 2009. "'New-Style' Judicial Campaigns and the Legitimacy of State High Courts." *Journal of Politics* 71, no. 4 (October): 1285–1304.

Gibson, James L., and Gregory A. Caldeira. 2009a. *Citizens, Courts, and Confirmations: Positivity Theory and the Judgments of the American People.* Princeton: Princeton University Press.

———. 2009b. "Knowing the Supreme Court? A Reconsideration of Public Ignorance of the High Court." *Journal of Politics* 71, no. 2 (April): 429–41.

Gibson, James L., Gregory A. Caldeira, and Vanessa Baird. 1998. "On the Legitimacy of National High Courts." *American Political Science Review* 92 (June): 343–58.

Gibson, James L., Gregory A. Caldeira, and Lester Kenyatta Spence. 2003. "The Supreme Court and the U.S. Presidential Election of 2000: Wounds, Self-Inflicted or Otherwise?" *British Journal of Political Science* 33 (October): 535–56.

Gillman, Howard. 2001. *The Votes That Counted: How the Court Decided the 2000 Presidential Election.* Chicago: University of Chicago Press.

Goldberg, Deborah, Sarah Samis, Edwin Bender, and Rachel Weiss. 2005. *The New Politics of Judicial Elections 2004: How Special Interest Pressure on Our Courts Has Reached a "Tipping Point"—and How to Keep Our Courts Fair and Impartial.* Washington, DC: Justice at Stake Campaign.

Heagarty, J. Christopher. 2003. "Public Opinion and an Elected Judiciary: New Avenues for Reform." *Willamette Law Review* 39, no. 4 (Fall): 1287–1311.

Iyengar, Shanto. 2002. "The Effects of Media-Based Campaigns on Candidate and Voter Behavior: Implications for Judicial Elections." *Indiana Law Review* 35: 691–99.

Jamieson, Kathleen Hall, and Bruce W. Hardy. 2008. "Will Ignorance and Partisan Election of Judges Undermine Public Trust in the Judiciary?" *Dædalus* 137, no. 4 (Fall): 11–15.

Jamieson, Kathleen Hall, and Michael Hennessy. 2007. "Public Understanding of and Support for the Courts: Survey Results." *Georgetown Law Journal* 95, no. 4 (April): 899–902.

Kimball, David C., and Samuel C. Patterson. 1997. "Living up to Expectations: Public Attitudes toward Congress." *Journal of Politics* 59, no. 3 (August): 701–28.

Kritzer, Herbert M. 2001. "The Impact of *Bush v. Gore* on Public Perceptions and Knowledge of the Supreme Court." *Judicature* 85, no. 1 (July–August): 32–38.

———. 2007. "Law Is the Mere Continuation of Politics by Different Means: American Judicial Selection in the Twenty-First Century." *DePaul Law Review* 56, no. 2 (Winter): 423–67.

Lipset, Seymour Martin. 1981. *Political Man: The Social Bases of Politics.* Enl. ed. Baltimore, MD: Johns Hopkins University Press.

Nicholson, Stephen P., and Robert M. Howard. 2003. "Framing Support for the Supreme Court in the Aftermath of *Bush v. Gore.*" *Journal of Politics* 65, no. 3 (August): 676–95.

Price, Vincent, and Anca Romantan. 2004. "Confidence in Institutions, before, during, and after 'Indecision 2000.'" *Journal of Politics* 66, no. 3 (August): 939–56.

Rizzo, Louis, J. Michael Brick, and Inho Park. 2004. "A Minimally Intrusive Method for Sampling Persons in Random Digit Dial Surveys." *Public Opinion Quarterly* 68, no. 2: 267–74.

Wenzel, James P., Shaun Bowler, and David J. Lanoue. 2003. "The Sources of Public Confidence in State Courts: Experience and Institutions." *American Politics Research* 31, no. 2: 191–211.

Whittington, Keith E. 2003. "Legislative Sanctions and the Strategic Environment of Judicial Review." *International Journal of Constitutional Law* 1, no. 3: 446–74.

Yates, Jeffrey L., and Andrew B. Whitford. 2002. "The Presidency and the Supreme Court after *Bush v. Gore*: Implications for Legitimacy and Effectiveness." *Stanford Law and Policy Review* 13, no. 1: 101–18.

12 The Rule of Law Is Dead!
Long Live the Rule of Law!
Keith J. Bybee

IN THEIR CLASSIC DISCUSSION of legal reasoning, Carter and Burke argue that the rule of law, in its essence, is a matter of requiring people to "look outside [their] own will for criteria of judgment" (Carter and Burke 2007, 147). Whatever the specific features of a given political order may be, the rule of law directs individuals to organize their lives and reconcile their disputes according to independent, publicly shared principles outside the sphere of personal attachments and private beliefs. The highly charged conflicts that end up in courts will certainly tempt people to evaluate a judge's decision by their own feelings and convictions. But the rule of law asks us to push beyond individual preferences. "[If] you stop and think about it," Carter and Burke write, "judging a legal result simply in terms of one's own sense of right and wrong won't do. The whole point of the rule of law is to set standards of governance that transcend individual moral feelings. If all we have are our moral feelings, we are no better than Islamic or other religious fundamentalists who insist that *their* moral scheme justifies destroying other incompatible moral systems" (ibid., 3; emphasis in original).[1]

Judged by this definition, the United States is arguably experiencing a rule-of-law crisis. Public opinion polls show that substantial majorities of Americans consider judges at every level to be influenced by political preference. The belief that judges decide cases and issue rulings on the basis of partisan interests is supported by scholarship that shows the judicial process to be permeated by political claims and commitments. Rather than attempting to "look outside their own will for criteria of judgment," participants in the judicial process appear simply to be advancing their personal political agendas.

And yet, at the same time, the rule of law in the United States also appears to be alive and doing very well. Many of the same polls that reveal a significant public belief in the political nature of judicial decision-making also indicate a substantial public faith in the impartiality of judges. Large majorities of Americans consider judges at every level to be fair and trustworthy arbiters, properly shielded from political pressure and allowed to reach decisions based on their own independent reading of the law. The public belief in judicial impartiality conforms with the conventional picture of the judiciary that is typically advanced by the American Bar Association and by judges themselves. Moreover, the belief in impartiality is supported by scholarship that shows the judicial process to be infused with legal principle. From this perspective, judges do indeed seem to "look outside their own will for criteria of judgment"—except, of course, when they appear to be doing the opposite.

When confronted with a tension between ideas, the natural tendency is to attempt to resolve it. In this spirit, there are many efforts to demonstrate that the American judicial process must ultimately be either legal or political, and not remain some uneasy mix of the two. In this chapter, I adopt a different approach following the lead of Judith Shklar. Over four decades ago, Shklar suggested that clashing perceptions of the judiciary may never be resolved into a single, internally consistent understanding because we expect our courts to perform contradictory functions (Shklar 1964). As Shklar noted, people often insist that "the impartiality of judges and of the [legal] process as a whole requires a dispassionate, literal pursuit of rules carved in spiritual marble." This insistence on legal principle "may seem ridiculous" because "most thoughtful citizens know that the courts act decisively in creating rules that promote political ends." Yet Shklar warned against the conclusion that political claims should eclipse legal understandings. The mix of political and legal factors is "not at all socially or psychologically indefensible," Shklar wrote. "Indeed, if we value flexibility and accept a degree of contradiction, this paradox may even seem highly functional and appropriate" (ibid., x).

Taking my cue from Shklar, I use the contradictory elements of the judicial process as my starting point. My goal is to understand how such a half-politics-half-law system of courts may endure.

I begin with a survey of the basic tensions that characterize the American judiciary, outlining the mixed view of the courts found in public opinion and in scholarly studies. To better understand how this house divided may stand, I then turn to the work of the legal realists. Formed in the early part of the twentieth century, the legal realists were a group of jurists who devoted themselves to exposing the role played by politics and other nonlegal factors in judicial decision-making. The realist critique called into question conventional efforts to render judicial authority strictly as a matter of legal principle. As a result, the legal realists found themselves squarely presented with the challenge of making sense of a judicial system in which political preference and personal belief occupied a central position. This is the same challenge that faces commentators today.

My particular interest is in Thurman Arnold, the legal realist who was most clearly committed to understanding how and why the tension between different elements of the judicial process was sustained. I argue that Arnold's vision of a contradictory-yet-durable legal system ultimately rested on a specific understanding of human motives as a mix of emotional impulse, rational thinking, and moral inclination. Although parts of Arnold's thinking are problematic, his mixed portrait of human nature holds promise. As we seek an account of how our rule of law functions, and attempt to explain how it remains possible for individuals to look beyond their own insistent will for criteria of judgment, I argue that we should begin with an understanding of citizens that makes room for the contradictory set of motives on which Arnold relied.

A House Divided

To begin, consider the distribution of public opinion mapped by the Maxwell Poll on Civic Engagement and Inequality. In the fall of 2005, the Maxwell Poll posed a battery of court-related questions as part of a nationwide survey (Maxwell School of Citizenship and Public Affairs 2005).[2] According to the poll, 82 percent of those surveyed believed that the partisan background of judges influences court decision-making either somewhat or a great deal. This view was shared by very different groups. An overwhelming majority of liberals, conservatives, people who attend religious services several times a week, and people who never attend religious services all agreed that partisanship does not switch off when judicial robes are put on.

For many, a belief in the political nature of judicial decisions seemed to translate directly into doubts about the sincerity of judicial pronouncements. A majority of poll respondents agreed that even though judges always say that their decisions flow from the law and the Constitution, many judges are in fact basing their decisions on their own personal beliefs. Judges may consistently "talk law," but most Americans appeared to suspect that judges were simply "doing politics."

Given the widespread agreement that partisanship skewed judicial decision-making, one might expect large segments of the public to view judicial selection in political terms. The Maxwell Poll confirmed this expectation. In a period when Republicans controlled Congress and the executive, the poll showed that Republicans were eight times more likely than Democrats to trust the president and Senate to pick good federal judges. Moreover, three-quarters of survey respondents rejected the idea that fewer judges should be subject to popular election. Most Americans appeared to view judicial selection as a political process and, as a result, thought it made sense to organize judicial selection in a political way.

Even so, the Maxwell Poll also provided evidence of strong support for the idea that independent judges are impartial guardians of our constitutional rights. In spite of the widely shared belief that judging was influenced by politics (a belief that was coupled with the commonly held opinion that judges often merely pretend that their decisions are derived from the law and the Constitution), most of those surveyed did not appear to think that the rule of law was simply the rule of men. Next to the finding that an overwhelming majority of Americans believed partisanship to have an influence on judicial decision-making, the most lopsided majority tapped by the Maxwell Poll came in response to a question about the value of judicial independence. When asked whether judges should continue to be shielded from outside pressure and allowed to make decisions based on their own independent reading of the law, 73 percent of those surveyed agreed.

The large majority in favor of shielding judges from politics held straight across party lines: three-quarters or more of Democrats and Republicans agreed that the courts should be independent. The same was true of self-described liberals, moderates, and conservatives. Similar results held for daily television news watchers and daily newspaper readers—two groups that the poll showed were otherwise inclined to see judging in political terms. In fact, even among those respondents who *disagreed* with the statement "You can generally trust public officials to do the right thing," the idea that judges should be insulated from outside pressure received a high level of support.

The widely shared desire to preserve judicial independence appeared to reflect a popular aspiration—and, according to the Maxwell Poll results, it also appeared to reflect a broad-based recognition that, whatever else might be said about the politics of judging, a wide variety of citizens relied on the courts to resolve disputes. When asked why so many conflicts end up in the courts, only a small percentage of Americans blamed politicians for failing to deal with the controversies in the first place, and an even smaller percentage blamed judges for actively reaching out to decide hot-button issues. Instead, almost half of those surveyed said that courts were at the center of so many conflicts because the people themselves demanded that the judiciary get involved. Many Americans appeared to believe, in other words, that the courts responded to the demands of the citizenry as a whole. Given this belief, judicial independence would appear to be quite sensible: it is by allowing judges to make decisions without pressure from specific groups or parties that the judiciary is able to preserve the trust and interests of its broad public.

The overall picture painted by the Maxwell Poll is decidedly mixed. On one hand, large majorities of Americans seem to see the influence of partisanship on the judicial process. On the other, large majorities of Americans appear to believe that the courts are special venues in which political pressure and partisan squabbling have no place. A faith in the importance of judicial independence and impartial decision-making is alive and well, but so too is the suspicion that judges are advancing political goals under the cover of legal principle.

How much weight should these results be given? Although the Maxwell Poll provides only a single snapshot of public opinion, it is also the case that the poll's findings are echoed in many other surveys taken at different times. In 2006, the year after the Maxwell Poll, the Annenberg Foundation Trust at Sunnylands released a national poll that found the same set of ambivalent opinions about the judicial system (Annenberg Foundation Trust at Sunnylands 2006). The Annenberg survey found that large majorities of Americans (a) trust the judiciary to operate in the best interests of the people, and (b) believe that state courts and the U.S. Supreme Court have the right amount of power. At the same time, the Annenberg survey also found (a) that 75 percent of respondents believe that judges are influenced by their personal political views to either a great or moderate extent, and (b) that more than two-thirds of those surveyed consider the influence of judges' personal political views to be either "not too appropriate" or "not appropriate at all."

The Maxwell and Annenberg findings have been repeatedly reproduced by polls designed to survey public attitudes about state courts (as opposed to public attitudes about "the courts" more generally). In his contribution to this volume, James L. Gibson finds that substantial majorities of Kentuckians believe (a) that their Supreme Court can be trusted to make decisions that are right for the state as a whole, and (b) that this same court is inevitably mixed up in politics and needs to be more tightly controlled. Gibson's findings can be broadly confirmed. Nine separate surveys of public opinion on state courts were conducted in the ten-year period from 1998 to 2008 (University of New Orleans Survey Research Center 1998; Connecticut Judicial Branch and the Connecticut Commission on Public Trust and Confidence 1998; National Center for State Courts 1999; Office of the Administrator of the Courts, State of Washington 1999; New Mexico Administrative Office of the Courts 2000; Anderson, Niebuhr and Associates 2000; Greenberg, Quinlan, Rosner Research 2001; Illinois Campaign for Political Reform 2002; Justice At Stake 2008). Two of the polls drew from a national sample and the other seven were conducted in individual states (two of the statewide polls were conducted in Minnesota eight years apart). All of these polls contained similar questions about judicial fairness (for example, "How well does the word 'impartial' describe judges?") and similar questions about the impact of politics on judicial decision-making (for example, "Are judges' decisions influenced by political considerations?"). In every one of the nine surveys, clear majorities expressed their belief that state judges were impartial *and* their belief that politics was at work in the state judicial process.[3]

Polls designed to measure public opinion about the federal judiciary show similar results, indicating that the public simultaneously believes in the even-handedness of the federal courts and doubts the degree to which the federal judges actually stick to the law. Consider the political view. When asked whether federal judges "rise above politics and hand down fair decisions" or "hand down decisions that reflect [the judges'] own political leanings," more than 60 percent of those surveyed agreed that federal court decisions generally reflect political preferences (Belden, Russonello, and Stewart 1998). Matters are not much different for the highest federal court. A large portion of the public believes that the Supreme Court operates with too little regard for either legal principles or impartiality: national surveys regularly find a near-majority of respondents agreeing that the Supreme Court is "too mixed up in politics" (Gibson and Caldeira 2007, 51, table 1; see also Gibson et al. 2003, 358; Scheb and Lyons 2001, 184–90; Gibson et al. 2005). Indeed, some polls suggest that up to 70 percent of Americans agree that the Court favors some groups more than others (McGuire 2007, 203). With the Court widely viewed as a political institution, the public often rates the Court's performance in partisan terms. A large number of polls show that Americans routinely evaluate the Court from the perspective of their own individual party affiliation (Gallup Poll News Service 2007).[4] In this vein, positive opinions of the Court have fallen among Democrats and conservative Republicans because the former have found leading decisions to be too conservative while the latter believe that the Court has not been conservative enough (Pew Research Center for the People and the Press 2005).[5]

And yet the public also thinks of federal judges in terms of fairness and neutrality. Polls show that large majorities of Americans expect federal judges to apply the law impartially and distrust federal judges who advance narrow ideological interests (Russonello 2004; Scheb and Lyons 2001; Gibson and Caldeira 2007). Studies have shown that the Supreme Court in particular has received a good deal of public goodwill because it is generally thought to be an evenhanded guarantor of basic democratic values for all (Caldeira and Gibson 1992; Gibson et al. 2003; Gibson and Caldeira 2007). On the whole, Americans seem to believe that the federal judiciary uses its independence to make fair decisions. Sixty-four percent of Americans surveyed in 2006, for example, trusted the Supreme Court to operate in the best interests of the American people either a "great deal" or "a fair amount" of the time (Annenberg Public Policy Center 2006; McGuire 2007). When asked whether federal judges should be subject to greater political control by elected officials, over two-thirds of those surveyed said no (CNN.com 2006).

In sum, whether the subject of discussion is the state courts, the federal courts, or courts in general, a wide range of surveys suggest that most Americans share the same conflicting mix of legal and political perceptions, leading them to view judges as fair arbiters and political agents all at once. The consistent message conveyed by these opinion polls is reinforced by the seminal research on popular legal consciousness performed by Patricia Ewick and Susan Silbey (Ewick and Silbey 1998). Based on a series of in-depth interviews with 430 individuals, Ewick and Silbey's work demonstrates that ordinary Americans typically define, use, and understand law in conflicting ways: on one hand, law "is imagined and treated as an objective realm of disinterested action ... operating by known and fixed rules," and, on the other hand, law "is depicted as a game, a terrain for tactical encounters through which people marshal a variety of social resources to achieve strategic goals" (ibid., 28). The same people hold these contradictory conceptions simultaneously. Law is popularly understood to be "both sacred and profane, God and gimmick, interested and disinterested" all at the same time (ibid., 23).

The Stability of Contradiction

Competing renderings of the judiciary also fill the annals of contemporary scholarship—a fact to which this entire volume eloquently testifies. Rather than rehearse the research reviewed in other chapters, I limit myself here to observing that the existence of well-developed academic literatures with conflicting legal and political conceptions of the judiciary helps to reinforce and confirm the divisions in public opinion.[6]

This convergence between scholarly and public views prompts a question: how can a judicial system that appears to be shot through with conflicting legal and political considerations endure?

One response to this question is to deny the significance of the conflict by arguing that the American judicial process is ultimately consistent, and not some uneasy mix of incongruent factors. Judges themselves often insist that even though they may have differences of political opinion, their work remains fundamentally legal, a matter of applying preexisting principle to the facts and argument of a given case. As Judge J. Harvie Wilkinson has argued, it is the law that in the final analysis provides "a medium through which judges of disparate beliefs can often find common ground" (Wilkinson 2009). Others maintain that the assertion of legal principle in judicial opinions is a mere pretense designed to protect judicial prerogatives by papering over court politics. According to Shapiro and Stone Sweet (2002), lawyers and legal academics generally work together to promote the judiciary's reputation for independence and impartiality. It is left to others to speak the hard truth that the emperor has no clothes: "Political scientists do not have the duty to defend the courts that lawyers have, and they do have an inclination to celebrate rather than disguise politics when they see it, in courts as well as elsewhere" (Shapiro and Stone Sweet 2002, 6; see also Segal and Spaeth 2002).

The idea of ultimate judicial consistency is appealing, but unfortunately it is not particularly helpful. To demonstrate that the judicial process rests on a single set of internally consistent factors, one must interpret away views endorsed by substantial public majorities and large scholarly literatures. This may be the right course in a general sense, and perhaps one day further research and study will lead to the repudiation of contradictory understandings (indeed, several of the contributions to this volume see an internally consistent, synthetic conception of judicial action emerging). In the meantime, however, conflicting perceptions of the courts are still with us. These perceptions matter because the legitimacy of courts rests on the ability of judges to convey the impression that their decisions are dictated by the impersonal requirements of legal principle (Geyh 2007; Brown and Wise 2004; Gibson et al. 1998). Judges must visibly appear to play the role of neutral umpire, for it is by maintaining appearances of impartiality that judges reinforce their claim of actually being impartial and worthy of receiving public support.

There is a developing empirical debate about precisely which aspects of judicial behavior appear political to the public (Gibson 2008a; 2008b; 2009). At the level of state courts, for example, some evidence suggests that campaign contributions and negative campaign advertisements detract from popular beliefs in judicial impartiality, while policy statements by judicial candidates do not have a similar effect (at least in those states that rely on elections to select or retain their judges). As this empirical debate refines our understanding of how different kinds of judicial action trigger different public responses, it also underscores the point I have made here: we live in a time of Janus-faced judicial appearances, with large majorities of the public and significant bodies of scholarship seeing judges as impartial arbiters *and* as political actors. Whatever the "real" nature of the judicial process may ultimately be, judges seem to be projecting images of their work that at once sustain and undermine their claims to legitimacy. And so the question remains: how can the judiciary continue to function when courts are widely viewed in contradictory ways?[7] I suggest that we turn to legal realism for the beginnings of an answer.

Legal Realism

Developed during the early decades of the twentieth century, legal realism encompassed a complex range of related ideas and theories (Purcell 1973; Kalman 1986; Horwitz 1992; Schelegel 1995; Duxbury 1995; Feldman 2000). Yet one theme that threaded through much of legal realism was a specific critique of judicial reasoning: most realists were skeptical that court rulings were derived solely from legal principles, and they insisted instead that the true origins of judicial decisions were to be found in the judges' circumstances and motivations. "We know, in a general way," Felix Cohen wrote in his description of the realists' common knowledge, "that dominant economic forces play a part in judicial decision, that judges usually reflect the attitudes of their own income class on social questions, [and] that their views on law are molded to a certain extent by their past legal experience as counsel for special interests" (Cohen 1935, 845). Behind judicial pronouncements about what the law is, most realists saw a tangled set of social pressures and political preferences at work.

By virtue of their shared critique of judicial reasoning, the realists were confronted with the task of understanding how the mix of legal and nonlegal factors attending the judicial process might fit together. In other words, the realists, like commentators today, faced the problem of determining how judges could appear to be motivated by something other than the law and, at the same time, remain legitimate legal actors. And like many in our own time, a number of realists responded by claiming that it was possible somehow to overcome the apparent contradictions of the judicial process. Felix Cohen, for example, thought that the values and preferences driving judicial decisions could be coherently systematized and ranked according an ethical understanding of the good life (Cohen 1933). Walter Wheeler Cook called on lawyers and judges to reorganize their thinking around the rigorous scientific study of social and economic life (Cook 1927). For his part, Jerome Frank advocated psychological transformation: he urged jurists to dispense with their childish need for certainty and to confront indeterminacies of decision-making with an adult sense of candor and responsibility (Frank 1970, originally published in 1930).

None of the various realist proposals for reconciling law and politics were realized—a fact that has led many to consider realism's most lasting contribution to be its critique of judicial reasoning (for example, Kalman 1986; Horwitz 1992). In this sense, scholars have considered legal realism to remain relevant today mainly as a set of standing questions, challenging us to explain how a judicial process driven by politics can be consistent with the rule of law (Fischer 1991, 284–86).[8]

I agree that legal realism does not tell us how to overcome the tensions between legal and nonlegal elements in the judicial process. But I disagree that the relevance of realism is limited to its critical analysis. In this body of thought, we can find arguments that help us understand how conflicting factors may hang together, creating a judicial process that does not need to overcome its internal inconsistencies in order to remain intact. Indeed, even though no legal realists were able to find a way out of the contradiction between law and politics, there was one particular figure in the movement who provided a way in: Thurman Arnold.

The Symbols of Government

In a number of ways, Arnold's work reflected the commitments of the legal realists that surrounded him at Yale Law School in the 1930s. As his biographer notes, Arnold wrote in the "slash-and-burn style" favored by a number of realists as a means of distinguishing themselves from the meticulous, formalistic legal scholarship produced by other legal academics (Waller 2005, 50; see also Duxbury 1995, 112). In this spirit, Arnold included few footnotes in his work and generally took a cavalier approach to citation: in one article, he "simply turned over one of the footnotes to a colleague" who used the opportunity to criticize points Arnold had made in the text (Waller 2005, 50). Substantively, Arnold also accepted the realist critique of judicial decision-making and argued that the legal system could not be explained in logical, impersonal terms that judges offered in their opinions. He "shared with most realists an abhorrence for abstract concepts and the view that the law was inconsistent, if not incoherent, as to any individual doctrine or set of doctrines" (ibid.).

Yet Arnold also departed from other realists in one key respect: he did not argue that inconsistencies in the law had to be resolved (Waller 2005; Fenster 2003, 2007). With one glaring exception that I will discuss below, Arnold did not attempt to work out the contradictions in the judicial process. In this way Arnold differed from his contemporaries (and from many commentators today). He considered the tension between impartial principle and political preference less as an obstacle to be overcome than as an indication of how the rule of law actually operated and endured.

Arnold developed his somewhat unique position with greatest force and originality in his book *The Symbols of Government* (Arnold 1935).[9] In *Symbols*, Arnold claimed that people have a strong rational bent, with a penchant for framing life and experience within coherent systems of principles. "Rational thinking compels us to seek complete and rounded systems of doctrine and principles," Arnold wrote. "The intellectual who makes one of these systems necessarily believes that it represents the 'truth'" (ibid., 5). It is the motive force of rational thinking that leads people to disparage actions that appear to contravene systematized principles or seem to operate without principles at all.

Arnold argued that rational thinking produces the same love of logical system when applied to law. We consider the development and application of enduring, impartial principle to be the very essence of law—such that the term "law" embodies for the public "the belief that there must be something behind and above government without which [government] cannot have permanence or respect" (ibid., 44). Actions that cast doubt on this belief in impartial principles are strongly criticized even when the actions may have beneficial effects. As Arnold noted, "[A] court of law which achieves a desirable result by an inexact use of legal conceptions arouses more criticism from legal scholars than one which achieves an undesirable result in a learned way" (ibid., 5).

Unfortunately, our rational systems tell us little about how law and society work. "Actual observation" indicates that the "great constructive achievements in human organization have been accomplished by unscrupulous men who violated most of the principles we cherish" (ibid.). If we look at the world as it is, Arnold argued, we will see that we cannot discover how problems actually get solved by scrutinizing doctrines and abstract philosophies. Regardless of what legal principles we may believe govern courts, judicial decision-making in actuality will be driven by preferences and feelings that cannot be traced back to doctrine. Rational thinking leads to the production of principled systems, but reason does not fully explain or motivate human conduct.

According to Arnold, judges caught up in the articulation of legal principles will remain blind to the fact that their reasoned arguments are disconnected from the process by which their decisions are actually reached. These judges are like the ancient Egyptian priests who never developed a rigorous understanding of medicine in spite of embalming thousands of cadavers because they "opened up the body in the light of their accepted principles [and] were unable to observe what was before their very eyes" (ibid., v). Arnold suggested that the legal realists recognize the limits of legal principle that "the priests" do not. Indeed, it is "child's play for the realist to show that law is not what it pretends to be and that its theories are sonorous, rather than sound; that its definitions run in circles; that applied by skillful attorneys in the forum of the courts it can only be an argumentative technique; that it constantly seeks to escape from reality through alternate reliance on ceremony and verbal confusion" (ibid., 44).

The legal realists are wrong, however, to extend their insight about the limits of principle into a claim that principles are entirely meaningless. Impartial, logically ordered principles do not wholly explain or motivate conduct, but that does not mean that these principles are dispensable window dressing. Arnold claimed that ideals and doctrines give "purpose, beauty, and symmetry to the drab business of life" (ibid., iv). Law, like any human institution, cannot be concretely organized and implemented on the basis of consistent principles. Yet individuals nonetheless place the utmost importance on principled coherence. "In spite of all the irrefutable logic of the realists, men insist upon believing that there are fundamental principles of law which exist apart from any particular case, or any particular human activity; that these principles must be sought with a reverent attitude; that they are being improved constantly; and that our sacrifices of efficiency and humanitarianism in their honor are leading us to a better government" (ibid., 32–33). People tenaciously cling to the importance of principle, even though the validity of such an understanding cannot be demonstrated. The truth is, Arnold wrote, that the belief in rational principle "exists only because we seem unable to find comfort without it" (ibid., 33).

In calling principles matters of "comfort," Arnold did not mean that they were luxuries. As a matter of basic emotional need and deeply ingrained habit, every individual imposes order and purpose on life by "constructing for himself a succession of little dramas in which he is the principal character" (ibid., iv). When conflicts emerge between the role a person has created and her actual behavior, the conflicts are not resolved so much as they are "escaped" either by generating a "maze" of obscuring rituals or jumping into an altogether "different and inconsistent role" (ibid.). People never arrive at some moment of clarity and directness where they are simply themselves; instead, they always live in a world of theories, systems, and performances that give shape and direction to their experience. "Those who are unable to construct a worth-while character for themselves in any particular situation lose morale; they become discouraged, ineffective, confused" (ibid.).

Arnold argued that institutions operate like individuals writ large, giving meaning to their actions by constantly creating unifying ceremonies and symbols. It is this institutional process of elaborating "little dramas" about law and other official practices that "make up the story of government" (ibid., v). In actual fact, of course, law will be made to suit the agenda of interested parties and there will be no straight line of causation leading from legal principle to judicial decision. But that does not mean that only "dupes" or "unconscious hypocrites" will insist that legal principle still matters (ibid., 7). The great mass of people are neither fools nor liars; yet they insist on the truth of "the story of government" in spite of evidence to the contrary because rational systems of principle remain important ordering mechanisms even if no one can quite conform to their terms. Arnold argued that the legal realists fail to understand the enduring importance of such principles because they fail to understand the basic "personality" that individuals and institutions share: these "living organisms" are "molded by habit, shaken by emotional conflicts, turned this way and that by words, constantly making good resolutions which affect them but not in the way that the terminology of the resolutions might indicate, and never quite understanding themselves or the part they are actually playing because of the necessary illusions with which they must surround themselves to preserve prestige and self-respect" (ibid., 25–26).

As a matter of logic, contradictions between the practical politics of judicial decision-making and the impartial principles of law are a source of frustration. But a contradictory system is the only one that will work given the way people and institutions are. Law is a tool that will be made to function in the interests of its users; and yet this tool will only be accepted by and have value for people if it is enveloped by overarching principles that convey a message of unity and impartiality, independent of the law's diversity of partisan uses. Thus, as one might expect given his talk about "little dramas," Arnold suggested that the best way to think about the judicial process is not from the vantage point of logic, but from the perspective of dramaturgy:

> An admission by a judicial institution that it was moving in all directions at once in order to satisfy the conflicting emotional values of the people which it served would be unthinkable. It would have the same effect as if an actor interrupted the most moving scene of a play in order to explain to the audience that his real name was John Jones. The success of the play requires that an idea be made real to the audience. The success of the law as a unifying force depends on making emotionally significant the idea of a government of law which is rational and scientific. (Ibid., 49)

Arnold's Significance

The argument in *Symbols* suggests that it is a mistake to evaluate the judicial process on the basis of whether people succeed or fail in their search for criteria of judgment outside of their own will. The judicial process cannot be reduced to the rule of law or to the rule of men, for it is both at once. Arnold grounds this conclusion on a specific understanding of human nature. It is because individuals have a practical need to advance their own particular interests and an emotional need to feel that they are living up to impersonal, coherent standards that the law must operate on two conflicting planes at the same time.

The resulting system endures not in spite of the contradiction between instrumental action and impartial principle, but because this contradiction suits the law to the people who are governed by it. This arrangement is not necessarily connected to justice. The judicial process is stable because it recognizes and responds to competing human needs, not because it ensures that we live in a fair society. As Arnold put it, "From a practical point of view [law] is the greatest instrument of social stability because it recognizes every one of the yearnings of the underprivileged, and gives them a forum in which those yearnings can achieve official approval without involving any particular action which might joggle the existing pyramid of power" (ibid., 35).

Arnold thus provides us with a place to start to think about how and why the tensions in the American judicial process persist. He locates unresolved contradictions within people themselves—contradictions that in turn are used as the raw materials for dramatizing public life, creating roles for both legal principle and political preference. Arnold's portrait of people as being attuned to high principle, yet being unable to practice what they preach, suggests a connection to an old notion of human nature that stretches back to Machiavelli (for example, Grant 1997). Arnold's dramaturgical understanding of the way in which the passions and interests of each individual are played out suggests a connection to more contemporary readings of social performance (for example, Goffman 1959 and 1963). These two streams of thought are not central to current scholarly assessments in either the legal academy or political science, and Arnold's work gives us some reason to elevate their profile (Bybee 2010).

It is a thought-provoking beginning, but not one on which Arnold himself built. At the end of *Symbols*, Arnold unveiled a *deus ex machina* "philosophy for humanitarian politicians" to suggest that a truly unitary system of law might be created after all (Arnold 1935, 232). Rather than living with a judicial process that is at once driven by specific interests and held up to standards of impartial principle, Arnold argued that officials ought to adopt the perspective of physicians running an insane asylum. The doctors in such an institution do not argue with the patients about the validity of delusions nor do they try to persuade patients about the soundness of medical therapies. Since the staff's sole "aim is to make the inmates of the asylum as comfortable as possible," the doctors are free to experiment with different approaches without worrying about whether their doctrines are mutually consistent (ibid., 233). There is no tension in the asylum between what the physicians actually do and how they talk about what they do because the physicians feel no need to dramatize their work as a principled system.

In order for this insane-asylum-inspired spirit of unabashed experimentation to take hold, Arnold argued that the "humanitarian philosophy for politicians" must be matched by a new set of attitudes among the public, otherwise people will continue to demand the comfort of believing that government is rational and moral. Borrowing from the legal realists that he otherwise scorned, Arnold claimed that ordinary people could in fact be transformed by a "new creed called psychiatry" (ibid., 269). "A new conception of an adult personality is bringing a new sense of tolerance and common sense to replace the notion of the great man who lived and died for moral and rational purposes" (ibid.). Arnold hoped that once this new understanding of adult personality took root and a new kind of citizen had emerged, then a new "competent, practical, opportunistic governing class may rise to power" (ibid., 271).

The resolution that Arnold tacked on to the end of *Symbols* drew some critical fire when the book was published and has continued to irk the book's readers (Fenster 2003 and 2007). Arnold's biographer, for example, closes his very favorable overview of *Symbols* by excoriating the book's conclusion: "It was as if a brilliantly engaging and complex movie ends with a jarring, happy ending tying up all the impossible loose ends or just concluded because the studio refused to advance further funds to the director" (Waller 2005, 58). The criticism is well deserved. If we accept Arnold's basic argument, then the resolution he suggests at the end is almost impossible to achieve. Throughout his book, Arnold presents the desire for rational, principled order as a fundamental human need. As a result, the tolerance for uncertainty and experimentation that marks psychiatry's "adult personality" does not represent just another set of symbols; it represents a sea change in basic human behavior and an abandonment of the dramaturgical understanding of personal and public life on which Arnold depends. Rather than join Arnold in the impossible position where he concludes, I would suggest that we follow the promising direction in which the rest of his argument points.

Conclusion

As I have argued, surveys show that a significant proportion of the public considers judges to be political. This result holds whether Americans are asked about Supreme Court justices, federal judges, state judges, or judges in general. At the same time, a large majority of the public also believes that judges are fair and impartial arbiters, and this belief also applies across the board. The public is hardly alone in its views: divisions among scholars indicate that when the academy looks at the judicial process it sees versions of the same tension that members of the general public do.

It would be intellectually cleaner if the judicial process were not beset by conflicting perceptions; indeed, many appear to hope that further research and study will lead to a single, internally consistent view of judicial activity. Yet, rather than joining the chorus of voices that are calling for the development of a consistent view, I have outlined a way of thinking about how contradictory legal and political elements of the judicial process might cohere.

My source has been Thurman Arnold, a figure who accepted the legal realist position that judicial reasoning was driven by interests and nonetheless insisted that claims about the importance of legal principle have real significance. Arnold's argument is far from perfect, but it helps us begin to conceptualize how legal and political perceptions of the courts may coexist by complicating our understanding of individual beliefs and motives. More specifically, Arnold's argument depends on the claim that individuals value moral principles and rational systems, and yet remain unable to conduct their lives in complete accordance with either one. Thus the law is made to serve different purposes: on the one hand, the law is pressed into service by interested parties trying to solve their problems; and, on the other, the law is shaped into a rational structure in order to give "the story of government" meaning. The law operates in both registers at the same time, even though they point in incompatible directions.

Thus Arnold helpfully provides us with the elements necessary to build on Judith Shklar's old observations (noted at the outset of this chapter) about the usefulness of contradictions in the legal process. The next step, I would argue, is to move forward from this promising beginning and fashion a theory that accounts for the half-politics-half-law system that we have (see Bybee 2010).

Notes

The author thanks Ellen Palminteri and Kyle Somers for their valuable research assistance.

1. Carter and Burke take the injunction to "look outside [their] own will for criteria of judgment" from Robert Cover.

2. My discussion of the Maxwell Poll draws on Bybee (2007). The Maxwell Poll was conducted in October 2005. The sample size was 609 and the margin of error was ±5 percent. The codebook and datasets for the different iterations of the Maxwell Poll, 2004–2007, may be found at <http://www.maxwell.syr.edu/campbell/programs/The_Maxwell_Poll/>. Accessed June 15, 2010.

3. Averaging across all nine polls, 70 percent of those surveyed agreed that state judges were fair and impartial, while 75 percent thought that politics influenced judicial decision-making.

4. Specifically, thirteen polls conducted by Gallup from 2000 to 2007 show that Americans' overall rating of the Court is clearly related to their party affiliation. See Gallup Poll News Service 2007.

5. Subsets in the population may come down differently on this issue. The less educated are more likely to see the Court in political terms, while lawyers admitted to practice in federal appellate courts are more likely to see the high bench in legal terms (see McGuire 2007). For discussions of how opinion elites and African Americans evaluate the Court in political terms, see Caldeira and Gibson 1992, 655–58; Gibson and Caldeira 1992.

6. This is not to say that the general public is familiar with law-and-courts scholarship.

7. It is possible to synthesize the conflicting perceptions into a seamless view of the psychology of judicial decision-making (see Feldman 2005). Yet such reconciliations leave the fact of conflicting public and scholarly perceptions unexplained.

8. The challenge posed by realist thought is not only considered to be a challenge for commentators. Charles Geyh, for example, has argued that the realist critique today threatens norms and customs that have long underwritten judicial independence in the United States (Geyh 2006).

9. Arnold's best-selling work was *The Folklore of Capitalism* (Arnold 1937). I nonetheless focus on *Symbols* because it more squarely addresses rule-of-law questions and because *Folklore* simply repeats many of the basic claims from *Symbols*. (Arnold himself considered *Folklore* to be a repetition of *Symbols* "with different examples," and throughout his life he continued to think *Symbols* was his best work. See Waller 2005, 69, 75.)

References

Anderson, Niebuhr and Associates. 2000. "1999–2000 Minnesota Supreme Court Public Opinion of the Courts Study." Arden Hills, MN: Anderson, Niebuhr and Associates.

Annenberg Foundation Trust at Sunnylands. "2006 Annenberg Judicial Independence Survey." Princeton, NJ: Princeton Survey Research Associates International.

Annenberg Public Policy Center. 2006. "Judicial Independence, Final Report September 2006." Available at http://www.annenbergpublicpolicycenter.org/. Accessed June 15, 2010.

Arnold, Thurman W. 1935. *The Symbols of Government*. New Haven: Yale University Press.

———. 1937. *The Folklore of Capitalism*. New Haven: Yale University Press.

Belden, Nancy, John Russonello and Kate Stewart. 1998. "Americans Consider Judicial Independence: Findings of a National Survey Regarding Attitudes Toward the Federal Courts." Washington, DC: Belden, Russonello, and Stewart Research and Communications.

Brown, Trevor L., and Charles R. Wise. 2004. "Constitutional Courts and Legislative-Executive Relations: The Case of Ukraine." *Political Science Quarterly* 119: 143–69.

Bybee, Keith J. 2007. "Introduction: The Two Faces of Judicial Power." In Keith J. Bybee, ed., *Bench Press: The Collision of Courts, Politics, and the Media*. Stanford: Stanford University Press.

———. 2010. *All Judges Are Political—Except When They Are Not: Acceptable Hypocrisies and the Rule of Law*. Stanford: Stanford University Press.

Caldeira, Gregory A., and James L. Gibson. 1992. "The Etiology of Public Support for the Supreme Court." *American Political Science Review* 36: 635–64.

Carter, Lief H., and Thomas F. Burke. 2007. *Reason in Law*. Updated 7th ed. New York: Pearson Education.

CNN.com. 2006. "Poll: Americans Don't Want Politicians Constraining Judges." Available at http://www.cnn.com/2006/POLITICS/10/27/activist.judges/. Accessed June 15, 2010.

Cohen, Felix S. 1933. *Ethical Systems and Legal Ideals*. Camden, NJ: Falcon Press.

———. 1935. "Transcendental Nonsense and the Functional Approach." *Columbia Law Review* 35: 809–49.

Connecticut Judicial Branch and the Connecticut Commission on Public Trust and Confidence. 1998. "Statewide Public Trust and Confidence Study." Trumbull, CT: Center for Research and Public Policy at Central Connecticut State University.

Cook, Walter Wheeler. 1927. "Scientific Method and the Law." *American Bar Association Journal* 13: 303–9.

Duxbury, Neil. 1995. *Patterns of American Jurisprudence*. New York: Oxford University Press.

Ewick, Patricia, and Susan Silbey. 1998. *The Common Place of Law: Stories from Everyday Life*. Chicago: University of Chicago Press.

Feldman, Stephen M. 2000. *American Legal Thought from Premodernism to Postmodernism: An Intellectual Voyage*. New York: Oxford University Press.

———. 2005. "The Rule of Law or the Rule of Politics? Harmonizing the Internal and External Views of Supreme Court Decisionmaking." *Law and Social Inquiry* 30: 89–135.

Fenster, Mark. 2003. "The Symbols of Governance: Thurman Arnold and Post-Realist Legal Theory." *Buffalo Law Review* 51: 1053–1118.

———. 2007. "The Folklore of Legal Biography." *Michigan Law Review* 105: 1265–82.

Fischer, William W., III. 1991. "The Development of Modern American Legal Theory and the Judicial Interpretation of the Bill of Rights." In M. J. Lacey and K. Haakonssen, eds., *A Culture of Rights: The Bill of Rights in Philosophy, Politics, and Law, 1791 and 1991.* New York: Cambridge University Press.

Frank, Jerome. 1970. *Law and the Modern Mind.* Gloucester, MA: Peter Smith, reprint of the 1930 edition.

Gallup Poll News Service. 2007. "Slim Majority of Americans Approve of the Supreme Court." Available at http://www.gallup.com/poll/28798/Slim-Majority-Americans-Approve-Supreme-Court.aspx. Accessed June 15, 2010.

Geyh, Charles Gardner. 2006. *When Courts and Congress Collide: The Struggle for Control of America's Judicial System.* Ann Arbor: University of Michigan Press.

———. 2007. "Preserving Public Confidence in the Courts in an Age of Individual Rights and Public Skepticism." In Keith J. Bybee, ed., *Bench Press: The Collision of Courts, Politics, and the Media.* Stanford: Stanford University Press.

Gibson, James L. 2008a. "Challenges to the Impartiality of State Supreme Courts: Legitimacy Theory and 'New-Style' Judicial Campaigns." *American Political Science Review* 102: 59–75.

———. 2008b. "Campaigning for the Bench: The Corrosive Effects of Campaign Speech?" *Law and Society Review* 42: 899–928.

———. 2009. "'New-Style' Judicial Campaigns and the Legitimacy of State High Courts." *Journal of Politics* 71: 1285–1304.

Gibson, James L., and Gregory A. Caldeira. 1992. "Blacks and the United States Supreme Court: Models of Diffuse Support." *Journal of Politics* 54: 1120–45.

———. 2007. "Supreme Court Nominations, Legitimacy Theory and the American Public: A Dynamic Test of the Theory of Positivity Bias." Available at http://ssrn.com/abstract=998283. Accessed June 15, 2010.

Gibson, James L., Gregory A. Caldeira, and Vanessa Baird. 1998. "On the Legitimacy of National High Courts." *American Political Science Review* 92: 343–58.

Gibson, James L., Gregory A. Caldeira, and Lester Kenyatta Spence. 2003. "Measuring Attitudes toward the United States Supreme Court." *American Journal of Political Science* 47: 354–76.

———. 2005. "Why Do People Accept Public Policies They Oppose? Testing Legitimacy Theory with a Survey-Based Experiment," *Political Research Quarterly* 58: 187–201.

Goffman, Erving. 1959. *The Presentation of Self in Everyday Life.* Garden City, NY: Doubleday Anchor Books.

———. 1963. *Behavior in Public Places: Notes on the Social Organization of Gatherings.* New York: Free Press.

Grant, Ruth W. 1997. *Hypocrisy and Integrity: Machiavelli, Rousseau, and the Ethics of Politics.* Chicago: University of Chicago Press.

Greenberg, Quinlan, Rosner Research. 2001. "Justice at Stake National Survey of American Voters, October 30—November 7, 2001." Washington, DC: Greenberg, Quinlan, Rosner Research.

Horwitz, Morton J. 1992. *The Transformation of American Law, 1870–1960: The Crisis of Legal Orthodoxy.* New York: Oxford University Press.

Illinois Campaign for Political Reform. 2002. "2002 Illinois Statewide Survey on Judicial

Selection Issues." Springfield: University of Illinois at Springfield Institute for Public Affairs.

Justice at Stake. 2008. "Minnesota Statewide Poll." Minneapolis, MN: Decision Resources.

Kalman, Laura. 1986. *Legal Realism at Yale, 1927–1960.* Chapel Hill: University of North Carolina Press.

Maxwell School of Citizenship and Public Affairs. 2005. "Maxwell Poll on Civic Engagement and Inequality (2005)." New York: Campbell Public Affairs Institute, Syracuse University.

McGuire, Kevin T. 2007. "The Judicial Branch: Judging America's Judges." In Kathleen Hall Jamieson, ed., *A Republic Divided: The Annenberg Democracy Project.* New York: Oxford University Press.

National Center for State Courts. 1999. "How the Public Views the State Courts: A 1999 National Survey." Presented at the Conference on Public Trust and Confidence in the Justice System. Washington, DC.

New Mexico Administrative Office of the Courts. 2000. "How New Mexicans View the State Courts: How Do We Compare to the National Picture and How Perceptions Have Changed since 1997." Santa Fe, NM: Shaening and Associates.

Office of the Administrator of the Courts, State of Washington. 1999. "How the Public Views the Courts: A 1999 Washington Statewide Survey compared to a 1999 National Survey." Bellevue, WA: GMA Research.

Pew Research Center for the People and the Press. 2005. "Court Critics Now on Both Left and Right: Supreme Court's Image Declines as Nomination Battles Loom, National Survey Conducted June 8–12, 2005." Available at http://people-press.org/report/247/supreme-courts-image-declines-as-nomination-battle-looms. Accessed June 15, 2010.

Purcell, Edward A., Jr. 1973. *The Crisis of Democratic Theory: Scientific Naturalism and the Problem of Value.* Lexington: University Press of Kentucky.

Russonello, John. 2004. "Speak to Values: How to Promote the Courts and Blunt Attacks on the Judiciary." *Court Review* (Summer): 10–12.

Scheb, John M., II, and William Lyons. 2001. "Judicial Behavior and Public Opinion: Popular Expectations regarding Factors That Influence Supreme Court Decisions." *Political Behavior* 23: 181–94.

Schelegel, John Henry. 1995. *American Legal Realism and Empirical Social Science.* Chapel Hill: University of North Carolina Press.

Segal, Jeffrey A., and Harold J. Spaeth. 2002. *The Supreme Court and the Attitudinal Model Revisited.* New York: Cambridge University Press.

Shapiro, Martin, and Alec Stone Sweet. 2002. *On Law, Politics, and Judicialization.* New York: Oxford University Press.

Shklar, Judith N. 1964. *Legalism: Law, Morals, and Political Trials.* Cambridge, MA: Harvard University Press.

University of New Orleans Survey Research Center. 1998. "Citizen Evaluation of the Louisiana Courts: A Report to the Louisiana Supreme Court, Volume I, The Survey." New Orleans, LA: University of New Orleans.

Waller, Spencer Weber. 2005. *Thurman Arnold: A Biography.* New York: New York University Press.

Wilkinson, J. Harvie, III. 2009. "Storming the 4th Circuit." *Washington Post*, January 23, 2009, A14.

13 Three Views from the Bench

Frank Sullivan

Nancy Vaidik

Sarah Evans Barker

A T THE CONFERENCE where the authors whose work appears in this book first presented their ideas, three judges were invited to attend and comment on the role law plays in their decision-making. Those comments were transcribed and are reproduced below.

Remarks of Justice Frank Sullivan, Jr., Indiana Supreme Court

What's law got to do with it? Everything.

For me, who forsook making decisions based on politics when I took the oath of office as a judge fifteen years ago, the critique of some in the political science academy that judicial decision-making is not based on law but on politics is disheartening.

And I think that critique is wrong.

I propound the following three examples from my own court:

(1) In 1988, the four Republican members of the Indiana Supreme Court denied Republican governor Robert Orr's request that Democratic gubernatorial aspirant Evan Bayh be declared ineligible to run for governor because he did not meet the state's constitutional residency requirement.

(2) In 2003, each of the members of the Court—three Democrats and two Republicans—voted to reject the competing plans of the Democratic and Republican parties for redrawing the boundaries of twenty-five Indianapolis city council districts. Instead, the Court unanimously redrew the boundaries without regard to the political composition of the districts.

(3) Shortly before the 2008 general election, two of the three Democrats on the Court voted to approve the Republican Party's request that jurisdiction over a dispute involving early voting sites in Lake County be transferred from one court to another.

In my fifteen years on the Indiana Supreme Court, no dispute between the Democratic and Republican parties or between Democratic and Republican candidates has been decided on a party-line vote.

Think about the Federal District and Courts of Appeals judges in the South following *Brown v. Board of Education*. These appointees of President Eisenhower followed the law, not politics, in deciding school desegregation cases even though it caused them to be ostracized in their home communities and threatened with violence.

Do you know the story of Alabama County Court Judge James Horton who in 1933 presided over the retrial of one of the Scottsboro Boys after the U.S. Supreme Court had reversed the first conviction and death sentence entered in the case? After the new jury convicted the defendant and sentenced him to death, Judge Horton set aside the verdict and the death sentence. (The next spring, Judge Horton was defeated running for re-election.)

What's law got to do with these decisions? Everything.

So what are we to make of the studies that show judicial decision-making correlated with judges' political orientation to a statistically significant degree? I have three separate answers.

First, if we disaggregate the data from which these correlations have been drawn and set aside all of those cases in which an individual judge has voted consonant with his or her political orientation, there will still be an extremely large number of cases in the data set. Those remaining cases will fall into one of two categories: cases in which the judge voted contrary to his or her political orientation or cases that are not scored either way because the subject matter of the case is not subject to being categorized politically. That is, acknowledging a correlation between judicial decision-making and political orientation, that correlation exists only with respect to an extremely small proportion of the total corpus of judicial work.

Second, when we drill down into the lyrics of Tina Turner's song, she tells us that love "scares" her. Instead, she's "been thinking of a new direction"— she's "been thinking about [her] own protection." No doubt some judges think about their own protection and decide cases based on some political calculation. It would not be credible to say that this does not happen.

But when it does happen, I think the principal reason is that judges must run for election on partisan ballots—or, with respect to Article III judges, the role that their ideology plays in their selection (to use Vice President Biden's unfortunate formulation). As such, the correlation that does exist between judicial decision-making and political orientation is to me an argument for the merit selection of judges—at the state and federal level. Here in Indiana, we use a merit selection process to choose trial-level judges in two counties; we should use it in all. And I would hold out as a recent felicitous example of the merit selection of an Article III judge President Bush's nomination and the Senate's confirmation of Judge D. Tinder to the U.S. Court of Appeals for the 7th Circuit.

Third, today's debate between political scientists and law professors closely resembles a debate that has taken place within the legal academy for least a century—from formalism to Legal Realism to Progressivism to legal process and beyond. And reflecting on the contours of that debate, I conclude, as have several of the authors in this volume, that politics and law are not mutually exclusive but rather inextricably bound.

Holmes once said:

> The felt necessities of the time, the prevalent moral and political theories, intuitions of public policy, avowed or unconscious, even the prejudices which judges share with their fellow-men, have had a good deal more to do than the syllogism in determining the rules by which men should be governed.

Judicial decision-making is not syllogism; it is the result of the factors Holmes identified, including politics—politics in the sense that the very statutes and constitutional provisions that judges must interpret are products of politics and so cannot be interpreted without taking politics into account.

With all that has been written and said about President Roosevelt's "court-packing plan," one thing that is often not remembered is that Justice Brandeis, the New Deal's staunchest supporter on the Court, authorized his name to be used in Chief Justice Hughes's letter to the Senate that proved to be influential in defeating the plan. Justice Jackson later explained Brandeis's position as follows:

> He believed with all the intensity of his being that the country needed the institution he served, and that a court of courage, character, and independence could exist only in an atmosphere of freedom from political pressure. But he believed the Justices maintain it by self-restraint and open-minded-

ness, by unbiased patient and accurate application of the law, and by freedom from political ambition or partisanship.

These are my ideals as a judge.

Or are they? Am I really that good? Or, if only a perfect attitudinal or strategic model could be constructed, would political scientists be able to explain what's really going on in Sullivan's decision-making?

Perhaps I think I'm deciding cases according to law but that a fulsome empirical analysis would demonstrate otherwise. So let me describe some of the things I do in deciding cases. Maybe this self-description of one judge's decision-making will be helpful to scholars as they refine their models explaining judicial behavior. (I assume for this purpose issues or cases of first impression—that is, issues where precedent is of limited utility.)

First, I try very hard to avoid deciding any case on constitutional grounds, recognizing that people's elected representatives in a democracy, not unelected judges, are entrusted with the lawmaking power. This is the countermajoritarian difficulty. I strongly believe that courts should leave policy decisions to the executive and legislative branches unless the challenged policy is within the scope of the Bill of Rights, is directed against discrete and insular minorities, or restricts those political processes that can ordinarily be expected to bring about repeal of undesirable legislation. I have on several occasions decided not to reach the merits of a state constitutional challenge solely based on my assessment that the challenged policy was the product of normal democratic processes working as they should. For example, in one challenge to an annexation statute's constitutionality, the bill had passed the one-hundred-member Indiana House of Representatives with fifty-one votes; the fifty-member Senate with twenty-seven. The closeness of the vote told me that the bill had passed only after a tough fight; that because the statute was the product of normal democratic processes, judicial intervention was not required.

Second, when it comes to statutory interpretation, I try very hard to make a good faith determination as to how the legislature that enacted the statute in question would want the statute interpreted. To be sure, an enactment of a multimember legislative body has no single intent or purpose. But by studying the legislation at issue as a whole and any available legislative history, a general intent or purpose can often be discerned.

Let me use a fabulous 7th Circuit case decided in 1987, first called to my attention by Professor Bill Popkin, as an example. The Wisconsin legislature protected from the reach of bankruptcy creditors farm equipment called "mowers" and "hay loaders." It did this in 1935. But "mowers" and "hay loaders" were no longer in use in 1987. By then, farmers were using farm implements called "balers" and "haybines" to do what "mowers" and "hay loaders" had done a half-century earlier. Could the court consider the modern balers and haybines to be exempt property even though not listed in the exemption statute?

(I might say that Professor Popkin used this great case as an illustration of problems in statutory interpretation. I have also seen studied this case in jurisprudence as an illustration of indeterminacy.)

I would look at the 1935 Wisconsin statute in total, its legislative history, who voted for and against it. If that examination showed a general intent or purpose of the statute to provide protection to farmers from creditors for certain basic farm implements, then I would treat balers and haybines as exempt. But if the general intent or purpose of the statute appeared to give creditors greater access to their security, then I would not.

Third, I am constantly on the lookout, particularly when deciding common law issues, for "neutral principles"—that is, rules of decision that "swing both ways," that operate the same way on parties of opposing ideologies. For example, under Indiana law, children over the age of fourteen are chargeable with exercising the standard of care of an adult. It is a neutral principle of law, operating irrespective of whether the over-age-fourteen child is a plaintiff injured in an accident or a defendant driver who caused an accident. In either case, the law holds the child to the standard of care of an adult.

In summary, I think that if one wanted to analyze how I make decisions— apart from the significant influence of precedent that I have not addressed— one would need to factor into the analysis a sensitivity to the countermajoritarian difficulty, an attention to legislative intent and purpose at almost an operational level, and an effort to forge neutral principles in the common law arena. I hope that's of some help.

I've been more personal here than I usually am—and I'm going to finish on a highly personal note.

A little more than eight years ago, a prominent American found himself on the losing end of a highly politically charged 5–4 decision of the U.S. Supreme Court. This man, who was not a lawyer, could well have invoked the political science literature we have heard about today and attacked the judges in the majority for casting their votes based on their politics rather than law. But this man who, I repeat, was not a lawyer, did just the opposite. "[T]he motto: 'Not under man, but under God and law' . . . [is] the ruling principle of American freedom, the source of our democratic liberties," Al Gore said. "I've tried to make it my guide throughout this contest, as it has guided America's deliberations of all the complex issues of the past five weeks. Now the U.S. Supreme Court has spoken. Let there be no doubt, while I strongly disagree with the court's decision, I accept it." He concluded, "Now [this long and difficult road] has ended, resolved, as it must be resolved, through the honored institutions of our democracy."

Al Gore's conclusion that *Bush v. Gore* was decided "not under man, but under God and law" inspired and motivated me to rededicate myself to deciding the cases entrusted to me under law as well.

Remarks of Judge Nancy Vaidik, Indiana Court of Appeals

What do Lauren Hutton, Dave Letterman, and Madonna have alike? They all have gaps in their teeth. Please hold that thought. I'm Nancy Vaidik. I am an intermediate Court of Appeals judge here in Indiana, where we have no docket control at all. We take every case that is appealed to us. We have 2,500 cases a year out of the 1.8 million that are heard by the trial courts in Indiana. I am reviewed by the Honorable Justice Frank Sullivan and his colleagues. This is my perspective on what law has to do with it. And I agree with Justice Sullivan that it has a lot to do with it.

There has been an underestimation of the role of precedent in our discussions here. It's very important this thing called precedent. What we have been trained to do is follow precedent. We do not go outside of precedent. I recently voted on an opinion where we said we don't like the precedent at all. It's been around since 1884, we don't think that it is good, but we're constrained by it. That is but one illustration of how much we're controlled by precedent. And the vast majority of our trial and appellate courts may not deviate from precedent; generally only the U.S. and state supreme courts may. Even so, looking at recent empirical studies (such as that authored by Professor Lindquist in Chapter 7), I see that rarely in the state supreme courts is precedent reversed. Texas appears to be the leader in reversing precedent in fifteen cases per year, but most states reverse precedent in zero to six cases per year. And Justice Sullivan has told us that of the 1,100 cases the Indiana Supreme Court reviews in a year, it reverses precedent in an average of two cases. So, precedent is very, very important to us.

In most cases, my court and most courts are bound by precedent. That is, we have no discretion to rule any other way but to follow precedent. Nevertheless, there are cases where there is no precedent and we may exercise discretion. There is a gap, if you will, where we do have discretion, but there has to be a perfect storm of events in order for me and my colleagues to exercise that discretion within the gap. In order to do so, of course, the case first has to have been appealed. So in Indiana, of the 1.8 million cases heard in the trial courts in a year, 2,500 cases are appealed, or 0.14 percent. But it does not stop there. The case not only has to have been appealed, but the parties must have raised the issue in the lower court. That issue must be raised again before us. Further, when that issue is raised before us, it must be cogently argued. Additionally, there has to be ambiguity in the law. The appeal must be based on a legal issue and not a factual issue, and on top of all that the issue has to be outcome determinative because if it is not, we're going to say we don't even have to reach the merits of the claim if it is subject to harmless error analysis.

In other words, a perfect storm of events has to come together in order for us to be able to exercise this discretion. This discretion is like the gap in the teeth of David Letterman, Madonna, and Lauren Hutton. It's a small gap, but it happens to be right in the middle of their face. In some sense, the literature I have read puts an increased importance on this gap, but it's a gap that is tiny, that we celebrate, and that we find very important. Our legal system does not want judges to be like computers who simply intake the facts, apply the law stored in the computer, and press enter while at the same time ignoring individual circumstances. We want and celebrate that discretion. There is this space, but it's not a very big space, and in this space there are considerations other than the law that naturally come into play.

But when I'm confronted with the proposition that it's just political considerations, it bothers me a lot, because it's not just political considerations. I know it is probably meant in the broadest sense of the term, but there are a lot of things in that little gap that we think about. We think about the balancing of social issues. We think, in part, with our heart when we look at a case: how do we feel about this case?; what's the right thing to do?; and what's the justice of the cause? We look at it through the prism of our personal and professional experiences. I may look at a criminal case, having been a former prosecutor, a little differently from my colleagues, who may not have experience. In this space, the quality of the lawyering makes a difference. Look at *Gideon v. Wainwright*, which makes the point perfectly. Abe Fortas was representing an indigent client who wanted quality legal representation, against a state attorney general who was not very effective. Fortas personified the very principle of good lawyering for which he was arguing. The quality of the advocacy matters within this gap.

The receptivity of our colleagues to what we are thinking about the case matters too. We want to have consensus with our colleagues on the issue, so that we don't have three separate decisions or a two-to-one decision. We really try hard, because precedent and predictive value are very important for our society and we know that.

In this space also is the ability to write the opinion. We might feel one way, and think that in this little discretionary space there is ambiguity enough for us to go with our feelings, but then we try to write it and "it doesn't write." And if it doesn't write, we can't exercise the discretion to act on our leanings. And then yes, we do think of the likelihood of reversal. We do think about Justice Sullivan and his colleagues and how they might react to this. Lower court judges do not want to lose their credibility with reviewing judges.

All of these things are considerations that we are thinking about in this space of discretion. Many times these considerations are conflicting. If I were to rule on a criminal case, maybe I may tend to identify with the prosecutor because I've been a prosecutor, so maybe that's where I'm coming from. On the other hand, if my experience says that what the police did here is so outside of what I've seen in my personal experience, then there are conflicting things going on. Add to it that maybe my colleagues might feel differently about what is going on. So there are all these colliding motivations in this little space. Ultimately that makes me wonder about the efficacy of models of judicial decision-making, and it just seems to me that such models are much too simplistic.

Scholars, such as Professor Segal writing in Chapter 1, have stated that their objective is to come up with a model to capture the essence of what judges do. Whoa! I just can't even imagine it ever being possible to find my essence or Judge Barker's essence, or Justice Sullivan's essence in a model. It's too simplistic a view. There is some value in, if you will, naming behavior, as psychologists have done. Freud did it—the patient is acting in thus and so way because he is regressing, or he is repressing bad experiences, or there's transference, or any number of other named psychological behaviors. That may be valuable, but I'm not sure how much value there is in saying we're going to superimpose a preset model or formula on top of behavior that is obviously so complex, so complex that sometimes we judges don't even realize what our own motivations are. I know there are some that might be thinking, well what she is saying right now—that law is really important and all these other factors are not so important—is "motivated reasoning," and I know there are those who have answers to all of this. But I'm not so sure that they really do fit.

There may be value too in isolating one variable or one factor and making statistical correlations with outcomes. Even defining an outcome is problematic, in that the outcome can be the result or the reasoning to reach the result. But, even so, let's take the attitudinal model, which seems to be a model that people are really happy with. They say, well, there is a correlation between a judge's ideology and the outcome of a case. And I think, well that's nice. But I hearken back to a certain American celebrity. Her name is Holly Madison. Holly is the former girlfriend of Hugh Hefner and she's been a Playmate for numerous months. She is on "Dancing with the Stars" right now. She was dancing a couple weeks ago when one of the judges said, gee, your chest is really interfering with your dancing, and she replied, "Well, duh!" And just as this premise was too simplistic to Ms. Madison, so too is the attitudinal model too simplistic. Well of course, to some extent, in this small gap, in very limited instances, a judge's ideology is going to affect his ruling. But duh!

So finally, in the end here, what are we trying to do? Why are we trying to do this? Are we trying to predict behavior of judges in the future? I have been told that experts just can't predict behavior as well as empiricists. I want to say, "I'll take you on." Let's look at Justice Sullivan's voting. I can predict how he is going to vote better than they can because I've studied—I've done the hard work, I've lived on the court for nine years, I've read everything he's written, I've been to conferences where's he talked. I study his philosophies, how he thinks. There is no way that an empiricist can predict how he will rule better than I. So the bets are on. The best predictor of how judges are going to rule is to look at their writing, to do the hard work.

If our point is to duplicate this wonderful system of justice that we have, there is no easy way to do that either. I think we've got to do it the hard way, and that is to go into Third World countries, which judicial and legal organizations, as well as law schools have been doing, and teach people about the system. I don't think that saying, okay, we have these models and now we can re-create why our judges decide cases is very helpful—so I wonder, to what end are we trying to create the perfect model to predict judicial behavior?

In conclusion, there is a gap that allows a judge discretion. It's overstated—in some senses it's been made a gorge instead of a gap. The discretion that we have in this gap includes things that we really do welcome in our system of justice: considerations that are diverse, considerations that are more expansive than merely political considerations, and considerations that seek and result in justice. To empiricists, I say, God love you, good luck, but I think judicial behavior defies being perfectly fit in a perfectly shaped model.

Remarks of Judge Sarah Evans Barker, U.S. District Court for the Southern District of Indiana

I've been thinking about what the take-homes are from this discussion. For me, one of them is to try not to let my chest get in the way of my dancing. It's never been a problem, frankly, but I never had my consciousness raised in that respect. I must say I have come to the end of this conversation feeling a little like a lab rat being analyzed. I feel a bit as if some of the authors here are trying to figure out what lies behind the beauty of a butterfly by looking at it when it's been pinned down in a display box. It doesn't work that way. Nobody knows anything about butterflies who hasn't watched butterflies—empiricists need to get as close as they can to what they are seeing to let their theories better inform their observations. I once had a professor request to come watch mediations in our court. He said this would help him with his teaching. I said, "You bet, and we can make those arrangements," and I thought that it was a very good sign.

Based on all the research recounted here, I have to say that if you were to come to me and ask me how I'm feeling, I'd probably answer, "I feel fine. . . . Don't I?" I am reminded of one of those little e-mail blurbs that come in the afternoon to keep you absolutely up-to-date on everything that is happening. It told about a judge in Chicago who had reversed a Chicago ordinance that gave some sort of protection to the architecture up there and cited as the reason for the judicial ruling that ordinance unconstitutional, that the judge found it was "vague, ambitious and overly broad." We usually say "ambiguous," instead of ambitious, but that's Chicago justice. Part of what you need to do, if you are looking at justice, is to look at Chicago justice, look at the paradigms, look at where it's coming from. People will snooker you into thinking that it's all alike everywhere, but it's very much local. That's what you are seeing when you see these things—they are variations on the theme, and it's because judges are indigenous.

This is one of the complaints that federal district court judges had with the sentencing guidelines—that it was a template that attempted to remove all the discretion from the judges and ignored the regional differences. Back when

I was a U.S. attorney, we used to try to get Miami, Florida, law enforcement to cooperate with us on wire-taps between Miami and Indianapolis. By our standards we had a big case and we wanted to apply the resources that Miami had to man a wire-tap and get the approvals and so forth. We had a big case, but in Miami it was regarded as chicken-feed, and we just couldn't get their attention—that's what I mean by a regional difference. So when you get a judge in southern Indiana, that judge is going to see things slightly differently than a judge in Miami, Florida. In research and in thinking about the way a judge decides, you have to look at these very important local differences. They're not all base behaviors. They're not all culpable behaviors. They're real reflections of the people who live in a particular locale. In that regard, you know there's an awful lot of just bumping into people in your local community when they know you have been assigned a big case. Sure, they're not supposed to ex parte you but the public isn't in on all these nuances. They find out you have some major criminal case, and they'll say, "Man, give them life," and they don't know anything more about it. It's just that they know there was a disruption to the fabric of their community caused by the crime. Of course, if it is somebody they know or somebody they are related to, it's a lot of "Now, you ought to take into account some of these special, individualized facts." So it's a much more nuanced and interactive process than judges sitting in court or in chambers trying to impose a template.

So in answer to the question of what difference law makes, what does law have to do with it, I would say, "Something." But I wouldn't say, "Everything." I would say, "A lot," but I wouldn't say, "Everything." That is what Judge Vaidik means when she talked about "the gap." Justice Sullivan got to it too, even though he answered the question differently, because if law really was everything, he could have stopped at that. But he gave a beautifully nuanced explanation of what he does and how he decides.

There is a little remark that gets bantered about between judges when we get together at our conferences. Someone will say, "I know all the judges in this room. You've all been appointed pursuant to a political process. It's because of the people you know, and the route that you took to the office. Everybody here is a political appointee. But me I'm merit." It's a pure joke, because the truth is we all know we were appointed through a political process, and the miracle is that having gone through a highly politicized process to become judges, almost instantly we have to step back from that. And so what you need to measure is how successful we are in doing that. Can we move back from it, and if so how do we do that? We do it with a whole series of disciplines, internal and external. Legal scholars and political scientists have looked at some of these. The ethics, the canons, really do matter, and they get internalized quickly. A judge doesn't have to read them every day; you know them, because you live by them. You know because you read about other judges who didn't follow them, and you don't want to be that sort of judge. You have a certain amount of professional pride on the line to do the right thing for the right reasons.

There are, of course, reversals. None of us like a reversal—not because we don't expect it sometimes. People see things differently, or the law will shift. We need that check on our exercises of power because we've really poured ourselves into our decisions, we've worked hard, and we thought we had it right. That's the only reason a reversal on an appeal matters to a trial court judge.

So, let me describe, in an itemized way, the climate in which we are doing our judging so that when data is gathered, others can use this as sort of reality check. First of all, the case loads are huge, the numbers of cases are huge, the legal problems are huge, as are the complications and the implications. At any given moment on my current docket, I'm carrying between 500 and 550 civil cases—and remember my job is to shepherd them through the process. Some of them are mortgage foreclosures where you just have to put your name on those, but on all the cases that require adjudication, it's often several adjudications, its requires several ways of being involved, and several levels of involvement. And so we move the cases through to some sort of acceptable conclusion, maybe adjudication, maybe a settlement, maybe a dismissal on a motion, but they take a lot of judicial intervention.

Since the case loads are huge, a judge has to figure out ways to promote efficiency. Twenty-five years ago, no less a scholar than Judith Resnik discussed the role of managerial judging that we are imposing on the federal district courts requiring them to shepherd their case through the pipeline with all kinds of little tricks and devices to get all them adjudicated, in federal court especially. You pays your money, you proves your jurisdiction, and you takes your chances. That's what judges must manage. I use the word "management" in the most active verbal tense because a judge can't just let the cases sit there on the docket. Sometimes, we judges think we are the only ones working the case; the lawyers have forgotten about it, the litigants are having trouble coming up with the money to pay their lawyers, and we're the only ones saying, "Hey, don't you want a hearing? Hey, aren't you going to file a motion? Hey don't you want to come in and talk about this?" So, we often have to push hard. And Judith Resnik says there is a problem in that. One of the problems is that case management occurs way below the radar—only the parties in that case know about it. You have a lot of flexibility with respect to how you manage your cases; it can become a way in which the judge can take over the case. I know I've made lawyers wince by saying, "In two weeks, we go to trial." I know if I say that, a lot of those cases are going to settle. But there's no appeal from that scheduling order. Judge Barker is simply managing her docket, she's got to get all those cases resolved, and we can't tie her hands says the Court of Appeals.

There are as well lots of routine cases, and when we have so many cases, we have to draw on decisional help wherever we can find it. So we have law clerks, we have interns, and we have borrowed law clerks, if and when there is a judge who isn't using his clerks at the moment. It's not a district court judge in each instance who is going through a disciplined analytical process to come up with merits-based decisions. You don't let decisions go out that are not yours—don't misunderstand—but ordinarily a person learns the case by working the case, and we simply cannot do that on every case. So one of the first things a district court judge does is look at the case to see if it is routine. If it is routine, you apply the decisional paradigm, for example, for a section 1,983 case, or for an Americans with Disability Act case, or for an employment discrimination case, or for an excessive force case. When it's routine, I read through those facts to make sure I've got it, before I move to apply the template. Because we get a lot of decisional help, when you are looking at the output of a district court judge, a reader can tell if the district court judge has written a decision, because the district court judge will write it with more fluidity. It's the difference between recipe cooking and gourmet cooking, and generally you can tell by tasting the results. So if you want a measure of what the district court judges are doing, you can't necessarily just read all those cases; you have to read to determine who likely wrote the case and figure out how it was cranked out. Ask yourself: is it run of the mill? Is it sort of business as usual?—And remember that the pressure is on the judge to move through cases.

Judge Vaidik mentioned the importance of the role of lawyers. They are in the trenches with us. They're our yoke-fellows, you might say—if they don't move fast, we can't move fast, and if they want to move slowly, we have to move slowly. So we're very dependent upon them. And she is right, there are great variations in quality, which is something we have to learn to live with. How they position the dispute can be very important.

Whatever biases there are—whatever subconscious motivations there are for decisions—more often than not, such views are usually imputed to the judge; they don't ordinarily arise in any conscious way from the judge. For example, I know things get said about me by lawyers and others. I've been on the court for twenty-five years. I don't know what that means, maybe that just means I'm old, but it's a fact that gets mentioned as a way of signaling something about me. "Oh, she's our only woman judge." "Oh, she was a Reagan appointee." "Oh, she is a Hoosier." "Oh, she is something else." And none of these things comes consciously to my mind when I am deciding . . . . How would a woman, Hoosier, twenty-five years on the bench decide this matter? And the same is true of the great principles of judicial independence, disciplined adherence to the canons and so forth: we don't think about those, they simply are part of what we do and who we are. When you are cold and you put a blanket on at night, you don't look to see how it is woven. You are looking for what it can do and what you need it to do at that time and you are grateful for a Pendleton blanket if you are cold, or a little flimsy blanket, if it's springtime. So you have to realize that these characteristics are part of the fabric, but they are not really telling you about what we are doing. I was recently talking to a good friend, and I made a passing reference to the fact that a lot of things get imputed to judges, especially by the party that loses. "Well isn't she dumb," "She didn't get it," "She didn't pay attention," "She's never had to worry about losing a job," "She's never had to worry about whatever," "Well, she was a Reagan appointee." So the person, who is a wonderful professor, asked: "What do you mean?" and I said because other people seem to make something of the fact that I am a Reagan appointee. I don't know what difference that makes, but I do know that when I move to the left in making some decision (and you know the weakness of all these characterizations), it's not perceived by a lot of people as being terribly to the left because I was a Reagan appointee. Or if I move to the right, well, they say, what do you expect? She was a Reagan appointee. I don't make decisions because I was a Reagan appointee. I frankly don't know what President Reagan would've wanted me to do. I really don't know what he wants me to do now. But that isn't how we judges make our decisions, and part of the reason is we don't have the luxury of that because there simply are too many decisions to make.

Judge Posner says in his wonderful book that most judges would deny that they have preconceptions about the outcomes of the cases when they get them. In our courts, we have control over the specific cases assigned to us. Each of us takes one-fifth of the filings in the Southern District of Indiana. Judges would deny that we have that kind of subjectivity, but we would admit that we likely are subject to certain subconscious factors. Researchers rely on subconscious factors too when they evaluate us. And that's what I mean by imputation—researchers are thinking things about me when they ascribe motivations to me, so they have to be just as pristine as they want me to be when I am making the decisions that they analyze.

When we decide cases in the district court, we decide them not on the basis of preconceived outcomes and views, but with huge attention to the facts. I can't emphasize this enough: the facts, the facts—that's our primary job. We must find honest facts. The law will change as a case goes up on appeal, but our job in the trial court is to find honest facts, so you should look to see if we left something out. I tell my clerks that if there is a gap in the facts, don't leave fact of the gap unaddressed in the opinion. Rather, say we too were left wondering about such and so fact, to signal that we know that it likely would matter, if somebody had taken the time to tell us. Maybe they don't know either. At our level, the facts drive most of the specific decisions because, if you start analyzing all the 1,983 cases, for example, you'll come up with a yearly compendium hundreds of pages long that tracks all the 1,983 decisions. So, the law is fairly settled, but the facts change all the time. And the facts typically have a push to them that leads us to apply the controlling legal principles. Does the law matter? Of course. But, not completely, and that is because some of these other factors I have mentioned are also very important.

About the Contributors

Sarah Evans Barker is Judge, U.S. District Court for the Southern District of Indiana.

Lawrence Baum is Professor of Political Science at the Ohio State University.

Eileen Braman is Associate Professor of Political Science, Indiana University.

Stephen B. Burbank is the David Berger Professor for the Administration of Justice, University of Pennsylvania School of Law.

Keith J. Bybee is the Paul E. and the Hon. Joanne F. Alper '72 Judiciary Studies Professor, Syracuse University.

Frank Cross is the Herbert D. Kelleher Centennial Professor of Business Law, University of Texas.

Barry Friedman is the Jacob D. Fuchsberg Professor of Law, New York University School of Law.

Charles Gardner Geyh is Associate Dean for Research and John F. Kimberling Chair in Law, Indiana University Maurer School of Law.

James L. Gibson is the Sidney W. Souers Professor of Government in the Department of Political Science and Professor of African and African American Studies in the Department of Political Science at Washington University in St. Louis. He is also the Director of the Program on Citizenship and Democratic Values and Weidenbaum Center on the Economy, Government, and Public Policy, and Professor Extraordinary in Political Science, and Fellow, Centre for Comparative and International Politics, Stellenbosch University (South Africa).

Melinda Gann Hall is Professor of Political Science and Distinguished Faculty, Michigan State University.

Stefanie A. Lindquist is the Thomas W. Gregory Professor of Law, University of Texas Law School.

Andrew D. Martin is Professor of Political Science and Professor of Law, Washington University in St. Louis.

Mitchell Pickerill is Associate Professor of Political Science at Northern Illinois University.

David Pozen is Special Assistant to the Legal Adviser, U.S. Department of State.

Jeffrey A. Segal is SUNY Distinguished Professor, Department of Political Science, Stony Brook University.

Matthew J. Streb is Associate Professor of Political Science, Northern Illinois University.

Frank Sullivan, Jr. is Justice, Indiana Supreme Court.

Nancy H. Vaidik is Judge, Indiana Court of Appeals.

Index

ABA, *see* American Bar Association
Abortion rights, 24, 102, 207, 237, 270, 287
Accountability: electoral, 9, 224, 235–36, 250–51, 284; judicial independence and, 46, 52, 59, 236–38; of legislatures, 265; mechanisms, 250–51; public expectations of, 282, 298; research on, 46
Activist judges, 10, 109, 253
Administrate Procedure Act, 96
Affirmative action, 26–27, 102–3
Alabama Supreme Court, 179, 207
Alito, Samuel, 29
American Bar Association (ABA), 196, 238–40, 307
Annenberg Foundation Trust at Sunnylands, 310
Appeals courts: circuit courts, 49, 100–101, 103, 162; federal, 29, 33–34, 49, 58, 76–77, 159–60, 330; institutional design, 176, 177–78; norms, 173, 175–78; panel effects, 49–50; precedents followed, 160–61, 175–78; relations among judges, 49–50, 82, 175–78; strategic behaviors, 49, 51. *See also* Intermediate appellate courts; State supreme courts

Appointments, judicial: arguments for, 9; drawbacks of system, 241, 262–63; legislative confirmation, 239, 251; legitimacy, 216n18; nomination process, 98, 109, 234, 239, 251; performance of judges, 262; political considerations, 97–98, 234, 239, 338–39; to state supreme courts, 239, 270–71
Arnold, Thurman W., 308, 315–21, 322
Attitudinal model: consequences, 59–60; criticisms of, 47, 48, 50, 51, 102, 336; description, 26–29, 150; development, 1–2, 150; expected voting patterns, 27–28, 28 (fig.); ideological space, 26–27, 27 (fig.); implications, 74–75; importance, 156; legal realism and, 43; measures, 150; motivated reasoning, 104; performance, 150–51; policy preferences of judges, 26, 73, 74, 150, 152; pure, 73; research using, 148; strategic choice models and, 73–74, 152; Supreme Court as domain, 150

Baird, Vanessa A., 286
Barghothi, A. J., 237